POLITICS AND POETRY
IN RESTORATION ENGLAND

POLITICS AND POETRY

IN RESTORATION ENGLAND

The Case of Dryden's *Annus Mirabilis*

MICHAEL MCKEON

Harvard University Press
Cambridge, Massachusetts, and London, England
1975

Copyright © 1975 by the President and Fellows of Harvard College
All rights reserved
Publication of this volume has been aided by a grant from the
Andrew W. Mellon Foundation.
Printed in the United States of America

Library of Congress Cataloging in Publication Data

McKeon, Michael, 1943–
   Politics and poetry in Restoration England.

   Bibliography: p.
   Includes index.
   1. Dryden, John, 1631–1700. Annus mirabilis.
   2. Great Britain—History—Restoration, 1660–1688.
   3. Political poetry, English—History and criticism.
   I. Title.
PR3416.A73M3   821′.4   75-4508
ISBN 0-674-68755-8

To Betty
and to the memory of
Michael Alssid (1927–1975)

ACKNOWLEDGMENTS

I would like to acknowledge the aid—including permission to quote from manuscript holdings—given to me by members of the staffs of the British Museum and the Public Record Office (London), the Bodleian Library (Oxford University), the collection of the marquis of Bath (Longleat, Wiltshire), Chetham's Library (Manchester), and the Houghton Library (Harvard University). Transcripts of Crown-copyright records in the Public Record Office appear by permission of HM Stationery Office, London. Quotations from Rachel Trickett, *The Honest Muse: A Study in Augustan Verse*, copyright Oxford University Press, 1967, appear by permission of the Oxford University Press, Oxford. I am grateful to Columbia University for generous fellowships during the main period of my research on this study.

I am indebted especially to a number of individuals. Hugh Amory provided the initial inspiration for a study of *Annus Mirabilis*. During the period of research and composition, Howard Schless and Ronald Knowles gave me the aid of sensitive critics who are also accomplished scholars of Restoration history and literature. From the former I received much good advice and invaluable guidance through the complexities of historical research and argument. To the latter I owe many of the references on which that argument is based, and the opportunity to read the draft of his forthcoming edition of John Ogilby's *The Entertainment of . . . Charles II* (1662), volume 6 in the series *Renaissance Triumphs and*

Magnificences, published by Theatrum Orbis Terrarum (Amsterdam). The rough manuscript of this book was immeasurably improved in appearance by the skillful typing of Evangeline Goodwin. During the period of its preparation for publication, I benefited greatly from the diverse criticism, suggestions, and support of James Clifford, Richard Neugebauer, Tom Treadwell, Keith Stavely, Helen Vendler, and John Wallace. Finally, from the conception of this study to its completion as a book I have relied frequently on the intelligence of Elizabeth Falsey, who has discussed its critical and scholarly difficulties with unfailing wisdom and generosity.

CONTENTS

ILLUSTRATIONS

ABBREVIATIONS

Add.	Additional (when used without library name refers to BM Additional MSS.)
AM	*Annus Mirabilis*
Amer. Hist. Rev.	*American Historical Review*
App.	Appendix
ARS	*Augustan Reprint Society*
Ashm.	Ashmole, Ashmolean
BM	British Museum, London
Bod.	Bodleian Library, Oxford
brs.	broadside
Bull. IHR	*Bulletin of the Institute of Historical Research*
Camb.	Cambridge
Camb. Hist. Jour.	*Cambridge Historical Journal* (later *Historical Journal*)
Chet. Lib.	Chetham's Library, Manchester
CJ	*Commons Journal*
Clar.	Clarendon
Cov.	Coventry
CSP Clar.	*Calendar of the Clarendon State Papers*
CSP Col.	*Calendar of State Papers, Colonial Series*
CSPD	*Calendar of State Papers, Domestic Series*
CSPD Add.	*Calendar of State Papers, Domestic Series, Addenda*
CSP Ire.	*Calendar of State Papers, Ireland*
CSP Ven.	*Calendar of State Papers, Venetian*
Curr. Intell.	*The Current Intelligence*
DNB	*Dictionary of National Biography*
Econ. Hist. Rev.	*Economic History Review*
Eg.	Egerton
Eng. Hist. Rev.	*English History Review*
Harl.	Harleian
Harl. Misc.	*Harleian Miscellany*
Hist. Jour.	*Historical Journal* (formerly *Cambridge Historical Journal*)
HMC	*Historical Manuscripts Commission Reports*
Intell.	*The Intelligencer*
JHI	*Journal of the History of Ideas*
Jour. Warb. and Court.	*Journal of the Warburg and Courtauld Institutes*
King. Intell.	*The Kingdome's Intelligencer*
LJ	*Lords Journal*
Merc. Pub.	*Mercurius Publicus*

MLQ	*Modern Language Quarterly*
N&Q	*Notes & Queries*
n.d.	no date
n.p.	no place
OHEL	*Oxford History of English Literature*
PC	Privy Council
POAS	*Poems on Affairs of State*
PQ	*Philological Quarterly*
PRO	Public Record Office, London
Pubs.	Publications
Rept.	Report
RES	*Review of English Studies*
Scott. Hist. Rev.	*Scottish History Review*
SP	State Papers
SP	*Studies in Philology*
SR	*Statutes of the Realm*
Steele no.	Number assigned to royal proclamation by Steele, *Bibliography of Royal Proclamations* (1910)
Trans. APS	*Transactions of the American Philosophical Society*
Trans. RHS	*Transactions of the Royal Historical Society*
T.T.	Indicates that the date following is as given by George Thomason, seventeenth-century collector of tracts (cf. *Thomason Tracts* [1908])

POLITICS AND POETRY

IN RESTORATION ENGLAND

All references to Dryden's poetry and translations are to Dryden, *Poems* (1958), for which volume and page numbers are not given. All references to *Annus Mirabilis* are to stanza numbers, not to line numbers.

Dates are given in the English Old Style, ten days behind the Continental New Style, but the year is taken to have begun on January 1, not on March 25.

I have modernized seventeenth-century manuscript usage in two respects: superscriptions have been brought down to the line; and tildes ($\sim$) have been omitted without altering the spelling of the words they abbreviate. I have not modernized or "corrected" language in manuscript and printed sources, nor have I used the notation "[*sic*]."

INTRODUCTION:
"POLITICAL POETRY"

It is a fact of some relevance to the way we understand poetry of the past that in the contemporary climate of academic criticism, "political poetry" is a particularly troublesome phrase, one which approaches the status of a contradiction in terms. This has not been so in other times and places—most significantly, for the purposes of the present study, in the England of the late seventeenth century. My concern with "political poetry" in this study will be twofold. First and foremost, it is with John Dryden's *Annus Mirabilis* (1667) and with the historical context of that poem. The questions which proceed from this concern provide the framework for the argument that follows. How does contemporary criticism understand the nature and meaning of political poetry of the Restoration, and of *Annus Mirabilis* in particular? What problems are apparent in this criticism? What sort of critical and scholarly method will facilitate the understanding of *Annus Mirabilis* as a political poem whose political qualities are not discontinuous with its poetic qualities?

Because the aim of this study is not only to provide answers to these questions but also to demonstrate the application of an alternative method to a specific poem, the following discussion will descend quite deeply into the concrete detail of Restoration belief and behavior. Nevertheless, a second major concern underlies these specific investigations into political poetry and provokes its own, more general questions. What are the philosophical premises which provide the basis for a separation of poetry and politics in literary criticism? What are the broadest consequences of such a separation for the understanding of the nature and function of poetry? What might be the benefits of a literary criticism which perceives all poetic achievement as a complex function of political achievement, rather than as a negation or transcendence of it? Whether this broader concern with political poetry is expounded adequately in the following argument will depend greatly on the adequacy with which Dryden's poem is explained, but it is a subject which extends ultimately beyond the boundaries of specifically Restoration poetry and politics.

Generality vs. Particularity, Poetry vs. Politics

Recent criticism of Restoration poetry frequently judges it according to what might be called a "generality theory of value." In his introduction to the first volume of *Poems on Affairs of State*, George deF. Lord remarks that

satire has often been granted only a grudging and precarious status as a literary genre . . . satire directed at ephemeral issues and persons seems above all to lack the autonomy or universality of true poetry . . .
The richest satire, as the example of the Augustans reminds us, is that which transmutes concrete historical realities into universals. Its fictions include but transcend historical fact . . .
[A good poem] has the autonomous poetic life of true satire . . . [it] exemplifies the formal and stylistic features by which satire can transmute history into poetry.
. . . the critical question remains the same: has the satirist succeeded, by his masks, his indirections, his ironies and his myths, in freeing his poem from the trammels of historical circumstance and in bestowing upon it the poetic autonomy of true satire?[1]

As Sanford Budick has explained, "the modern revaluation of Augustan poetry has learned to ask one question su-

1. *POAS* (1963), pp. xlix–l, li, lv.

premely well: what is the real scope of the artist's subject and achievement? Is it only personal and occasional or does it also have timeless, universal concerns to which local details are, in the end, made subordinate? Dryden's poetry has been late in benefiting from this kind of question, but even in the last decade it has become common to speak of his satires in terms of the same issues that occupy our attention in *Paradise Lost*."[2] Reuben Brower thinks Dryden to be a good poet because he is successful in transcending the "parochial," "provincial" qualities of the poetry of his time. "The particular issues involved are of little concern for us at present; but we can recognize their importance in the late seventeenth century, and see that the general issues involved are of a sort that is central in any conceivable society."[3] Critics who think highly of *Annus Mirabilis* choose terms of praise which are suggestive of this underlying poetic standard of generality. The people who appear in *Annus Mirabilis*, Earl Miner says, share "a world of tragic potential, a possibility of triumph but in a life precarious amid such disasters as war and fire. The two actions of the poem are, therefore, whole in their view of life, to which danger is a common element in varying experience . . . The threat of disaster, with the promise of continuing life, enters the poem at its beginning . . ."[4]

The supposition behind these statements seems to be that poetry, especially good poetry, is known to be poetic by its generality—that is, by its transcendence of particularity. Literary works which lack this innate capacity for transcendence remain something else, "concrete historical realities." How has this central distinction between generality and particularity affected criticism of *Annus Mirabilis*?

In an article which was first published in 1946, Edward N. Hooker presented evidence that the genesis, and hence the understanding, of that poem was too deeply involved in its

2. *Dryden and the Abyss of Light* (1970), p. xi.
3. *Dryden Collection* (1963), "An Allusion to Europe: Dryden and Poetic Tradition," pp. 51–52.
4. *Dryden's Poetry* (1967), p. 16.

immediate political context to be separated from it. The very title of the poem, Hooker claimed, was derived from the seditious *Mirabilis Annus* tracts which had been printed a few years earlier, and the poem itself must be seen as a refutation of the enthusiastic antimonarchal and anti-Anglican doctrine expressed in those tracts. *Annus Mirabilis*, then, "was a piece of inspired journalism . . . the poem must be taken as part of a pamphlet-war." It "stands as a political document as well as a poem . . ."[5] Ten years later Hooker reformulated these conclusions by observing that "*Annus Mirabilis* is remarkable for the skill by which an urgent, practical problem is raised to a subject of universal meaning."[6] Many critics have made approving, if passing, reference to Hooker's thesis that Dryden's intention in writing *Annus Mirabilis* was "political."[7] A "political reading" of the poem, however, has usually been rejected, sometimes by the same critics, as insufficient to do justice to the poetic breadth of Dryden's intention and vision, or irrelevant to large parts of the poem which are "nonpolitical" in content.[8]

Thus, despite certain differences in language, it is not altogether clear that "political" approaches to *Annus Mirabilis* constitute a real alternative to those based on the generality theory of value. For even the many critics who acknowledge the value of Hooker's research seem to hold the fundamental principle that if a poem is understood politically—as a political document or as a piece of journalism—it is seen in its particularity, and its meaning is limited by the localized instrumentality of the poem and by the parochial

5. *Essential Articles* (1966), Hooker, 'The Purpose of Dryden's *Annus Mirabilis*," pp. 298, 293.

6. Dryden, *Works* (1956), I, 258.

7. See, e.g., Butt, *Augustan Age* (1950), p. 13; Kinsley, *RES*, n.s., 7 (1956), 30; Cope and Jones in Sprat, *History* (1667), p. xiv; Schilling, *Dryden and the Conservative Myth* (1961), p. 272; van der Welle, *Dryden and Holland* (1962), pp. 15ff; Lord in *Restoration of the Stuarts* (1960), p. 65, *POAS* (1963), p. xxxiv; Nevo, *Dial of Virtue* (1963), p. 158; Rosenberg, *PMLA*, 79 (1964), 255; Watson in Dryden, *Essays* (1964), I, 93; Wedgwood, *Poetry and Politics* (1964), p. 143; Miner, *Dryden's Poetry* (1967), p. 8n; Davison, *Dryden* (1968), p. 92; Sutherland, *OHEL* (1969), VI, 183.

8. Cf. Butt, *Augustan Age* (1950), p. 13; C. Ward, *Life of John Dryden* (1961), p. 44; Miner, *Dryden's Poetry* (1967), pp. 8, 26.

response of its audience. The significance of the poem is no
larger than the circumscribed political occasion which it
aims to influence. In the context of literary criticism, it
would seem, the political capacity of a work is a relatively
inferior or insignificant one; relative, that is, to its poetic
capacity, in which the work, if it is "good," rises to the
opposite values of generality and plurisignificance, transcending the limitations of its political occasion. The critic
who demonstrates the poetic value of a poem operates in a
sphere of inquiry which is distinct from that available to
the student of a poem's political capacity, and the poet's
achievement of poetic excellence may be sharply distinguished from whatever strategies of his are responsible for
his political effects. In fact, poetic excellence often will seem
to consist precisely in the negation of the political capacity,
in the final, "nonpolitical" quality of the poem.

By asserting that certain reciprocal attitudes of the poet
and of his audience—those involving the effect of political
strategies—are inoperative for the critic who understands
the poem "as poem," this approach transforms the poetic and
the political capacities of a work into categories which are
quasi-objective solely by virtue of their assumed disjunction
prior to the act of critical definition by which the work is
first understood. In the remainder of this Introduction I will
broaden my investigation of recent criticism in an attempt to
show why I find this conception of the critic's task a limited,
and ultimately an unsatisfactory, basis for critical practice.
In the process, I will try to formulate a theoretical foundation for an alternative practice.

Didacticism and Generic Differentiation

Modern criticism's disjunctive categorization of poetic
and political strategies is closely related to its characteristic
attitude toward the system of generic differentiation—despite the fact that Dryden and his contemporaries provide a
quite different perspective on both matters. At first consideration, of course, today's generality theory of value

would seem to be well suited to the prevailing critical temper of the period studied. Modern critics evidently are in accord with the neoclassical theorists who believed that generality is indispensable for poetic excellence. The agreement, however, is not as close as it appears to be. In neoclassical theory, generality is valued as a means of ensuring that poetry will be morally educative. The successful communication of the poet's moral purpose is dependent on the generality of its expression, on a clarity and representativeness which make his moral purpose immediately apprehensible. The generality theory of value is thus a function of the fundamental didactic purpose.[9] But as we have seen, modern critics tend to value generality in poetry as a means to transcend poetically the nonpoetic capacity of the poem, its historical, political, or moral dimensions. To assert the poetic value of a poem by arguing its generality is to ignore or exclude—to rise above—didactic considerations. While in neoclassical theory the aim of generality unites poetic and didactic value, in modern criticism it separates them.

The many categories of the neoclassical system of generic differentiation had a common basis in didacticism. All good poetry, no matter what its specific kind, had to be educative, to inculcate moral virtue, to lead or persuade the reader toward the conclusions which the poet advocated. All genres could be subsumed under the fundamental rhetorical concerns of praise and blame.[10] All genres were seen as didactic. Yet to say that a system of discourse proceeds on the general assumption that all statements are pedagogic, persuasive, or "political" is not to deny that many statements will seek to convince their auditors that they are innocent of instructive, rhetorical, or political purpose. The stance of the antirhetorician was an important one in the arsenal of rhetorical strategies, and it lent support to the tendency of genres,

9. On the meaning of "generality" during the Restoration see Youngren, *ELH*, 35, no. 2 (1968), 158–87. Pace Youngren, however, the neoclassical demand for generality in poetry is not *in itself* opposed to modern expectations of poetry (see p. 158), as I hope to document in the present discussion.
10. See Hardison, *Enduring Monument* (1962), pp. 28, 51.

shared by other types of constructed categories, to harden into exclusive, quasi-objective entities.

In the prefatory "Account" of *Annus Mirabilis* to his brother-in-law Sir Robert Howard, Dryden writes: "I have call'd my Poem *Historical,* not *Epick,* though both the Actions and Actors are as much Heroick, as any Poem can contain." The reason for this decision, he continues, is that "the Action is not properly one . . ." It is "broken action, ti'd too severely to the Laws of History," a phenomenon which Dryden illustrates by alluding to the example of Lucan, who should be ranked "rather among Historians in Verse, then Epique Poets."[11] It would not be difficult to find very similar discussions of "historical poetry" in Renaissance and seventeenth-century literary theory, nor would it be unprofitable to place Dryden within this literary tradition.[12] Yet it must be remembered that the neoclassical genres were very flexible, not least because they were characterized by a strain of didacticism whose commonness to all genres prevented any from being unique or entirely exclusive. When Dryden defines the literary kind within which he will perform, he simultaneously defines for his readers both the way he will persuade them and the way he will—in the cause of better persuasion—create the illusion of writing nonrhetorically. Thus, his poems characteristically are poised between their quasi-objective existence in an autonomous genre which transcends didacticism, and their rhetorical function which effaces the categorial boundaries between genres. In the same way, Dryden both intends to write a historical poem and intends to write a work which will be taken as a historical poem by his reader. Furthermore, both strategies invite the reader to enter into the illusion that Dryden's poem, however heroic, is "ti'd too severely to the Laws of History," invite him to suspend his consciousness of this statement as a rhetorical assertion of objectivity or im-

11. For a similar judgment of Lucan see Dryden, *Essays* (1964), "Of Heroic Plays" (1672), I, 160.
12. See, e.g., Hardison, *Enduring Monument* (1962), pp. 45–51.

partiality, a claim that the poet is telling the truth. The neo-classical system of generic differentiation was flexible enough to accommodate the frequent negative responses to this sort of invitation, as the popularity of the mock-heroic genre testifies. The mock-heroic customarily mocks not true heroism, nor even the heroic genre, but those unworthies who pretend to it, and Dryden himself possessed a mock-heroic perspective more than sufficient to subvert his own claim that in *Annus Mirabilis* "both the Actions and Actors are as much Heroick, as any Poem can contain." When he observed that Homer "forms and equips those ungodly man-killers whom we poets, when we flatter them, call heroes,"[13] Dryden demonstrated a capacity, which he shared with his age, to work within a system of poetic genres whose status as categories never threatened to obscure their provisional character.

The same may not confidently be said, however, of modern critics. By giving only nominal recognition to the didactic function of neoclassical poetry, modern criticism hardens the boundaries between each poetic genre and between poetry itself and political persuasion. The poet's definition of his genre, an act which implies a certain didactic strategy, becomes simply a description of what his poem "is," and precludes any understanding of its poetic meaning that is not explicitly accounted for in the terms of the generic description. Critics point out that Dryden developed the habit of attaching to his poems prefaces which explain to the reader what genre he is attempting and what his purpose will be.[14] Our understanding of the poems, it is argued, must derive from these explanations, even though modern critical presuppositions have deprived them of their implicit didactic significance. From this perspective, problems of persuasion and its strategies do not exist, because their solution must be found outside the system, predefined as exclu-

13. Dryden, *Essays* (1964), preface to *Examen poeticum* (1963), II, 167.
14. See, e.g., Nichol Smith, *John Dryden* (1950), p. 9; Jack, *Augustan Satire* (1965), p. 6; Kinsley, *English Studies,* 34 (1953), 549.

sively poetic, in which a poem's manner of presentation constitutes its own justification and meaning.

In the case of *Annus Mirabilis,* critics have been unusually zealous in embracing the antirhetorical implications of Dryden's prefatory remarks, since what he says there about the genre of the poem is frequently misconstrued or ignored. The "Account" to Howard has a good deal to say about epic form, but at crucial points Dryden makes clear his preference for the historical poem and the georgic as models for *Annus Mirabilis.*[15] By far the greatest amount of attention, however, has been paid to the poem's epic pretensions. Dryden's most recent biographer, Charles E. Ward, has argued against Hooker's interpretation of the political occasion of the poem by saying that "the tenor of Dryden's 'Account' to Howard shows clearly that his thoughts are employed upon the epic poem and upon the details of a poetic art which can encompass a modern treatment of heroic actions. Indeed one may seriously doubt the narrow, political purpose as is suggested by this interpretation."[16] Another critic takes similar exception to Hooker's thesis: "Dryden calls *Annus Mirabilis* an Historical Poem, but it is clearly to be considered as a preliminary exercise in the epic manner by a poet who has wider ambitions in that field. Its subject matter is contemporary, the events of the year 1666 . . . But clearly Dryden is doing more than writing a journalist's report on these; he is attempting to give them the wider and timeless context of epic poetry . . . *Annus Mirabilis* then may be considered primarily as a Lucanian poem, though Dryden also acknowledges his debt to Virgil . . ."[17]

In Earl Miner's analysis of the poem, the generalizing process by which Dryden brings together the English and the Dutch results less in "tragedy or irony than epic sorrow

15. For a discussion of some of the reasons for this preference, see below, Chapter 5.
16. *Life of John Dryden* (1961), p. 44.
17. *Dryden's Mind and Art* (1969), John Heath-Stubbs, "Dryden and the Heroic Ideal," p. 5.

and epic exaltation . . . the irony and the tragedy are part of the full epic awareness, of a Homeric view of war."[18] By trying to avoid the "narrowness" of a "political interpretation," critics guarantee that their own understandings of *Annus Mirabilis* will have the narrowness of a unitary perspective on what constitutes the "poetic." H. T. Swedenberg's interest in the generic discussion found in Dryden's "Account" yields no more than the observation that the poem "was an avowed effort to achieve epic grandeur."[19] The repudiation of didactic considerations excludes vast stretches of explanation and interpretation. Rachel Trickett, observing that "Dryden's poems suggest that he saw all tragic or heroic occasions in life as part of a common and inevitable human fate," allows her understanding of his poetry to be limited by a total acceptance of this suggestion. In Dryden's formal panegyrics, she writes, "we can recognize what he most admired in the epic manner—its magnitude, its being so much larger than life." He sometimes makes use of a "reflective generalizing tendency . . . , sententious commonplaces and generalized reflections . . . to show how every event is part of the general pattern of existence. Here was a way of elevating the trivial and exhibiting the great or tragic event in its true perspective in history."[20] By defining didacticism out of the sphere of poetry, Trickett precludes an understanding of how a "reflective generalizing tendency," by raising poetry to the level of epic generality, also serves a very particular use as rhetorical strategy.

The relation between celebrations of generality and the strict categorization of poetry and poetic genres can be seen in recent comparisons between Dryden's and Andrew Marvell's poetry. According to D. W. Jefferson, Dryden's "superiority in satire over his predecessors lies mainly in his large approach to his material and complete imaginative adjustment to it. The world of politics is in many respects a little world, full of confusing details. Marvell, for the most part, was

18. *Dryden's Poetry* (1967), p. 18.
19. *SP*, extra ser., no. 4 (1967), 16.
20. *Honest Muse* (1967), pp. 71, 33, 35.

unable to rise above this littleness and confusion. His *Last Instructions to a Painter* is composed chiefly of obscure references to insignificant people and their forgotten deeds."[21] Reuben Brower agrees with Jefferson that "breadth of vision and sureness of rhythm are missing in *Last Instructions to a Painter*, although the poem has some of the obvious earmarks of epic satire. The spectacle is rather painful: the earlier Marvell could not address this world without sacrificing many of his virtues as a poet."[22] The principle which is established by these critics is implicitly retained in John M. Wallace's "political" comparison between *The Last Instructions* and *Annus Mirabilis*. Given the separation of poetry and politics, and the poetic excellence of Dryden's poem owing to its "epic generality," it follows that a reading of the poems "as political documents" should reveal Marvell's particularity to be politically superior—revelatory, that is, of a sounder understanding of the complexity of the political situation. Thus Wallace writes that "politically, the farsightedness of *The Last Instructions* makes *Annus Mirabilis* look myopic."[23] Jefferson and Brower regard the poems they discuss as the outcome of a striving toward excellence in the sharply delimited sphere of poetry. Wallace regards them as the outcome of an attempt to assess the political climate realistically. It seems more reasonable, however, to explain them comprehensively as poetry that is the outcome of a political experience whose nature dictates which cause will profit from a strategy of "poetic transcendence" (Wallace's "myopia") and which from a strategy of "political specificity" (Jefferson's "confusing details").

Rhetoric and Rhetorical Analysis

The critical attitudes toward didacticism and generic differentiation which I have been describing are all the more

21. *Dryden's Mind and Art* (1969), "Aspects of Dryden's Imagery," p. 39.
22. *Dryden Collection* (1963), "An Allusion to Europe: Dryden and Poetic Tradition," p. 51. Cf. Trickett, *Honest Muse* (1967), p. 37.
23. *Destiny His Choice* (1968), p. 173.

surprising when it is remembered that in recent years critics
have become very interested in "rhetorical" approaches to
the understanding of the meaning of English literature—in
the use, that is, of classical rhetoric for literary analysis. The
application of a system whose function it was to prescribe
the proper literary techniques for influencing an audience in
specific ways to the task of describing the literary techniques of a poet requires an interest in the kinds of effects
the poet wishes to produce and hence in his understanding
of the nature of his audience.[24] There has been general
agreement, for example, that Dryden's poetry is in some
manner peculiarly "public" or "occasional," that it occurs,
and therefore should be read, "in context." This sort of reading, which requires more than the explication of isolated
allusions or the tracing of literary traditions, might demand
the temporary adoption, by the critic, of the perspectives of
those of Dryden's contemporaries who are taken to constitute his audience.

At this point in the discussion it may be useful to intro-
duce some terms to describe the attitudes which contribute
to a rhetorical approach to literature. Generally speaking, it
might be said that literary criticism whose "definitions"
approximate those of the poet whose poem it studies tends to
understand the poem in its own terms, that is, from the perspective which the poet requires of his "ideal audience." On
the other hand, literary criticism whose definitions diverge
from those of the poet whose poem it studies tends to understand the poem in different terms, from a different perspective. Neither of these approaches is wrong in itself, but in
their most simple and uncompromising forms they are no
more than partial ways of understanding the poem as a
rhetorical event. Hence the pejorative connotations of the
labels I will attach to each, dogmatism and reductionism,
are meant to emphasize the deficiencies of these approaches

24. Although Horace and other rhetoricians tend to base their prescrip-
tions on a knowledge of emotions and reactions which are common to all
people, the prototypical rhetorical relationship between orator and audience-
jury demands a more precise and specific understanding of the case to be
argued in relation to the beliefs of those before whom it is argued.

as they remain totally separate from one another. Rhetorical analysis, as it might be practiced by the critic, would understand the meaning of poetry as the product of the interaction between the definitions of the poem and those of, not the poet's ideal audience, but the historical audience whose perspective is taken at the outset to differ in some manner from that of the poet because a difference in perspective is implicit in rhetoric's fundamental task of persuasion. In other words, rhetorical analysis might constitute a synthesis of dogmatism and reductionism, an analysis which is neither dogmatic nor reductive. It would proceed according to an understanding of poetry as a confrontation of perspectives. It is important to emphasize that the implication of adopting the perspective of the audience is not that the poet's definitions have been discarded but that the poem is thereby recreated in its original rhetorical capacity. In fact, it is only the adoption of the audience's perspective which gives meaning to the idea that the poem is written from the poet's perspective.

The interest which modern critics have shown in rhetorical approaches to literature, one might expect, should obviate the problem of the separation between poetry and politics: by understanding both poem and audience one balances them against each other and begins to appreciate how poetry is also politics. Unfortunately, an interest in classical rhetoric and its devices need not have much to do with rhetorical analysis as I have described it.[25] Very often, terms whose greatest use would be to facilitate description of the factors involved in a rhetorical relationship are taken ultimately to refer to quasi-objective entities created by the poet and related exclusively to the interaction between him and the poem. George deF. Lord, for example, discusses satire in terms of "structural forms," "structural and tonal variety," "fictional and poetic devices," and treats all of the

25. Although I find his analysis of *AM* in *Dryden's Poetic Kingdoms* lacking in this respect, Alan Roper's characteristic approach to Dryden's poetry seems to me unusually conscious of its rhetorical dimensions, and, for this reason, unusually persuasive literary criticism.

following as fairly discrete and noncontingent techniques employed by the satirist: the *persona*, the butt, the fictional audience, "scene," "action," "masks," "indirections," "ironies," and "myths."[26] The most notable example of this objectification of rhetorical terminology is the way in which the rhetorical idea of the "ethical argument" has been transformed by critics into the idea of the autonomous persona.[27] The idea of the ethical argument evolved from the dialectic between orator and audience, as the orator's understanding of how his particular audience would best—vis-à-vis the case to be argued—understand the character of the orator. Transferred to the realm of poetic description rather than rhetorical prescription, this idea would therefore necessitate a knowledge of the audience as understood by the poet outside the poetic fiction in which that understanding is mediated for rhetorical purposes. The persona, however, is a fictional poet who speaks to a fictional audience, both of which fictions are generated by the real poet, whose act of generation is defined as external to the realm of critical discourse.

The positive value of the idea of the persona is entirely owing to what it derives from the idea of the ethical argument. Literary criticism often treats the poet's expression of ideas reductively, by taking these poetic ideas as if they directly represented the state of the poet's mind. The concept of the ethical argument counters this reductionism by implying a distinction between the poet's instrumental self-characterizations, which occur in a particular instance of rhetorical expression, and a more complex species of belief, which would require the reconciliation of this one instance

26. *POAS* (1963), pp. li, liii, lv.

27. Some documents in the continuing controversy over the term *persona* are Maynard Mack, "The Muse of Satire," *Yale Review*, 41 (1951), 80–92; Irvin Ehrenpreis, "Personae," in *Restoration and Eighteenth-Century Literature: Essays in Honor of A. D. McKillop*, ed. Carroll Camden (Chicago, 1963), pp. 25–37; James L. Clifford, "The Eighteenth Century," *MLQ*, 16 (1965), 119–22; "Symposium: The Concept of the Persona in Satire," *Satire Newsletter*, 3 (Spring 1966), 89–153. The relevance of biography, more than that of the historical audience, is of major concern to the participants in this controversy.

with other instances and with other kinds of expression. Yet the transformation of the ethical argument to the persona has had a curious effect. Critics who have only an inconsistent commitment to rhetorical analysis find it difficult to maintain an equilibrium between dogmatism and reductionism for long, and frequently descend to dogmatic or reductive biographical assertions even while the recognition of rhetorical design is at its height.

Dogmatism and Belief

Dogmatic criticism involves the critical elevation of Dryden's definitions into universal truths which exist above the level of rhetorical interaction. Reductive criticism, on the other hand, takes the commonplaces of Dryden's rhetorical argument as evidence of his belief or of his place within a philosophical tradition.[28] Put in the same terms, the dogmatic critic treats the political rationale which underlies the use of those commonplaces as if its intention were automatically fulfilled, as if what the poet argued was an idea universally accepted as true by contemporaries.

The critical dogmatism which may result from an inconsistent commitment to rhetorical analysis is illustrated by the following comments on *Absalom and Achitophel:* "While not hiding his opinions the narrator assumes the stance of an urbane, impartial observer . . . The modulations of the speaker's voice allow Dryden to be objective in his treatment of his material. Throughout the poem the narrator seems only tentatively committed, recognizing faults in all parties . . . The urbane, cool wit of the narrator creates a buffer of civilized emotions between the action portrayed and our normal immediate response. It creates the aesthetic distance necessary for the poem as art object rather than propa-

28. Cf. Ronald S. Crane, *The Idea of the Humanities* (Chicago, 1967), I, 175–76, who calls A. O. Lovejoy's "unit-ideas" "commonplaces," "partly to suggest their affinity with the *topoi* and places of argument . . . , and partly to emphasize their character as more or less crystallized and discrete conceptual materials or devices of method that are capable, as their history shows, of being put to a great variety of uses."

ganda."[29] The creation of aesthetic distance is here seen as indistinguishably a rhetorical device and an ontological transformation. As Dryden's rhetoric takes hold, his alter ego "narrator" acquires a distinct and separate existence, a duality which allows Dryden not simply to seem, but to be, objective. The poem does not seem, but is, an "art object" rather than "propaganda."

This sort of vacillation may seem a strange critical phenomenon, but it is not so unusual in Dryden criticism. In the following passages, Rachel Trickett's rhetorical consciousness is evenly mixed with an impulse to make biographical assertions which contradict this consciousness, and qualities of sincerity, insincerity, honesty, dishonesty, truth, and falsehood are made to take each other's places with no sense of difference between them:

. . . those poets who were born into the contentious world of satire were unavoidably preoccupied with honesty and sincerity, and with the devices, the style, and the tone of voice which would appear to convey these qualities . . .

Dryden's pleasure in rising to the occasion of a panegyric was entirely sincere . . .

[The Hind and the Panther] is persuasive, and needs at least an assumed tone of sincerity, which Dryden, with his skill in adapting his manner to argument and in claiming forthright honesty, could easily command. But . . . may not the effect of candor here be simply a rhetorical device? . . . Yet there is some evidence of sincerity in this case . . .

Intense sincerity is present in all those parts of The Hind and the Panther where the poet speaks in his own person . . .

It is easy to imagine that when the poet writes like an orator with pomp and persuasion, or argues, or exchanges banter over the footlights, his verse reduces itself to empty rhetoric. But in Dryden's poetry the public tone mingles imperceptibly with personal feeling, and its peculiar principle of honesty sometimes extends from public declamation to private confession.

. . . from his life, and the significant evidence of his poetry, we can discover a general principle of sincerity which sprang from his convictions and was a matter of his sensitivity to the manner best suited to their expression . . .

29. *Dryden's Mind and Art* (1969), Bruce King, "*Absalom and Achitophel:* A Revaluation," pp. 79, 81, 82.

Dryden and his successors were equally concerned to be true to poetry as an art . . . Because of the widespread misuse of poetry for propaganda and the unavoidable competition with hack writers, serious poets were unusually sensitive about the dignity of their art. They were conscious of their craft as part of the high tradition of poetry, which set them apart from amateurs and journalists in verse alike.[30]

Again, some unstated process is taking place which transforms "sincerity" into a relevant, even an important, standard for the evaluation of Dryden's poetry. We do not see how Trickett has been able to distinguish between Dryden's "art" and the "high tradition of poetry" on the one hand, and "amateurs," "propaganda," and "journalists in verse" on the other. Hence we must assume that it has something to do with the way in which Dryden's customary ethical argument is accepted by her as the proper, apolitical, nonrhetorical criterion for understanding the meaning of his poetry. One reads the final quoted passage with the uneasy feeling that Trickett has failed to maintain sufficient distance from Dryden's rhetorical strategies to resist the process of persuasion which can transform the critic into an uncritical "convert"— blind to the way in which the poet's language aims to persuade because unconscious that persuasion already has occurred.

Another example of dogmatic criticism can be seen in the way the idea of political moderation has been handled by literary critics. A useful rhetorical technique for arguing any political position, the stance of "moderation" is frequently a means by which defenders of the status quo effect a mystical transformation of statistical normality ("the majority") from a quantitative into an evaluative concept. Unlike "majority," "moderation" commonly connotes not simply distinction but normative exclusion, opposed "extremes" between which the "moderate" majority moderates. The word "extreme," as well, has not only its accepted denotation but the connotation which links it with unreasonableness and wild-eyed fanaticism. Dryden would find little rhetorical use in refer-

30. *Honest Muse* (1967), pp. 21–22, 30, 62, 63, 64, 81, 82.

ences to "the moderate sort" of men[31] were he not hoping to capitalize on the evaluative connotation, as well as on the quantitative denotation, of the word. Yet an awareness of this fact makes critical statements like the following ones difficult to assess:

[In 1648], England to all moderate men appeared once again to have gone out of her mind . . .
    In [1681], the moderation of Dryden's opinions, which he emphasized in his preface [to *Absalom and Achitophel*] and in his additions to the second edition, was the guarantee of the satire's effectiveness.[32]

Although he did not thereafter express it in terms of the union of popular choice and divine right, this was the moderate political position Dryden regularly adopted in one form or another.[33]

Where do the critics stand in relation to the poet's rhetorical purpose? Clearly, the assertion of moderation does not prove moderation, except to an audience that does not require proof. It is important to note that what Dryden manifestly adopts is not a "moderate political position" but the name and language of moderation, and he does so in order to argue for a position which may or may not be moderate but whose moderation depends on its context and on the perspective from which it is viewed. An evaluative concept has no meaning without reference to an evaluative (not simply numerical) context, and the nature of the evaluation is a function of the particular context which is supplied. Thus it is obvious that from the perspective of many Englishmen of a certain political and religious persuasion, the execution of Charles I was evaluatively a "moderate" act: however extreme it was in the sense of infrequency, it was not extreme in the evaluative sense of wild-eyed fanaticism. From the royalist perspective, however, both the execution of Charles I and Hampden's refusal to pay ship money were extreme

31. See *Absalom and Achitophel* (1681), l. 75, "To the Reader," l. 16.
    32. Wallace, *ELH*, 36, no. 1 (1969), 279, 281–82.
    33. *Dryden Collection* (1963), Earl Wasserman, "Dryden: *Epistle to Charleton*," p. 81.

acts in both senses of the term. According to some atypical evaluative scales, deviation from the statistical norm may constitute deviation from extremism into moderation. For the critic to use the term "moderation" as Dryden uses it is to accept Dryden's political application of that term, which consists not only in the identification of his political opponents as extremists in both senses but also in the identification of Dryden himself as a man whose moderation—between two extremes—permits him a measure of apolitical impartiality.

Reductionism and Belief

Critical reductionism is likely whenever a critic makes an explicit attempt to derive Dryden's beliefs, in the largest sense of the word, from his poetry. Earl Miner, for example, has shown interest in the poet's attitude toward the idea of progress:

> Two types of imagery emerge from [Dryden's] progress-pieces, I believe, and suggest his dual concept of progress. There are images of progress as process—growth or motion, and progress as an end achieved—the goal of art reached, for which he often employs imagery of stasis that is often architectural or trans-cendant.
>   . . . apparently he felt that a good deal of progress is possible and desirable in time, but that perfection will come only when eternity begins at the Day of Judgment . . .
>   Dryden is not a simple progressivist, but he does not believe in historical decay.[34]

Two main points are worth mentioning. First, like most other modern critics, Miner normally is aware of the problematic nature of his inquiry owing to the rhetorical dimension of the poems from which he deduces this belief in progress. Dryden's use of the idea of historical decay, for example, is unwelcome evidence of contrary belief, and so Miner says that Dryden's "purely rhetorical purpose there is

---

34. *PQ*, 40 (1961), 124, 125; *Dryden's Poetry* (1967), p. 27n (on other beliefs see p. 34).

evident from his use of a cyclical theory of history as well."[35] The poet's expression of an "apocalyptic view," similarly, draws the response that "here, as always, . . . it is danger-ous to quote Dryden out of context."[36] This inconsistency, however, is no more striking than the insipid, colorless nature of Dryden's "idea" once it is extracted from its con-text. "Belief" is involuntarily reduced by Miner to a com-monplace whose meaning consists not in anything substan-tive but in its sheer construability. Another example of reductionism may be found in the many critical assurances that Dryden is a late, a narrow, or a full-fledged "Christian humanist."[37] The breadth and indeterminateness of this intellectual tradition, even as it is characterized by single critics, are enough to accommodate "beliefs" that would seem to be directly opposed to those with which Dryden is often associated. Thus one well-known writer considers Christian humanism incompatible even with "a real theory of progress."[38]

A final example of the simplification of beliefs which amounts to reductionism is the treatment, common in many modern studies, of the seventeenth century's attitude toward astrology and prophecy. The Restoration and eighteenth century have long been characterized by scholars as an age of rationalism. Or rather, it has become usual to distinguish, as prominent contemporaries often did, between the ra-tionalism of those figures whom posterity has designated "major" and of those institutions which maintained an ascen-dancy throughout the age, and the irrationality or "enthusi-asm" that marks the period's various forms of political, religious, and literary dissent. In literary history it is a

35. *PQ*, 40 (1961), 121n3.

36. Ibid., 126. The two sources are the dedicatory epistle to *Plutarch's Lives* (1683) and *A Song for St. Cecilia's Day* (1687).

37. See, e.g., Miner in Dryden, *Works* (1969), III, 304, 339, 345, 348; Miner, *Dryden's Poetry* (1967), pp. xiii, 29, 30, 34; *Dryden Collection* (1963), E. M. W. Tillyard, "Ode on Anne Killigrew," p. 147; *Dryden's Mind and Art* (1969), Elias J. Chiasson, "Dryden's Apparent Scepticism in *Religio Laici*," p. 85.

38. Herschel Baker, *The Wars of Truth: Studies in the Decay of Christian Humanism in the Earlier Seventeenth Century* (London, 1952), p. 78.

commonplace that the Augustan tradition has a great deal to
do with rationalism, and that the contemporary opponents
of this tradition necessarily represent an opposed spirit of
enthusiasm.[39] Terms like "rationalism" and "enthusiasm" are
dangerous tools in modern scholarship because it is difficult
to keep their contemporary ideological use as weapons of
absolute definition from obscuring the modern understanding of the past in its fullest complexity. But the problems
involved in this sort of analysis go far beyond those posed by
the use of seventeenth-century terminology, as the work of
an influential historian of religion demonstrates.

In his widely read study of medieval "revolutionary millenarianism," Norman Cohn seeks a correlation between
millenarian thought, revolutionary behavior, and certain recurrent social conditions by using the perspective of socio-
logical and psychological description.[40] The unfortunate
result is a picture of medieval society polarized, by the combined reductionism of contemporary social prejudices and
modern psychological categories, into two exclusive groups.
Millenarian prophets, if they also dissent from the current
social distribution of power, are seen as the victims of
pathological "fantasy." The millenarian fantasies of those
who wield power, on the other hand, are accorded the status
of sober "belief." Cohn's idea of fantasy wavers back and
forth between the realms of naive epistemology and politico-
historical hindsight. At times, for example, revolutionary
millenarian fantasy consists of using imaginative language
which cannot be translated literally into reality. At others,
any expectation or demand which is "unrealistic"—meaning
that it was neither fulfilled at the time nor vindicated by the

39. Two important documents in the modern discussion of Augustan
rationalism are George Williamson, "The Restoration Revolt against Enthusiasm" (1933), in *Seventeenth-Century Contexts* (Chicago, 1961), pp.
202–39; and Donald F. Bond, " 'Distrust' of the Imagination in English
Neo-Classicism" (1935), in *Essential Articles: For the Study of English
Augustan Background,* ed. Bernard N. Schilling (Hamden, Conn., 1961),
pp. 281–301.
40. *Pursuit of the Millennium* (1970). For the work of a scholar of
17th-century English sectarianism who adopts attitudes similar to some of
Cohn's, see Cooper, *Baptist Quarterly,* 18, 19 (1960, 1961), 351–62, 29–34.

developments of later history (as the subversion of papal power was but the creation of universal communism was not)—is thereby a fantasy as well. Cohn's standard for evaluating medieval revolutionary millenarianism, in other words, is a psychological theory of a severely selective nature. Social and historical phenomena which are seen to have been "dysfunctional" tend to be invalidated psychologically, whereas the socially dominant and the historically "progressive" tend to be favorably evaluated according to political rather than psychological criteria. It is therefore no wonder that Cohn's description of revolutionary millenarianism should agree so closely with the ideological categories preferred by the medieval status quo.[41]

The disjunction between rationalism and enthusiasm in Restoration studies is, I think, very similar to this one. For example, Hooker writes that in *Annus Mirabilis* "Dryden opposes the superstitious acceptance of the vulgar prophecies," implying that it was the superstition, and not the political significance of the *Mirabilis Annus* prophecies, which provoked Dryden's opposition.[42] And Charles Ward's argument with Hooker's "political reading" alludes to the gulf that is felt to exist between Dryden's Augustan rationalism and the suspect mental productions of dissenters: "The pamphlets and tracts advanced in evidence for this interpretation are few in number and obviously written by persons on the lunatic fringe."[43] When Miner encounters profound difficulty in reconciling his conception of Christian humanism with Dryden's apparent belief in astrology, the problem is solved by rejecting the latter,[44] and in E. M. W. Tillyard's judgment, "Dryden really believes in the social

41. I can do no more here than cite a number of passages from Cohn's book which I take to substantiate this brief critique: *Pursuit of the Millennium* (1970), pp. 29, 60, 62–63, 67, 75, 84, 88, 102, 105, 126, 206–7, 245, 247–48, 254, 268, 283–86.

42. *Essential Articles* (1966), "The Purpose of Dryden's *Annus Mirabilis*," p. 295. For related interpretations of Dryden's purpose and belief, see Wasserman, *John Dryden* (1964), p. 51; Elloway, *Dryden's Satire* (1966), p. xxi.

43. *Life of John Dryden* (1961), p. 342n5.

44. *Dryden's Poetry* (1967), pp. 31n, 31–32.

virtues of human civilization, but he does not really believe in astrology (as the 'advanced' men of his age did not believe in it) nor in the angels. In fact he uses both stars and angels primarily as ornaments."[45] From one perspective, these statements may be seen as a reduction of Restoration dissent through a dogmatic attachment to Dryden's beliefs, but they are more accurately understood as a reduction of both dissent and Dryden. The poet is not allowed to express those beliefs which critics think inconsistent with the beliefs that they are attributing to him.[46]

Compartmentalizing Experience

In the preceding pages I have been trying to formulate the basis for a rhetorical analysis of poetry by isolating the contradictions between rhetorical and nonrhetorical presuppositions in recent critical practice. Phillip Harth's book on Dryden's thought,[47] although an unusually systematic and often illuminating work of scholarship and criticism, provides a sustained example of how the theoretical disjunction of poetry and politics, and of other kinds of experience as well, may preclude a comprehensively rhetorical approach to poetry.

The aim of his work, Harth implies, is to counter the reductionism of critics who distort Dryden's ideas by placing them within a unitary "intellectual milieu" or "world picture." His method is to restore Dryden's religious thought to its appropriate contexts, both "primary" and "secondary." First, the primary or

logical contexts in which his terms acquire whatever meaning they possess, and the artistic contexts, or particular poems, in which Dryden's religious ideas appear . . . as the material ingredients of carefully planned formal structures . . . [Then, the] secondary contexts: the historical circumstances in which Dryden conceived and expressed them . . . , in which Dryden consid-

45. *Dryden Collection* (1963), "Ode on Anne Killigrew," p. 140.
46. For a fuller refutation of this sort of disjunction between Restoration rationalism and enthusiasm see below, Part II.
47. *Contexts of Dryden's Thought* (1968).

ered certain clearly defined questions familiar to his contemporaries and offered answers with which they were also acquainted . . . my procedure has been to begin in every case with Dryden's own ideas as expressed in their particular literary contexts and then to search for individual historical movements of thought which can help to define his own thought more precisely and to identify its specific orientation.[48]

It is of fundamental importance in understanding the necessities of Harth's antireductionism to see that these two "contexts" are taken to comprehend all of what must be known in order to establish the meaning of Dryden's poems, and that both of them are defined from the poet's perspective—that is, according to what he self-consciously "intends," logically, aesthetically, intellectually. "Intention" is limited to the poet's consciousness of what his audience should make of the poem, and excludes his consciousness of the strategies that underlie this rhetorical injunction. "Meaning" is exclusively what Dryden means to mean, not what he might mean to others.

Harth's consciousness of the rhetorical dimensions of Dryden's poetry, although frequently discerning, clearly must conflict with his more fundamental approach, which tends to objectify the individual decisions and choices which Dryden came to as a complex human being into formalistic, "clearly defined" categories of behavior and belief accepted by contemporaries as familiar social "things." Thus, for example, Harth derives from the writings of Dryden and other founding members of the Royal Society a terminology for making a schematic distinction between the epistemologies of the various disciplines of knowledge. Skepticism (modesty and diffidence and freedom of inquiry) is proper to the discovery of truth in literature and the sciences; dogmatic belief is proper to the attainment of truth in politics and religion, at least to the extent that skepticism is definitely improper to these disciplines. Hence skepticism is a scientific method implying a certain state of mind, which Dryden feels is proper to some questions. But as Harth recognizes, it

48. Ibid., pp. viii–ix.

is dangerous to assume that state of mind wherever skeptical inquiry seems to be in operation—for example, in the *Essay of Dramatic Poesy*.[49] Yet in the following observations the idea of skeptical inquiry as an epistemological method is replaced by the idea of skeptical inquiry as a rhetorical method. What distinguishes skepticism is revealed to be not the mind which uses it but certain formal techniques of argument: "If Dryden's diffidence is minimal it is nevertheless sufficient to justify his comparing the *Essay* to 'the modest inquisitions of the Royal Society.' He has preserved the character of a modest inquirer by . . . studiously avoiding any appearance of partiality in rendering a decision . . . Such detachment is appropriate and even desirable on questions such as these, which are the proper subject of free inquiry."[50] Thus the skepticism of Dryden and the Royal Society—that is, the means of knowledge proper to literary and scientific inquiry and sharply distinguished from that proper to religious and political belief—consists of the *appearance* of detachment, diffidence, free inquiry. It consists, that is, of the rhetorical expertise of the persuasive ethical argument.

Harth does not acknowledge that this kind of "skepticism" is in the end all but indistinguishable from the dogmatism which characterizes Dryden's mode of inquiry in such a poem as *Religio Laici*, where the poet "defends what he considers to be certain and indubitable truths": "His role . . . is very different from that of the skeptical critic who, in the essays, exhibits the wary caution of an independent inquirer . . . Dryden's conception of the poet as 'a kind of Law-giver' [in *Religio Laici*] is . . . a conception of the poet as a rhetorician."[51] The difference in role is not a difference in mode of inquiry but a difference in ethical argument. Dryden's conception of the poet as lawgiver is no more one of the poet as rhetorician than his conception of the essayist as skeptic is one of the essayist as rhetorician. In the *Essay*

49. For the arguments summarized here see ibid., pp. 13, 30, 32, 33.
50. Ibid., p. 34.
51. Ibid., p. 42.

(the discipline of "literature") Dryden asserts his impartiality by assuming the role of "skeptical scientist." In *Religio
Laici* ("religion") he asserts his impartiality by assuming the
role of the lawgiver who will reason his reader into truth
(that is, impartial reason will disclose the law-truth). In
Absalom and Achitophel ("politics") he asserts his impartiality by assuming the role of historian, chronicler of "what
happens." In none of these works is the critic's artificial distinction between epistemologies and disciplines reflected in
any meaningful way. It is only through an inconsistent
consciousness of the rhetorical dimensions of Dryden's
poetry that he is able to invest his compartmentalization
with plausibility. Dryden would, no doubt, regard scientific
method as entirely unsuitable to the main concerns of his
life, which after all did not literally include scientific experi-
mentation. In this respect he would be like most people: the
application of scientific method to the totality of human life
only appeals to those who would use it to comprehend
others than themselves. Like most people who write on controversial issues, Dryden tries to persuade his audience of
what he at each separate moment, it may be said, takes "on
faith" as true. To do this he finds it useful to adopt stances
which suggest impartiality, such as that of "skepticism." To
admit that his skepticism may be seen as a "stance" does
nothing to malign Dryden's own desire or ability to achieve
intellectual objectivity.

Harth's tendency to compartmentalize kinds of knowledge
and experience runs throughout his book, most often serving
to designate as purely "religious" or "poetic" subjects and
attitudes which a different perspective might regard also as
political. He argues, for example, against Earl Wasserman's
thesis that the "Epistle to Charleton" has "political meaning"
by asserting its generic identity. The genre of the "com-
mendatory verse epistle" dictates the use of certain poetic
conventions such as metaphors that contain political language, but these are exclusively poetic devices ("conceit,"
"similitude," "encomiastic analogy") whose language follows
from poetic—and by implication not from political—prem-

ises and traditions.[52] This kind of approach to Dryden's poetry is clearest in Harth's treatment of his main subject, *Religio Laici* and *The Hind and the Panther:* "The fact that politics and religion were closely connected in the Restoration period does not mean that Englishmen could not separate the two when they became topics for discussion. To see *Religio Laici* as a political poem and its publication as a political act is to fail to appreciate this distinction. The poem, as we have seen, is a contribution to religious apologetics . . ."[53] The acceptance of Harth's distinction was a luxury to be enjoyed only in certain circumstances, and only by those of Dryden's contemporaries whose political security permitted it. To others it would have seemed a disingenuous attempt to suggest that the ontological complexity of experience could be simplified by careful attention to labels. In denying political significance to religious topics, Harth either reduces Restoration thought to a twentieth-century compartmentalization or dogmatically allies himself with the political argument of which Dryden frequently would have been one proponent. (Although the separation of politics and religion would have been unconvincing to Dryden as a general proposition, any attempt to depoliticize the issue of religious persecution under Charles II, and thereby elevate it above the temporal protests of religious dissenters, might well have met with his polemical approval.)

In countering the traditional reductionist charge that Dryden's motives in converting to Roman Catholicism "were political and pragmatic rather than religious and intellectual," Harth characteristically suggests that a reappraisal which can be based on nothing more absolute than the sympathetic assumption of Dryden's human complexity is in fact based on certain well-known, articulated laws of social behavior:

. . . the movement of influence was usually from religion to politics, and seldom in the opposite direction. Many Englishmen

52. Ibid., pp. 21–25.
53. Ibid., p. 228.

took their politics from their religion, as Dryden was fond of
pointing out . . . But neither Dryden nor his contemporaries
were in the habit of suggesting that many Englishmen took their
religion from their politics . . .

The temptation to seek clues to Dryden's religion in his politics
is understandable. In the first place, while his religious beliefs
changed, his political convictions did not. His Toryism is a
principle of continuity in the changing world of Dryden's convictions . . .[54]

Despite his language, Harth seems to be referring not to
religious and political belief but to sect and party affiliation.
During the Restoration, the well-developed terminology of
sectarian distinction was conventionally understood to comprehend the spectrum of religious belief, but the same cannot be said of the embryonic system of party distinction and
the spectrum of political belief. Furthermore, "religious conversion" is a social formula for which there is no corresponding term in "politics." Social formulas of affiliation are not
the same as substantive belief, and to point out that Dryden
never made a formal change of political party is not to
demonstrate that his politics did not change. The difference
between Dryden's authoritarian monarchism in *The Medall*
and his insistent advocacy of limited monarchy in "To
Driden of Chesterton" is one which in the religious sphere
might well dictate a conscientious change of faith—that is,
of sect.[55] The question of whether the comprehensive
change, from 1682 to 1699, in Dryden's attitude toward God,
king, and country was *primarily* political or religious is not
necessarily a meaningless one, but it has the complexity
which is implied in the inescapable recognition that as
substantive beliefs, politics and religion in this period were
only artificially separated. This does not mean that they
were literally "the same thing," but that their interpenetra-
tion requires that the conventional distinctions between the
realms of politics and religion be suspended and that the

54. Ibid., pp. 228, 229. For typical complaints of the opposite movement
of influence see below, Chapter 6.

55. See Roper, *Dryden's Poetic Kingdoms* (1965), pp. 71–73, on the
flexibility of Dryden's belief in "limited monarchy."

attractions of mechanistic determinism be resisted. Thus, the more interesting question regarding Dryden's conversion is not whether it was motivated by an expectation of political profit but from what perspectives it could be said to have had political significance for Dryden and for his contemporaries.

In the final pages of Harth's book, the uncritical acceptance of Dryden's "moderation" is combined with the equally familiar phenomenon by which the very uncertainty that rhetorical consciousness confers on biographical speculation somehow legitimates, if acknowledged explicitly, assertions regarding character:

Another attitude no less consistently maintained is Dryden's habit of moderation . . . At times this takes the form of a self-conscious appeal to the moderation of his own view by presenting it as a *via media* between unwelcome extremes . . . Such explicit appeals serve an obviously rhetorical function, of course . . . [However] they appear so often without fanfare . . . that we must assume they were habitual with Dryden . . .

His attitude had no appeal for the fanatics of either church, "for sects that are extremes, abhor a middle way"; but it was entirely appropriate to one who believed that "a Man is to be cheated into Passion, but to be reason'd into Truth."[56]

What can be seen unequivocally to have been habitual with Dryden is, however, not his moderate attitude but his moderate stance. It is noteworthy that as an index of moderation in the evaluative sense—and the contrast with "fanatics" makes it clear that this is the sense intended—Harth should prefer a nonrhetorical analysis of Dryden's poetic language to, for example, an investigation of the concrete policies and actions for which his poetry argues.

Poetic and Rhetorical Belief

It is clear enough from the nature of the subject that any critic who wishes to understand poetry rhetorically, didacti-

56. *Contexts of Dryden's Thought* (1968), pp. 290, 291.

cally, politically, or the like will be concerned with the strategic intention of the poet. Yet it is equally clear from the foregoing discussion that many critics, once having adopted a rhetorical approach to Dryden's poetry (perhaps even out of frustration at simplistic assertions made about his belief), choose to ignore the rhetorical instrumentality of Dryden's intention and transform it into a species of belief which transcends the sphere of rhetorical discourse altogether. What is the explanation for this puzzling phenomenon? Why has the renewal of interest in rhetorical approaches to the study of poetry paradoxically generated so much of the dogmatism and reductionism which it might be expected to obviate? In his recent book on Edmund Waller, Warren L. Chernaik takes rhetorical consciousness in reading late seventeenth-century poetry further than other critics I have discussed so far, and in doing so he suggests some answers to these questions.[57] I will try to summarize his argument in the process of its development.

Like most modern critics of Restoration literature, Chernaik initially distinguishes between the political and the poetic capacities of a poem in terms of particularity and generality. "The occasional nature of the poem gives it specificity, while the heroic and artistic qualities—the existence of the poem as poem and as part of a poetic tradition —seek to give it universality." This distinction implies a similar, epistemological one for the critic: "Waller's political poems must ultimately be judged not as politics but as poetry." Yet Chernaik's argument suggests that conventional distinctions such as these, necessary in any discussion of poetry or politics, may have a particular use in creating the conditions for their own dissolution. Waller's poems should "reflect their circumstances as they transcend them . . . If they do not, their failure is artistic as well as persuasive." What Chernaik calls poetic effects "all subserve the poem's essentially persuasive purpose and as such find their artistic justification." Thus a comprehensive understanding of poetic

57. *Poetry of Limitation* (1968).

production reveals that "occasion, rhetorical purpose, and purely artistic qualities are inseparable."[58]

Because he makes these connections, Chernaik's basic expression of rhetorical consciousness promises more than those which I have quoted from other critics, even though its substance may be the same:

> Satire, like panegyric, must be effective both as persuasion and as literature; it must convince in two different ways. The author writes as a partisan, yet in a sense he must disguise his partisanship; satire and panegyric are often most effective when they create the illusion of objectivity . . . it is the satirist's responsibility to show that what he considers a vice is one, and that correction is possible or desirable—in other words, to validate his standards. His position is anything but detached, yet through various devices he gives his partisan arguments the objectivity of wit, point, precision, and aesthetic distance.[59]

Since the "creation" of aesthetic distance in effect "creates" objectivity, the two different kinds of conviction, rhetorical and poetic, have a close causal relation, whatever the conventional distinctions between these two spheres of discourse. The factors that are responsible for rhetorical and poetic conviction are, in fact, the same: rhetorical validation is coextensive with poetic validation.

One implication of this argument is that the literary critic who judges this kind of poetry to be "good" is indistinguishable, both in his evaluation *and in the proof which he alleges for it,* from the politically partisan reader who judges it to be "good." Poetic evaluation requires the blind leap of conviction made by the politically committed. The critic must be politically persuaded that the poem transcends its political limitations, thereby attaining a state for which evaluation may be regarded as "purely poetic." The poet's "illusion of objectivity" must become objectivity for the critic, at which

58. Ibid., pp. 130–31, 134, 134–35, 136, 137. Cf. Kinsley on *AM* in *RES*, n.s., 7 (1956), 32: "In accordance with the demands of the 'Historique and Panegyrique,' which are branches of epic poetry, and in the interests of policy, Dryden passes over incidents which detract from the heroic dignity of his characters and reshapes events to a glorious end."

59. *Poetry of Limitation* (1968), p. 187.

point the critic is free to understand his own act of evaluation as objectively poetic. However much Chernaik may
perceive this conceptually, as a literary critic he evidently
feels it necessary to make what he can regard as autonomous
"aesthetic" evaluations of Restoration poetry. The only solution is to proceed to the accepted tasks of criticism with a
double consciousness. Chernaik praises an episode in Marvell's *The Last Instructions* for its "amplification, aesthetic
distance, and satiric point. The episode contains an abundance of names, most of them now unfamiliar, and much
direct personal satire. Yet, through his use of a heroic fiction,
Marvell is able to preserve these flies in amber." For
Chernaik, Dryden's "best poems are characterized by the
attempt to lend highly ephemeral particulars an air of per-
manence, to turn briars and thorns into fine flowers." In
these poems, the reader finds that the "standards for judgment are implicit in the heroic framework of the satire and
are made explicit in the author's manipulations of levels of
style," and like the critic, one must assume, he judges them
accordingly.[60]

Chernaik's consciousness of what critical evaluation
means is necessarily double, because it partakes of two,
mutually exclusive, conceptions of poetic and critical activ-
ity. The first is the idea of poetic generality with which I
began this discussion. The second is a rhetorical conception
of poetry and criticism: "Dryden's satires are based on the
assumption that artistic skill and persuasive effectiveness are
inseparable . . . The poet's art is directed at having the
reader take his positives and negatives as absolute, objective,
indisputable, rather than simply partisan."[61] This statement
implies that poetry is a function of political particularity and
that literary critics are readers who are persuaded to elevate
the works they study into a transcendent sphere of generality. Rhetorical consciousness of this consistency prohibits
the critic from evaluating poetry according to the generality
theory of value. For an absolute and autonomous standard of

60. Ibid., pp. 194–95, 175, 196.
61. Ibid., p. 200.

poetic value it substitutes a relativistic standard of rhetorical instrumentality whose evaluations always are prior to, and comprehend, whatever judgments of poetic value the critic may make. The solution to this contradiction of double consciousness which Chernaik adopts is, in the end, the same as that which we found so curious in other critics. This puzzling phenomenon may be understood in the following manner. The critic dissolves his own rhetorical consciousness by allowing the poet his aesthetic distance, by embracing the poetic illusion created by the poet's antirhetorical stance—in short, by believing the poet. Such belief is a kind of conversion, and it requires that the critic become, at the crucial moment, uncritical: for clearly articulated criteria of judgment as to truth, merit, or the like he substitutes the naked fact of belief itself. The assertion of the critic's own credence is made most directly when he affirms those beliefs held by the poet—his honesty or sincerity—which simultaneously imply an act of belief on the part of the critic. But this end is also achieved indirectly, I think, when the critic claims to have established certain "objective" biographical facts about the poet's intellect in which he himself is not so apparently implicated (the belief in progress, moderation, Christian humanism, and so forth), for here the assertion of the poet's belief serves more effectively to rationalize and objectify—but really only to mystify—the fact of belief on the critic's part, his abdication of critical judgment. What is gained in both cases is the same. The dependable beliefs of the poet come finally to provide a firm foundation for the critic's belief in the aesthetic solidity of his evaluation of the poem before him, a piece of dry land by which to escape, with gratitude, the ceaseless flow of critical relativism.

Levels of Discourse: Commonplace and Ideology

But if this escape is often a satisfying one, the kinds of criticism to which it leads do not, as the foregoing discussion has suggested, do satisfactory justice to the uncompromisingly political nature of "political poetry." It is not that the sympathetic and admiring critic should be prohibited from coming finally to "believe" the poet; we would expect nothing less of serious literary evaluation than an identification with that which it values. The problem is rather that the sort of belief I have been describing is characteristically expressed through the critic's abandonment of his position outside the rhetorical realm within which the poet's propositions are by definition self-fulfilling, and the result is a necessarily circular form of affirmation. In particular, it involves no attempt to account for the value of the concrete political and moral implications of the poetry it affirms, and yet the necessity of such an account to the assessment of value in poetry must be a fundamental premise of rhetorical consciousness in literary criticism.

A clear alternative to this dissolution of rhetorical consciousness is, of course, the repudiation of the generality theory of value and the disjunction between poetry and politics. Whether critical relativism is an unavoidable concomitant of this alternative is a question of great importance which must be deferred until the potential interpretative benefits of rhetorical analysis have been explored in the body of this study.[62] A more immediate problem with rhetorical analysis is how to convert it from a theoretical attitude to a practical method of criticism. Since it has proved relatively easy to select examples of dogmatism and reductionism from recent critical practice, the sharpening of these terms and of the attitudes they represent will provide a likely means for developing a practice of rhetorical analysis. If dogmatism and reductionism can be practiced by method, rhetorical analysis will be constituted by their relation.

In his study of *Absalom and Achitophel,* Bernard N. Schilling is primarily interested in describing what he calls the "conservative myth" which characterizes the thought of the Restoration:

. . . Dryden . . . can rely on a complex of ideas, feelings, attitudes of mind—a whole way of looking at things that people

62. See below, Conclusion.

were going to accept without consciously deciding whether these things were true or not . . .

Dryden works from an inherited set of symbols and responses to them that make up a general interpretation of life. This might be called a mythology of order . . . Dryden . . . combines various mythical elements with his own views . . . to make something that everyone who matters will see at once to be true . . . Writing mythically, poetically, Dryden draws close to his readers by replying on a shared consciousness . . .

[Dryden] reflects the age and shares its temper . . .

In these sentences, Schilling portrays the "conservative myth" as a largely unconscious, inexplicit, virtually unquestioned world view or set of values which is so universally accepted that it characterizes the age. Dryden is a significant spokesman of this world view, which centers around an appreciation of conservatism and order. Yet the following sentences, meant to describe the same myth, give a totally different picture of it:

It is said that conservative ages are defensive . . . Only when it seems threatened, as in the late seventeenth century . . . , does conservatism seem compelled to state its principles or declare its own meaning . . .

. . . the chief commandments of Dryden's age are those beginning "Thou shalt not" from the Old Testament, [which] set a tone of negative prohibition as against the radical urge to act . . .

. . . like most conservatives, [Dryden] does not allow the opponents of order the benefit of doubt . . .

In the conservative myth, it is literally insane to do anything which might possibly overturn the established order.[63]

Schilling clearly is talking about two different kinds of conservatism and two different kinds of order. The second kind, unlike the first, is not an unconscious, inexplicit, unquestioned value of the age, but an outgrowth of one of the age's political institutions, whose interest lies precisely in convincing others to identify "the established order" with the greater "mythological order" which all people value.

63. *Dryden and the Conservative Myth* (1961), pp. 1, 2, 4, 5, 10, 65.

Schilling's intellectual identification with this interest is automatic, insofar as he accepts the formula whereby opponents of Dryden or opponents of the Stuart-Anglican order are necessarily opponents of that greater, cosmic order.

One outcome of this confusion is the idea that Dryden need only embed his "own [political] views" in "various mythical elements" for them to be universally accepted. It must be recognized, however, that "mythical elements" of the kind Schilling discusses—genuinely common to the age —were "politically neutral" rhetorical commonplaces, capable of being put to very different ideological purposes and capable of being understood by contemporaries in both their neutral and their ideological capacities. As the contrast between "commonplace" and "ideology" will indicate, I use the latter term to characterize that dimension of an idea which is taken to define and maintain the interests of one social group against the interests of other social groups. The neutral or commonplace dimension of an idea, on the other hand, is part of what Schilling would call a "shared consciousness," a rhetorical fundamental which is therefore "assumed unconsciously," a cohesive rather than a definitive force which unites in common belief what the ideological dimension distinguishes in particular belief.[64] Public discourse, in other words, may be said to occur simultaneously on two different levels: on the primary level ideas are like commonplaces, aids to thought and expression, "mythic" in their unconscious reception and in their suprapolitical quality; on the secondary level of discourse, ideas are invested with the specific meaning of conscious political and social usage, with ideological significance. The totality of "belief" is suggested by, if not contained in, the composite of primary and secondary meanings.

An example of this schematic distinction may be seen in the difference between the dimensions of the idea of order

64. In this sense of the term, then, "ideology" implies a consciousness of group identity and interest. For a discussion of the relation of group or class consciousness to ideology see John Plamenatz, *Ideology* (London, 1971), chap. 5.

which refer to Order and to the established political order. In taking the second for the first, Schilling dogmatically accepts Dryden's definitions, at the same time implicitly reducing all other ideologists to the acceptance of a world view that they do not share. The critic who takes the first for the second, or for the totality of Dryden's belief, reduces Dryden's ideology or his total mental state to a set of commonplaces—the chain of being, Renaissance correspondences, progress, and so forth. The danger of forgoing any distinction such as this one is the inconsistency and inadequacy of descriptions like those which Schilling makes. An example comparable to these is provided by E. M. W. Tillyard, who describes Dryden's "general belief" in the two following, irreconcilable, passages:

> . . . those general matters of faith in which Dryden sincerely believed and of whose value no reasonable person can have any doubt: . . . the faith in the value of good manners and of an ordered way of life.
> . . . a belief in civilization . . . which includes the beliefs in solid craft against empty ingenuity, in reason against fanaticism, in order against disorder, in monarchy against mob-rule, in established religion against arbitrary and undisciplined nonconformity.[65]

In terms of the distinction between levels of discourse which I have introduced, the first passage describes the primary, or "commonplace," level of Dryden's language, whereas the second passage describes its secondary level, or its "ideological" dimension. Each level exists separately in Dryden's public discourse; to ignore their distinctness by treating both either as commonplace or as ideology involves the critic in the error of dogmatism or reductionism.

The "analytic" quality of rhetorical analysis derives from its relation to the two basic critical approaches, whose uncompromising forms are dogmatism and reductionism: it constitutes both approaches at their most valuable, as they tend toward each other. Rhetorical analysis is "rhetorical,"

65. *Dryden Collection* (1963), "Ode on Anne Killigrew," pp. 148, 139.

on the other hand, because the confrontation which it seeks as a source of poetic meaning compares the poet's definitions with those of his historical audience. Rhetorical analysis requires the distinction between primary and secondary levels of discourse because it is necessarily conscious of the provisional utility of both Dryden's, and his audience's, perspectives for the understanding of the meaning of poetry. It is conscious that "meaning" is a relative term in that all knowledge is relative to the knower posited. The idea of "meaning" in rhetorical exchange implies both a meaner who intends a certain meaning, and the intended recipient for whom that meaning does indeed mean something, but not necessarily what the meaner has intended. In this basic respect, the definitions of the poet and those of the oppositional audience which he seeks to persuade are mutually determinant of meaning. Yet in fact, the poet's intention itself may be seen to imply meaning in this complex, dual sense. The poet's production is conditioned by his conception of the audience that he intends to consume his work, and this conception comprises both the ideally persuaded audience which will receive the poet's meaning and the oppositional audience the perception of whose distance from the poet has provided the impetus for this particular act of persuasion. Poet and audience depend upon one another, which is to say not only the obvious—that literary production creates the conditions for a certain kind of consumption—but also the less obvious—that consumption creates the conditions for a certain kind of production. Thus, by taking seriously the historical context of poetry, rhetorical analysis restores to the poet's words not simply the background circumstances of their composition but the very framework within which they are enabled to assume complex meaning. The aim of rhetorical analysis is the comprehensive understanding of public discourse as both commonplace and ideology which is both spoken and heard—that breadth of perspective which perceives poetry to be not just expression or product or effect, but a historical event.

Rhetorical Analysis as Critical Practice

Recent ways of understanding the meaning of *Annus Mirabilis* might be divided roughly into two types. First there is the "political reading," which regards the poem as an ingenious and effective "political document," a rationalist refutation of sectarian enthusiasm and sedition. This kind of reading must be distinguished from the "poetic" even though both may be maintained by the same critic, since poetic transcendence depends on the effacement of political particularity. Political readings require a "narrow" concern with the very specialized issues of political motive and division; proof of the poet's political motive requires proof of the real existence of political division and consciousness.[66] Similarly, poetic readings understand the meaning of poetry in a way which requires certain positive assumptions about (if not demonstration of) the uniformity and homogeneity of its historical audience's self-consciousness. Their reliance on the generality theory of value determines that their main concern will be to demonstrate that what Dryden says has "general" meaning for all people and all times, a demonstration which often excludes, as we have seen, the possibility that what he says may have had "particular" meaning for anyone at any time as well. The picture of *Annus Mirabilis* that results from this poetic type of reading is of Dryden's experimental epic, a bold and colorful compendium of classical literary devices applied to a modern theme. Such a reading may well acknowledge, with Dryden, that the poem's narrative is too fragmented to claim poetic unity. Even so, it is replete (according to this view) with felicitous effects which, if they sometimes descend into extravagant

---

66. Cf. C. Ward (*Life of John Dryden* [1961], p. 342n5) in refutation of Hooker's discussion of the political importance of the *Mirabilis Annus* tracts: "Are there any others [i.e., tracts] to suggest a widespread dissatisfaction with Charles and the royal Parliament? Where is the fear of the populace to be found? . . . Do we not need more evidence to demonstrate that the government was so weak as to need to fear opposition pamphlets? After all, were such tracts not a constant factor in seventeenth-century England?"

bathos, nevertheless succeed in converting history to poetry and point ahead to Dryden's masterpiece of the poetic generalization of politics, *Absalom and Achitophel*. An evaluation such as this will have little use for evidence of political divisiveness.

These two common readings of *Annus Mirabilis*, the poetic and the political, provide us with the basis necessary for constituting a rhetorical analysis of the poem. The dogmatism of the poetic reading must be balanced by a reductive reinterpretation of the public discourse with which it is concerned, just as the reductionism of the political reading requires the dogmatic reinterpretation of the relevant public discourse.

In each case, "reinterpretation" consists, first, in giving a reading of the poem which is opposed to the common one; and second, in "confirming" it by showing the probability that such a reading would have been made by many of Dryden's contemporaries. Rhetorical analysis assumes at the outset the oppositional nature of the audience addressed, and attempts to discover the quality and the degree of this opposition to the poet's ideology. The end of this historical confirmation is not so much an assessment of the poet's probable success or failure in either persuasive or aesthetic terms, but a well-founded understanding of the extent to which—given the premises of rhetorical analysis—a perspective quite distinct from the poet's must be acknowledged as partially constitutive of the meaning of his poetry. For the purposes of this kind of study, the composition of Dryden's audience might be gauged according to our knowledge of whom Dryden intended to read *Annus Mirabilis* or of who actually read it, but neither source of information is in fact available. And I am finally more interested in the documentation of a historically specific context of discourse, behavior, and belief than I am in Dryden's actual readership, for Dryden no doubt hoped that his ideological argument would gain general acceptance, and in this sense he "spoke" to many more people than he might have expected to read *Annus Mirabilis*. Yet I am also sensitive to the limitations involved in identifying Dryden's specific audience, however we may define it, with a very general sort of "public opinion," and I am aware of the potential contradiction involved in trying to document public opinion solely through written records. Neither danger can be avoided entirely, but I have sought to mitigate both to some extent. Thus, my research procedure has been to investigate a wide and varied assortment of documents in order to gain access to a diverse range of Dryden's contemporaries—diverse in political, social, and economic status. At the same time, rather than taking "the mind of the age" as my province, I have focused my attention throughout on the particular concerns with which Dryden seems to be especially preoccupied in *Annus Mirabilis*.

This basic plan of combining reinterpretative readings of *Annus Mirabilis* with historical confirmations of their probability is carried out in the following manner. The common "poetic" approach is countered by one which assumes in the contemporary reader a high degree of group consciousness and a sharp sensitivity to the depoliticizing effects of Dryden's generality (Chapter 1). This consciousness constitutes in itself an alternative to the "poetic" reading, whose meaning depends precisely on an unconsciousness of political motive, and hence on an absence of political division. Similarly, the common "political" approach is countered by one which assumes in the contemporary reader an appreciation of Dryden's ingenuous and nonironic indulgence in prophecy and eschatological speculation, for purposes which are evident enough in themselves and which require no knowledge of similar, specifically sectarian, indulgences (Chapter 5). Each of these readings is followed by its confirmation. The inadequacies of the "poetic" approach are shown, by reference to contemporary documents other than *Annus Mirabilis*, to owe to a dogmatic acceptance of secondary- for primary-level discourse (Chapters 2–4). In the same way, contemporary writings are used to demonstrate that the common "political" approach to the poem errs reductively in taking primary- to be secondary-level discourse (Chapters

6–9). It will be noticed that the defining concern—or "sphere of discourse"—of the first common reading and of my reinterpretation of it is quite different from that of the second common reading and of my reinterpretation of it. Whereas the former has to do with matters of group consciousness, interest, and unity, the latter relates to the language of, and belief in, eschatological prophecy.

Because my point of departure is these two (respectively dogmatic and reductive) common readings of Dryden's poem, the former reinterpretation stresses secondary- over primary-level discourse while the latter stresses primary- over secondary-level discourse. Modern criticism has done more than justice to these two common readings, and I hope to be excused for assuming the reader's understanding of their general character. It is of the first importance to remember throughout this study, however, that both of the spheres of discourse which my two reinterpretations consider are composed of both of the levels of discourse: Dryden spoke both commonplace and ideology, and he was understood accordingly by his contemporaries. So too a rhetorical analysis of Dryden's poem will require both dogmatic and reductive understandings of any given sphere of discourse. Furthermore, it must be kept in mind that the two spheres of discourse whose separation is made here to facilitate analysis were experienced by Dryden's audience within the total relationship of the poem as a rhetorical encounter. To return, finally, to the troublesome term with which I began this investigation of modern treatments of Restoration poetry, the analysis that follows will seek to understand "political poetry" as the outcome of an interaction of perspectives, neither "poetry" nor "politics" alone but the product of their convergence.

A final word is necessary. It is an irony, perhaps unavoidable, that a study whose concern is to expand the meaning of a poem by reuniting it with its historical context should appear, because of its form, to do just the opposite. The argument which is to come draws widely on the diverse literature of the Restoration period for the purpose of under-standing one single product of it. For this reason, Dryden's poem may seem at times to rise and hover above the dense undergrowth of documentation, may seem even to demon-strate its transcendence of relatively obscure names and titles despite my avowed intention to return it to its origins. The problem derives largely from the formal demands of historical research and literary explication. Yet it is clear that English literary history and tradition, as we have both received and created them, have determined that the subject of this study should be *Annus Mirabilis* rather than one or more of the works that are now relegated to footnotes or preserved in only partial quotation. As the premises which underlie this Introduction would suggest, I am convinced that traditional distinctions between classics and ephemera are neither absolute nor desirable. Our present ideas of literary tradition are the result of complex historical de-mands and decisions, as much social and political as literary, whose existence and force we often only dimly perceive. The great majority of the works that I use to analyze *Annus Mirabilis* have become for us mere instruments by which to understand, not subjects to be understood. One consequence of too ready an acceptance of received literary tradition may be a blindness to the value of works which, but for the all-important exigencies of intervening history, might now be in dire need of the rhetorical analysis that I am seeking to provide for *Annus Mirabilis*. As it is, much of the literature to which I am indebted suffers the even harsher fate of virtual oblivion. I can only trust that if the form of this study seems to perpetuate attitudes which its substance aims at dissolving, the reader will recognize the dilemmas of such an undertaking and will make the necessary allowances for it.

I

GROUP CONSCIOUSNESS,
INTEREST, AND UNITY

So that a man had need, if possible, to know somewhat of
the temper of his Historian, before he know what to think
of his relations; such especially, as have somewhat of
incredibleness in them.

Meric Casaubon, *Of Credulity and Incredulity*
(1668), p. 312

[A] mischief by which the greatness of the *English* is
suppress'd, is a want of union of *Interests,* and *Affections.*
This . . . has bin heighten'd by our *Civil differences,* and
Religious distractions. For the sweetning of such
dissentions, it is not best at first to meet, and convers about
affairs of state, or spiritual controversies . . . But the
most effectual remedy to be us'd is, first to assemble about
some *calm,* and *indifferent* things . . .

Thomas Sprat, *History of the Royal Society* (1667), p. 426

The expedient to oblige them to forbear disputing one with
another about their particular differences, is to divert their
thoughts and put them upon publick tasks, wherein they
shall have no cause to dispute with any for a victory, but
onely to shew their abilities for the service and good of all.

John Dury, *Plain Way* (1660), pp. 4–5

1

ANNUS MIRABILIS
FIRST READING

A "political" understanding of *Annus Mirabilis* demands in the reader a fundamental state of consciousness which amounts to a sustained concern for seeking intelligibility on what I have called the secondary level of discourse. The function of this chapter will be to develop a conceptual context in which Dryden's poem can be seen to have "political" meaning.

Annus Mirabilis is introduced by Dryden's dedication of the poem to the City of London "in its representatives," and by his "Account" of it to his brother-in-law Sir Robert Howard. These documents provide a useful summary of the poem's characteristic arguments. The dedication defines the nature of the human units with which Dryden will deal. They are institutional and collective; at his most particular, they are representative: typical of civil, royal, and national virtue. London is one such human unit, a "pattern" of fidelity ("Loyalty," "Courage," and "Constancy"), an "Emblem of the suffering Deity." Another is Charles II, England's "Prince." And a third is the unit formed by the mutuality of "Prince" and "People," whose common "sufferings" determine a common "reason to love each other." The metaphor which Dryden uses to realize this bond of affection in adversity casts prince and people as "a pair of matchless Lovers": Charles, the male and active half, frustrated in his desire for possession by fortune and a long exile; London, the female counterpart, ravished and withheld from him by "many Rivals." London's virtue is, appropriately, the familial one of piety. Her many sufferings—war, plague, fire, and lack of trade—are as much "occasions for the manifesting of [her] Christian and Civil virtues" as "the effects of God's displeasure." This is to say no more than that they are as much divine "trials" as "Judgments" and that the "Providence" which reunited prince and people in Charles's restoration cannot fail to reunite virtue and fortune in the case of London. Although virtue sometimes goes unrewarded in individuals, this is a matter not of a single human being, nor even of one city, but of a "vertuous Nation," and "Providence is engag'd too deeply, when the cause becomes so general."[1] In other words, the salvation of England depends on, and is guaranteed by, the generality of her cause. Because he is confident of the national unity which is implicit in this generality, Dryden is able to prophesy what "all true *Englishmen*" wish for, London's restoration from her ashes.

The "Account" to Howard develops some aspects of this theme of collective character. London is praised again for her faithfulness, her "courage, loyalty and magnanimity." Here it is Charles who exhibits the virtue of piety, and the exemplary familial emotion is paternal, "the Piety and Fatherly Affection of our Monarch to his suffering Subjects." The prince aids his people; the people are obliged equally to aid their prince, and Dryden offers the final part of his poem, which concerns the Second Anglo-Dutch War, as "a due expiation for my not serving my King and Country in it." In this conventional phrase the identity of interests of king and country is assumed. The reciprocity of familial ties overrides whatever differences might result from the natural and inevitable hierarchy of the family.

---

1. Vincent, *Gods Terrible Voice* (1667), p. 61, wrote that the plague and fire were "National Judgments," largely "because *London* was the Metropolis of the Land," and therefore "National sins have been the cause of them . . ." Hardy, *Lamentation* (1666), p. 17, said of the fire: "*Private*, but much *more Publick* Calamities require our *Sympathy*; for *such* was this, not over a particular *Person* or *Family*, but a *City*." The "public" nature of the fire encouraged others besides Dryden to trace it to providential, rather than human, causation: see below, Chapter 4.

   Dryden's digressive description of his poetic subject in the
"Account" is a striking example of his characteristic assertion
of national unity by unobtrusively obviating potential divisiveness. Early in the "Account" Dryden speaks of the war as
"the most heroick Subject which any Poet could desire" and
of the fire as "the greatest Argument that can be imagin'd."
Later on he digresses into praise of Prince Rupert and the
duke of Albemarle, "incomparably the best subject I have
ever had, excepting onely the *Royal Family*." Dryden begins
to develop an extended agricultural metaphor in order to
elaborate on his fortune in having so praiseworthy a poetic
subject: "I have been forc'd to help out other Arguments,
but this has been bountiful to me." Yet when he comes to
specify the poetic value of his "subject" the word momen-
tarily takes on a double meaning: "All other greatness in
subjects is onely counterfeit, it will not endure the test of
danger; the greatness of Arms is onely real: other greatness
burdens a Nation with its weight, this supports it with its
strength. And as it is the happiness of the Age, so is it the
peculiar goodness of the best of Kings, that we may praise
his Subjects without offending him: . . . for the Good or
the Valiant are never safely prais'd under a bad or a degen-
erate Prince." Dryden's "subject" is simultaneously poetic
and civil. The effect of the process by which the one imperceptibly becomes the other is that Rupert and Albemarle,
Dryden's poetic subjects, become equated with Charles's
civil subjects, the people of England. Dryden seems to
demonstrate that the people are truly "represented" by
Rupert and Albemarle; that his topic in *Annus Mirabilis* is
the praise of the people; that his license to praise the prince
and the general is proof not only of Charles's virtue but even
of England's felicity in having a king and people—potentially and traditionally at odds with each other—who constitute a unity of affection. The device suggests a reconciliation
of opposites, tacitly denying that Rupert and Albemarle may
be seen simply as administrative extensions of the king.
   Themes of unity and mutuality dominate the "Verses to
her Highness the Dutchess" which Dryden includes at the

end of his "Account" to Howard. The marital devotion of the
duke and duchess of York provides a central perspective on
the relation between civil leaders and those who are led. The
"chaste vows" which unite husband and wife involve not
only mutual love but mutual aid—that is, interest. In terms
of the national macrocosm this interest is ultimately mercantile, a matter of "where the wealth of Nations ought to flow."
In one sense the duchess is clearly distinguished from the
people, a distinction which entails the demonstration that
York's activities are a function of the collective national
interest: she resigns him "for our sakes," which presupposes
that she lodges her "Countries cares within [her] breast." In
another sense the inestimable value which the duchess sets
on her husband identifies her with the people whose beloved
admiral he is:

> Ships, Men and Arms our Country might restore,
> But such a Leader could supply no more.

In this context the pangs of separation of husband and wife,
which only emphasize the naturalness of being together,
parallel the pain that is felt by a nation whose husband/
leader must leave for a time to defend her honor:

> Ah, what concerns did both your Souls divide!
> . . . . .
> And 'twas for him much easier to subdue
> Those foes he fought with, then to part from you.

In taking to heart her "Countries cares," the duchess becomes her country, at least with regard to the husband from
whom she is divided.

This particular dimension of the duchess is not emphasized throughout the "Verses," however. Once separated
from York she is quite capable herself of assuming the role
of leadership which, after all, is natural to her social position
as duchess. In her progress north she leads an army of
cupids; she commands an entire court of nobility; she is a
"new-born *Phoenix*," a "Queen" adored by her "feather'd

Subjects." Yet the familial framework of the poem operates even in these images to soften the harshness of command. Her role, noticed earlier, as passive helpmate and only metaphorical ruler (for example, of York) colors the expression of her political function, her power over others, so that her rule is never more than that of a woman, a coy similitude for power. In this way the political relationships of ruler and ruled are tempered by the ethics of family structure, according to which the convenience of political arrangements is understood as the necessity of nature. The family, embodiment of unity and nexus of interest, is a suitable starting point for formulating an alternative perspective on *Annus Mirabilis*.

Dryden's portrait of the ideal monarchy in *Annus Mirabilis* is frequently a portrait of the ideal family. Albemarle, exhausted after the Four Days Battle, refuses to suspend his larger paternal functions:

> Return'd, he with the Fleet resolv'd to stay,
> No tender thoughts of home his heart divide:
> Domestick joys and cares he puts away,
> For Realms are housholds which the Great must guide.
>
> (138)

Albemarle refuses, that is, to divide his attention between the public and the private, the general and the particular, the national and the individual. The good ruler is a good father, and the familial unit is nothing smaller than the nation. Albemarle the general is "like a Father of the War" to his men (73), most cheerful when danger is nearest. But he is still only a surrogate father: Charles is the real ruler of England and therefore its real patriarch. He is "the Father of the people" (286), whose power does not preclude the gentleness of a mother who, distressed by the ruin of the phoenixlike Londoners, "will hatch their ashes by his stay" (288). Similarly, Charles's other naval surrogate, Prince Rupert, comes to the rescue of Albemarle as a mother eagle might interrupt her foraging for her "callow Infants" in order to return and save them from disaster (107–8).

If the parental role in the good family-state is filled by Charles and his deputies and their "children" are variously citizens and sailors in distress, the collectivity London embodies the ideal woman whose characteristic competence, elegance, and haughty pride are properly (if sometimes only tacitly) not ends in themselves but means to her ultimate possession by another. As the symbolic extension of the newly launched *Loyal London* ("the *Phoenix* daughter of the vanish'd old"), the rebuilt city

> Like a rich Bride does to the Ocean swim,
> And on her shadow rides in floating gold.
>
> (151)

As "Empress of the Northern Clime" (212), London contains within herself the promise of resurrection. And as "Augusta" she undergoes, in prophecy, the metamorphosis from rude "Shepherdess" (295, 296) to the fabulous, semidivine "Maiden Queen" who beholds

> From her high Turrets, hourly Sutors come:
> The East with Incense, and the West with Gold,
> Will stand, like Suppliants, to receive her doom.
>
> (297)

It is part of Dryden's purpose to portray London in times of crisis, and familial associations are serviceable to him in describing not only ideal national relationships but also those that are not all they should be. There is, for example, the risk that paternal power, brought to the test, may be proved impotent. Dryden's war is often sexual. At Bergen (25–28), the rich Dutch traders are "like hunted *Castors*, conscious of their store,"—conscious, that is, of the valuable contents of the mysterious sacs situated in their groins. They are a "perfum'd prey" whom the English trace by their "scent." Protecting this effeminate enemy is well-fortified Denmark, with its "murdering Canon" which "at once . . .

threaten and invite the eye." Englishman confronts Dane
with exclusive enjoyment of the Dutch prizes as reward.

> These fight like Husbands, but like Lovers those:
> These fain would keep, and those more fain enjoy:
> And to such height their frantick passion grows,
> That what both love, both hazard to destroy.
>
> (28)

In the face of English virility, even powerful nations reveal
their effeminacy:

> And threatning France, plac'd like a painted *Jove*,
> Kept idle thunder in his lifted hand.

> That Eunuch Guardian of rich Hollands trade,
> Who envies us what he wants pow'r t'enjoy!
>
> (39–40)

Other naval encounters extend the theme of sexuality.
Albemarle does his best for England during the disastrous
Four Days Battle, and when his "batter'd rigging their whole
war receives,"

> All bare, like some old Oak which tempests beat,
> He stands, and sees below his scatter'd leaves.
>
> (61)

Dryden converts the ridiculous destruction of Albemarle's
breeches into an occasion for celebrating his manliness—the
fact that his ship still "Steeple high stood propt upon the
Main," his "excess of courage" which amazes "the foremost
of his foes" (62, 63). Yet courage alone is not enough to
lead his men in war, and on the third day of battle Albemarle finds himself sadly deficient in the instruments of
power:

> But now, his **Stores of** Ammunition spent,
> His naked valour is his onely guard:
> Rare thunders are from his dumb Cannon sent,
> And solitary Guns are scarcely heard.
>
> (103)

He is saved at the last moment by Rupert's "new stores" and
"loud Guns" (118, 120), a salvation which underscores the
need for potency in a leader. It is England's felicity that
paternal power is a matter of positive interest and delight to
her potent leader Charles II. At the refitting of the fleet,

> Our careful Monarch stands in Person by,
> His new-cast Canons firmness to explore:
> The strength of big-corn'd powder loves to try,
> And Ball and Cartrage sorts for every bore.
>
> (149)

Thus Dryden illustrates the familial crisis of impotent
authority with direct reference to England's collective
progress in the war with the Dutch. Other crises—familial
divisions and estrangements, broken households—are ex-
exemplified by individual but representative families in the
United Provinces or England, whose sufferings constitute a
glass through which the reader may view larger developments in the national macrocosm. One such case is that of
the Dutch boy who, having set to sea to fight the English,
now sees from an English ship "the *Holland* Coast, / And
Parents arms in vain stretch'd from the shore" (33). His fate
may have been repeated by the long-departed "carefull
Husband,"

> Whom his chast wife and little children mourn;
> Who on their fingers learn'd to tell the day
> On which their Father promis'd to return.
>
> (34)

These instances of the disruptive and tragic effect of war on
families are a forceful argument for the traditional pattern
of familial integrity as a standard by which the good life
may be judged. The Great Fire of London is another divisive
disaster, the apprehension of whose most poignant effects
requires a sensitivity to the blessings of family ties. "Homes"
are destroyed in cruel parodies of "the Vestal fire" (255–57).
Mothers are separated from their infants (226), or find

themselves helpless to care for them as nature requires (258–59). Even orphans are deprived of that public charity which was meant to assuage their pathetic lack of parental love (274). And when Charles's prayers finally move God to mercy, the result is described first in terms of the reestablishment of the family seat, the home:

> Each houshold Genius shows again his face,
> And, from the hearths, the little Lares creep.
>
> (282)

These familial crises may appear to be unavoidable necessities of existence. But Dryden sometimes uses metaphorical language to suggest that the evil that man does can be understood profitably as an unnecessary perversion of natural familial relationships. A minor example of this is the deadly duplicity of France:

> And, while his secret Soul on *Flanders* preys,
> He rocks the Cradle of the Babe of *Spain*.
>
> (8)

More memorable are the terms in which Dryden describes the generation and growth of the Cromwellian fire (213–22). Like the usurper whose "birth" and "Cradle" are hidden from public view, the fire is "obscurely bred":

> In this deep quiet, from what source unknown,
> Those seeds of fire their fatal birth disclose.
>
> (217)

Its birth is uncertain and unnatural; it grows into an "infant monster" whose sexual attack upon the female London, an act of "usurpation," has incestuous overtones:

> The winds, like crafty Courtezans, with-held
> His flames from burning, but to blow them more:
> And, every fresh attempt, he is repell'd
> With faint denials, weaker then before.

And now, no longer letted of his prey,
He leaps up at it with inrag'd desire:
O'r-looks the neighbours with a wide survey,
And nods at every house his threatning fire.

(221-22)

And like the "Prince" who is "surpriz'd" by the usurper and powerless to oppose him, Charles—the father of the people—sleeps quietly through the fire's first ravishments (224).

The state, then, is like a household: the usurper is an unnatural child whose growth to stature is a perverse actualization of Oedipal fantasy, symptomatic of a profound imbalance in the natural hierarchy of rule and reciprocity. In the rationalization and justification of this hierarchy which is Dryden's aim in *Annus Mirabilis,* the family is of primary importance because it provides a conventionally acceptable perspective for understanding civil structures as "natural" unities whose internal organization should command the unquestioning assent not only of nature but of all of their human participants. Dryden's argumentative task clearly extends beyond the limits of a purely authoritarian demand for obedience, although this consideration is not to be ignored. His concerns in *Annus Mirabilis,* as they have emerged thus far, may be summarized under four headings: (1) *Hierarchy:* the people must be persuaded to accept, so far as possible, their natural subordination. This aspect of Dryden's theme is apparent from nothing more methodologically sophisticated than the preponderance of the word "subject" over the word "people" in describing the commoners of England. (2) *Mutual interest:* the attractions of hierarchy become increasingly clear as it is demonstrated that only this relationship can guarantee the perpetuation of the interchanges which determine the civil and economic interests of every citizen. (3) *Mutual love:* if self-interest is dependent on interest in others, then genuine love between subject and monarch, so far from being inconsistent with pragmatism, is inextricable from it. (4) *Unity:* mutuality is only another way of expressing the idea of oneness with a larger, encompassing entity, a conviction of which it is

Dryden's aim to inculcate in his audience. "Us" must be a perpetually inclusive category. All of these themes are contained within the emotive complex of "the family," but Dryden makes efficient use of a variety of related frames of reference as well, which may be classified, for convenience, as the natural, the customary, the literary, and the providential.

The force of familial analogy derives largely from the fact that patriarchal structure is so customary as to appear "natural." Dryden's emphasis on the primal "necessities" of sexuality adds to the plausibility of this assumption. His other uses of the argument from nature entail an appeal to the example of animal behavior. The Virgilian portrait of Proteus, the nautical shepherd, is based upon human custom, but it also implies that if Charles assumes the role of shepherd, his herd of ships conforms naturally to the practice to sheep (15). More exclusively animal is the epic simile, mentioned above, of Rupert as mother eagle protecting Albemarle as callow infant (107–8). In this case the action is indisputably instinctual—that is to say, natural. The same could be said of Charles's later approximation to a mother bird, were not the phoenix a figure of unnatural natural histories and Dryden's maternal scene a departure from the requisite mystery of phoenix generation (288).

Dryden's most important allusions to animal lore are his comparisons of the people to bees and of the state to a beehive. A common emblem of industry and loyalty,[2] the beehive functions in Annus Mirabilis to characterize the civil and economic unit as a highly efficient, almost mechanized

2. See, e.g., Ogilby, Entertainment (1662), p. 39, explicating the meaning of the first of the triumphal coronation arches; Rolls, Londons (1668), pp. 122, 226; Welch, History of the Monument (1893), facing p. 25, print of C. G. Cibber's sculpture on the fire monument explaining its iconography. Ogilby cites Pliny's testimony "that of Animals none, but a Bee, ha's a King . . . The Obedience of the Communalty is to be admired. Whensoever the KING goes forth, the whole Hive accompanie him, gather round about him, encompass him, protect him, and suffer him not to be seen. Whensoever the Communalty is at work, he oversees them, and is alone free from the labour." Goodman, Fall of Man (1616), p. 100, wrote that the bee "seemes to teach vs a platforme and president of a perfect Monarchie . . ."

example of interdependent labor. In the georgic passage on
the refitting of the fleet, the repetition of "some," "some,"
"another," "one" emphasizes the division and diversification
of labor, the perfect intermeshing of skilled workers
(144–48). The same device is used later when the Londoners, like bees in a "waxen City," work in unison to stop
the spread of the fire (228–29). In both cases the figure of
the swarming beehive expresses an idea of limited diversity
and of a greater unity of purpose: differentiation among
individuals extends no further than the necessary fulfillment
of diverse functions directed toward a common end. And in
both cases the hierarchy of the hive is well enough understood to preclude any impression that this is a leaderless
state or a democracy.

The behavior of bees is instinctual. Many of Dryden's
other metaphors for the government of nations are drawn
from customary, human institutions which provide, as few
natural structures can, precise analogies for different aspects
of the civil relationship for which Dryden argues. The ship
of state figure is used sparingly and without emphasizing the
authoritarian function of the captain (35, 304). In the face
of "Armies" of fire, the Londoners spontaneously seek a
general in their masterful ruler by forming "an Army worthy
such a King" (235–37, 243). Thus Charles in domestic setting is no less literally a leader of men than Charles in battle
dress (cf. 14). In struggle with the fire he is compelled to
"lay waste / That Country which would, else, the foe maintain" (244).

Dryden uses other familiar metaphors of social interaction
in a similar manner, to suggest that the beneficent hierarchy
of the English state is the rational choice of everyone,
whether superordinate or subordinate. He modifies the
image of the body politic so that Charles is not head or belly
but the doctor whose sole care is to "bind the bruises" of the
country's limbs (263; also 142). Charles's altruism and
selflessness are here all the more evident in that his own
welfare is entirely independent of the body which he treats
so lovingly. In another metaphor, Charles as chivalric knight

Engraving of C. G. Cibber's allegorical sculpture on the west front of the Monument, erected in the 1670s to commemorate the Great Fire of London. On the left the city is in flames and ruins; on the right it is rebuilt under the guidance of England's monarch and the civic and technological virtues. The divisiveness of the anti-Catholic inscription represents a more drastic solution to the problem of national unity than the familiar beehive emblem (P) and the technique of allegorical generalization. Reprinted by permission of the Guildhall Library, City of London.

accepts the Dutch challenge "In *Britain's* right," acting as her representative in "wedding" the sea.[3] As a "Mighty Nation" striving within the "Lists" of combat, she is thus constituted by the leaders who defend her name. All that is English and all that is Dutch is concentrated within the actions of the opposing admirals, "the two bold Champions of each Countries right" (20, 39, 187).

Dryden's continuing effort to reduce England into one or two entities whose relationship is clearly defined by nature or social custom can be seen in his treatment of the idea of friendship. False countries make false alliances. France seeks not only to thwart Spain's "timely friendship" with us but ultimately to betray that weakened power "whose cause he seems to take in hand" (8, 9). After "the attempt at Bergen," Dryden warns that Denmark's "weak assistance will his friends destroy" (40). And the perfidy of the bishop of Münster, England's single and short-lived ally, is the occasion for Dryden's melancholy reflection on the undependability of friendships that ignore considerations of interest:

> Happy who never trust a Strangers will,
> Whose friendship's in his interest understood!
> Since money giv'n but tempts him to be ill
> When pow'r is too remote to make him good.
>
> (38)

In the end the fault lies not with the faithless Bishop von Galen but with the human condition, "which oft, for friends, mistaken foes provides" (36).

But if nations seem incapable of keeping faith, England contains within herself examples of the cohesion which true friendship embodies, and her internal bonds of friendship maintain her in unity against all the attempts of divisive foreigners. Albemarle and Rupert are equals, "mighty Partners" who are "each able to sustain a Nations fate," identical in "duty, faith, and int'rest" (47–48). They symbolize

3. On the derivation of the conceit whereby Charles weds the sea from 17th-century Venetian ceremonial see Hooker's note in Dryden, *Works* (1956), I, 283.

that dual unity which characterizes the best of friendships and civil relationships. The division of the fleet (54) is not simply a naval catastrophe but, much more, an enactment of what may happen once the bonds between friends, or between prince and people, are temporarily severed. This first cleavage entails others. While the Dutch rejoice at the sight of reinforcements, Albemarle contemplates the sad necessity of sending his wounded ashore, who "think them happy who with him can stay" (72, 74). (After the battle he resolves to stay with his fleet rather than allow thoughts of home to "divide his heart" [138].) Yet the division has, in Dryden's version, a happy ending. The friends are reunited in friendship, Rupert's "inbred worth" and "Heroique virtue" guiding the rescue of his "friend" from the foreign enemy (115–16) in much the same way as providence might direct a prince to the rescue of his people from a usurper.

> But, when approach'd, in strict embraces bound,
> *Rupert* and *Albemarl* together grow:
> He joys to have his friend in safety found,
> Which he to none but to that friend would owe.
>
> (117)

So Charles, in prayer, recalls how "unfriended" he wandered in exile until God restored him to his kingdom and taught him to "recompense, as friends, the good misled" (262, 264).

Dryden uses literary precedents to generate the same atmosphere of beneficent unity in hierarchy which derives from his application of natural and customary paradigmatic relationships. The significance of epic and georgic conventions, language, and reminiscences in a rhetorical analysis of *Annus Mirabilis* has been touched on in the Introduction; it is relevant to note here how Dryden exploits the Virgilian ideas of familial piety and patriarchal care. *Annus Mirabilis* is headed by two classical epigraphs. The first derives from an epistle of the Emperor Trajan to Pliny, and distinguishes military campaigns into two categories: those which are motivated by prudent policy considerations and those which arise from a more personal ambition for imperialistic expansion. It is significant for Dryden's general purpose that the distinction comes in the context of the emperor's reassurance that his only guide for action is the public interest.[4] The second epigraph, from the *Aeneid*,[5] Dryden later translated as "An ancient and imperial city falls." This line encapsulates the first great action of the *Aeneid* as it does the second half of *Annus Mirabilis*. In combination with many echoes and the explicit comparison of Berkeley to the "lost *Creüsa*" (67) it points the reader's attention to Aeneas's departure from burning Troy in the second book of Virgil's poem. On a sign from heaven Aeneas sets off, Anchises on his shoulders protecting the household gods, Ascanius led by one hand, and his wife, Creusa, trailing behind. In his wanderings out of the city Aeneas loses his wife, searches for her in vain, and, to his horror, soon encounters her ghost; but it calms him and prophesies the eventual restoration of Troy in Rome.

The theme of familial devotion which is portrayed in this passage is reinforced by Dryden's concentration on the virtues of piety and care as characteristic of the actors in his poem. Piety is a virtue of familial affection—father for children, children for parents—which is associated particularly with the "pius Aeneas." In *Annus Mirabilis*, Albemarle's comrades-in-arms display piety toward him; London's present to Charles is "piously design'd"; and Charles sheds "pious tears" for his subjects during the fire just as Aeneas shows pious devotion to his family while Troy burns (64, 154, 240). "Care" is an epithet of paternalistic concern, as frequently used by Dryden in his *Georgics* and their scenes of rural domesticity as it is in his *Aeneid*. Dryden casts Rupert as a mother eagle of "pious care"; Albemarle is a "careful

4. Dryden's "Multum interest res poscat, an homines latius imperare velint" changes the word order slightly. Cf. Pliny, *Letters*, trans. W. Melmoth, rev. W. M. L. Hutchinson (London, 1915), II, 304–5 (10.22): "Multum interest, res poscat an homines imperare latius velint. Nobis autem utilitas demum spectanda est" (It is very material to distinguish between what the exigency of affairs requires and what an ambitious desire of extending power may think necessary. As for ourselves, the interest of the public must be our only guide).
5. 2.363.

General"; the Royal Society exhibits "auspicious care" in transmuting God's intentions to human use (107, 99, 165). Most of all, and especially in connection with the disastrous effects of the fire, Charles is truly Virgilian in his care for his people.[6]

I have been considering metaphorical systems or frameworks that Dryden uses as overlapping alternatives to the familial in order to characterize England as a hierarchy united by its sense of mutual benefit and devotion. So far I have mentioned the natural, the customary, and the literary. A final frame of reference may be called the providential. In *Annus Mirabilis* the idea of providence operates in three distinct ways: God the Father is seen in relation to his children the English; English leaders are likened to God the Father, implying that the common people assume the role of children; finally, the power of heavenly providence is equated with that of fate.

The conventional view of the English as God's chosen people echoes throughout *Annus Mirabilis*. Albemarle tells his men that they are Heaven's choice (75), and the parallel with the Israelites is a frequent one.[7] When Dryden imagines a depopulated Continent

> Were Subjects so but onely by their choice,
> And not from Birth did forc'd Dominion take,
>
> (44)

he reminds the reader that for both God and the godlike, their choice of people does not necessarily correspond to a similar choice by the people of them. The divinity who chooses England in *Annus Mirabilis* is first of all an authoritative one. He is the "Judge" who puts "judgments" upon the land, "sentences" which may prove "unconditional" (263–69). God's ministering angel chastises undutiful flames

6. See sts. 13, 142, 149, 238, 242, 260, 263. On the piety and care which Charles exhibited during this crisis see also *Gazette*, no. 87, Sept. 13–17, 1666; Roger Boyle, *Collection* (1742), Boyle to Ormonde, Sept. 21, 1666, p. 181.

7. See, e.g., sts. 92, 94, 114, 290.

(272) with the same dispatch that God himself manifests in punishing his people. At the same time, he is troubled enough to accommodate his judgments to the capacities of human comprehension: St. Paul's is "purg'd" by the flames "since it was prophan'd by Civil War" (276). And in the end God's "pity" and "mercy" for his people overrule his anger, and judgment is converted to the necessary trial of a beloved nation (280).

This is the God that England, the national collective, sees in *Annus Mirabilis*. In respect to God, Charles is only the greatest of His subjects, but in respect to the English he and his deputies are only slightly lesser divinities. Intervals in the fire's smoky gloom reveal Charles's "Sacred Face." The Dutch start back in amazement at Albemarle's courage, just as the invading barbarians gazed in awe at the Roman Senate's "God-like Fathers." Rupert sails to his fellow admiral's rescue like a resurrected and avenging Christ.[8] Like God himself, Charles creates the surrogate rulers Albemarle and Rupert, who will act in his stead until the refitting of the fleet: "With equal pow'r he does two Chiefs create" (47). The two chiefs to whom Charles's authority has been delegated imitate their maker by stamping in turn their followers with their own virtue:

> Their valour works like bodies on a glass,
> And does its Image on their men project.
>
> (53)

This process is carried to its extreme in the case of the Royal Society, creation of the royal Charles, whose declaration of "your wise Creator's praise" (165) is therefore amiably ambiguous.

> O truly Royal! who behold the Law,
> And rule of beings in your Makers mind,

8. Sts. 239, 63, 105, 114. Reference is made to an alternative reading of st. 105 in the first few printings, which Dryden eventually altered, perhaps to avoid imputations of blasphemy: "For now brave *Rupert*'s Navy did appear,/Whose waving streamers from afar he knows:/As in his fate something divine there were,/ Who dead and buried the third day arose."

And thence, like Limbecks, rich Idea's draw,
To fit the levell'd use of humane kind.[9]

(166)

The chain of creation and imitation extends from God down to the lowest levels of humanity. Charles creates in the pattern of the Creator—and like the Creation, Charles's work is ultimately for his people, whose only task is to maintain their faith:

Heav'n ended not the first or second day,
Yet each was perfect to the work design'd:
God and Kings work, when they their work survey,
And passive aptness in all subjects find.

(141)

As the Londoners are finally justified, in their patient endurance of the fire, by God's removal of it, so they are gratified in the end by the corresponding mercy of God's anointed:

The Father of the people open'd wide
His stores, and all the poor with plenty fed:
Thus God's Annointed God's own place suppli'd,
And fill'd the empty with his daily bread.

(286)

In *Annus Mirabilis*, Charles and even God are personal enough representatives of abstract Justice and Mercy. But for the working out of the affairs of 1666 Dryden gives much more important roles to the figures of heaven and fate, whose operation obviates the consideration of human intention, agency, and motive. It is well for the subject to see how

9. Thus some of the practical uses of the Royal Society's transmutations from its "Makers mind" were naturally compatible with the king's practical delights as Dryden describes them (142–49). Sprat, *History* (1667), p. 150, reported that the society "have employ'd much time in examining *the Fabrick of Ships*, the forms of their *Sails*, the shape of their *Keels*, the sorts of Timber, the planting of Firr, the bettering of Pitch, and Tarr, and Tackling. And in all *Maritime* affairs of this Nature, his *Majesty* is acknowledg'd to be the best *Judge* amongst Seamen, and Shipwrights, as well as the most powerful amongst *Princes*."

his individual contribution fits into the larger scheme, but finally he must understand that to question the scheme is only to reveal the narrowness and inadequacy of his own vision, which tries to gain an individual perspective on something that is beyond the comprehension even of the collective. Dryden's use of the terms "Heaven," "Fate," and "Fortune" synonymously has the added effect of morally legitimating otherwise amoral exigencies. The understanding of events not only as inevitable, impersonal, and universal but also as "for the best" guarantees a total and unqualified acquiescence in things as they are.[10] In his dedication of *Annus Mirabilis* to London, Dryden envisioned a city whose happiness would be owing to a beneficent providence which in the end united virtue with good fortune. According to the same expectations, the virtuous Albemarle's fortune cannot be bad forever, and Dryden achieves poetic and providential justice simultaneously in Rupert's fortuitous advent (104–5).

This is not to say that the good cause always gets what it deserves in *Annus Mirabilis*. It often does: in York's victory off Lowestoft "Heav'n our Monarch's fortune did confess" (19); and although the implications cannot be known "till time digests the yet imperfect Ore," the Four Days Battle seems to Charles—trusting in heaven and heavenly in his patience—a comforting token of future successes "which all-maturing time must bring to light" (139–40). When things go badly for England, agency is depersonalized and universalized. In aiding the Dutch to rebel against Spain, England sought to check one power but failed to foresee the dangerous rise of France, and even of the Provinces themselves.

> In fortunes Empire blindly thus we go,
> And wander after pathless destiny:
> Whose dark resorts since prudence cannot know
> In vain it would provide for what shall be.
>
> (200)

10. The equation of fortune with providence was not necessarily normal usage during the period: cf. Lluelyn, *To the Kings* (1660), p. 6; Davenant, *Poem* (1663), p. 5.

This universal helplessness in the face of the future is a useful means of avoiding questions of personal responsibility for disastrous national policies. At Bergen, for example, the neutrality of Denmark was sacrificed in an adventuristic and unsuccessful attempt to waylay Dutch traders. In the treaty with the bishop of Münster, money was spent uselessly to finance an invasion of Holland that never took place. For Dryden, the lesson to be drawn from these fiascos is addressed to no one more immediate than "Mortals" (32), and concerns nothing more concrete than the mutability of all things. Here fate equals heaven: the force is one, inscrutable, unavoidable, and hence necessarily acceptable:

> Such are the proud designs of human kind,
> And so we suffer Shipwrack every where!
> Alas, what Port can such a Pilot find,
> Who in the night of Fate must blindly steer!
>
> The undistinguish'd seeds of good and ill
> Heav'n, in his bosom, from our knowledge hides;
> And draws them in contempt of human skill,
> Which oft, for friends, mistaken foes provides.

(35–36)

Thus events which might divide the national unity necessitate an abstraction of the collective from the national to the international level. There the Dutch are no longer foes but fellow members of suffering humanity. Differences shrink to insignificance in the context of cosmic forces.

These passages indicate that Dryden has no difficulty in attributing naval misfortunes to the inscrutable will of God. The fire is also a divine judgment, but one whose quite specific application to London precludes the plausibility of cloudy allusions to the tragedy of the human condition. Inscrutability cannot always be a satisfactory explanation of causality. Dryden overcomes this problem by restricting his discussions of cause to the general level of the national unity—only descending from this level to locate the fire's cause in the factionalism of the distant and unchangeable past—and by holding out the promise that God's judgment has the instrumental, Old Testamentary significance of a trial. Therefore what seems a very specific disaster, understandable by reference to individual human causality, is explained away either as a general and unavoidable condition or as a personal triumph for London and England, a trial rather than a judgment. The former rationale is evident when Dryden says that our joy at naval victories tempted "Heav'n" and "Fate to lay us low" (209, 210):

> Each Element his dread command obeys,
> Who makes or ruines with a smile or frown;
> Who as by one he did our Nation raise,
> So now he with another pulls us down.
>
> (211)

Charles speaks comprehensively for his country, "this mourning Land," asking God to remove His judgments: for "we all have sinn'd, and thou hast laid us low" (265, 266). The specification of some who might have sinned more than others—usurpers, traitors and fanatics, and Civil War desecrators (213–14, 223, 276)—is extremely casual and oblique and constitutes an interpretation of past history rather than a fragmentation of present unity. Dryden uses the second means of avoiding division when he observes that the national sin is inseparable from the national redemption, a mark of being specially chosen by God for future glory:

> Yet, *London*, Empress of the Northern Clime,
> By an high fate thou greatly didst expire;
> Great as the worlds, which at the death of time
> Must fall, and rise a nobler frame by fire.
>
> Already, Labouring with a mighty fate,
> She shakes the rubbish from her mounting brow,
> And seems to have renew'd her Charters date,
> Which Heav'n will to the death of time allow.
>
> (212, 294)

London's "high and mighty" fate is the beneficent will of heaven; whatever is, is right.

Dryden argues his case in *Annus Mirabilis* by means of the highly significant metaphors and frames of reference whose rhetorical implications have now been made explicit. How else do the terms and categories of the poem contribute to the argument that England is a national homogeneity, a unity of love and interest?

In Dryden's Anglo-Dutch War, all of England is galvanized against the foreigners, the outsiders, the "foe." In treating the fire as a manifestation of providence, Dryden implicitly affirms the propriety of understanding it by its first cause—but war is sometimes a different matter. Charles prays to God for an end to the judgments of plague and fire,

> But, if immutable and fix'd they stand,
> Continue still thy self to give the stroke
> And let not foreign foes oppress thy Land.
>
> (270)

This distinction between "biblical" disasters (the direct castigation by God) and warfare (the product of both first and second causes) was not unusual at the time, but it was by no means standard.[11] It allows Dryden both to refrain from potentially divisive speculation on the identity of the second causes of the fire and to work upon the patriotism of the common Englishman whenever naval disappointments do not demand suprahistorical meditations on the inscrutability of heaven and fate. A foreign enemy is an obvious means of defining a national collectivity because it characterizes what is common to the group by exhibiting, in itself, what is alien to it. Despite the fact that France and Denmark had been in the war for a year Dryden gives strong emphasis to the United Provinces as England's arch-enemy,

11. See, e.g., *Gazette*, no. 85, Sept. 3–10, 1666, and Roger Boyle, *Collection* (1742), Boyle to Ormonde, Sept. 21, 1666, p. 181, where the distinction is exploited in Dryden's manner; and Add. MS. 4182, fol. 34v, Aug. 17, 1665, Colenbrander, *Bescheiden* (1919), I, 343, "Notes upon the June Fight, 1666," and Vincent, *Gods Terrible Voice* (1667), p. 152, where it is not.

classicizing the confrontation as "our second Punick War" (5).[12]

Given Dryden's rhetorical strategy as we have understood it thus far, it is not surprising that over and over the units of discourse and action in *Annus Mirabilis* are "us" versus "them," the English versus the Dutch. (Later on, Dryden's treatment of the fire-fighting Charles as a general who opposes the "foe" [244] adds this same flavor of wartime solidarity to London's united opposition to the fire.) The war is one between "two Nations" (7). Each navy is supported by entire "Nations" (124). Battles are won by "the braver Nation" (170), and fought with so much noise that they seem to be meetings between, not fleets, but "Lands unfix'd, and floating Nations" (57). *Annus Mirabilis* is a poem of national, not individual, entities. Dryden's canvas is crowded with different members of the international family: France, Spain, Flanders, Denmark, Germany, Norway, Guinea, and Turkey, not to mention England and the Provinces.[13] Real diversity exists only on this international scale; single countries are regarded as unities, none more so than England:

> But when with one three Nations joyn to fight,
> They silently confess that one more brave.
>
> (42)

In fact it is this very virtue of courage which is seen as England's national characteristic, the distinguishing mark of a discrete entity.[14]

War and the apprehension of a destructive fire provide occasions for the manifesting of economic, as well as civil, unity. As England's justification for entering the war against

12. And see st. 50. The English-Dutch Rome-Carthage parallel was a popular one, although the correspondence of terms did not remain fixed. For examples of the metaphor, see Cornelius, *Way propounded* (1659), p. 4; Z. G., *Excise* (1659), pp. 8–9; *CSP Ven.*, July 10, Aug. 14, 1665, pp. 154, 175–76; *Dutch Armado* (1665); W. Smith, *Poem On the famous Ship* (1666), p. 4; Dryden, "Epilogue" to *Amboyna* (1673), l. 22.
13. See sts. 7–9, 39–42, 143, 206–7, 299.
14. See sts. 76, 101, 170, 176, 192–96.

the Provinces, Dryden offers an argument of enlightened internationalism, implying that in such matters self-interest is dependent on the interest of others:

> Trade, which like bloud should circularly flow,
> Stop'd in their Channels, found its freedom lost
> Thither the wealth of all the world did go,
> And seem'd but shipwrack'd on so base a Coast.
>
> (2)

This argument is greatly extended in the "Digression concerning Shipping and Navigation" (155–64), where a *translatio studii* becomes an understated *translatio imperii* as England's rightfully inherited dominion of the seas is manifested in her mastery of navigational techniques. But Dryden's message is international, and not strictly imperial. He imagines a world economically one, a universal collective resembling a city like London but comprehending the entire earth. At this point the units of discourse expand with our perspective, comprehending not just nations but heavenly bodies:

> Instructed ships shall sail to quick Commerce;
> By which remotest Regions are alli'd:
> Which makes one City of the Universe,
> Where some may gain, and all may be suppli'd.
>
> Then, we upon our Globes last verge shall go,
> And view the Ocean leaning on the sky:
> From thence our rolling Neighbours we shall know,
> And on the Lunar world securely pry.
>
> (163–64)

The international scope of this utopian vision is only an extension of the collectivizing tendency of a zealous nationalism which recognizes the general necessity of mercantile cooperation. The nation remains the significant unit in *Annus Mirabilis*, and the general necessity of cooperation has many particular exceptions. One of these exceptions is the war itself, whose ultimate justification, Dryden makes clear, is mercantile. From one perspective it is precisely the

Dutch disruption of the international trade flow which requires that England temporarily suspend her own internationalism to engage the Provinces in war. From another, it is
simply a case of two opposed national interests which cannot be reconciled: "What peace can be where both to one
pretend?" (6). By offering these two economic interpretations of the war—the benevolent and the pragmatic—Dryden appears to seek a comprehensive understanding of the
event. Yet it is significant that his pragmatism does not
analyze self-interest into units smaller than the national:
there is no question that the war is in the economic interest
of every Englishman. Thus it is not surprising that in *Annus
Mirabilis* a more prevalent utopian conception than that of
the international state is the mercantile *locus amoenus*
whose amenities are the fruits of others' labors or of none at
all. After the St. James' Day Fight, Sir Robert Holmes sails
among the Dutch islands:

> Now on their coasts our conquering Navy rides,
> Way-lays their Merchants, and their Land besets:
> Each day new wealth without their care provides,
> They lie asleep with prizes in their nets.

> (202)

Seen historically, the present may be the necessary period
of economic rivalry which separates the prenationalist
Golden Age (158) from the postnationalist Universal State
(163). The Golden Age inaugurated by Saturn was one in
which natural wealth was available to all, one which precluded the getting and spending of the competitive modern
mercantile state and the sophistications of the monarchal
beehive.[15] But with the invention of coin and commerce,

15. Cf. Dryden, *Georgics* (1697), 2.777ff, and *Aeneis* (1697), 8.425–32.
Cf. the Virgilian description of the restored Golden Age in the *Fourth Eclogue*:
Dryden, *Pastorals* (1697), 4.37–48. Although st. 158 of *AM* is ambiguous,
it is generally accepted that the invention of commerce marked the end
of the classical Golden Age rather than having been a part of it: see Lovejoy
and Boas, *Primitivism* (1935), index, s.v. "Navigation." The ambiguity
probably owes to the fact that by the 17th century, commerce, classically a
mark of the "post-lapsarian" state of man, was displacing agriculture—both
imaginatively and practically—as the means for attaining the peace and
plenty which were traditionally associated with the Golden Age.

unfallen man of pastoral simplicity became *homo econo-micus*. The present age of acquisitiveness is one in which wealth, "stores," gold are difficult to obtain and easy to lose.[16] The nation-state is the basic acquisitive agent and war the fundamental means to acquisition: this is the Rome not of Saturn but of the Punic Wars. Yet as wealth accumulates, knowledge progresses, until that time is reached when one nation masters "Arts Elements," learns to control nature, and teaches its discoveries to other nations.[17]

The technological superiority which Dryden attributes to England at the dawn of this new age owes to the understanding of the newly created Royal Society, the alchemical alembic that transmutes the ideas of God and the laws of nature into gold "to fit the levell'd use of humane kind" (166).[18] The knowledge of Charles and the Royal Society, spread to all nations, will re-store forever England's "stores" and obviate the endless competition for gold, because it will make "one City of the Universe, / Where some may gain, and all may be suppli'd" (163). The resurrected London typifies this restored and final Golden Age. The "Chymick flame" of the fire purges her dross and reveals her, "all divine with Gold," not as the rude, pastoral "Shepherdess" of primitive abundance but as the fantastic "Maiden Queen" of prophecy to whom incense and gold are brought as suppliant offerings (293, 296–97). The crisis in this historical progression has passed, Dryden tells London. Now we need only finish the war, trust in our "constant Trade-wind," and

16. Cf. sts. 32, 139, 173, 208–9, 250–52.
17. Cf. Mede, *Key of the Revelation* (1643), "Preface" by William Twisse, sig. A3r, who says of Dan. 12:4 ("many shall run to and fro, and knowledge shall be increased"): "I lighted some times upon a wittie interpretation of this passage in a certain *Manuscript;* and the interpretation was this. That the opening of the world by Navigation and Commerce, and the increase of knowledge, shall meet both in one time, or age."
18. On the use of alchemical material in *AM* see Rosenberg, *PMLA*, 79 (1964), 254–58. The Royal Society's acquisition of useful knowledge is related to the theme of internationalism. Thomas Sprat wrote that the society learned a great deal by discoursing with world travelers and merchants. Furthermore, its members "openly profess, not to lay the Foundation of an *English, Scotch, Irish, Popish,* or *Protestant* Philosophy; but a Philosophy of *Mankind*" (*History* [1667], pp. 155, 63).

welcome the second Golden Age, when trade and war will be eternally obsolescent.[19] England will lead the way into the future in which rivalry will no longer be necessary, but she has no intention of forsaking the means of economic preeminence until they are literally outdated. The vanity of acquisition is a theme of some importance in *Annus Mirabilis,* but its moral force is greatly mitigated by the fact that vanity seems to apply only to those who cannot hold on to their riches.[20] There is nothing wrong with the secure possession of newfound wealth, and the shortly anticipated completion of the war will make national the luxury, foreshadowing the Golden Age, which Holmes's men fleetingly enjoyed:

> A constant Trade-wind will securely blow,
> And gently lay us on the Spicy shore.

(304)

To say that the basic units of *Annus Mirabilis* are national is not to deny that Dryden sometimes divides England into smaller entities. The question is whether these entities are seen to differ at all as to civil or economic interests. Individuals are specified: Charles, Albemarle, Rupert, Lawson, Berkeley, the bishop of Münster, the captains of the St. James' Day Fight. Simple distinctions are made: between king and merchants, between king and capital city (1, 154). Individual but indistinguishable citizens are seen united in work (144-48, 228) or in suffering (225-26, 255-59). These distinctions are all, as it were, cohesive ones. Even Dryden's oblique allusions to past rebellion[21] seem to dispose of a divisive, yet unavoidable, subject in a very efficient manner. The same cannot be said of his apparently gratuitous contrast between the conduct of rich and poor during the fire:

> The rich grow suppliant, and the poor grow proud:
> Those offer mighty gain, and these ask more.

19. See sts. 300, 301, 303, 304.
20. See, e.g., sts. 32, 208-9.
21. See sts. 213-14, 223, 276.

So void of pity is th' ignoble crowd,
When others ruine may increase their store.

(250)

Yet Dryden's point is, as ever, a positive, ultimately conciliatory one. The poor are ignoble in that they seek what they
mistake for their self-interest at the expense of the national
interest. Profiting from the misfortunes of others is permis-
sible only on the level of national units. Within the state, all
interests are identical because all are interrelated as in a
beehive, subsumed under the greater, national purpose. The
authorities God and Charles show the requisite "pity" which
the poor lack (240, 280), and justify the claim that the state
incorporates the interests of everyone by freely supplying to
the poor precisely that plenty which they had sought at the
expense of the rich (286).

The temporary transgression of the poor only emphasizes
the proper mutuality of relations between fellow Englishmen. It is this mutuality which Dryden's most frequent
analysis of the national unit—into prince and people—exemplifies. His analytic division of England has the effect of
unifying it. Only a superficial kind of mutuality is implicit in
the equilibrium of wise king and headstrong people:

The loss and gain each fatally were great;
And still his Subjects call'd aloud for war:
But peaceful Kings o'r martial people set,
Each others poize and counter-ballance are.

(12)

And something less than real reciprocity is manifested in the
partnership between godlike king and subjects whose es-
sence is "passive aptness" (141). These passages, although
important reminders of hierarchical structure, do not convey
the ideal relation of mutual love and interest between prince
and people which is Dryden's ultimate vision. He uses the
avarice of the bishop of Münster as an example of interest at
variance with love (38). In the English, on the other hand,

love for their prince is not distinguishable from concern for
their own interest, since his interest is theirs:

> The doubled charge his Subjects love supplies,
> Who, in that bounty, to themselves are kind:
> So glad *Egyptians* see their *Nilus* rise,
> And in his plenty their abundance find.
>
> (46)

In the same way, the famous friendship between Albemarle
and Rupert is owing to their identity of interests, to the fact
that

> Their duty, faith, and int'rest too the same,
> Like mighty Partners equally they raise.
>
> (48)

If subjects could choose which prince might rule them,
Charles would know the devotion of everyone; Solomon's
test would prove the mercy which Charles manifests in
"inviting" the unity, and not the mortal division, of French
and Englishmen (43–44).[22] In time of disaster, suffering
London is gratified to have its love fully reciprocated by
Charles:

> He wept the flames of what he lov'd so well,
> And what so well had merited his love.
>
> (241)

The *Loyal London*, like the parliamentary vote of war supplies, is a bounty which bespeaks simultaneously the city's
love and its apprehension of its own best interest:

> This martial Present, piously design'd,
> The Loyal City give their best-lov'd King:
> And with a bounty ample as the wind,
> Built, fitted and maintain'd to aid him bring.
>
> (154)

22. See 1 Kings 3:16–28.

Charles reciprocates by studying "how they may be suppli'd, and he may want" (261), and later, by putting his study into action:

> Thus God's Annointed God's own place suppli'd,
> And fill'd the empty with his daily bread.
>
> (286)

He discovers that to supply the people, far from causing his own want, actually amounts to supplying himself: "This Royal bounty brought its own reward," the reward of loyalty, constancy, and wealth in his subjects (287, 289–90). The people find their own abundance in their leader's plenty, and Charles finds his own reward in his people's supply. "Augusta" is indistinguishable from Augustus.[23] Mutuality of love and interest are perfect, national unity is inviolable.

The final understanding of *Annus Mirabilis* which results from the present reading is of a poem whose constant aim is to use the categories of love and interest and a wide range of literary conventions to depict England as a collective whose cohesiveness will admit no serious fragmentation of national unity so long as the policies and leadership of Charles and his court are unquestioningly embraced, as they have been thus far. The Anglo-Dutch War and the Great Fire have only strengthened the natural unity which exists between prince and people by defining Englishmen's unique status in the eyes of God and their national solidarity against the alien enemy. Yet instead of unconsciously acceding to these rhetorical strategies, my reading has, through its very willingness to regard and to analyze them as such, made explicit the strategic purposes by which they are motivated. In doing so, the reading has altered the "meaning" of the poem by precluding the response of unquestioning conviction which Dryden hopes to elicit from his audience, in favor of a

23. See st. 295. For derivations of "Augusta" as signifying London see Hardy, *Lamentation* (1666), p. 21; Kinsley's note in Dryden, *Poems* (1958), IV, 1840.

self-conscious awareness of how the poet has aimed at creating this conviction. Such an awareness necessarily undermines the reflex assent sought by Dryden, thereby converting "poetry" into "politics," and it provides a counterbalance to the exclusively "poetic" implications of the first "common reading" of the poem. Taken together, the two readings comprehend an epistemological range which consists of not only the primary level, on which *Annus Mirabilis*'s categories are perceived as commonplaces and command the unconscious assent they seek, but also the secondary level, on which "commonplace" is consciously apprehended as ideological strategy.

Such an apprehension implies, even presupposes, alternative perspectives among Dryden's contemporaries from which the events and conditions that *Annus Mirabilis* describes may be viewed, and it is now my task to confirm the likelihood of my political reading by investigating the historical context of the poem. Is it plausible to suggest that a large historical audience existed for *Annus Mirabilis* which was capable of understanding the poem's perspective on English affairs in this radical manner, that is, from the fundamentally different perspective which would permit the analysis of its political purpose? And if the existence of such an audience can be demonstrated by reference to contemporary opinion, what kind of alternative perspective would make plausible this understanding of the meaning of *Annus Mirabilis*?

2

FACTIONALISM:
THE CIVIL WAR LEGACY

A few weeks after his restoration to the throne of England, Charles II addressed the following words to the House of Commons: "How wonderfull, and miraculous soever the great harmony of Affections between Us and Our good Subjects is, . . . yet, We must not think that God Almighty hath wrought the Miracle to that degree that a Nation, so miserably divided for so many Years, is so soon, and entirely United in their Affections and Endeavours as were to be wished . . ."[1] Three years later his chief minister echoed these words in a tract whose anonymity permitted a degree of frank pessimism: "we enjoy this Universal Harmony only in our Wishes, (diversity of Opinions in Matters of Religious Worship having held so long a possession in the Minds of the People)."[2] The divisions of the Civil Wars, rather than lessening, had reached such a height during the settlement crisis which directly preceded the king's return that a correspondent wrote from London: "The confusions here are so great that it is not to be credited; the Chaos was a perfection in comparison of our order and government; the Parties are like so many floating islands, sometimes joining and appearing like a Continent, when the next flood or ebb seperates them that it can hardly be known where they will be next."[3] And George Monck, the man most singly responsible for

1. *His Majesties Gracious Message* (June 20, 1660), p. 4.
2. Clarendon, *Second Thoughts* (1663), p. 2.
3. *CSP Clar.*, June 3, 1659, III, 479.

Charles's restoration, summarized in convincing terms the demands which the legacy of the past twenty years would make upon future decades:

Before these unhappy Wars the Government of these Nations was Monarchical in Church and State: these wars have given birth and growth to several Interests both in Church and State heretofore not known; though now upon many accounts very considerable, as the *Presbyterian, Independent, Anabaptist* and *Sectaries* of all sorts as to Eccleciasticks; and the Purchasers of the Kings, Queens, Princes, Bishops, Deans and Chapters, and all other forfeited Estates; and all those engaged in these Wars against the King as to civils. These Interests again are so interwoven by Purchases and intermarriages, and thereby forfeited; as I think upon rational grounds it may be taken for granted; *That no Government can be either good, peaceful or lasting to these Nations, that doth not rationally include and comprehend the security and preservrtion of all the foresaid Interests both Civil and Spiritual . . . If this be so, Then that Government under which we formerly were both in State and Church, viz. Monarchy cannot possibly be admitted for the future in these Nations . . . That Government then that is most able to comprehend and protect all Interests as aforesaid must needs be Republique.*[4]

That four months after this letter was written Monck would welcome Charles back to England testifies to the unlikelihood that the Restoration, in itself, was capable of composing Englishmen into a harmony of affections and interests. The history of the first eight years of Charles II's reign is the history of successive and concurrent attempts to unify England, to isolate and efface the causes of divisiveness. As the decade wore on these causes were identified increasingly with particular groups or "conspiracies." It became clear to many who were concerned about the lack of national unity that the only way to achieve the reconciliation of diverse interests was to agree on which few interest groups were irreparably inconsistent with the national interest. The nature of this agreement in the 1660s had a great

4. Monck, *Collection* (1660), "A Letter of General George Moncks . . . directed unto Mr. Rolle . . . [and] the rest of the Gentry of Devon," Jan. 23, 1660, p. 19.

deal to do with the nature of the events which comprise the Exclusion Crisis and the Glorious Revolution.

The fundamental factor in the post-Restoration search for unity was the structure of affiliation and opposition bequeathed by the Civil War years. By granting formal recognition to developments of the interregnum, the Act of Indemnity and Oblivion of 1660 and related legislation necessarily alienated those who had looked to the Restoration for a just retribution. By reestablishing Anglicanism, the religious settlement necessarily alienated those who had enjoyed the latitude of the Commonwealth and Protectorate experiments.

The Cavaliers' dissatisfaction with the lot apportioned them at the Restoration owed most to the fact that only certain, exclusive categories of land sold or forfeited during the Civil Wars were made subject to the laws of restoration to prewar owners. The rest of the landowners went uncompensated.[5] In the early 1660s, discontent at this compromise became a commonplace. One Cavalier observed in 1664 that "we have been a table-talk in most parts of Christendom these three years past . . ."[6] Another was bitter that Commons voted a royal benevolence in 1661, "which, if every man's affections must be measured by their abilities in giving, will fall heavy upon the poor Cavalier, whose good will to His Majesty hath already drained their purses too much to be able to come in competition with the gaining Presbyter or saveing neuter . . ."[7] Anthony Wood commented that "Presbyterians for their money must be served, while the Royall party, that have endured the heat of the day and become poore, be putt off with inconsiderable nothings."[8] Pepys gave the following account of a meeting with a royalist: " 'Ah!' says he (I know [not] whether in earnest or

5. See Feiling, *History of the Tory Party* (1965), pp. 100–101.
6. Hammond, *Truth's Discovery* (1664) (*Somers Tracts* [1812], VII, 558).
7. *HMC* 5th Rept., letter of May 30, 1661, pp. 203–4.
8. *Life and Times* (1891), Sept. 1660, I, 333.

jest), 'this is the time for you,' says he, 'that were for Oliver heretofore; you are full of employment, and we poor Cavaliers sit still and can get nothing.' "[9] A *Cavaliers Complaint* prayed

> That since the Starres are yet unkind
> To Royalists, the King may find,
> More faithfull Friends then they.[10]

And "the Royal and Loyal Party" complained to Charles "that having ruined their fortunes, they now find themselves altogether slighted, for want of favour to obtain offices; that those who were the greatest opposers to Kings are preferred to the chief places."[11]

Many of the Cavalier petitions to the king were restrained and modest appeals for due recognition.[12] In others, the bitterness of this final disappointment threatened to occasion the change of allegiance which twenty years of quiet suffering could not.[13] " 'Whigism,' " said the earl of Ailesbury, "really sprung by degrees from the discontent of noble families" and gentry whose ancestors suffered for their "steadfast loyalties."[14] He blamed Clarendon for the advice that "his Majesty must reward his enemies to sweeten them, for that his friends were so by a settled principle, and that their loyalty could not be shaken."[15] Burnet gave his version of the bitter Cavalier joke that "the king had passed an act of oblivion for his friends and of indemnity for his enemies," and added that "to load the earl of Clarendon the more, it was given out that he advised the king to gain his enemies, since he was sure of his friends by their principles." This policy "laid the foundation of an implacable hatred in many of them, that was completed by the extent and comprehen-

9. *Diary* (1904), Dec. 15, 1665, V, 174.
10. *Cavaliers Complaint* (1660).
11. *CSPD*, Aug. [?] 1660, p. 217.
12. See Davies, *Restoration* (1955), p. 317. Cf. *Humble Representation of the sad Condition* (1661); *Plea, Case* (1663); Hammond, *Truth's Discovery* (1664).
13. See, e.g., *Cavaleer's Letany* (1661).
14. *Ailesbury Memoirs* (1890), I, 5. Cf. Milward, *Diary* (1938), p. xx.
15. *Ailesbury Memoirs* (1890), I, 5–6.

siveness of the act of indemnity."[16] These careless distinctions between friends and enemies could end in persuading all of the former to join the latter: "If any internal accidents should occur, as they threaten to do, it is not easy to see how the king could escape, with few supporters at home and fewer friends abroad, all having great occasion for disgust since his return . . ."[17] Cavalier rage was nowhere stronger than in Roger L'Estrange: "It was a jolly saying betwixt Jest and Earnest, of a *Presbyterian* to a *Cavalier, You told us Wee were Rebells once, but wee'll make You so now, before we have done with you . . .*"[18] But the future surveyor of the press was generally representative of the "Cavalier Party" in preferring, to rebellion, the utter suppression of the Presbyterians and sectarians as a means toward making good the Restoration settlement.

It was widely acknowledged that many Presbyterians had given their support to the royalist movements which culminated in Charles's restoration,[19] and many were almost indistinguishable from the Cavaliers in their desires for policy and employment when the Restoration was first accomplished.[20] Thus the term "new Royallists," used by Commonwealthsmen to describe Cromwellians during the Protectorate, was revived for a while to designate Presbyterians.[21] The returns to the Convention Parliament of 1660, however, were seen by contemporaries to favor the Cavalier interest in distinction from the Presbyterian.[22] From this point on, although diverse groups played a minor role, the controversy regarding domestic dissidence centered on the

16. Burnet, *History* (1897), I, 288–89.
17. *CSP Ven.*, July 14, 1662, p. 161.
18. *Caveat* (1661), p. 23.
19. See Kitchin, *L'Estrange* (1913), pp. 44–46, 74; Davies, *Restoration* (1955), chap. 8, especially on Sir George Booth's rising.
20. See Abernathy, *Trans. APS*, n.s., 55, pt. 2 (1965), 59.
21. See Davies, *Restoration* (1955), p. 125. Cf. *A Lively Pourtraict of our New-Cavaliers, Commonly Called Presbyterians* (1661). On the ambiguity of terminology and affiliations aimed at distinguishing Anglicans from dissenters—especially Presbyterians—owing to the widespread practice of "occasional" and "partial" conformity to the Anglican settlement, see Lacey, *Dissent and Parliamentary Politics* (1969), chap. 2.
22. See Abernathy, *Trans. APS*, n.s., 55, pt. 2 (1965), 50–60.

question of whether or not the Presbyterians and sectarians constituted a united interest. As far as the latter were concerned, royalists and Anglicans were increasingly content to overlook denominational differences in the face of common marks of disaffection. If royalists like Evelyn were indignant at the "*Schismes,* and *Heresies,* . . . and a thousand severall sorts of *Blasphemies* and professed Atheists"[23] spawned by the Protectorate, many others were equally unable to tell them apart: "And truly how to distinguish between the Anabaptists is difficult, Fleetwood being one, and Sir H. Vane one, yet they in high opposition; next, the Quakers and Fifth Monarchy men are Anabaptists, yet highly incensed at Sir H. Vane, so that to give you a true account of these subdivisions is too hard a task . . ."[24]

White's Plot, which was revealed on the dissolution of the Convention Parliament in November 1660, may be taken as the first of the many incidents which were to provide Restoration polemicists with occasions for the discovery of conspiracy inimical to English unity.[25] The arrest of this obscure officer and others who were implicated afforded a model for future discoveries, in which modest or questionable plots assumed grave proportions and implications. It also initiated the complex charges and countercharges of sham plotting which engrossed the attention of contemporaries and partisan historians.[26] There was no question,

23. *Apology for the Royal Party* (1659), p. 4.
24. *CSP Clar.,* Mordaunt to Hyde, June 7, 1659, III, 484. In ensuing discussions I use, at different times, the following terms to comprehend the entire spectrum of non-Anglican English Protestant belief and affiliation: Presbyterians and sectarians; nonestablished Protestantism; dissent; and nonconformity. My use of these terms, and of those denoting particular sects, unavoidably will reflect the same ambiguity which I am trying to document in post-Restoration usage of group terminology.
25. See Ludlow, *Memoirs* (1894), II, 328–29; Ashley, *Wildman* (1947), pp. 161–63.
26. See Ludlow, *Memoirs* (1894), II, 329n, on the use of his name in connection with plots in 1660–1663, and II, 376; also Echard, *History of England* (1718), III, 65–66, 72, 111, 150; Oldmixon, *History of England* (1730), pp. 503, 504; Ralph, *History of England* (1744), I, 35; Kennet, *Complete History* (1706), III, 236. On the alleged role played by Clarendon in shamming plots see Oldmixon, *History of England* (1730), pp. 504, 505, 509; Baxter, *Reliq. Baxt.* (1696), III, 20–21; Burnet, *History* (1897), I, 326; Clarendon, *Continuation* (1759), p. 192.

Portrait of the Fifth Monarchy Man Thomas Venner, in battle dress. He is charged with sedition, libertinism, and religious hypocrisy, and directly associated with the Quakers and Anabaptists. Reprinted by permission of the Trustees of the British Museum, London.

however, of the reality of the notorious Thomas Venner's Fifth Monarchist rising in the second week of January 1661. Twice he and his men swept through the streets of London to the cry of "King Jesus" before they were finally surrounded and overcome, leaving twenty soldiers and civilians dead and the city under martial law. The duke of York and the duke of Albemarle (the former General Monck) led mounted noblemen, soldiers, and the Life Guard in what proved to be unnecessary aid of Lord Mayor Brown and the trained bands of London and Westminster. A week later twenty men were arraigned for treason, of whom thirteen were executed, among them Venner.[27]

Public and official reaction to the plot was extraordinary. At least nine printed tracts of diverse origin were devoted entirely to condemning Venner's insurrection, which was portrayed in the most extreme and undiscriminating terms imaginable.[28] Royal proclamations of January 10 and 22, 1661,[29] prohibited seditious meetings of "*Quakers, Anabaptists,* and *Fifth-monarchy-men,*" and drew replies from groups of Anabaptists, Quakers, and Independents protesting their innocence of the recent insurrection and deploring the harassment for which the rising provided an excuse. The Anabaptists made the following complaint: "But that which wounds us most, O King, is the late *Proclamation,* wherein there is no Difference made, but as though all were alike in the Transgression, and had all made an ill use of thine Indulgence . . ." The Quakers were also disturbed at the arbi-

27. On Venner's rising see *CSPD,* Jan. 10, 11, 1661, pp. 470–71; *Merc. Pub.,* nos. 1, 3, Jan. 3–10, 17–24, 1661; *King. Intell.,* no. 4, Jan. 21–28, 1661; Add. MS. 10116, fols. 148v, 149v–150v; *Relation of the Arraignment and Trial* (1661), passim (*Somers Tracts* [1812], VII, 469–72); Kennet, *Register* (1728), I, 361–63; Sharpe, *London and the Kingdom* (1895), II, 387; Whiting, *Studies in English Puritanism* (1931), p. 238.

28. See, e.g., Clarendon's words to Parliament in *His Majesties Gracious Speech* (May 8, 1661), p. 17; Tanner, *Angelus Britannicus* (1662), sig. B2r; Pagitt, *Heresiography* (1662), pp. 285–86, 291, 292; *Merc. Pub.,* no. 1, Jan. 3–10, 1661. The nine tracts are: Clarke, *Plotters unmasked* (1661); *Last farewel* (1661); *Judgment and Condemnation* (1661); *Phanatiques Creed* (1661); *Renuntiation and Declaration* (1661); *Londons Glory* (1661); *Holy Sisters Conspiracy* (1661); Marriot, *Rebellion Unmasked* (1661); *Advertisement As touching* (1661).

29. *By the King* (Jan. 10, 1661); *Proclamation* (Jan. 22, 1661).

trariness of official conduct: "Our Meetings were stopped and broken up in the daies of *Oliver,* in pretence of Plotting against him; and in the daies of the *Parliament,* and *Committee of Safety,* wee were looked upon as Plotters to bring in KING CHARLES; and now we are called Plotters against KING CHARLES."[30] The memory of Venner's rising was useful in arguing for the necessity of the Militia Act (1662)[31] and even in justifying, according to some historians, the Clarendon Code in general.[32] More immediately, the news of it spread quickly throughout England. Oxford was in a state of alarm, numerous arrests were made in Chester and Canterbury, and in Lincolnshire there was discovered an Anabaptist plot timed to coincide with Venner's in London; "So as the same bad Spirit was for the City and Country . . ."[33] Venner's rising, like future plots, came to symbolize the evil which those united by their manifold disappointment at the Restoration settlement were capable of committing.

. . . there are many prophane Meetings . . . that had need to be taken great heed of; Namely, (that I may speak plain) those of the discontented Papists, Prisoners, Souldiers, Officers, Courtiers, Lawyers, Scholars, Royalists, Schismaticks, Seperatists, Merchants, Servants and Peasants; and specially all such of them as are the more sullen and desperate, for that they have lost, or have not gained their expectations. It was (I am afraid) the malecontentednesse of all these, that gave no small fewel and fire to these mens audacious and nefarious attempts [i.e., in Venner's rising] . . .[34]

30. *To the King . . . , the Humble Representation of . . . Anabaptists* (1661); Fox et al., *Declaration from the . . . Quakers* (1661), p. 6. See also *Humble Apology Of . . . Anabaptists* (1661); *Renuntiation . . . of the Congregational Churches* (1661). In fact, the first proclamation was instituted four days before Venner's rising in the form of orders "to be read in every parish church, forbidding meetings, held under the pretence of teaching, except in public churches and chapels" (Bate, *Declaration of Indulgence* [1908], p. 16).

31. See *His Majesties Declaration* (Dec. 26, 1662), pp. 3, 5–7; Kenyon, *Stuart Constitution* (1966), p. 374n.

32. See Oldmixon, *History of England* (1730), p. 495; Ralph, *History of England* (1744), I, 34, 52; Bate, *Declaration of Indulgence* (1908), p. 16.

33. *King. Intell.,* no. 3, Jan. 14–21, 1661; *Merc. Pub.,* no. 2, Jan. 10–17, 1661.

34. *Advertisement As touching* (1661), p. 6.

In March 1661 a momentary sensation was caused by the
return of two Presbyterian and two Independent London
aldermen in the elections for the new Parliament.[35] Many
took this development as proof of the disturbingly disaffected temper of the country and as a court defeat.[36]
Presbyterians saw it as a successful combination of sectarian
and Presbyterian power:

> . . . if so be it all the Fanatics . . . can agree together, as here
> they did, to choose any sober Presbyterians, it will do well.

> The bishops' interest fell before the conjunctive interest of
> honest men, . . . we all agreed unanimously, and carried all
> clearly and fully, so much that their party is exceedingly vexed,
> and swear the Devil united the Presbyterians, Independents, and
> Anabaptists.[37]

The king's reaction suggests that his interpretation of the
significance of the elections was similar to that of the Presbyterians. First, he resolved to strengthen the guard and
reserve the militia—"very needful," it was said, "seeing the
Presbyterians, Independents, and Anabaptists, are leagued
together in the plottings."[38] Second, Charles agreed to renew London's charter unchanged only on the condition that
he might replace certain offensive aldermen with certain
others of his choice. United opposition to this tactic was in
vain: "the presbiters, independents, anabaptists, and quakers
joined together in abundance, but could not carry it," and
the city was deluged with reports of the king's treachery.[39]
As the settlement of church and state slowly turned
against the interests of Protestant dissenters, there was a

35. See *CSPD*, Mar. 18–19, 1661, p. 536; Sharpe, *London and the
Kingdom* (1894), II, 391–93. Other sources (e.g., Bosher, *Making of the
Restoration Settlement* [1951], pp. 208–9) say all four were Presbyterians.
36. See *CSPD*, Mar. 19, 1661, pp. 537ff; Sharpe, *London and the Kingdom* (1894), II, 393; *HMC* 5th Rept., letter of Mar. 23, 1661, p. 151;
Loyall Subjects Lamentation for Londons Perversenesse (1661).
37. Letters quoted in Bosher, *Making of the Restoration Settlement*
(1951), p. 209.
38. *HMC* 5th Rept., letter of Mar. 23, 1661, p. 170.
39. Sharpe, *London and the Kingdom* (1894), II, 394–96, 403; *HMC*
5th Rept., letter of Apr. 9, 1661, pp. 181–82.

marked increase of court informations that non-Anglican groups were praying and plotting in unity: ". . . I have intelligence that [the Presbyterians] are so united with the Anabaptists and Fifth Monarchy men as at their meetings of late they preach one after another in the same churches and meeting houses . . ."[40] The discovery of the Worcestershire Plot in late 1661 alleged the unlikely combination of the famous Richard Baxter and other Presbyterian ministers, with the republican Major-General John Lambert.[41] The revelation of this conspiracy may have been influential in securing passage of the Corporations Act in December 1661,[42] although by this time the fear of "an universal Conspiracy against the Kingdom"[43] was being fed from many sources. One such source described the "central committee" of the conspiracy in the following manner: "There were seaven interests taken in, which are opposite to the present government. These seaven had each three representatives; the Commonwealth men three, whereof Harrington and Wildman were two; the purchasers of King's lands, &c. three; the Londoners three; the Anabaptists and Independents three; the disbanded officers three; the Rumpe three; and the Long Parliament three. All which, except the three last, met constantly . . ."[44] One of the "seaven interests" had been secured in November, with the arrest of several former members of the Rota Club, including Praisegod Barebones, John Ireton, John Wildman, and James Harrington himself. The charge of participating in the grand committee included the revelation of a further "Inner Council of Seven," and of the Rota's instrumentality in obtaining

40. Secretary Nicholas to Clarendon, Sept. 13, 1661, quoted in Bosher, *Making of the Restoration Settlement* (1951), p. 238.
41. See Abbott, *Amer. Hist. Rev.*, 14 (1908), 507–8; *HMC Hastings*, letter of Nov. 19, 1661, IV, 119; *CSPD*, Nov. 12, 16, 1661, pp. 143, 148, 149; Baxter, *Reliq. Baxt.* (1696), II, 383; Ashley, *Wildman* (1947), pp. 172–75.
42. See Abbott, *Amer. Hist. Rev.*, 14 (1908), 508; Ashley, *Wildman* (1947), p. 175.
43. Commons' warning to the king on Dec. 11, 1661, in Kennet, *Register* (1728), I, 576.
44. *HMC Beaufort*, letter of Dec. 19, 1661, p. 51.

the victories of the four offensive aldermen in the recent parliamentary elections. A joint committee of Parliament appointed to examine the matter soon transferred its attention to the more compelling business of uniformity debates.[45]

Shortly after the elections to what was to become known as the Cavalier Parliament, George Wither wrote hopefully of its inability to accommodate the diverse groups which constituted English society:

> Dissatisfide men of all judgment are,
> The Rich, the Pore, the Roundhead, Cavaleer,
> And they who at the first did in their choice
> Of such as these much glory and reioice.[46]

But Parliament soon showed itself to be almost totally united in blaming the disunity of England on nonestablished Protestantism. The Act of Uniformity of 1662 can be seen as the use of religious legislation to define strictly the nature and limits of England's interest. If Uniformity had the effect of uniting the Church of England, it also—according to many observers—strengthened solidarity among dissenters. Some long-suffering Presbyterians only continued to wonder at the irony of divisiveness: ". . . The Royalist's throw us am[ong] ye Phanaticks bec[ause] of Piety. The Phanaticks throw us to them bec[ause] of our Loyalty. These 2 extremes harden one another, & both hate us."[47] But others were said to regard the act as the final straw: "The Independents and Presbyterians who could scarcely give each other a good word, on the publishing of the Act of Uniformity, held a great meeting at St. Bartholomew's, Thames Street, received the sacrament together, and appointed a fast."[48] At his execution for treason in June 1662 Sir Henry Vane's scaffold speech was silenced by royal trumpet blasts. Charles is reported to have said that Vane's intention was to reveal that he and the marquis of Argyle (executed in the

45. See Ashley, *Wildman* (1947), pp. 175–82.
46. *Vox Vulgi* (1661), p. 21.
47. Chet. Lib. MS. Mun. A.3.123, June 11, 1662, p. CXLVII.
48. *CSPD*, June 1, 1662, p. 396.

previous year) had been "the father and mother of the
Covenant . . . By telling the people this . . . he meant a
piece of sedition, to unite the Presbyterians and the Congre-
gationalists against the present government."[49] Charles's
new secretary of state, Sir Henry Bennet, was convinced that
"the dissatisfaction towards ye present Government . . . is
become soe universal that any small accident may put us
into new troubles . . ." The Cavalier Parliament had become "ye onely bulwarque now betwixt the disaffected
people and the government."[50]

The plots, real or alleged, followed in swift succession. In
November 1662 Ensign Tong and other obscure military
men were arrested for conspiring to seize the Tower, burn
London, murder (according to different reports) Charles,
York, Clarendon, and Albemarle, and institute a republic—
all of which was revealed by the Reverend William Hill
shortly before the plot's expected fruition.[51] Two Councils
of Forty were said to exist in Holland and England, the
latter of which had been reduced to a Council of Six that sent
agitators to each county to coordinate what was to have
been a national rebellion under the command of Major-
General Edmund Ludlow.[52] (In fact Ludlow was in
Switzerland throughout this entire period, and he under-
standably regarded Tong's conspiracy as another sham
plot.)[53] Charles identified the rebels as "Anabaptists." Another contemporary described them as *Fifth-Monarchy
Men, Anabaptists,* and fighting *Quakers;* of which the *Fifth
Monarchy-men* were to lead the Van." A third believed "it is
not unlikely that the Presbyterians have had a share in these

49. *HMC Hastings,* letter of June 17, 1662, IV, 134.
50. Lister, *Clarendon* (1838), letters of ca. June 1662, III, 199, 198.
51. See *CSP Ven.,* Nov. 10, 1662, p. 209; *True and Exact Relation*
(1662); *Brief Narrative* (1662, 1663); *HMC* 7th Rept., letter of Oct. 30,
1662, p. 463; Kennet, *Register* (1728), I, 839–41; Abbott, *Amer. Hist.
Rev.,* 14 (1908), 513–15; Muddiman, *King's Journalist* (1923), pp. 152–53.
52. See *King. Intell.,* no. 50, Dec. 8–15, 1662; *Merc. Pub.,* no. 50, Dec.
11–18, 1662; *HMC* 7th Rept., letter of Oct. 30, 1662, p. 463; *HMC Portland,* letter of Nov. 25, 1662, III, 270; *CSP Ven.,* Nov. 1, 1662, p. 205;
Muddiman, *King's Journalist* (1923), p. 153.
53. See Ludlow, *Memoirs* (1894), II, 341–42.

contrived dissensions . . ." And a fourth observer was shocked by the breadth of the alleged conspiracy, "a very great designe amongst the fanaticks, Commonwealth men, and those kind of people."[54] Several months after the execution of Tong and his cohorts, Lord Lieutenant Ormonde foiled a plot led by Colonel Thomas Blood to take the Castle of Dublin, a plan rumored, once again, to have been part of a larger conspiracy reaching as far as London.[55] And once again, as the year wore on, the Council of Six idea gained prominence: but now there were two of them in England, one led partly by Colonel Blood, the other by Wildman (who was still in prison) and others, some of whom were arrested in October–November 1663.[56] The king's brother later attributed to this period a confederacy of dissidents which "could not agree about what sort of government to declare for, in church and state; and they always broke up in a heat . . . their council consisting of all sorts of dissenters, quakers, &c. Their number was, at length, reduced to six; yet they seldom met, without running into some inconvenience."[57] In July 1663 Charles himself promised Parliament that he would bring two bills against fanatic and popish sedition "if I live to meet with you again, as I hope I shall."[58]

The Yorkshire Plot, according to Arlington a "remnant" of the Castle of Dublin Plot, was known in detail weeks before October 12, the day on which "the fifth monarchy men, the Anabaptists, Independents, Presbyterians, and a great many of the old soldiers, are resolved upon a rising."[59] One hun-

54. Bryant, *Letters* (1935), Charles to Madame, Nov. 4, 1662, p. 136; *King. Intell.*, no. 50, Dec. 8–15, 1662; *CSP Ven.*, Nov. 17, 1662, p. 212; *HMC Portland*, letter of Nov. 25, 1662, III, 270.

55. See *HMC Ormonde*, n.s., H. Coventry to Ormonde, Mar. 20, 1663, III, 46. Marvell, *Poems and Letters* (1952), Marvell to Mayor Wilson, June 6, 1663, II, 36. On the Dublin Castle Plot see *HMC Ormonde*, II, 251–53.

56. See Ashley, *Wildman* (1947), pp. 195–96; *Misc. Aulica* (1702), Arlington to Buckingham, Nov. 5, 1663, p. 320; Clarendon, *Continuation* (1759), p. 192.

57. Macpherson, *Original papers* (1775), "Life of James II," I, 24. See also Clarke, *Life of James the Second* (1816), II, 396.

58. *His Majesties Most Gracious Speech* (July 27, 1663), p. 5.

59. *Misc. Aulica* (1702), Arlington to Ormonde, Nov. 3, 1663, p. 320; *HMC Lonsdale*, letter of Oct. 1663, p. 93.

dred of the alleged conspirators were seized in August, and despite panicky rumors of the plot's universality and of the intention of taking Albemarle, York, Clarendon, and Lord Treasurer Southampton, the countryside was calmed and the militia dismissed through the efforts of the duke of Buckingham and Lord Belasyse.[60] For the next nine months the remainder—and the real substance—of the plot consisted in the well-publicized collection of damning evidence and the prosecution of the plotters. With the new year came news of the trial, and conviction for high treason, of ten conspirators.[61]

The quashing of the Yorkshire Plot was evidently considered by Roger L'Estrange to be a vindication of his convictions regarding the unity of domestic sedition. In one of his newspapers, he assured his readers that "the Plot is now believ'd even by the most Incredulous, having been traced upon the very heel, and proved to be in Agitation in these *Northern* Parts ever since *February* last: begun by the Anabaptists; hatch'd by the *Fifth-Monarchy-men;* foster'd by the *Congregated* Churches; favour'd by the *Purchasers;* supported by the *Souldiers* of *Olivers old Army;* and in Fine, carryed on by the Concurrence of all *Dissenting Sects* against the *Royall Interest* . . ."[62] It was L'Estrange's own belief that there was an intimate relationship between the actions of conspirators and the workings of the seditious press, which had become his special province. The trial and execution of the printer John Twyn were based upon the charge that he was responsible for the *Treatise of the Execution of Justice,*[63] which was in turn charged with having

60. See *CSPD*, Oct. 10–24, 1663, pp. 293–312; *Intell.*, no. 8, Oct. 19, 1663; *Newes*, no. 8, Oct. 22, 1663, and following numbers; Walker, *Yorkshire Archaeological Journal*, 31 (1934), 348–59; Abbott, *Amer. Hist. Rev.*, 14 (1908), 522–26; Gee, *Trans. RHS*, 11 (1917), 125–42; Muddiman, *King's Journalist* (1923), pp. 168–71.

61. See *Newes*, no. 4, Jan. 14, 1664; *HMC Ormonde*, n.s., letter of Jan. 16, 1664, III, 140.

62. *Intell.*, no. 5, Jan. 18, 1664.

63. See Hart, *Index Expurgatorius* (1878), no. 223, p. 192; and the partial copy in PRO SP 29/88(76). Twyn was said to have been secured before copies of the *Treatise* could be disseminated.

constituted a call to rebellion in Yorkshire.[64] The implications of these developments were clear to L'Estrange:

> . . . the Generality of all the Separate Factions, within the Kings Dominions, are Engaged in the Conspiracy, And it is no more wonder to find a People *Distemper'd*, that's entertain'd with *Poyson*, instead of wholesome *Nourishment*, then to see the *Sea Rage*, when the *Winds blow* . . .

> It would be well to have an Eye to the Traders This way in that kind of Commodity [i.e., seditious papers]. By the Tenour of the Accompt we have of the Phanatiques Design, compar'd with the Dictates of many Printed Discourses lately scatter'd up and down the Kingdome It seems to me reasonable to believe, that the Authors of many of Those Treatises, and the Chiefe Menagers of their Military Designs, understand one another and Act by Confederacy . . .[65]

In the final estimate, the Yorkshire Plot was said to have been the work of a central council situated in London. It was "but a Branch" of the continuity of plots in progress for the last few years; it was, presumably with the Dublin Castle attempt, "to have begun in *Ireland*, to have followed in *England*, and then in *Scotland*."[66] Either Ludlow or Lambert—the one still in Switzerland and the other in the Tower—was to have led the general rebellion.[67] In May 1664 the Conventicle Act went into effect. Directed against those "who under pretence of Tender Consciences doe at their Meetings contrive Insurrections as late experience hath shewed,"[68] the act sought to dissolve practically those groupings of dissidents which other government policy was doing so much to unite conceptually.

---

64. See *Exact Narrative* (1664), passim; Heath, *Chronicle* (1676), p. 521; Echard, *History of England* (1718), III, 111.

65. *Exact Narrative* (1664), sig. A3v; *Newes*, no. 8, Oct. 22, 1663. Although it has not been attributed to him, "To the Reader," which prefaces the *Exact Narrative*, sounds very much like L'Estrange's work.

66. *His Majesties Most Gracious Speech* (Mar. 21, 1664), pp. 4, 5; Add. MS. 33770; Heath, *Chronicle* (1676), p. 521.

67. See *CSPD*, Oct. 13, 1663, p. 299; *CSP Ven.*, Nov. 5, 1663, p. 269; Heath, *Chronicle* (1676), p. 521; Oldmixon, *History of England* (1730), p. 515.

68. *SR* (1819), V, 516.

The foregoing discussion should have clarified the kind of response which Englishmen made to one basic factor in the post-Restoration problem of national unity, the divisive legacy of the Civil Wars. It is necessary to consider only a few of the ways in which this divisiveness continued to manifest itself during the last two years of the period with which we are most concerned.

In the plague year of 1665, the nonconforming clergy succeeded in taking over the London pulpits that had been vacated by Anglican ministers who followed Charles and the court into the country as the plague increased in intensity. As a result, the stature of the dissenting clergy rose in the eyes of the people, while that of the Anglicans suffered proportionately.[69] In the pamphlet controversy over the culpability of those from all professions who fled the plague, the Anglican clergy received the major criticism.[70] The Five Mile Act of 1665 was in part a response to this unprecedented threat of concentrations of dissenters in municipal corporations and in part a continuation of legislation aimed at preventing armed rebellion.

Amid the many plots and alarms of plots reported in the *Calendar of State Papers, Domestic* for 1665–66, there are two which stand out not only for their notoriety but also for their relevance to the kind of development in public consciousness which we have been tracing. On October 10, 1665, Clarendon revealed to Parliament that a plot to take the city had been foiled recently: "you had heard of them in all places upon the third of the last month (their so much celebrated Third of September)" had not the "Seditious Leaders" of it been apprehended just in time; "some of the Principal

69. See Burnet, *History* (1897), I, 400–401; Baxter, *Reliq. Baxt.* (1696), III, 2; Ellis, *Original Letters*, letter no. 312, to Dean Sancroft, Aug. 10, 1665, 2nd ser. (1827), IV, pp. 27–28; Bell, *Great Plague* (1924), pp. 149–52, 227; Nuttall and Chadwick, *From Uniformity to Unity* (1962), Roger Thomas, "Comprehension and Indulgence," pp. 195–96.

70. See, e.g., J. B., *Shepherds Lasher* (1665); *Pulpit to be let* (1665); *Londini Lachrymae* (1665); *Run-awayes safe Refuge* (1665); *Run-awayes Routed* (1665); J. W., *Friendly Letter* (1665); *Lamentatio Civitatis* (1665), pp. 5, 24–25.

Persons are not yet taken . . ."[71] Except for this speech little or no reference is made to Rathbone's Plot until the following April, when Joseph Williamson printed in his *Gazette* the account of it—occasioned by the plotters' conviction for high treason—which for the first time mentioned by name Colonel Rathbone and the seven other republican soldiers convicted of the conspiracy.[72] In this polished version, the plot was to have accomplished the seizure of the Tower, the burning of London, and the murder of Charles as well as Albemarle. The conspirators allegedly testified that they were directed by a central council in London, which in turn received orders from a council in Holland. Ludlow again was said to have planned to lead the insurrection.[73]

The most substantial and widely publicized uprising of 1666 was the Scottish Rebellion. It broke out in the land in which the Covenant had originated—"the most disaffected part of the Kingdom"[74]—in November 1666, when Dryden was finishing the "Account of the ensuing Poem" prefixed to *Annus Mirabilis*. A proclamation of October 11 had ordered stricter usage of legislation directed against Protestant and Catholic dissenters. On November 15 the royal enforcer of this proclamation was seized by Protestant rebels, an event which precipitated twelve days of battle between royalist and rebel forces culminating in the defeat of the "fanatic whigs" on November 27 at Pentland Hills.[75] During the rebellion and even after it had subsided, observers were

71. *His Majesties Gracious Speech* (Oct. 10, 1665), p. 18. For other possible allusions to this plot see Clarendon, *Continuation* (1759), p. 290, and st. 16 of the anon. poem printed in Bell, *Great Plague* (1924), pp. 339–51. Cromwell won victories at Dunbar (1650) and Worcester (1651), and died (1658), on the third of September.

72. *Gazette*, no. 48, Apr. 26–30, 1666.

73. See *Gazette*, no. 48, Apr. 26–30, 1666; Heath, *Chronicle* (1676), p. 550; Echard, *History of England* (1718), III, 167; Oldmixon, *History of England* (1730), pp. 523, 524.

74. *Arlington's Letters* (1701), Arlington to Sir R. Southwell [?], Nov. 15, 1666, II, 208. Cf. Airy's note in *Lauderdale Papers* (1884), I, xi–xii.

75. See *CSPD*, Oct. 18, Nov. 15, 17, 27, 1666, pp. 205, 262, 268, 294–95, and 1666–67 "Preface," pp. xix–xxiii; *HMC Le Fleming*, Nov. 15, etc., 1666, pp. 42–44; *Gazette*, no. 106, Nov. 19–22, 1666, and following numbers.

concerned that sympathetic risings in other parts of the island might convert it into an unmanageable revolution.[76]

The contradictions inherent in official policy regarding Protestant dissent during the early 1660s can be seen in the polemical activities of that hardworking public servant Roger L'Estrange, surveyor of the press. It was inevitable that for men like L'Estrange the task of achieving a united and stable England would be defined in the inexhaustible terms of factionalism of the previous twenty years. But with so many interests opposed both to the king and to each other, the problem of a rational reconciliation became at the same time much too large and much too amorphous. The solution that L'Estrange adopted consisted in attributing group coherence to—"reconciling"—a large number of disparate factions on the basis of their presumed dissatisfaction with the restored monarchy. The wholesale suppression of this artificially created group would then lead to the unification of England. Several factors determined the failure of this policy. First, L'Estrange was never able to carry out the total suppression of Protestant dissent on which the success of his policy depended. This being the case, the conceptual polarization of England into two basic camps had the effect of hastening a substantive disunity which was only potential as long as the "interest of England" remained diverse and fragmented. The attribution to individual factions of a common interest in opposing the government made those factions more conscious of how they might increase their power through combination without at the same time forsaking their separate self-interests as they conceived them. Thus legislation frequently sought to dissolve that unity which reports of plots and seditious writings simultaneously conferred on dissidence.

It is notable that *Annus Mirabilis* is concerned very little with the kinds of group divisiveness which we have exam-

76. See *CSPD*, Nov. 27, Dec. 5, 1666, pp. 293, 322.

ined so far. This fact is explicable both from the perspective of the material which prefaces the poem and from that of the reading made in the previous chapter. A different context of group definition, the Anglo-Dutch War, has arisen once or twice in the preceding discussion, and it is obvious that a distinction between this context and that of the Civil War legacy can be made only for purposes of analysis. The war with the Dutch and the Great Fire were selected by Dryden as the "subject" for his poem, but in the larger context of post-Restoration history they constituted the decisive factors in the court's failure to unite England by focusing the blame for division on dissenting conspiracies.

3

NAVAL WAR AND TRADE

A popular point of wisdom adopted by Englishmen from the writings of the influential duc de Rohan was the maxim that *"England is a mighty Animal, which can never dye except it kill it selfe."*[1] The application of this maxim to recent history was clear enough: civil war divides and destroys England from within; foreign war provides the external catalyst for English unity and strength. "Warfare" with the United Provinces of the Netherlands, in the sense of commercial rivalry, was a constant factor in seventeenth-century English foreign policy and economic debate. English writers, by turns admiring and querulous, balance again and again the natural disadvantages of the Provinces against their infuriating achievements and seek to point the moral for England's less spectacular commercial development. In the early 1660s, resentment against the Dutch for their peaceable usurpation of English trade was only one aspect of the growing hostility to the Provinces. A sense of their irritating ingratitude to England pervades anti-Dutch polemics. Their thanks to Elizabethan England for its aid to the rebel republic against Spain had been the massacre at Amboyna (1623) and Dutch maintenance of trade relations

---

1. Rohan, *Treatise* (1663), p. 55. Cf. Corbet, *Second Part* (1661), p. 156; *CSP Ven.*, Apr. 10, 1665, p. 97; Humfrey, *Proposition* (1667), epigraph; Trigge, *Calendarium* (1667), sig. A6v; *Interest of England* (1669), pp. 1–2.

with Spain during the Anglo-Spanish War (1655–1659).[2]
Even more galling was the impunity with which the Provinces ignored the imperialist pretensions of the doctrine of
Mare clausum, to the extent of outfishing the English in
their own Narrow Seas, the British sovereignty of which was
demonstrated by incontestable historical precedent.[3] The
Navigation Act of 1660 and its subsequent modifications and
extensions[4] sought by prohibitions to encourage the trade of
England and decrease that of other countries, especially the
carrying trade of the United Provinces. And for five years
after its legislation, related policy for the improvement of
trade grew out of the recommendations of the Privy Council
Committee for Trade and Plantations, the Council for
Trade, and the Council for Foreign Plantations.[5] Anglo-
Dutch rivalry reached its height in the Africa and East India
trades, where there was a lengthy history of mutual seizure
of ships and property. Article XIV of the commercial treaty
of 1662 stipulated that a catalogue of past damages between
set dates be prepared by both nations, exchanged, and in
effect consigned to the oblivion of diplomatic adjudication.
Volatile incidents, however, continued after the treaty's
ratification.[6]

When Dryden prophesies British dominion of the seas
(155–64) or recalls English aid to the new republic (198),

2. See W. W., *English and Dutch Affairs* (1664), title and pp. 9ff; Darell,
True and Compendious (1665), title; Cliffe, *Abreviate* (1665), pp. 31–37,
46–52; Eliot, *English-Duel* (1666); Codrington, *His Majesties Propriety*
(1665), pp. 121–25, 150–69.

3. See J. Smith, *Trade & Fishing* (1661), p. 16; Ogilby, *Entertainment*
(1662), p. 52; *John Keymors Observation* (written 1601, printed 1664);
Dutch Drawn to Life (1664), pp. 75–81; W. W., *English and Dutch Affairs*
(1664), pp. 26–36; Codrington, *His Majesties Propriety* (1665), p. 1 and
passim; Cliffe, *Abreviate* (1665), pp. 44–45; *Hollanders Unmasked* (1665);
Royal Victory (1665), second sheet. On the history of this controversy see
the standard authority on the subject, Thomas W. Fulton, *The Sovereignty
of the Sea* (London, 1911).

4. See 13 Car. II c. 14 (1661) confirming the Navigation Act; 15 Car.
II c. 7 (1663), act for the encouragement of trade; *By the King* (Aug. 26,
1663).

5. Established July 4, Nov. 7, and Dec. 1, 1660, respectively. See
Andrews, *British Committees* (1908), pp. 62, 66–67, 76, 85.

6. See *Articles of Peace & Alliance* (1662) and *Catalogue of Damages*
(1664). See Feiling, *British Foreign Policy* (1930), pp. 105–8.

or when he confidently and consistently assumes the rightness of a national effort against the Provinces, it is on this strongly felt rivalry that he tacitly bases his argument. *Annus Mirabilis* attempts to heal England's internal divisions through the sheer force of its persuasive thesis of nationalist coherence. This thesis received valuable support from the popular mercantile dogma of the times that the index to prosperity was the national balance of trade, the ratio between imports and exports: if the latter exceeded the former, the difference constituted monetary profit for all.[7] One economic projector recalls Dryden's characteristic metaphor in *Annus Mirabilis* when he explains the balance of trade theory first in terms of the family—"and soe a Comonwealth, which in itt's Politique Capacitie is, or ought at least to bee consider'd but as one family, and to bee Governed by a like Method."[8] Scholars have noted that a corollary of the quest for a favorable balance of trade was a strictly nationalist conception of economic intercourse, a view that the world held only a certain, fixed amount of wealth and that the impoverishment of one nation necessarily entailed the enrichment of others.[9] When Dryden asks, "What peace can be where both to one pretend?" (6), he echoes earlier advocates of a war with the Dutch: ". . . there is but a certain proportion of Trade in the world, and *Holland* is prepossessed of the greater part of it . . ."; ". . . the trade of the world is too little for us two, therefore one must down . . ."[10]

The war provided Charles and his court with an issue which, as Rohan's maxim suggested, might serve to unite

7. See, e.g., Cradocke, *Expedient* (1660), pp. 8, 9; Fortrey, *Englands Interest* (1663), p. 14; Mun, *England's Treasure* (1664), p. 11; Hodges, *True and onely* (1666); Milward, *Diary* (1938), Sept. 22, 1666, p. 5; Manley, *Usury* (1669), pp. 43, 66; Temple, *Observations* (1673), p. 206. Cf. Viner, *Studies* (1937), pp. 6–57.

8. PRO SP 29/19(20), paper of Oct. [?] 1660.

9. See Heckscher, *Mercantilism* (1935), II, 24; Lipson, *Economic History* (1948), III, 4; Clark, *Seventeenth Century* (1947), p. 26; Buck, *Politics of Mercantilism* (1942), pp. 28–30.

10. Graunt and Petty, *Natural and Political* (1662), p. 21; Pepys, *Diary* (1904), Feb. 2, 1664, IV, 31, quoting Capt. George Cocke.

men who through other circumstances had good reason for increasing divisiveness. Although Charles observed the form of claiming that England's part in the war was from the start defensive,[11] official court policy was closer to Dryden's position in stanza 12 of *Annus Mirabilis:* "And still his Subjects call'd aloud for war." In court circles the proximate cause of the war was said to be the joint patriotism and enlightened self-interest of the people of England;[12] thus as early as 1662 a medal was struck showing English and Dutch ships in battle and bearing the legend "NON · MIHI · SED · POPVLO."[13] It was further claimed that the mercantile community in particular was strongly in favor of a war which would recover trade lost to the Dutch. This claim received most of its apparent justification from the report of a parliamentary committee which met in 1664.[14]

On March 26 a committee headed by Sir Thomas Clifford was "impowered to inquire into Reasons of the general Decay of Trade; and to consider, how the same may be advanced and improved." With the Privy Council this parliamentary Committee of Trade was to assume the functions of the moribund Council for Trade.[15] After hearing the testimony of merchants, Clifford informed Commons of the Committee of Trade's agreement "that ye seuerall Wrongs

11. See Add. MS. 32094, fol. 165, reply of Oct. 4, 1666, to a letter from the Provinces of Sept. 16 concerning peace and the causes of the war. Cf. Temple, *Lettre* (1666), p. 3. The *Lettre* was commissioned by Charles via Arlington; see *Arlington's Letters* (1701), I, 90–91.

12. See Bryant, *Letters* (1935), Charles to Madame, June 2, Sept. 19, 1664, pp. 159, 164; Macpherson, *Original papers* (1775), "Life of James II," I, 25; Hartmann, *Clifford* (1937), Clifford to W. Coventry, Nov. 25, 1664, p. 37; Harl. MS. 7010, fol. 231v, Arlington to Fanshawe, Apr. 6, 1665; Barbour, *Arlington* (1914), Cominge to Lionne, Dec. 29, 1664, pp. 82–83; *Recueil des instructions* (1929), Courtin to Lionne, Apr. 23, 1665, XXIV, 377; Eg. MS. 627, fol. 92, "Relation D'Angleterre," 1666; PRO SP 29/159(108), letter of court informer, June 24, 1666.

13. See Hawkins et al., *Medallic Illustrations* (1969), I, 495, "Charles II," no. 123.

14. For earlier evidence of merchant support for a war with the Provinces see *CSP Ven.*, May 5, July 14, Aug. 18, Aug. 25, 1662, pp. 138, 161, 174, 180 (all letters of one ambassador); letter to de Witt and statement of Clarendon, mid-1662, quoted in Wilson, *Profit and Power* (1957), p. 106; Josselin, *Diary* (1908), Nov. 9, 1663, p. 144.

15. *CJ*, Mar. 23, 26, 1664, VIII, 535–36, 537; *CSPD*, Mar. 26, 1664, p. 531; Andrews, *British Committees* (1908), p. 85.

dishonors and Indignytyes done to his Matie. by the subjects of the united Provinces . . . bee reported to ye Howse as the greatest Obstrucon of Our Forreigne Trade, that is the Opinion of ye Committee." To the committee's request that Charles take "speedy redress" of these grievances, Commons added their own pledge—"with their Lives and Fortunes, [to] assist his Majesty against all Oppositions whatsoever" —and passed the resolution.[16] The court and its apologists took this decision to be clear proof of popular and mercantile enthusiasm for a war with the Dutch.[17] Parliament's voting of an unprecedented war supply the following November, although the result of a hard-fought political battle,[18] was seen as a vindication of this view. Thus one year later, after war had been declared and its first ill effects had been felt, Charles was able to remind both Houses (and, by implication, the people in general) that "I entered upon this War by your Advice and Encouragement . . ."[19]

There is a perceptible tendency in modern accounts of the first decade of the Restoration to confirm what was the court's official position on the state of the nation. Of course, this picture of national amity and the intimate accord of prince and people is not positively asserted by historians. Even so, we sometimes are left with the general impression that despite the difficulties of the 1660s, it is only at the beginning of the next decade that the seeds of the severe discord manifested in the Exclusion Crisis of 1678–1681 may be seen to be sprouting.[20] My argument in the preceding chapter may have helped to correct this impression by showing the growth of domestic discontent even as patriots were

16. PRO SP 29/97(15), Apr. 21, 1664; *CJ*, Apr. 21, 1664, VIII, 548; *CSPD*, Apr. 21, 1664, p. 562. Lords voted in favor of the resolution and Charles accepted it: *LJ*, Apr. 22, 1664, XI, 599–600; *CJ*, Apr. 29, 1664, VIII, 553; *CSPD*, Apr. 29, 1664, pp. 572–73.

17. See, e.g., W. W., *English and Dutch Affairs* (1664), p. 51; *Dutch Drawn to Life* (1664), pp. 4–5; Codrington, *His Majesties Propriety* (1665), sig. A5r; Clar. MS. 83, fol. 374, paper by Sir Richard Ford.

18. See Witcombe, *Charles II* (1966), pp. 29–31.

19. *LJ*, Oct. 10, 1665, XI, 684.

20. See, e.g., Wilson, *Profit and Power* (1957), p. 156; and cf. Ogg, *England in the Reign of Charles II* (1934, 1963), p. 351, and Witcombe, *Charles II* (1966), pp. 178–79, who imply a similar interpretation.

celebrating the return of their king. The present argument will attempt to sharpen this reassessment by considering the negative response of contemporaries to Charles's foreign policy, which was strengthened by the court's failure to deal consistently and successfully with the Civil War's legacy of discord. The origins of the Second Anglo-Dutch War in popular and mercantile clamor for a confrontation, the absence of mercantile or popular enthusiasm for peace—these are articles of court dogma which, on the face of it, are difficult to refute, and they continue to find routine acceptance in the writings of modern historians who may rightly see their consistency with the ideal type of what we have come to call the theory of "mercantilism."[21] I hope to show, however, that interested observers were capable of reiterating the theoretical principles of strict nationalism and the efficacy of trade wars at the same time that they were obliged, by practical experience and common sense, to denounce the ill effects of war on trade and to question seriously the official equation of governmental with national interest.

As long as the war seemed both popular and a likely means of uniting Englishmen against an external enemy, Charles was content to regard it as an expression of popular, mercantile, and royal solidarity. But when the war began to go badly for England and it became necessary to lay the blame for it in some quarter, Charles was left in an uncomfortable position. The Dutch could not be blamed: when wars are unsuccessful people look to home for the causes. Antiwar opposition sought to assign responsibility not simply for the failure of the war, but, even more, for its origins. Like the Restoration settlement, the Anglo-Dutch War only exacerbated the divisiveness which it might have cured, and Englishmen quickly agreed that the only way to rectify the harm it had done was to decide which group bore responsi-

---

21. See, e.g., Feiling, *British Foreign Policy* (1930), pp. 83–84, 130; Geyl, *Netherlands in the Seventeenth Century* (1964), p. 84; Haley, *First Earl of Shaftesbury* (1968), p. 172. Despite these demurrals, I have of course benefited greatly from the works which I cite here and in the preceding note.

bility for it. Many contemporary observers had ideas on the proximate causes of the war with the Dutch which conflicted sharply with those that were encouraged by court propaganda: Charles's and Albemarle's hatred of the Dutch; the duke of York's "military Genius" and the king's love of sea affairs, so that "a war of that kind was rather an entertainment then any disturbance to his thoughts . . ."; Sir George Downing's machinations as ambassador to the Provinces; Sir Thomas Clifford's "Violence in the House of Commons"; the general court conviction that money might be obtained from Parliament "by only threatning a War, without Intention of seeing it brought to Effect."[22] Charles was unable to take the initiative in determining the internal interest which was to be blamed and punished for what was now seen as a national disaster. In the end he was obliged to accept the judgment of the Parliament and people concerning how the interest of England might best be salvaged. To understand the significance of this judgment, we must have a look, closer than that afforded by Dryden's and the court's perspective on the origins of the war, at the relations between trade, war, and the mercantile community in the 1660s.

The existence of trading companies with more or less monopolistic rules of association and licenses to trade was opposed by unprivileged merchants, foreign and domestic, throughout the seventeenth century.[23] The model for this kind of monopolistic enterprise was the "joint-stock" company, a corporation in which trade was managed and profits distributed as a common venture, out of the pool of capital subscribed by a limited number of members for the pur-

22. See Cov. MS. 102, fols. 5–7, W. Coventry's paper on the causes of the war (1667?); Clarendon, *Continuation* (1759), pp. 198–99; Temple, *Letters* (1700), Temple to John Temple, Sept. 30, 1667, I, 125–26, reporting Dutch gossip on causes of the war; *CSP Ven.*, Mar. 12, 1665, p. 89; Burnet, *History* (1897), I, 357–58 (cf. Feiling, *British Foreign Policy* [1930], pp. 85–93); *POAS* (1963), p. 33n, quoting Buckingham.

23. See *Select Charters* (1913), pp. xxiv–xxv, lxviff; Scott, *Constitution and Finance* (1912), I, 105–28; Buck, *Politics of Mercantilism* (1942), pp. 63–70.

chase of shares, with profits divided accordingly at the end of each voyage. The joint-stock enterprise was especially necessary, it was most often argued, in the case of distant foreign trade, which required large, guaranteed outlays of capital both to finance expeditions and to defend ships, outposts, and factories. The incentive for these regularly exacted payments was the profit to be made by the trade monopoly which came with incorporation and the attractive guarantee against competition among members themselves. "Regulated company" was a much more elastic term. It generally characterized a loose association of independent merchants, each trading with his own capital and on his own account, and each paying levies according to when and how often he set to sea. Yet although regulated companies were less exclusively organized than joint-stock enterprises, they too might enjoy monopolistic privileges to varying extents.[24]

In the early 1660s a dispute arose over the restrictive organization of the regulated Company of Merchant Adventurers. Company representatives argued that if their privileges were contrary to the commercial interests of a few merchants, they were to the general benefit of the nation as a whole.[25] Unaffiliated merchants, however, observed of the Merchant Adventurers' price fixing that "though it be a benefit to that Company, yet [it] must needs . . . be . . . a detriment to this Kingdom."[26] Restrictive monopolies lessen the number of merchants and amount of trading stock and hence the enterprise and volume of trade. The merchant is discouraged from joining such companies by their excessive regulations—restricted numbers of shippings and regions open to trade, exorbitant membership fees, extravagant oaths, even outright exclusion—yet without membership he is debarred from trading.[27] Restrictive companies

24. See K. G. Davies, *Royal African Company* (1957), pp. 25–26, 28, 37; Heckscher, *Mercantilism* (1935), I, 381, 384, 399, 409–10; Lipson, *Economic History* (1948), II, 195–96; *Select Charters* (1913), p. xxi; Scott, *Constitution and Finance* (1912), I, 272–73, 442–63; Holdsworth, *History of English Law* (1903), VIII, 202–3.
25. See *Reasons offered* (1662); *Advantages of the Kingdom* (1662?).
26. *Reasons Humbly offered* (1662?), p. 2.
27. See ibid., pp. 3, 5–7.

are therefore (according to this argument) not only detrimental to England's commercial interest, they are an instrument of exclusive privilege and a monstrous inequity: "It is
repugnant to the very Law of Nature, to give the chief and
general Commodity of a Country to a few; in which every
free born Inhabitant may claim a material interest."[28] The
freedom sought by the enemies of trade regulation, however, was not necessarily an entirely unregulated one: "It is
not to be imagined by the desiring of a free Trade, that all
sorts of people should be permitted to exercise the mistery of
a Merchant, but such only who have been bred Merchants,
or served an Apprentice, or used the Trade of a Merchant
for seven years past, and no others."[29] This particular encounter ended in a compromise relaxation of the Merchant
Adventurers' monopoly on the transport of woolens.[30] A
more famous complaint by unaffiliated merchants—in a petition to Parliament in 1666 against the monopoly of the
Company of Merchants trading to the Canary Islands—resulted in a revocation of the company's charter and a restoration of free trade.[31] The special significance of the Canary
Company's case, which will be discussed below, probably
explains this appeal to Parliament:

> Tread all *Monopolies* into the Earth,
> And make provision that no more get birth.
> In this a Prince's danger chiefly lies,
> That he is forc'd to see with others eyes.
> From hence our Troubles rose in *Forty-one*,
> When that Domestick War at first begun.[32]

A parliamentary petition by the officers and several merchants of the City of London in 1662 provides a convenient
summary of the position of those who were opposed to joint-

28. Ibid., p. 2.
29. *Remonstrance* (1661).
30. See *CJ*, Mar. 24, Apr. 16, 1662, VIII, 394, 400; proclamations of
May 14, 1662, Apr. 8, 1663, Apr. 15, 1666, and Mar. 29, 1667 (Steele nos.
3354, 3380, 3458, 3489).
31. See Skeel, *Eng. Hist. Rev.*, 31 (1916), 529–44; Witcombe, *Charles
II* (1966), pp. 48–49.
32. *Vox & Lacrimae* (1668), p. 10.

stock and exclusive regulated trading companies. The
officers, whose petition comes first, wish not that trade be
"free," but that it "may be reduced under Government and
Regulation . . . and confirmed to English onely. And that
those Trades that are already under Regulation, may be
confirmed in such a manner, as may not exclude any English
Merchant that submits to the Government in all, or any the
respective Ports and places of this His Majesties Kingdom."
The merchants begin by complaining that while they spend
time and money apprenticing their sons to commerce, "sub-
tile and covetous men," lacking knowledge of trade but
possessing large amounts of capital, buy their way into
foreign markets and oppress "fair dealing Merchants" who
lack the stocks and credits to compete on equal terms. The
result is that "the whole Trade [comes] into a few hands
. . ." To remedy this situation the merchants make several
propositions which develop on the basic suggestion of the
Lord Mayor and his associates. Thus one of their provisos to
the regulation of trade is "that no Rule or By-law . . . shall
extend to the reducing of any foreign trade (other then that
to the *East-Indies*) into a Joynt-stock, nor to limit any, for
how much or how little they shall trade, nor at what price
they shall buy or sell; but that every one may trade for as
much or as little, and buy and sell his goods at such prices as
he pleaseth." It is this liberal understanding of commercial
regulation on which the merchants' description of its relation to England's interest is based: "whilst the Merchants
remain unassociated, and not under a general Regulation by
joynt counsel and consent, it may be supposed that every
man will be apt to make his own private interest and
profit . . . [but in association,] though a particular man
may intend his private profit in all his actings and advices,
yet it is sure that the generality will promote the general
concern of the Trade, which as it is their Interest, so it is also
the kingdoms interest."[33] "The kingdoms interest" may be
seriously at variance with "private interests" not only when

33. *Petition of the Lord Mayor* (1662), pp. 5, 8, 14, 9.

The Dutch Boare Dissected, or a Description of HOGG-LAND.

A *Dutch* man is a Lusty, Fat, two Legged Cheese-Worm: A Creature, that is so addicted to Eating Butter, Drinking fat Drink, and Sliding, that all the World knows him for a slippery Fellow. An *Hollander* is not an *High-lander*, but a *Low-lander*; for he loves to be down in the Dirt, and *Boar*-like, to wallow therein.

THe *Dutch* at first,
When at the worst,
The *English* did relieve them:
They now for thanks,
Have play'd base Pranks
With *Englishmen* to grieve them.
A Those Spider-Imps,
As big as Shrimps,
Doe lively Represent,
How that the States
Spin out their Fates
Out of their Bowels vent.
B The *Indian* Ratt
That runs in at
The Mouth of Crocodile,
Eates his way through,
And shews well how
All Nations they beguile.
C The Monstrous Pig,
With Vipers Big,
That Seven-headed Beast,
Shews how they still,
Pay good with ill
To th' *English* and the Rest.
The Vipers come
Forth of the Wombe,
With death of their own Mother:
Such are that Nation,
A Generation,
That rise by fall of Other.
D One of the Rout
Was Whipt about
Our Streets for telling lyes:
More of that Nation
Serv'd in such Fashion
Might be for Forgeries.
E Their Compass is
An *Holland* Cheese,
To steer a Cup of Ale-by:
The Knife points forth
Unto the North
The Needle these Worms sail-by.

F Their Quagmire Isle
('t would make one smile)
In Form lyes like a Custard:
A Land of Bogs
To breed up Hogs,
Good Pork with *English* Mustard.
G If any asks,
What mean the Casks?
'Tis Brandy, that is here:
And Pickle-Herring,
(Without all Erring:)
'tis neither Ale nor Beere.
H Those Two you see,
That yonder bee
Upon the Bog-Land Walking;
Are Man and Wife,
At woful Strife
About last Night's work talking.
He Drinks too long;
Shee gives him Tongue,
In sharp hot-scolding Pickle,
With Oyle so glib
The same for Tib,
Her tipling man to Tickle.
I spin all Day,
You Drink away
More then I get by Wheeling:
I do they part,
Sayes he, Sweet Heart,
For I doe come home Reeling.
I The *Holland* Boare,
Hath Stock-Fish store,
As good as can be eaten:
And such they are,
As is their Fare,
Scarce good till soundly beaten.
K Their State-House such is,
It stands on Crutches,
Or Stilts, like some old Creeple:
L Frogs in great Number
Their Land doth Cumber,
And such-like Croaking People.

Broadside printed in 1665 exemplifying chauvinistic anti-Dutch propaganda. Reprinted by permission of the Trustees of the British Museum, London.

all individual merchants remain unassociated but also when a few exclusive groups of merchants (such as those which constitute joint-stock companies) obtain the power and privileges necessary to turn public trade into a private monopoly.

These exchanges on the subject of trading companies in the early 1660s were not at all unique to the period. The purpose of giving them here is to provide a background for the brief history of the Royal Company of Adventurers Trading into Africa, an interest group whose fortunes and reputation are important in an assessment of the public reaction to the war.

First incorporated in 1660, the Royal Company soon received additional subscriptions and investments and was reincorporated on January 10, 1663, with an initial capital of £122,000 subscribed in 305 shares at £400 each, divisible into half shares. Its grant provided for the privilege of exclusive trade from Sallee to the Cape of Good Hope. Its motto, dismissed by Pepys as "too tedious," was public-spirited: "Regio floret, patrocinio commercium, commercioque Regnum."[34] In 1661 the Royal Company commissioned Sir Robert Holmes, later the hero of the Vlie and Schelling, to inform the Dutch of England's exclusive trade rights on the Guinea coast and to begin the dispossession of the Dutch holdings there. William Coventry was later to characterize the valiant Holmes as a man whose understanding was inversely proportional to his courage. When the Provinces protested against his actions, Charles denied having ordered them, but the Privy Council formally condoned Holmes's proceedings in a hearing of January 1662. The Dutch West India Company's seizure of the Royal Company's ships off

34. See Scott, *Constitution and Finance* (1912), II, 17, 18; K. G. Davies, *Royal African Company* (1957), pp. 41–42; Pepys, *Diary* (1904), May 23, 1663, III, 139. Add. MS. 6331, fol. 1, gives the following translation: "Commerce flourishes by royal protection, and the kingdom by commerce." On Feb. 16, 1663, the company allegedly invited subscriptions at a reduced minimum rate of £50 (for one-eighth of a share): *Several Declarations* (1667), pp. 9–10.

the Gold Coast in 1661 and 1662 was relegated to the catalogue of damages provided for by the treaty of 1662. But when the Dutch company renewed its blockade in October 1662 in response to English settlements near Cape Corse, Charles replied by loaning several ships to the Royal Company under the command of Holmes, whom he empowered in strict secrecy "to kill, take, or destroy such as oppose you" (September 5, 1663). In the first half of 1664 Holmes took Cape Verde and the island of Goree, reduced Cape Corse, and seized several Dutch ships and factories as well. When New Amsterdam was taken in August 1664 Charles openly acknowledged that it and the African settlements, with the exception of Cape Verde, had been seized on his order (October 28, 1664). The Dutch Admiral de Ruyter arrived at Cape Verde on October 22, 1664, and left the Gold Coast February 27, 1665, having recaptured all of the Dutch holdings except Cape Corse. The Royal Company appealed to Charles for aid, and received a verbal commitment on January 2, 1665. On February 22 war was declared on the United Provinces.[35]

The later history of the Royal Company does not fulfill the high expectations created by this early excess of royal aid. The losses sustained through de Ruyter's reconquests and the war's interdictment of trade proved fatal to it, the surplus of 1664 quickly becoming deficit. The Royal Company's petition to Charles in 1665 begging for royal support suggested that he give them Holmes's Dutch prizes, "as De Ruyter declares that the mischief he has done them is in retaliation for that loss." During the last eighteen months of the war, the Royal Company was forced by financial difficulties to issue trading licenses to private merchants. The cessation of hostilities did not sufficiently improve the company's economic standing, and in 1672 a new corporation,

35. See Cov. MS. 102, fol. 6, W. Coventry on the causes of the war; Zook, *Company of Royal Adventurers* (1919), pp. 30–65; Feiling, *British Foreign Policy* (1930), pp. 127–28; Ogg, *England in the Reign of Charles II* (1963), p. 251; Geyl, *Netherlands* (1964), pt. II, 84–85.

the Royal African Company, was chartered to undertake the Guinea trade.[36]

A final comment is necessary on the composition of the Royal Company. During the brief period of its ascendancy, the political connections of the company were powerful and diverse enough to ensure that what it took to be its economic advantage vis-à-vis the Dutch and domestic competition was regarded sympathetically by those in a position to further it. According to the royalist Thomas Sprat, this circumstance was the result of Charles's public-minded and laudable "Designe, which will infallibly make the English the Masters of the Trade of the world; . . . [i.e.] the bringing in of our *Gentry*, and *Nobility*, to contribute to [the Royal Company]."[37] In any case, the lists of charter members,[38] or "assistants," of the Royal Company indicate that an average of nine privy councilors (as well as assorted royalty, peers, and merchant princes) had a special relationship with a private organization whose success depended quite substantially on court officials.[39] The company's charter provided that the royal grantor be admitted to membership at any time in accordance with the rules of subscription which

36. Scott, *Constitution and Finance* (1912), I, 280; *CSPD*, 1666[?] (1666–67 vol.), p. 394; Pepys, *Further Correspondence* (1929), Pepys to Sandwich, Dec. 22, 1664, pp. 33–34; petition in *CSPD*, Jan. 2, 1665, pp. 159–60, and *CSP Col.*, Jan. 2, 1665, p. 266 (for similar petitions see *CSP Col.*, pp. 351, 435); Zook, *Company of Royal Adventurers* (1919), p. 21; *Answer of the Company* (1667), pp. 8, 9.

37. Sprat, *Observations* (1665), p. 165. Sprat urged English gentlemen to take a greater part in commerce and the new philosophy by supporting what he regarded as "Twin Sisters," the Royal Society and the Royal Company. See *History* (1667), p. 407.

38. *Select Charters* (1913), pp. 173–74 (charter of Dec. 18, 1660), pp. 178–79 (charter of Jan. 10, 1663); *Several Declarations* (1667), pp. 11–12.

39. The composition of the Privy Council changed continually, and there was a distinction between nominal and active membership. Cf. the lists in Turner, *Privy Council* (1927), I, 375–76; Carlyle, *Eng. Hist. Rev.*, 27 (1912), 257–58; Heath, *Brief Chronicle* (1663), pp. 813–14; and the lists which precede each volume and each day's minutes in the Privy Council Registers (PRO PC 2/). Among the privy councilors who were, at one time or another, simultaneously assistants of the Royal Company are Albemarle; Ormonde; St. Albans; Sandwich; Carteret; Charles Howard; Charles Berkeley; George, Lord Berkeley; Edward, earl of Manchester; Buckingham; Anglesey; John, Lord Berkeley; Arlington; W. Coventry; and Prince Rupert. York was a constant unsworn privy councilor.

Charles pledged to observe in 1662 and 1663.[40] The names of the admirals of the Anglo-Dutch War appear throughout the available lists of company assistantship—Albemarle (1660, 1667), Rupert (1663, 1667), Sandwich (1660, 1663, 1667), and York, the lord high admiral, who took over the company's governorship from Rupert around 1664. As for the favored merchant assistants of the Royal Company, their primary professions did not necessarily prevent them from seeking first-hand influence in other positions. When Sir William Rider, an assistant of the Royal Company, tried to obtain a navy commissionership, the conscientious Sir William Coventry advised Charles through his secretary of state that "when euer he admitts a Merchant to sit as an officer or Commissioner on the Navy office the reputation of that office is lost, & his exchecquer is charged deeper then if hee had giuen a Talley for 40000 l. I haue seene soe much of Merchants in the R[oyal] Company that I know if they gett into the Nauy, they will haue a share in all bargaines either one way or another . . ."[41] A representative of the company's court faction told Pepys that "Sir Richard Ford cannot keepe a secret, and that it is so much the part of a merchant to be guilty of that fault that the Duke of Yorke is resolved to commit no more secrets to the merchants of the Royall Company . . ."[42] Thus the main result of the Royal Company's mixed aristocratic-mercantile membership, of which Sprat had such high hopes, may have been less the advancement of England's commercial interest than a mutual antagonism according to which the nobility's and merchants' desire for money and power met head on.[43]

To what extent was the Royal Company identified as a private interest whose welfare conflicted with the interest of England? If such an identification was made, how closely

40. See *Select Charters* (1913), p. 181 and note, and *CSPD*, 1665–66 vol., pp. 136–37.

41. PRO SP 29/104, fol. 149, Coventry to Bennet, Nov. 16, 1664.

42. *Diary* (1904), Oct. 18, 1664, IV, 270. On the leaders of the court and merchant factions of the Royal Company see Cov. MS. 102, fols. 5–6, W. Coventry's paper on the origins of the war.

43. On this antagonism see also Clarendon, *Continuation* (1759), pp. 197–98.

was it related, in the minds of Englishmen, to the specific disaster of the Anglo-Dutch War and the paramount necessity of establishing guilt for its origins and mismanagement? These questions must be answered from several different directions. From 1663 to 1667 the Royal Company displayed a certain amount of sensitivity to attacks from antimonopolists. All English subjects, it was claimed, had been invited to join the company, "and therefore have no reason to complain of being excluded." Before the Restoration this trade was managed "by particular adventurers, who were so far from any possible design of having forts or asserting the honour of the nation that they were a constant prey to the Hollanders . . . The impossibility of carrying on the trade of Africa without a joint stock is too evident to be insisted on . . ."[44] ". . . . this Trade incorporated to this Company is in its Constitution National."[45] In 1667 the Royal Company printed a tract inviting new subscriptions. The tract consists of documents which are dated January and February 1663 and which remind the reader that these invitations are made by the company "in Conformity to the said Royal Intention of His Majesty, and to evidence to the whole World, that they intend not to confine the Benefit of the said Trade to a Few, or exclude any from it that will be governed . . . before such Subscriptions, [prospective subscribers] shall find such equal and indifferent Agreements prefixed, as may satisfie all rational persons, that nothing is designed but Publick Good, and the just Right of every Individual interessed."[46] The publication of these documents four years after their apparent composition suggests that the tract was designed as much to rebut charges of inefficiency and injustice as to aid in a campaign for new capital. In fact the original dates of the documents are called into question by the following allegation of several unaffiliated merchants: "If it shall be objected, That this Company doth not participate of a Monopoly, because their Books were laid open for

44. *CSP Col.*, 1663[?], pp. 122–23, 176; Oct. 24, 1666, p. 416.
45. *Answer of the Company* (1667), p. 17.
46. *Several Declarations* (1667), pp. 10, 2.

all men to subscribe that would? It is answered, That their Books indeed were for some time laid open, But not till upon good grounds it was generally believed that most part of their Stocks was consumed, And they had run themselves upon so many other Inconveniencies, That no prudent Merchant . . . would engage amongst them."[47]

Throughout the 1660s the Royal Company encountered opposition not only from unaffiliated merchants but also from British planters in America. The sale of African slaves to the American plantations had quickly become the Royal Company's most lucrative enterprise and the principal justification for its continued existence. The planters protested that the company's monopoly allowed the inequitable inflation of prices for slaves.[48] When the Royal Company complained to the Privy Council in 1664 regarding planters' nonpayment for "Negro Seruants," the council relayed the complaint to the governor of the Caribbean Islands introduced by judicious and conciliatory observations on Charles's eagerness "that all due Incouragemt be giuen to the Planters in the first Place, & to the Merchants in the next, well knowing that, in truth, their Interest is Joynct; . . . And Wee do all that is in Our power, upon all occacons, to informe and require the Merchants, not to take any Advantage of the necessity of the Planters, in setting un-reasonable & un-conscionable Prices upon the Comodities they send or carry to the Plantacons, of which Wee haue receiued some generall Complaints . . ."[49] A planters' petition presented to Commons and printed in 1667 charged that

formerly there hath alwaies been a freedom of Trade for all His Majesties Subjects for *Negroes* . . .

47. *Answer of the Company* (1667), pp. 14–16. For the company's refutation of this charge see pp. 15–17.

48. See Zook, *Company of Royal Adventurers* (1919), chap. 4; *CSP Col.*, 1661–1668 vol., index, s.v. "African Company, the Royal"; Scott, *Constitution and Finance* (1912), I, 271; PRO PC 2/57, fol. 66v, petition of June 15, 1664. A document dated Jan. 10, 1663, in *Several Declarations* (1667), pp. 8–9, specifies the original terms of the slave trade to the Caribbean. The Royal Company refuted all charges against it in *Answer of the Company* (1667).

49. PRO PC 2/57, fol. 101, draft of letter of Aug. 24, 1664.

. . . there is of late a new erected *Company* of *Adventurers* Trading into *Africa,* who claiming to themselves the sole and only Trade for *Negroes* on the coast of Guiney, has totally obstructed the former free Trade of all Adventurers thither . . . [and] do leave *English* Plantations in America . . . either ill supplied, and at excessive prices, or not at all supplied . . .
. . . unless such freedom be continued, the Plantations already compleated will soon decay, and those that are in their Infancy never advance.[50]

Material such as this provides evidence that the Royal Company was not exempt from attack by that segment of contemporary opinion which saw joint-stock companies as bastions of private interest inimical to the public interest. But did public discourse ever link directly and persuasively the private interest of the Royal Company with the private interest which bore responsibility for the war? Not in so many words—or at least, not in England. Intelligent court officials like William Coventry and Clarendon, of course, were well aware of the extent to which the greed of the Royal Company had provoked the outbreak of hostilities, and Henry Oldenburg reported that the same connection was being made publicly in the Provinces on the eve of war: "The Dutch use much of ye Foxe in asserting their cause agst ye English; . . . they insinuate into ye Body of our marchants, yt tis only to raise a particular Royall Company . . ."[51] For one thing, the Royal Company represented only one aspect of the total war disaster. For another, the company was not susceptible to open attack because Charles was not yet susceptible to open attack—yet it is noteworthy how many of the councilors and public servants associated with the company suffered at the hands of Parlia-

50. *Answer of the Company* (1667), pp. 1, 1–2, 6. The petition was presented on Nov. 15 (*CJ*, IX, 21; Grey, *Debates* [1769], I, 40–41) and answered by the Royal Company on Nov. 22, 1667 (*CJ*, IX, 24). Cf. Pepys, *Diary* (1904), Nov. 28, 1667, VII, 215–16.
51. *Oldenburg Letters* (1965), no. 348, Oldenburg to Boyle, Nov. 5, 1664, II, 292. For the views of Coventry and Clarendon on the Royal Company, see Cov. MS. 102, fol. 7 (1667?), and the latter's retrospection in *Continuation* (1759), pp. 197–98.

ment and the people for their part in the war. To say that the "ministerial" interest was blamed for the war implies that other interests were not. The court position, it will be remembered, asserted that Charles declared war "on the outcry of the nation," especially of the mercantile community. Before turning to the movement against Charles's ministers it is important to see how this movement was made possible by the popular and mercantile repudiation of the war.

The foundation of the court's argument that the merchants and people of England favored war with the Dutch was the 1664 report of the parliamentary Committee of Trade and Parliament's response to it. The representation of the resolution against the Dutch as the single and single-minded opinion of the committee and of the merchants who appeared before it would have been plausible only to observers who were entirely unacquainted with the realities of foreign trade and parliamentary management. The purpose of the committee was to hear testimony from trading companies and unaffiliated merchants on trade's "obstructions" and its "likely remedies." Of the complete transcript of meetings from March 26 to May 7, 1664, one-third of the testimony relates to Dutch obstructions and two-thirds relates to other causes, especially England's own policies of commercial interference. Evidence of the latter sort was temporarily set aside on April 5 so that the most decisive evidence against the Dutch might be heard at the next meeting, on April 18. This consisted of testimony exclusively from three joint-stock organizations, the Royal, East India, and Turkey Companies. On April 19 the committee heard the documentation of some English merchants whose ships had been seized by the Dutch. When this was completed, the resolution to advise Parliament of Dutch obstructions to trade was passed, and Clifford, the chairman of the committee, was sent to present it to Commons on April 21. In one of the later meetings from April 22 to May 7, a resolution was passed to advise Commons of the commercial benefit of a

naturalization bill to relax restrictions against alien merchants.[52]

The enormities of the Dutch, in other words, occupied a
comparatively small amount of the time and attention of the
committee, were not unique in attaining the sanction of a
resolution to advise Commons, and were most tellingly
documented not by privileged and unaffiliated merchants
equally but by joint-stock companies alone. On April 5 the
testimony seems to have been cut short by a concerted effort
to establish Dutch guilt, and it was resumed only on April
22, after the desired resolution had been obtained. It is natural to assume that Clifford, whom Charles had added to
Clarendon's committee for parliamentary management in
the previous year and who was Arlington's eager and capable protégé, had a great deal to do with the results of the
committee's inquiries.[53]

It cannot be assumed, however, that the merchants who
testified before the committee were pleased with these results. Edward Adams, one of the merchants whose complaint
against the Dutch seizure of his ship was read to the committee on April 19, printed a short tract later in the year, the
principal aim of which was to warn against the piratical
trade practices of the Dutch. At the end of the narrative of
his misfortunes, Adams adds the following comments,
prompted perhaps by the rabid response of the committee to
his report and of Parliament and the king to their resolution:

There is a rumor flies up and down the world, that in this
present conjuncture of affairs, the Merchants are great incendiaries to a Warre with the *Dutch,* and if there happen one, 'twill
be called the *Merchants Warre,* which I suppose is a great mistake; for to me it seems not rational for any intelligent Merchants
to be forward to that War, the maine dispute and decision

52. The complete transcript is in PRO SP 29/98(35). PRO SP 29/96(6)
contains fuller accounts of the testimony given on Apr. 1.
53. On Clifford's connections at this time see Vale, *Camb. Hist. Jour.,* 12,
no. 2 (1956), 108; *DNB,* s.v. "Clifford, Thomas, first Lord Clifford of
Chudleigh"; Hartmann, *Clifford* (1937), index, s.v. "Arlington"; Pepys,
Diary (1904), Apr. 26, 1667, VI, 289. And see Cov. MS. 102, fol. 5, on
the role played by George Downing in obtaining this parliamentary resolution.

whereof must be argued at Sea, the place where he is most concerned, and to the inconveniencies and hazards attending such
a War the Merchant of all other persons is most obnoxious. If any
such Merchants there be, that are so Warlike, and promise to
themselves great gain by Trading in troubled waters; I do declare
my self to be none of them . . .[54]

Insofar as Adams found himself at all in agreement with the
resolutions of the committee and Commons, war clearly was
not the basis of his conception of "speedy redress." Apparently this was true of the joint-stock East India Company as
well. In May 1664 a committee of their representatives
reported to the lord treasurer that as far as war was concerned, "the Company hopes it is in the interest of the
kingdome, for as to their private concerne as merchants they
must needs say that the worst of peace is better then the best
warr, by which they cannot expect but to bee present
sufferers in one kinde or other."[55] In a secret "paper about
the Dutch warre" written in the spring of 1665 Sir William
Coventry argued on commercial and other grounds that the
war would be at best useless and at worst overwhelmingly
detrimental to England.[56] A notable exception to this judgment, however, was the case of the East India and Africa
trades, which Coventry thought might be improved by war
with the Dutch.[57] In fact both trades suffered, but the East
India Company differed from the sponsors of Sir Robert
Holmes's actions on the west coast of Africa in its ability to
predict this outcome beforehand.

From beginning to end, the Anglo-Dutch War seemed so
detrimental to English trade that any pretense of a positive

54. *Brief Relation* (1664), pp. 12–13 [mispaginated 5–4].
55. Sainsbury, *Calendar* (1925), minute of May 25, 1664, p. 40; see also
East India Co. to Downing, May 27, 1664, p. 41. These fears were borne out
by the effect of the Anglo-Dutch War on the company's exports: see
Chaudhuri, *Econ. Hist. Rev.*, 2nd ser., 21 (1968), 482; fig. 1, p. 483; app.,
table 1, pp. 497–98.
56. See Add. MS. 32094, fol. 50–52v. Pepys records the development of
Coventry's—and, through the influence of Coventry, Pepys's own—private
opinions on the war, trade, and the Royal Company in *Diary* (1904), Apr.
7, 20, May 29, Dec. 22, 1664, Jan. 15, 1665, IV, 103, 114, 143, 144, 313, 332.
57. Add. MS. 32094, fol. 50v.

connection between it and the mercantile community was quite untenable. During the winter of 1664–65 mercantile shipping was already being reduced, merchant sailors were being pressed into men-of-war, and trade was felt to be suffering.[58] On March 1, 1665, Charles was compelled to issue "A Proclamation Forbidding Foreign Trade and Commerce" by unlicensed traders, in consideration of "the great perils and inconveniences that may happen . . . in these times of danger."[59] By autumn London was experiencing "the absolute destruction of trade . . . externally by the war."[60] Thereafter war vied with the plague in the reduction of commerce, which was expected to worsen with France's formal entry into hostilities against England. The secretary of the Royal Society wrote to Robert Boyle: "Now ye French king hath declared warre against England . . . we shall, I feare, meet with some interruption of our Philosophical Commerce, as we cannot but doe with a totall one of Marchant-trade."[61] In the spring of 1666, Sir George Oxinden, president of the East India Company at Surat, received a rash of letters from his colleagues in London bemoaning the utter deadness of commerce as the plague and the wartime interdiction of traffic continued.[62] Like the Royal Company eighteen months earlier, the Levant Company requested convoy protection for her traders against Dutch attacks—but now Charles had no ships to spare.[63]

By the end of the summer it was being proposed that

58. See *Barlow's Journal* (1934), I, 93; Scott, *Constitution and Finance* (1912), I, 276; *CSP Ven.*, Dec. 4, 1664, p. 63; *Oldenburg Letters* (1965), no. 360, Oldenburg to Boyle, Dec. 10, 1664, II, 332–33; PRO PC 2/58, fols. 2v–3v, directions for hiring merchantmen for conversion to men-of-war, Jan. 2, 1665; Josselin, *Diary* (1908), Feb. 12, 1665, p. 146.

59. *By the King* (Mar. 1, 1665), Steele no. 3409.

60. *CSP Ven.*, Oct. 30, 1665, p. 217.

61. *Oldenburg Letters* (1965), no. 487, Jan. 27, 1666, III, 33. See no. 492, same to same, Feb. 24, 1666, III, 46, for the same conceit.

62. See Add. MS. 40712, fols. 42, 41, 32v, 22, 18v, Jan. 3, Mar. 5 (2 letters), 6, 8, 1666. See also *CSPD*, Mar. 8, 1666, p. 292.

63. See PRO PC 2/57, fol. 66v, Royal Company petition of June 15, 1664; PRO PC 2/58, fols. 90v–91, petition of Levant Company and merchants trading to the Caribbean.

English trade be curtailed entirely "that the fleet might be better supplied with men and ships," and special shippings in "foreign vessels" had to be commissioned for the supply of the impoverished American colonies.[64] Clarendon wrote of these months: "And then, whereas the Advancement of Trade was made the great End of the War, it was now found necessary to suppress all Trade, that there might be Mariners enough to furnish the Ships for the carrying on the War . . ."[65] In November the pious Reverend Ralph Josselin recorded: "plague abates blessed bee God but ye war damps all Trade; the Lord drive his spiritual trade . . ."[66] The need to reduce navy expenditures over the winter of 1666–67 resulted in a new strategy which involved the substitution of small squadrons of cruisers and defensive shore works for war fleets, and a temporary ban on all importing and exporting merchantmen. Those that chose to venture into the high seas risked probable capture by unimpeded Dutch men-of-war.[67] Oxinden's correspondents found that even the passage of letters—not to mention trade—was extremely uncertain.[68] Thus by the time spring came the London mercantile community was desperate for a treaty. Pepys spoke with some acquaintances in the city: "they and all merchants else do give over trade and the nation for lost, nothing being done with care or foresight, no convoys granted . . . I to the Exchange, and there do hear mighty cries for peace, and that otherwise we shall be undone . . . Our merchants do much pray for peace . . ."[69] Contemporaries varied in their ability to absorb commercial disappointment, but all agreed that the cause of disappointment was the war:

64. *CSPD*, July 1, Oct. 16, 1666, pp. 488, 202.
65. *Miscell. Works* (1751), "Discourse by Way of Vindication of my self . . . ," p. 71.
66. *Diary* (1908), Nov. 11, 1666, p. 155.
67. See Scott, *Constitution and Finance* (1912), I, 278; Wilson, *Profit and Power* (1957), pp. 138, 139; Clarendon, *Miscell. Works* (1751), "Discourse by Way of Vindication of my self . . . ," p. 73.
68. See Add. MS. 40713, fol. 28v, letter of Jan. 8, 1667.
69. *Diary* (1904), Nov. 14, 1666, Apr. 9, 11, 1667, VI, 64, 264, 268.

. . . upon the Change, our Merchants are but in ill heart and hope very little of peace.

. . . ye dangers yt merchants now run at sea & ye litel satisfaction of expectations when goods arriue well, makes me resolve to doe litel in trade, untill I see an alteration . . .

. . . Wee have lost almost all our trade and moneys, but a happy peace will restore both togeather . . .[70]

When peace finally came, many were content to welcome it with heartfelt relief:

> Trades men rejoyce, whole streams of wealth shall flow,
> Into your shops, such good from Peace doth grow.[71]

But many others, looking back on the war experience, were unable to reconcile its official management with the national interest: "the Wealth which we formerly enjoyed, and rendred us so considerable in the World, beside the fresh Experiment of the Disorder and Interruption which the War brought into all the Traffick of the Land, hath made us clearly see, that for Merchant-mens Fleets to be changed into Naval Armies, and the Substance of the people melted into Magazins unusefully, which might more profitably be imployed in rich and gainful Navigations, cannot be the proper Interest of *England*."[72]

Thus a heroic national enterprise, which had once promised to knit together in common purpose all the limbs of the "mighty animal" England, degenerated into a catastrophe which demanded that Englishmen be divided into two camps: those who had suffered and those who had caused the suffering. This distinction was achieved in two different ways, both of them partial and unsatisfactory: the parliamentary inquiry into the causes of the misconduct of the war, which continued to the end of the decade and which

70. Marvell, *Poems and Letters* (1952), letter of Apr. 2, 1667, II, 297; Add. MS. 40713, fol. 62, letter to Oxinden, Apr. 20, 1667; Stowe MS. 744, fol. 160, M. Boyle, archbishop of Dublin, to Clarendon, from Dublin, May 14, 1667.
71. *Peace Concluded and Trade Revived* (1667).
72. *Free Conference* (1668), pp. 12–13.

did not result in any trials;[73] and the dismissal and parliamentary impeachment of the earl of Clarendon in 1667.

The first practical step in rendering the king responsible to Parliament in his choice of servants came in October 1665, when Sandwich was removed from his naval command in response to the reading of a bill against the embezzlement of prize goods for which Sandwich's indiscretions at Bergen were the obvious stimulus.[74] In June 1667 Sir William Coventry told Pepys that "my Lord Chancellor [Clarendon], my Lord Arlington, the Vice Chamberlain [Sir George Carteret] and himself are reported all up and down the Coffee houses to be the four sacrifices that must be made to atone the people."[75] In the Commons debates of the following year, members were generally agreed on the group nature of the war guilt under investigation. The major fiascos of the war proceeded not from "want of intelligence [i.e., information], . . . but . . . from evil counsel," and "strictly to examine this did not at all reflect upon the King, but only upon his Council, or some of them, whom it was fit should be rooted out of the Council, and others put in their places to the satisfaction of the people . . ."[76] Rumors had circulated in 1667 that Arlington had used his Dutch wife to betray to the Provinces England's intention of dividing her fleet in June 1666,[77] and in 1668 Andrew Marvell and other M.P.'s expanded on the theme of "evil counsel" with veiled allusions to Arlington's corruption.[78] Arlington had sensed the delicacy of his position in June 1667, after the final disaster of the Dutch sortie in the Medway. As privy councilors searched for someone to bear the blame and then fastened on Peter Pett, a commissioner of the navy, Arlington observed that "if he was not guilty, the world would think

73. See Witcombe, *Charles II* (1966), p. 65.
74. See ibid., pp. 37–38.
75. *Diary* (1904), June 29, 1667, VI, 400.
76. Milward, *Diary* (1938), Feb. 15, 1668, pp. 185, 186. The specific fiasco under discussion is the division of the fleet.
77. *POAS* (1963), *Third Advice to a Painter* (1667), ll. 281ff; Colenbrander, *Bescheiden* (1919), I, 339.
78. See Milward, *Diary* (1938), Feb. 15, 1668, p. 185; Pepys, *Diary* (1904), Feb. 17, 1668, VII, 324.

them all guilty."[79] Commons initiated an impeachment of
Pett (which was never completed) even though some M.P.'s
recognized that he was being forced to serve as a scape-
goat.[80] Carteret escaped the fury of Parliament with no
worse scars than the suggestion that he had accepted large
sums of money. The subject of more serious rumors of
corruption ever since the war had first been contemplated,
Coventry was obliged to vindicate himself before Parliament
in April 1668.[81]

The single great casualty of parliamentary vengeance was,
of course, Clarendon. Charles's prudent acquiescence in his
dismissal and prosecution; the anti-Clarendonians' lumber-
ing quest for grounds for impeachment; the degeneration of
proceedings into an inter-House dispute; Clarendon's flight
to France and his subsequent banishment; these events comprise one of the best-known episodes of Restoration history.[82] The charges against Clarendon touch on all of the
most divisive problems of the 1660s, problems whose symbolic solution was provided by the lord chancellor's downfall.[83] Some of these problems have not yet been considered
in the present context: the article which was accepted as
sufficient basis for impeachment held that Clarendon had
betrayed council secrets to the French,[84] and he was widely
charged both with being a papist himself and with accusing
Charles of popery. Other causes of division are familiar:
Clarendon suppressed the Cavaliers at the settlement and
was lenient with stubborn nonconformists;[85] he received

79. Pepys, *Diary* (1904), June 19, 1667, VI, 377.
80. See Milward, *Diary* (1938), Nov. 13, 14, 1667, pp. 127 and n3, 128;
POAS (1963), Marvell, *Last Instructions* (written 1667, printed 1689), ll.
765–90.
81. See Pepys, *Diary* (1904), Oct. 25, 1666, VI, 38; *POAS* (1963),
Second Advice to a Painter (1667), ll. 25–40; Vale, *Camb. Hist. Jour.*,
12, no. 2 (1956), 115–16.
82. For the best accounts see Roberts, *Camb. Hist. Jour.*, 13, no. 1 (1957),
1–18; Witcombe, *Charles II* (1966), pp. 64–77.
83. For the articles of impeachment see Milward, *Diary* (1938), Nov.
6–7, 1667, pp. 113–16 and 112n.
84. See Witcombe, *Charles II* (1966), pp. 71–72.
85. See Milward, *Diary* (1938), Oct. 26, 1667, p. 100. See above,
Chapter 2.

gratuities for passing the Canary Company's patent;[86] he countenanced arbitrary imprisonments; he was primarily responsible for the mishaps of the late war.

Thus there is some accuracy to the interpretation of Clarendon's fall as a national ritual, a symbolic sacrifice of one man for the weakness and disappointments of many. As John Vaughan said in Commons, "Were it no other than this good that we have in the remove of this great man, that now by some years' experience things have always gone worse and worse, by this change we may hope they will grow better."[87] But the mythic simplicity of this event has obscured the fact that even as Commons were debating the fate of Clarendon, they were concerned as well that the other fish might not escape their net. Movements against Arlington, Coventry, Carteret, and Pett have already been mentioned. In November 1667 one M.P. "alleged that if the article [of impeachment] should be sent up [to Lords] and made public it might give alarm to all that were engaged in the treason to make their escape and go away." Later, in free conference with Lords, Commons objected to specifying the nature of the treason charge since "it gave opportunity to all others concerned in the treason to make their escape from justice."[88] In the previous month the Presbyterian earl of Northumberland told York "that the laying aside of the Chancellor, who was very much hated, was not sufficient to Satisfy the Nation, for they also expected the disbanding of the Guards, and the redress of severall other Grivences."[89] The idea of group treachery, of conspiracy in high places, possessed the mind of the seaman Edward Barlow from the attempt at Bergen in 1665 to the Peace of Breda in 1667. Each naval disaster could be traced back to London and the combined "treachery of some of our English peers" and

86. Cf. Pepys, *Diary* (1904), Oct. 25, 1666, VI, 38, where the same charge is made against Matthew Wren, Clarendon's secretary and an assistant of the Royal Company.

87. Milward, *Diary* (1938), speech of Oct. 14, 1667, app. 2, p. 328.

88. Ibid., Nov. 16, 29, 1667, pp. 129, 146. Lords replied that it would hardly be a secret if 400 M.P.'s knew about it.

89. J. S. Clarke, *Life of James the Second* (1816), I, 426.

"English papists."[90] However unwilling at first, Charles came to accept with some enthusiasm the necessity of Clarendon's sacrifice as a means of making certain the perpetuation of the principle of English kingship *"that the King can do no wrong,* but his Ministers may, through whose mouths he pronounceth sentence."[91] And the poetic denunciations of Clarendon and court policy which appeared in 1667–68 frequently took advantage of the traditional license to denounce "evil counselors."[92]

The spirit which made Charles accountable to Parliament in his choice of servants was responsible for other curtailments of royal power. Commons had routinely claimed the functions of financial appropriation and the examination of accounts during the session of 1663. Three years later they exercised the second function on the Navy, Ordnance, and Stores accounts and succeeded in passing legislation that guaranteed their right to the first.[93] During the same session the embryonic "Country Party" managed to pass, against court opposition, the well-known bill restricting the import of Irish cattle in order to "protect the landed interest."[94] The final defeat occurred in the three-week debate on the method of parliamentary supply to the king, when the court

90. *Barlow's Journal* (1934), pp. 109, 116; see also pp. 119, 122, 123, 127, 129, 130, 134, 137. See also Pepys, *Diary* (1904), June 13, 14, 1667, VI, 363, 368–69. In *Growth of Responsible Government* (1966), p. 173, Roberts corrected the one-sidedness of his earlier view (*Camb. Hist. Jour.,* 13, no. 1 [1957], 9) that the charges against Clarendon arose exclusively from the ambitions of the anti-Clarendonian faction in Parliament.

91. Howell, *PROEDRIA* (1664), p. 13. Cf. L'Estrange, *Caveat* (1661), pp. 20–21; Evans, *Light for the Jews* (1664), pp. 32–33; *Vox & Lacrimae* (1668), p. 15. Despite the principle, see *POAS* (1963), *Fourth Advice to a Painter* (1667), ll. 129–36; Burnet, *History* (1897), I, 448.

92. See *POAS* (1963), *Third Advice to a Painter* (1667), ll. 257–66, 439–40, 443–44, *Fourth Advice to a Painter* (1667), ll. 17–18, Marvell, *Last Instructions* (written 1667, printed 1689), "Envoy"; *Vox & Lacrimae* (1668), pp. 5–6, 11, 13. Bundles of *Vox & Lacrimae* were presented at the door of Commons on Feb. 12, 1668: see Milward, *Diary* (1938), p. 183 and nl. See also *CSPD,* Feb. 6, 1668, p. 217.

93. See Witcombe, *Charles II* (1966), pp. 13–15, 40, 44, 53–58. Cf. Pepys, *Diary* (1904), Oct. 4, 1666, VI, 5.

94. Witcombe, *Charles II* (1966), pp. 38–39, 44. See the historian of this episode on its contribution to the erosion of the royal dispensing power: Edie, *Trans. APS,* n.s., 60, pt. 2 (1970), 24–25, 56–57, and passim.

preference of a general excise on domestic goods was rejected in favor of a combined hearth tax, foreign excise, and the land tax favored by the Country.[95] Thus as the war ended the assignment of responsibility for its failure was linked with a substantive change in the responsibility of the king to the Cavalier Parliament.

While many Englishmen were identifying Charles's evil counselors as the domestic conspiracy alien to England's interest and deserving of removal, Dryden was trying to unite the country in opposition to those who seemed naturally alien, the Dutch and French enemies. Yet many of his countrymen did not agree with this distinction of interests along purely nationalistic lines. Although some dissenters and republicans were eager to serve in Charles's fleet,[96] many disenfranchised Scottish rebels were in secret communication with the Dutch months after the Restoration, and the flow of dissidents from England was soon great enough to warrant the establishment of Independent, Anabaptist, and Quaker churches in Rotterdam.[97] Ludlow sought asylum in Switzerland, and in 1663 he and his circle were joined briefly by Algernon Sidney, who two years later showed up at The Hague, hopeful, like William Say in Amsterdam, about Dutch naval power and the prospects for an invasion. Shortly afterward, Sidney went to Paris to

95. See Milward, *Diary* (1938), Oct. 12, 16, 18, 29, Nov. 3, 8, 1666, pp. 21, 25, 27–28, 33–34, 36, 38–39; Witcombe, *Charles II* (1966), pp. 45–46. Clearly, it would be wrong to assume that the nascent parliamentary "opposition" of this period backed either the landed interest against the trading interest or the trading interest against the landed interest. The two were not economically separable. Liquid merchant capital was "indispensable to farmers, craftsmen and consumers." It allowed them "to realize their assets, notably primary assets in land and minerals and government revenue from taxation. London merchant capital made possible the survival of landowners who were in debt after the Civil Wars . . ." (Grassby, *Past & Present*, no. 46 [1970], 106).

96. See *CSP Ven.*, Dec. 4, 1664, p. 61; *CSPD*, July 15, 17, 28, 1666, pp. 537–38, 546, 587; *Arlington's Letters* (1701), Arlington to Sandwich [?], Aug. 23, 1666, II, 193.

97. See Macray, *Notes* (1896), Dec. 1660, p. 17; Lister, *Clarendon* (1838), Downing to Clarendon, June 14, 1661, III, 144.

discuss a possible Franco-Dutch-English republican alliance. Ludlow had refused Louis XIV's invitation, and Sidney's proposal of 100,000 livres as a minimum French subsidy to the exiles was unacceptable.[98] The reception of these men on the Continent caused outrage in court circles[99] and led to various official attempts to capture them[100] or to learn their plans or to undermine their organization.[101]

Rumors that invading forces in England would be seconded by domestic dissidents were a constant factor throughout the war. In March 1665 the Dutch were said to be relying on the aid of Scottish rebels,[102] but the "wonderfull victory" at Lowestoft in June was said to have temporarily postponed plans of widespread uprisings.[103] During the winter of 1665–66 the presence of a Dutch fleet off the southeast coast of England and a reported penetration into Louis XIV's secret cabinet meetings were responsible for repeated rumors of invasion by both nations and for Charles's readying of the militias "to march at an hour's notice."[104] In April 1666 one of Lord-Lieutenant Ormonde's deputies informed him that "there is no doubt, if the French send men, or arms and ammunition, into this kingdom, it is on assurance of parties here," and in May a government informer revealed that London and Dover dissidents were

98. See Ashley, *Wildman* (1947), pp. 199, 200, 202; Feiling, *British Foreign Policy* (1930), pp. 10–11; *CSP Clar.*, Downing to Clarendon, May 26, 1665, V, 487. Downing claimed that Ludlow and Sidney were in Amsterdam in 1665: Lister, *Clarendon* (1838), June 23, 1665, III, 388.

99. See, e.g., Clarendon to Parliament in *His Majesties Gracious Speech* (Oct. 10, 1665), p. 17.

100. See *Articles of Peace* (1662), arts. IV–VIII; *Speeches, Discourses, and Prayers* (1662), on three republicans betrayed into Downing's hands; *By the King* (Apr. 21, 1666); *CSPD*, July 31, 1666, p. 595.

101. See, e.g., the work of Aphra Behn as a spy in the Provinces, *CSPD*, Aug. 16–Dec. 26, 1666 (see index, s.v. "Behn").

102. See *CSP Clar.*, Downing to Clarendon, Mar. 10, 1665, V, 472–73.

103. *HMC Le Fleming*, letter of June 17, 1665, p. 37. See Clarendon, *Continuation* (1759), p. 290; *CSPD*, Aug. 12, 1665, p. 514.

104. See *CSPD*, 1665–66 "Preface," p. xviii–xix; *CSP Ven.*, Mar. 9, 1666, p. 269; *HMC Gawdy*, letter of Jan. 30, 1666, p. 200. For rumors of invasion see *CSPD*, Nov. 8, 1665, p. 46; *Misc. Aulica* (1702), Arlington to Ormonde, Jan. 30, 1666, p. 374; *Hatton Correspondence* (1878), letter of Jan. 30, 1666, I, 48; Foxcroft, *Savile* (1898), G. Savile to W. Temple, Jan. 26, 1666, I, 43.

confidently expecting a Dutch landing in Sussex.[105] Unlike York's victory a year before, the Four Days Battle of June 1666 was regarded by many Englishmen as a disaster, and England's public thanksgivings for it "a horrid mocking of God, and a lying to the world."[106] A rash of mutinies and seamen's discontents broke out, continuing to the end of the year,[107] and the rumors of invasion came with greater frequency and insistence than ever before. Thirty-five French ships were said to be circling Ireland to join the Dutch in raising rebel Irish support for a landing. The French and Dutch were about to invade all along the southwest coast of England. Old Covenanters looked hopefully for an invasion of Scotland "in a few days." In London, a Frenchman "heard from France they had a design to land 40000 French and 15000 Dutch, in hopes that they would find some rebel party here to join them."[108] The French had plans to free Lambert for the purpose of leading a rebellion in England, and the three allies—the Provinces, France, and Denmark—were set to divide England, Ireland, and Scotland between them.[109]

After a frantic few weeks officials began to feel they could relax their vigilance slightly, although the presence of the Dutch fleet at the mouth of the Thames in mid-July briefly brought panic near the peak it had reached a month earlier.[110]

105. Roger Boyle, *Collection* (1742), letter of Apr. 18, 1666, p. 141; PRO SP 29/156 (107I) (document taken from informer May 4, enclosed in letter dated May 23, 1666).

106. Burnet, *History* (1897), I, 409. Cf. Evelyn, *Diary* (1955), June 5, 1666, III, 440; *CSP Ven.*, June 29, 1666, p. 23; Pepys, *Diary* (1904), Oct. 28, 1666, VI, 41–42.

107. See *CSPD*, June 22–24, 28, 1666, pp. 452–55, 469; Pepys, *Diary* (1904), June 30, July 1, 2, 21, 1666, V, 347–50, 351, 369, Oct. 19, 31, 1666, VI, 27, 45; Clarendon, *Miscell. Works* (1751), "Discourse by Way of Vindication of my self . . . ," p. 73.

108. See *CSPD*, June 27, Aug. 11, 1666, pp. 465, 30; Pepys, *Diary* (1904), June 29, 1666, V, 347; *CSPD*, June 28, 29, July 1, Aug. 12, Sept. 9, 1666, pp. 470–71, 472, 487, 33, 109; *CSPD*, June 30, July 2, 1666, pp. 476, 488–89; *HMC Portland*, letter of Denis de Repas, July 4, 1666, III, 297.

109. See *Misc. Aulica* (1702), Arlington to Ormonde, July 3, 1666, p. 407; *Gazette*, no. 66, June 28–July 2, 1666; Colenbrander, *Bescheiden* (1919), Amsterdam newsletter of July 2, 1666, I, 398; Add. MS. 10117, fol. 167v.

110. See *CSP Ven.*, July 20, 27, 1666, pp. 36, 40.

The English gained a modest victory over the Dutch on St. James' Day (July 25), and their assault on the islands of Vlieland and Ter Schelling the following month, in which hundreds of Dutch ships and houses were burnt, seemed at the time a fitting, even divinely ordained, ending to the audacity of the United Provinces.[111] The burning of London only two weeks later was a painful irony which troubled many besides Dryden.[112] And when the dreaded invasion finally materialized in June 1667 the fact that native rebels did not join the Dutch was not sufficient to calm men's fears, "so great in Court and City, as if an Army of a Hundred Thousand Men had encompassed it."[113]

Thus in his attempt to apply the duc de Rohan's maxim to the problems of war in the mid-1660s, Dryden addressed a large number of Englishmen unreceptive to his ideas of strictly nationalist heroism. Furthermore, to the extent that Dryden's sort of patriotism was still widespread after 1665, popular execration seems to have switched from the Dutch to the French.[114] This visceral response was supported by an increase in apprehension regarding England's supposed unfavorable balance of trade with France.[115] Why Dryden

111. See, e.g., *Gazette*, no. 82, Aug. 23–27, 1666; *Sir Robert Holmes his Bonefire: or, the Dutch Doomsday* (Aug. 18, 1666). Holmes led the attack on the Dutch islands. Bonfires traditionally were lit in celebration of victories.

112. See *AM*, sts. 202–11. Cf., e.g., *CSPD*, Sept. 6, 1666, p. 102; Hardy, *Lamentation* (1666), p. 20; Guillim, *Akamaton* (1667), p. 13; *POAS* (1963), *Third Advice to a Painter* (1667), ll. 164–68, 415–16. It was said that many of the ships burnt at the Vlie were English merchantmen (*CSPD*, Sept. 27, 1666, p. 163), and even that the Great Fire was set by English merchants rendered bankrupt by this earlier fire (*CSP Ven.*, Sept. 28, 1666, p. 77).

113. Clarendon, *Miscell. Works* (1751), "Discourse by Way of Vindication of my self . . . ," p. 7.

114. See *CSP Ven.*, Feb. 12, 1666, p. 266; Barbour, *Arlington* (1914), Arlington to Ormonde, Feb. 17, 1666, p. 92; Temple, *Lettre* (1666), pp. 4, 8, 11 (commissioned July 30, 1666, by Charles via Arlington in *Arlington's Letters* [1701], I, 90–91); PRO SP 77/35, fols. 111v, 166, Temple to Arlington, Sept. 4, 28, 1666; *CSPD*, Aug. 26, 1666, p. 68; *CSP Ven.*, Nov. 12, 1666, pp. 100–101; *CSPD*, Aug. 7, 17, 1667, pp. 18, 48; *Omnia Comesta a Bello* (1667), pp. 4–5; Kennet, *Complete History* (1706), III, 258.

115. See Priestley, *Econ. Hist. Rev.*, 2nd ser., 4, no. 1 (1951), 37–52; R. Baker, *Marchants* (1659), p. 17; Fortrey, *Englands Interest* (1663), pp. 21–28; *By the Mayor* (Oct. 27, 1665); *By the King* (Nov. 10, 1666–

treated the Dutch as the principal enemy, why he was unable to give greater substance to the nationalist stance he had adopted by capitalizing on this growing anti-French feeling, depend upon developments related to, but distinct from, the Anglo-Dutch War. The Great Fire of London, Dryden's second poetic subject, obviously required an assessment of guilt much more swift and unequivocal than those which grew out of the war and the Restoration settlement. To understand the reasons for this particular assessment in 1666, we must return, once more, to the early years of the decade.

---

against French imports); *Free Conference* (1668), pp. 50–51; Manley, *Usury* (1669), sig. B1r-B1v; Bethel, *Observations* (1673), pp. 4–5, 13, 15, and app.

4

ROMAN CATHOLICISM
AND THE GREAT FIRE OF LONDON

In the twenty years which preceded Charles's return, the several governments of England maintained a consistently anti–Roman Catholic stance with regard to religious matters. The restoration of Charles II and, soon after, of the Church of England, did not preclude antipapist literature, but it temporarily impeded its flow, since the affinity between Anglicanism and Roman Catholicism had become a fundamental of most Puritan polemics. Even so, admonitions of Catholic intrigue were acceptable throughout the 1660s so long as the implication of Anglican or Stuart complicity was carefully avoided. More important than the presence of this literature, however, was the fact that the gulf between the powerful Anglican and the powerless nonestablished branches of Protestantism immediately after the Restoration was so great that the ties of "primitive Protestantism" seemed largely obliterated and the force of antipapism as a unifying factor completely nullified.

Thus after Cromwell died it became a commonplace in Anglican polemics against popery to point out that if Catholics and nonestablished Protestants were widely separated as far as theology was concerned, their common interests under Anglican rule drew them very close together. Catholic apologists might argue, as Presbyterians and Quakers did, that the absurdity of these conspiracy theories was clear from their need to be adjusted with each change in government,[1]

1. See, e.g., H. M., *Letter* (1663), p. 11. For Presbyterian and Quaker arguments see above, Chapter 2.

but others regarded papists, Jesuits, and militant Anabaptists, Independents, Quakers, and Fifth Monarchy men as virtually interchangeable.[2] The Presbyterian leader Richard Baxter saw a great variety of Protestant sects as *"Masked Papists."*[3] The usual rationale for such statements was given in a letter that discusses the rumor of "a conjunction between the Nuntio-popish party and the Fanatics": "though there is no seeming probability of such an association, yet when it is considered that both are alike desperate, and cannot propose a more hopeful way for their own advantage than by fishing in troubled waters, it is not altogether impossible, notwithstanding the distance they seem to be at in profession of religion, but that they may agree *in aliquo tertio* to create new troubles in these kingdoms."[4] To the despair of men like Baxter, the Presbyterians were in no way exempt from equally damning explanations: "I have heard very wise and great Politicians say, that *Jesuites* are but *Popish Presbiterians,* and *Presbiterians,* but *Protestant Jesuites:* and it is no wonder, that Cocks of the Game, bred up in the same Principles, should sometimes fight with one another, not coldly, as with some others, but with most sharp and deadly stroakes, provoked and enabled by the Spurs of Emulation and Pragmaticallness . . ."[5]

These associations between Roman Catholics and non-established Protestants were encouraged by the exclusive definition of the true Church which was contained in the Act of Uniformity. The Anglican settlement tried to restore religious unity by equating unity with Uniformity. As defenders of the settlement put it,

We hope the God of Order and Unity will conform the hearts of all people in this Nation, to serve him in this Order and Uniformity.

2. See *CSP Clar.,* letter to Charles Stuart, June 16, 1659, III, 489; *Prophecy, Lately found* (1659), p. 5; Owen, *Herod and Pilate* (1663), title; Poor Robin, *Almanack* (1664), sig. B7r; Moulin, *Vindication* (1664), p. 58 (the Civil Wars were caused by Jesuits masquerading as Protestant sectarians).
3. *Key for Catholicks* (1659), sig. a4r.
4. *HMC Ormonde,* n.s., letter to Ormonde, Dec. 26, 1663, III, 128.
5. *Dolus an Virtus?* (1668), p. 3.

. . . we do verily believe, That Uniformity if it were carefully
maintained, and diligently looked after, would in a few years
recall our ancient Unity . . .[6]

Even in 1660 the Independents were placing their faith in a
general toleration, but it was not until the Act of Uniformity
was passed in 1662 that the mainstream of the Presbyterians
abandoned hope of their comprehension within a national
church.[7] This hope drew strength from the "Liberty to
Tender Consciences" promised by the Declaration of Breda
in 1660, but when Charles amended the well-received Declaration concerning Ecclesiastical Affairs[8] to a general toleration which might include Catholics, Baxter requested a
distinction between "parties tolerable and parties intoler-
able," and the declaration, in the form of a bill, was defeated.[9] The only way in which Charles might hope to win a
limited freedom for Catholics was on the coattails of some
sort of toleration for nonestablished Protestantism; thus
comprehension of the Presbyterians could be no more part
of his plan than it was part of the Anglicans'. A hatred of
popery united Presbyterians and Anglicans but guaranteed
that the former were likely to receive no acceptable aid from
the king. As for the latter, neither comprehension nor toleration was likely to prove acceptable.

At the Commons' Uniformity debates in the spring of
1662, Charles laughingly chose to interpret the impatience
manifested by reformers at his obvious reluctance to concur
in an exclusive Anglican settlement as a suspicion that his
sympathies lay with nonestablished Protestantism: ". . . I
must tell you, I have the worst luck in the world, if, after all
the reproaches of being a Papist whilst I was abroad, I am
suspected of being a Presbyterian now I am come home:
. . . I am as zealous for the Church of *England*, as any of
you can be . . ."[10] In private Charles told Clarendon,

6. Turnor, *Speech* (May 19, 1662), p. 7; Tomkins, *Inconveniencies*
(1667), p. 6.
7. See Abernathy, *Trans. APS*, n.s., 55, pt. 2 (1965), 67, 76.
8. *His Majestie's Declaration* (Oct. 25, 1660).
9. See Bate, *Declaration of Indulgence* (1908), pp. 12–13.
10. *His Majesties Gracious Speech* (Mar. 1, 1662), p. 7.

"rebell for rebell, I had rather trust a papist rebell then a presbiterian one."[11] But in public he prudently suggested a trial indulgence—by royal powers of dispensation—of non-established Protestantism out of "compassion towards the weakness of the Dissenters."[12] The indulgence was defeated and Uniformity became law, leaving Charles to meditate on his evident powerlessness to dispense with an act of Parliament, and the Presbyterians to reflect that whatever freedom they might hope to attain thereafter would be mitigated by an equal indulgence of popery.

Charles's Declaration of Indulgence of December 26, 1662,[13] proposed a limited toleration, the inclusion of Catholics in which was justified in part by reference to the great debt owed by royalists to Catholics during the late Civil Wars.[14] Presbyterian opinion was opposed to an indulgence which would apply to papists, but the Catholics and many sectarians were pleased with the declaration and looked forward to Parliament's acquiescence in the will of the king at their next meeting.[15] The reaction of many others to Charles's appeal may be suggested by the titles of two tracts[16] which were printed in 1663, presumably in response to the indulgence controversy. In February 1663 Charles tried to soften the declaration by pointing out that what he intended was not at all a general toleration of Roman Catholics,[17] and the bill brought before Lords to allow the king dispensing power with regard to certain clauses of the Act of Uniformity specified that this power would relate only to matters of Protestant dissent.

11. Macray, *Notes*, Mar. [?] 1662, p. 65.
12. The wording of the proviso which proposed the dispensation: see Christie, *Shaftesbury* (1871), I, app. VI, lxxviii–lxxix; and I, 263–64. See also *CSP Ven.*, Mar. 31, 1662, pp. 124–25.
13. See Abernathy, *Trans. APS*, n.s., 55, pt. 2 (1965), 86–87, on its origin.
14. See *His Majesties Declaration* (Dec. 26, 1662), p. 10.
15. See *HMC Le Fleming*, letter of Feb. 6, 1663, p. 30; Baxter, *Reliq. Baxt.* (1696), II, 430, 433; Clarendon, *Continuation* (1759), p. 187; Abernathy, *Trans. APS*, n.s., 55, pt. 2 (1965), 88.
16. See *Fair-Warning* (1663), title; *Fair Warning: The Second Part* (1663), title.
17. *His Majesties Gracious Speech* (Feb. 18, 1663), pp. 4–5.

Indisposed with gout at the time of the bill's formulation, Clarendon returned in time to support Lord Treasurer Southampton in arguing against it. His contention that the indulgence would cause Charles to be suspected of intending to expand it to include Catholics precipitated a debate with Ashley on the reliability of Charles's Anglicanism, in the heat of which Clarendon let fall "some unwary Expressions"—such as that the bill was "Ship-Money in Religion, that Nobody could know the End of, or where it would rest."[18] The charge that Clarendon had covertly accused Charles of papism and of intending the alteration of the established religion—outlawed under the new Sedition Act[19]—later figured in the earl of Bristol's attempt to impeach Clarendon and in the successful impeachment of 1667. Commons' reaction to the bill showed an equal sensitivity to the subject of popery. They advised against an indulgence to nonconformity because "it will establish Schism by a Law, and make the whole Government of the Church Precarious, and the Censures of it of no Moment or Consideration at all . . . It will be a cause of increasing Sects and Sectaries, . . . and in time, some prevalent Sect, will at last contend for an establishment; which, for ought can be foreseen, may end in Popery."[20] The statement combines the dominant themes of opposition to Protestant dissent and to royal dispensations from acts of Parliament and Anglican policy, with an ambiguous reference to the ultimate danger of Catholic domination. The vague connection made between sectarian and papist threats denies real precedence to either. A few days later, however, Parliament informed the king of his subjects' apprehensions regarding popery and requested the banishment of Catholic priests and Jesuits.[21] Having been advised earlier by prominent Catholics that the time to retreat had

18. Clarendon, *Continuation* (1759), p. 248. See Haley, *Shaftesbury* (1968), pp. 164–66.
19. 13 Car. II c. 1 (1661): see *SR* (1819), V, 305.
20. *Votes and Orders* (taken Feb. 25, 26, 1663), pp. 7, 7–8. These objections were echoed by antitolerationists during the toleration debates of 1668: Milward, *Diary* (1938), Mar. 11, 1668, p. 214.
21. See *Humble Representation and Petition* (Apr. 1, 1663).

come,[22] Charles acceded to Parliament's request[23] and the campaign for indulgence was over.

The significance of this episode in the formation of group alignments in post-Restoration England is difficult to determine. The Cavalier Parliament's hostility to Catholicism was quite compatible with the continued repudiation of nonconformity within the well-defined categories of principled antitolerationism and the routine maintenance of domestic peace, and within these categories the identification of papist with Protestant dissent might continue to be made with conviction. But the flow and interaction of events made unavoidable the reassessment of old categories and precluded the formulation of a national interest whose coherence and stability rendered all alien interests easily distinguishable. Charles's delicate patronage of the Catholic cause blurred the appealing simplicity of a restored Church of England guided down the *via media* by a royal defender of the faith. It is not simply that the king's affection for popery was widely believed early in the new reign.[24] There were also suspicions that he and popish members of the court circle were at the least doing Catholic France unwarranted services, and at the most negotiating, with Louis XIV, the replacement of Anglicanism by Catholicism.[25] The degree to which "the popish interest" played a part in the machinations of the Queen Mother, Bristol, Arlington, Clifford,[26] and the duke and duchess of York disturbed many Protestants, within Parliament and outside of it. These

22. See Abernathy, *Trans. APS,* n.s., 55, pt. 2 (1965), 89.
23. See *By the King* (Apr. 9, 1663). The banishment took effect on May 14.
24. See Lister, *Clarendon* (1838), II, 198–201; *HMC* 5th Rept., letter of Apr. 9, 1661, pp. 181–82.
25. See *HMC Hastings,* letter of Apr. 19, 1664, II, 145; *CSPD,* Aug. 11, 1666, pp. 30–31; Pepys, *Diary* (1904), Dec. 24, 1666, VI, 113; *POAS* (1963), *Fifth Advice to a Painter* (1667), ll. 135–38; *Vox & Lacrimae* (1668), p. 8; Kennet, *Complete History* (1706), III, 264. Cf. *Door of Hope* (1661), p. 6, the paper scattered about London on the night of Venner's rising.
26. See W. Temple's confused catalogue of Dutch speculations on the causes of England's declaration of war; Temple, *Letters* (1700), letter to John Temple, Sept. 30, 1667, I, 125.

apprehensions of court intrigue prepared the way for the major reassessment of national interest which culminated when the outbreak of the fire made the plausible assignment of group guilt imperative.

Many Englishmen who meditated on the desolation caused by the fire preferred, like Dryden, not to search for its moral below heaven or beyond a generalized Christian repentance for the national sins of the people.[27] And many observers, also like Dryden, mixed this Christian humility with the sanguine suggestion that the judgment itself should not be allowed to obscure the saving mercy of God in stopping the fire when he did, the suggestion that the judgment was also a trial.[28] Contemporaries were well aware that to speculate on the specific nature of the sin which God had punished was to attribute "political" significance to the event. Thus one writer saw through "any party whose constructions of Gods meaning are calculated to the Meridian of their interest, which has couched in it a secret reak of enmity to their opposites, and of applause of themselves, Such as are on the one hand the outed party, who expound it to be for their ejection, or the other party, who averr it to be a punishment of Phanaticism . . ."[29] Another writer simply noted the universal applicability of this sort of interpretation: "The Quakers say, it is for their persecution. The Fanaticks say, it is for banishing and silencing their ministers. Others say, it is for the murder of the king and rebellion of the city. The Clergy lay the blame on schism and licentiousness, while the Sectaries lay it on imposition and their pride. Thus do many pretend to determine the sin aimed at in this punishment."[30]

27. See, e.g., Welch, *History of the Monument* (1893), letter of Sept. 8, 1666, p. 66; Rolls, *Burning of London* (1667), p. 79; Roger Boyle, *Collection* (1742), Boyle to Ormonde, Sept. 21, 1666, p. 181; Stillingfleet, *Sermon Preached Octob. 10* (1666), p. 4; *London Undone* (1666); Vincent, *Gods Terrible Voice* (1667), p. 48.
28. See *Gazette*, no. 85, Sept. 3–10, 1666; Couch, *New Englands Lamentation* (1667?); *Citizens Joy* (1667). Cf. *Lamentatio Civitatis* (1665), p. 38, on the plague as judgment and trial.
29. Waterhouse, *Short Narrative* (1667), p. 43.
30. Gough MS. London 14, undated letter, quoted in Malcolm, *Lond. Rediv.* (1807), IV, 80. Cf. Wither, *Ecchoes* (1666), p. 95, on the similar

However controversial, this line of thought by its nature discouraged punitive action because it treated the fire as a divine *fait accompli,* and in court circles it even produced a curious, inadvertent complacency regarding God's wrath: "the whole was an effect of an unhappy chance, or to speak better, the heavy hand of God . . ."; "Some have conceived it was a plott, but most, and ye King himself, believed yt it was only ye Hand of God."[31] And however widespread, this attitude was not representative of England's response to the disaster. The inevitable distinction between first and second causes was made,[32] and everywhere people demanded of each other:

> War, fire, and plague against us all conspire;
> We the war, God the plague, who rais'd the fire?[33]

The precise nature of the plot, unlike that of God's animus, did not long remain subject to diverse interpretations. Early suspicions of some branch of nonconformity[34] were soon overwhelmed by the conviction that the French and Dutch enemies were responsible for the fire, with the French receiving most of the blame.[35] And the passage from belief

casting of aspersions with regard to the plague: "And the result of all summ'd up together,/*Is this,* Each *shifts his guilt off to another."* Examples of specific sins blamed for the fire are: court libertinism: Waterhouse, *Short Narrative* (1667), pp. 25–26; Henry, *Diaries* (1882), Sept. 8, 1666, p. 193; Clarendon Code: Vincent, *Gods Terrible Voice* (1667), pp. 20–21; *Few Sober Queries* (1668), p. 4; *Et à Dracone* (1668), p. 18; Baxter, *Reliq. Baxt.* (1696), II, 385–86, III, 17; Civil War rebellion and contemporary dissidence (cf. *AM,* sts. 213–14, 223, 276): *Oxinden Letters* (1937), letter of Sept. 14, 1666, p. 311; letter of Sept. 18, 1666, quoted in Bell, *Great Fire* (1920), pp. 313–15; Hardy, *Lamentation* (1666), p. 29; Tabor, *Seasonable Thoughts* (1667), p. 42; Guillim, *Akamaton* (1667), p. 10.

31. *Gazette,* no. 85, Sept. 3–10, 1666; letter of ca. Sept. 10, 1666, quoted in Besant, *Survey of London* (1903), p. 266.

32. See, e.g., Rege Sincera, *Observations* (1667), pp. 9–10.

33. *POAS* (1963), *Third Advice to a Painter* (1667), ll. 417–18.

34. See *CSPD,* Sept. 3, 4, 5, 8, 14, 1666, pp. 95, 99, 100–101, 107, 124; letter from Buckingham, Sept. 6, 1666, quoted in Welch, *History of the Monument* (1893), p. 64; *Cosin Correspondence* (1872), letter to Bishop Cosin, Sept. 8, 1666, II, 155.

35. Besides the Buckingham and Cosin letters cited in the preceding note, see Pepys *Diary* (1904), Sept. 5, 7, 1666, V, 425, 429; letter of ca. Sept. 5, 1666, quoted in Bell, *Great Fire* (1920), p. 317; *HMC Le Fleming,* letter

in a specifically French to belief in a generally papist conspiracy was a natural and insensible one. The possibility of a
papist massacre, a topic of discourse months before the fire,
was of vital concern throughout England after that catastrophe had been identified as a popish plot.[36] On November
5 Pepys wrote that "never more was said of, and feared of,
and done against the Papists then just at this time," and for
the rest of the month he recorded alarms of new fires and
rumors of a "fatal day" when a papist massacre might be
committed.[37] Anthony Wood made the following entry in
his diary: "Papists at this time very insolent in most parts of
the nation; appear in publick; contrive the massacring of
many; hundreds of strang[e] knives being lately discovered
and found [in] a ruinous cellar at London which the Fire
had burnt."[38] Parallels were drawn between the present
disaster and the infamous Gunpowder Plot,[39] and it was
intimated that York—and even Charles—had been instrumental in setting the fire.[40]

This popular hysteria gave the Cavalier Parliament its
first real opportunity to express the united feelings of the
people whom it represented: "the Parliament its self, did
since the Fire manifest a greater zeale and hotter displeasure

---

of Sept. 6, 1666, p. 41; Evelyn, *Diary* (1955), Sept. 7, 1666, III, 461–62;
CSPD, Sept. 5, 7, 8, 10, 1666, pp. 101, 105, 108, 112; letter of ca. Sept. 8,
1666, quoted in Besant, *Survey of London* (1903), p. 365; Josselin, *Diary*
(1908), Sept. 9, 1666, p. 154; *HMC Portland*, letter dated Sept. 1666, III,
298; Add. MS. 40713, fol. 28, letter of Jan. 5, 1667; Clarendon, *Continuation* (1759), p. 348.

36. See Chet. Lib. MS. Mun. A.3.123, July 9, 1666, p. CC; *CSPD*, Sept.
9, 11, 15, Nov. 6, 1666, pp. 110, 116, 127, 242–43; letter written shortly
after the fire in *N&Q*, 1st ser., 12 (1855), 102; Tanner MS. 45, fol. 103v,
draft of letter from Anthony Wood, Sept. 15, 1666; *HMC Portland*, letter
of Oct. 20, 1666, III, 302; PRO SP 29/177(107), letter of Nov. 7, 1666;
PRO SP 29/178(103, 135), letters of Nov. 17, 19, 1666; Chet. Lib. MS.
Mun. A.3.123, Nov. 30, 1666, p. CCVIII.

37. *Diary* (1904), Nov. 5, 7, 9, 10, Dec. 2, 1666, VI, 53, 54, 56–58, 89.

38. *Life and Times* (1891), entry for end of Nov. 1666, II, 93. Cf. the
discovery made by the parliamentary committee to investigate the cause
of the fire, below, text at n46.

39. See *CSPD*, Nov. 6, 1666, p. 242; Ford, *Conflagration of London*
(1667), p. 27.

40. See Burnet, *History* (1897), I, 416, 448; *POAS* (1963), *Fourth Advice to a Painter* (1667), ll. 129–36; *Vox & Lacrimae* (1668), p. 7.

against the Papists then ever before . . ."[41] On October 26 they resolved to request Charles for a proclamation banishing all priests and Jesuits and executing existing laws against popish recusants.[42] The proclamation appeared on November 10 with another prohibiting the import of all French manufactures and commodities.[43] Two weeks after the fire, Commons had voted, following "a long and serious debate," to establish a committee to investigate the cause of the disaster, and committee examinations and reports continued into the next year.[44] In November two M.P.'s were utterly convinced of a plot by the findings of the committee, "things of extraordinary weight and which if they were not true might haue bin thought incredible."[45] One of the committee's discoveries was several hundred "ugly knives" found in a burned house which belonged to Catholics.[46] The most substantial result of the parliamentary examinations came in October, with the trial and execution of the Frenchman Robert Hubert, self-confessed papist arsonist and suspected lunatic.[47] So far from quieting public opinion by firmly assigning guilt for the fire, this event only "revived to the memory of the people the principles and former practices of those of that religion, and raised a fear in them of their being now designing farther mischiefs, that may reach their lives, by a massacre; which fears have run like wild-fire through the whole nation, and caused a loud cry, of the

41. Rolls, *Burning of London* (1667), sig. A5v.

42. See *CJ*, VIII, 641–42.

43. See *By the King. A Proclamation For Banishing; By the King. A Proclamation Prohibiting*. For publicity regarding the proclamations see *Gazette*, no. 103, Nov. 8–12, 1666; Add. MS. 10117, fol. 181; PRO SP 29/174(139), newsletter of Oct. 11, 1666.

44. See Milward, *Diary* (1938), Sept. 25, Oct. 1, Oct. 26, 1666, Jan. 22, 1667, pp. 7, 11, 32, 68–69. Milward himself remained skeptical about the idea of a Franco-papist plot.

45. Marvell, *Poems and Letters* (1952), letter of Nov. 13, 1666, II, 44; Pepys, *Diary* (1904), Nov. 5, 1666, VI, 52, on the reaction of Sir Thomas Crew.

46. Pepys, *Diary* (1904), Oct. 27, 1666, VI, 39–40; Milward, *Diary* (1938), Oct. 26, 1666, p. 32.

47. See *CSPD*, Oct. 11, 21, 1666, pp. 191, 209; Add. MS. 40713, fol. 29, letter of Jan. 8, 1667; Clarendon, *Continuation* (1759), pp. 352–53; Baxter, *Reliq. Baxt.* (1696), III, 18; Bell, *Great Fire* (1920), pp. 191–95.

papists having the greatest part of the arms in their hands
. . ."[48]

The rest of the evidence assembled by the parliamentary committee, as well as purported prophecies indicating that the firing of London was the climax of a successful papist plot which had been in planning for some years, were printed in at least two different forms in 1667.[49] One of these was said to make "the reader believe the fire was designed by the Papists, executed by the Frenchmen and their Jesuits, [and] countenanced and approved by the whole Court,"[50] perhaps the same source as that "now common in the City which tries to prove that the King and the Papists burnt London, [and which] will do much harm if not well answered."[51] In 1667 and 1668 several other tracts seized the occasion of the burning of London and Parliament's apparently zealous attempt to prosecute the plot, for fulminations against popery and harrowing recapitulations of the major papist atrocities of the past two centuries—Marian martyrdoms, the St. Bartholomew's Day Massacre, the Spanish Armada, the Gunpowder Plot, the Irish Massacre of 1641.[52] One tract summarized the Stuart and Anglican Restoration by observing "that the number of professed Papists, hath increased more within these six Years, then it had for near sixty before."[53]

It is not surprising, then, that Clarendon was suspected

---

48. Robert Boyle, *Works* (1772), letter of Nov. 13, 1666, VI, 531.
49. See *True and faithful Account* (1667) (*Somers Tracts* [1812], VII, 615–33, and Malcolm, *Lond. Rediv.* [1807], IV, 46–73); *Londons Flames Discovered* (1667) (*State Tracts* [1693], pt. II, 27–48). Perhaps the most famous piece of evidence from the *Account* is the poem beginning "Couer la feu ye Hugonotts," reportedly scattered about the streets of London toward the end of Dec. 1666: see variant copies in Add. MS. 10117, fol. 182v; Add. MS. 34362, fol. 26; Eg. MS. 2982, fol. 169; Chet. Lib. MS. Mun. A.4.14, fol. 23v; *N&Q*, 1st ser., 12 (1855), 102.
50. *CSPD Add.*, July 15, 1667, p. 205. The writer refers to *Londons Flames Discovered* (1667).
51. *CSP Clar.*, anon. information of June 23, 1667, V, 618.
52. See *Pyrotechnica Loyolana* (1667); *Looking-Glass for England* (1667); Rolls, *Burning of London* (1667), sig. A5r, and *Londons Resurrection* (1668), p. 175; Philoprotest, *Protestant Almanack* (1668); *Vox & Lacrimae* (1668), pp. 6–7, 8, 16.
53. Stirling and Stewart, *Naphtali* (1667), sig. A5v.

Frontispiece to *Pyrotechnica Loyolana* (1667), depicting the seditious activities of the international Roman Catholic conspiracy. Reading clockwise from the top, the pope fans the flames of London, which, like Troy, burns only to be reborn from its ashes; Guy Fawkes prepares his gunpowder, Robert Hubert dispenses a fireball, and Loyola dispatches the hounds of Hell (?) with firebrands tied to their tails, while his fellow Jesuits manufacture the fireballs which, in the center, are spread throughout the world. Reprinted by permission of the Trustees of the British Museum, London.

not only of having accused Charles of popery but of being a
papist himself.[54] Roman Catholicism came to represent so
effectively the nemesis of England that the author of so
many national disasters could not fail to be a papist in dis-
guise. As Parliament dealt justice to Catholics and court
ministers in 1666 and 1667, they seemed to be forging a
national unity which the Restoration settlement and the
Anglo-Dutch War, as they were officially conceived, had
been unable to attain. And it was a unity whose basis was
very different, despite his advocacy of limited toleration,
from what Charles would have wished. A Presbyterian minister returned to his home in Manchester in early November
1666 to find "men in gt expectations of some good at this
time from ye Parliamt, from some Votes agst ye Papists . . .
Now yt god should, wn he hath his people on ye list, slake
his wrath, is very wonderfull. And if he shld now discovre ye
Popish party & defeat it, & therby make way to unite ye
Protestants in ye nation, wld be a wonderfull mercy . . .
And this Parliamt & Bps yt have yet been sad Instrumts to ye
Ch[urch] of god, he can make even ym ye Deliverers of his
people."[55] The unification of England would require not
only the suppression of alien interests but also the reincorpo-
ration of those groups which past parliamentary policy had
mistakenly thought the cause of disunity. In 1667 Pepys
discussed "the sad state of the times" with his cousin, who
believed that "nothing but a union of religious interests will
ever settle us . . ." A friend told Pepys that "there have
been great endeavours of bringing in the Presbyterian interest, but that it will not do." Another thinks "nothing but the
reconciling of the Presbyterian party will save us," to which
Pepys adds, "and I am of his mind."[56]

Of course the Presbyterians remained unreconciled and
the nation remained disunited, but the cause of the divisive-

54. See, e.g., *CSP Clar.*, Apr. 27–28, 1667, V, 605.
55. Chet. Lib. MS. Mun. A.3.123, diary of Henry Newcome, Nov. 6, 1666,
pp. CCVI–CCVII.
56. *Diary* (1904), June 29, 17, 1667, VI, 401, 374, 373.

ness which most Englishmen felt to exist in 1667 was now as likely to be found in the private, incorrigible interests of the court circle as anywhere else in the kingdom. When peace with the Provinces was declared, Pepys did "not find the 'Change at all glad of it, but rather the worse, they looking upon it as a peace made only to preserve the King for a time in his lusts and ease, and to sacrifice trade and his kingdoms only to his own pleasure: so that the hearts of merchants are quite down."[57] The analogy with 1641 became a frequent means of expressing the current atmosphere of popular and parliamentary anger. Commons raged against papists and balked at the court-sponsored general excise, "which these courtiers do take mighty notice of, and look upon the others as bad rebells as ever the last were."[58] Confrontations like these led Pepys to reflect that "upon the whole, God knows we are in a sad condition like to be, there being the very beginnings of the late troubles."[59] William Prynne, aging but irrevocably anti-Catholic, thought it wise to look back into the actions of "English Jesuits at Rome . . . at the time of the late King's murder."[60] Lord Conway told a correspondent that "the temper of the House of Commons is strangely altered, and grown like to that in 41. Nothing but discontents in Parliament, court, and kingdom. And now we are proceeding with as great severity against the Papists upon such like jealousies and apprehensions as in the beginning of the long Parliament."[61] And early in 1667 another interested critic of the state of the nation believed that "unless the King do do something against my Lord Mordaunt and the Patent for the Canary Company, before the Parliament next meets, . . . there will be a civil war before there will be any more money given, unless it may be at their perfect disposal

57. Ibid., July 27, 1667, VII, 39.
58. Ibid., Dec. 14, 1666, VI, 101.
59. Ibid., Oct. 27, 1666, VI, 40. After the Four Days Battle and the fire, the prudent Pepys took the precaution of converting his holdings into cash and dividing his money into separate lots, "if a storm should come": see *Diary* (1904), June 28, V, 346, Oct. 24, 30, 31, 1666, VI, 37, 43, 46.
60. *CSPD*, Dec. 4, 1666, p. 318.
61. *Rawdon Papers* (1819), letter of Oct. 30, 1666, pp. 200–201.

. . ."[62] The parallel with 1641 had not, at this time, the
status of a reflex equation between old and new rebellion
which it achieved by the early 1680s, and these statements
must be taken as fairly nonpartisan attempts to place the
current crisis within a familiar framework. Yet the Exclusion
Crisis has an obvious relevance to the events which we have
been examining. In 1667 one writer commented: "if indeed,
and in truth that Fire either came, or was carried on and
continued by their [papists'] treachery [I desire] that the
Inscription of the Pillar may consign over their names to
perpetual hatred and infamy."[63] The papist treachery of the
Great Fire, immortalized by the Monument's altered inscrip-
tions,[64] was to become the foundation of the Whig mythology which Shaftesbury used to mold an opposition of
awesome unity and strength. As William Bedloe later expressed it, "let therefore the Remembrance of SIXTY SIX be
engraven in Indelible Characters on the Hearts of the Posterity, To make them abhor Popery, and detest such vile
Incendiaries . . ."[65] Far too much had occurred in the
twelve years which separate these two pleas for the second
to be of any use in illuminating the conditions out of which
the first germinated, but it is interesting to observe how
opposition to special group interests in 1667—the French,
the Catholics, the power of royal dispensation, mercantile
monopolies, court elitism—coalesced in the issue of the duke
of York's exclusion from the succession in 1678–1681.[66]

The court ideology which Dryden expresses in Annus
Mirabilis involves the abolition of division by subsuming
group interests under that of the court. His portrait of
England entailed the effacement of the group distinctions

62. Pepys, Diary (1904), Feb. 17, 1667, VI, 184, recalling the opinion
of Captain Cocke. The issue of Mordaunt's impeachment had the general
significance of preparing the way for Clarendon's: see Witcombe, Charles
II (1966), pp. 49–50 and 50n4.
63. Rolls, Burning of London (1667), pt. III, 198.
64. See CJ, Jan. 10, 1681, IX, 703.
65. Narrative (1679), sig. A1v.
66. For different treatments of this idea see Priestley, Bull. IHR, 29
(1956), 205–19; Witcombe, Charles II (1966), pp. 173ff.

and alignments which had grown up in the seven years of restored Stuart rule and which the historical Charles II was forced to exploit as best he could. The English society of *Annus Mirabilis* is not, of course, a "groupless" one. Dryden's national collectivity assumes the existence of a traditional stratification of society according to status, uncomplicated by these special distinctions which undercut the traditional structure and challenged its authority by providing a rational alternative to it. If the ideal of national interest and unity was a commonplace for Dryden and his contemporaries, the proper means for its attainment was subject to diverse and conflicting ideological interpretations. The conventional language of national interest and unity in the 1660s expresses a sustained consciousness of how commonly held national aims may entail preferences for widely differing policies, preferences which depend on the group perspective from which the aims are examined. That Dryden's conciliatory vision of public interest and unity in *Annus Mirabilis* amounts to a defense of private court ideology is a plausible reading not only because that vision would seem to have been largely inconsistent with the prevailing consciousness of group division. Insofar as informed public opinion could conceive, at this time, of an end to divisiveness and a conciliation of private interests, the kinds of solutions which seemed best suited to achieving these goals and most congruent with the public temper were very far from those which form the ideological basis of *Annus Mirabilis*.

II

ESCHATOLOGICAL PROPHECY

But the Pen to describe this unparalell'd Fire, should be like its Flames, to soar high, and be perspicuous too; mounting above its own smoak, and not to wrap it self up in sheets of obscurity . . .

Joseph Guillim, *Akamaton* (1667), sig. A2v

. . . all trading is a Sleepe & a little waking houres, nothing but warre with Holland & France, they are so pfectly growne Deaf yt all the Cryes of merchants will not awake them, indeed Sr the times are very sadd, 666 is at hand & yet I have ventured to marry . . .

Add. MS. 40712, fol. 17v, Mary Escott to her uncle George Oxinden in Surat, Mar. [?] 5, 1666

O *Sixty-six!* Thou center of human Prophecies! Thou Ocean, into which all the Rivers of Conjectural Predictions did run! If I live to see thee end, as thou hast continued hitherto; for thy sake, if for nothing else (yet, upon other considerations too,) if men will find confidence to make a thousand Prophecies, no wayes countenanced by Scripture, I shall not find Faith to believe one of them.

Samuel Rolls, *Burning of London* (1667), pt. III, p. 96

5

ANNUS MIRABILIS
SECOND READING

By juxtaposing the first reading of *Annus Mirabilis* with an analysis of the context from which it emerged, we have seen that Dryden's poem would have had the simultaneous significance of "poetry" and "propaganda" for contemporaries. Its meaning as a "political poem" is a product of the indissoluble fusion of the conventionally distinct languages and epistemologies of politics and poetry. Rhetorical analysis of poem and context has provided a way of penetrating the dogmatism of modern criticism which, by identifying Dryden's secondary advocacy of court policy as the primary level of the language of public interest and unity from which it developed, located the "poetic" aspects of *Annus Mirabilis* in its transcendence of the particular. When the simultaneous reality of both levels of language is affirmed, the status of *Annus Mirabilis* as a "political poem" is understood.

Similar conclusions will grow out of the present discussion, but from a somewhat different direction. The "political" dimension of *Annus Mirabilis* is generally seen in modern criticism as distinct from the "poetic": not necessarily incompatible with it, but a kind of inferior existence, a bridge between the concreteness of history and the capacity of poetic transcendence. And it is in this distinct and final "poetic" capacity, critics are largely agreed, that the excellences or deficiencies of *Annus Mirabilis* are to be assessed and understood. The poem's "political" capacity, its grappling with concrete historical factors, is generally located in its tacit discrediting of contemporary antimonarchal groups. This intention to discredit has been substantiated by reference to the historical context of the poem (the *Mirabilis Annus* tracts) and by assumptions that the language of, and belief in, prophecy and eschatology are specifically sectarian or antimonarchal preoccupations. Thus, if the end of rhetorical analysis so far has been to counter the dogmatism which understands the secondary implications of Dryden's language in a primary manner, in the present discussion it will aim at demonstrating that common understandings of *Annus Mirabilis* in its "political" dimension erroneously reduce a system of language and belief primary to the age—that of prophecy and eschatology—to the secondary status of ideology peculiar to one separate group. In other words, the primary dimension of Dryden's use of the language of prophecy and eschatology in *Annus Mirabilis* customarily has been reduced to a secondary, ideological repudiation of the beliefs which the very use of that language is taken to imply.

This demonstration will be carried out, once again, in two stages. First, it will be argued that the poem uses the conventional language of, and reveals conventional beliefs in, prophecy and eschatology. Second, Dryden's language and the beliefs that are implied by its use will be set in the context of Restoration prophetic literature in order to show that what Dryden says and believes regarding prophecy—distinguishing this primary level from the secondary, ideological ends to which language and belief are directed—is broadly characteristic of all contemporary groups, royalist, Anglican, Presbyterian, sectarian, republican. From this it will be concluded that what Dryden discredits is not the peculiarly dissenting *habit* of prophecy and eschatology, but the peculiarly dissenting *policies* which this virtually universal habit may be used to advocate. The present reading will seek an understanding of *Annus Mirabilis* as an expression of this universal habit, always bearing in mind the secondary application which Dryden makes of primary discourse. Here, as with the language of interest and unity, the perception of both levels of discourse determined in his contemporary audience an integrated response to what was experienced as simultaneously "political" and "poetic."

Dryden's meditations on the uncertainty of heavenly fate in *Annus Mirabilis* were understood earlier to be a means of generalizing uncomfortable human particulars and hence to be a device instrumental in the universalization of interest and unity. In the present reading the poem's reflections on fate will be understood from a different perspective. Dryden's didactic admonitions against trying to read the future are made in three principal contexts of *Annus Mirabilis* and are evoked by three combinations of historical developments: the attempt at Bergen and the bishop of Münster's treachery (35–36); the conclusion of the Four Days Battle and the refitting of the fleet (139–41); the recollection of England's aid to the Dutch rebels, the burning of the Dutch fleet in the Vlie, and the Great Fire of London (200, 209–11). On the most basic level, the common message of these passages is that all prophecy is vain: the effort that is wasted in attempting to guess God's will would be better spent in cultivating an appreciation of its ultimate goodness. Yet alternating with these prudent sentiments are Dryden's several bold and explicit assertions of what the future holds for England: the opening prophecy of "a second Punick War" (5); the prediction that England will lead the world in perfecting navigational techniques (161–64); the closing prophecy of England in a rich and glorious future Golden Age (293–304). Dryden seems, in other words, to ignore his own advice against tempting fate. This striking antithesis is perhaps hinted at by his observation in the dedication to London that "one part of my Poem has not been more an History of your destruction, than the other a Prophecy of your restoration." The more that sobering instances of destruction are presented as reasons to despair of ever comprehending history, the greater the need to make history symmetrical by balancing past destruction with discovered or prophesied restoration. This antithesis lies at the center of

Annus Mirabilis, the Year of Wonders. We may begin to understand it by examining Dryden's concern with wonder as an emotion evoked by natural, literary, and historical phenomena.

In his "Account" of *Annus Mirabilis* to Sir Robert Howard, Dryden tells the reader that the proper response to "heroick" or "Epique" poetry—and to its branches, "the Historique and Panegyrique"—is admiration. A conventional Renaissance conception of epic poetry was that its function consisted in calling forth *admiratio* by aptly describing magnificent and sublime subjects. A different sort of literary wonder was associated with the effect achieved by the witty conceits of such poets as Donne and Marino. Here the reader's admiration consists largely of astonishment at the surprise and audacity of incongruous couplings; the wonder of the subject matter cannot be separated from the wonder of the way in which it has been described. The effect of admiration in this sense depends upon the apprehension that natural and generic rules of decorum in discourse are being violated intentionally. A milder form of this violation than that of "metaphysical" poetry can be seen in Virgil's *Georgics*, the basic fascination of which derives from the detailed, almost pedantic description of "low" subjects in "high," heroic, language.[1] The georgic style has been called "antithetical" because it juxtaposes incongruous moods and subjects, viewpoints which contrast with each other but which are maintained simultaneously.[2] Yet in Dryden's opinion the *Georgics* were notable not only for "metaphysical" antitheses but also for the heroic *admiratio* proper to their sublime language (if not to their subject). In the "Account" to Howard he acknowledges his debt to Virgil

1. See Chalker, *English Georgic* (1969), pp. 20–21, 24, 27. It is in this sense that Chalker uses the term "mock-heroic" to describe the georgic style, and not necessarily to imply satiric intention.

2. See ibid., pp. 209–10. Cf. Robert Boyle, *Occasional Reflections* (1665), sig. a5r–a5v.

quite exhaustively—not only to the *Aeneid*, but also to the *Georgics*, "which I esteem the Divinest part of all his writings." And it is apparently to these which he alludes when he says that Virgil "has been my Master in this Poem." In the *Georgics*, Virgil deals with natural subjects "most of which are neither great in themselves, nor have any natural ornament to bear them up: but the words wherewith he describes them are so excellent." The admiration of *Annus Mirabilis* arises, in part, from its imitation of the *Georgics* and of their blend of heroic and "metaphysical" wonder.

Dryden chooses to call *Annus Mirabilis* not heroic, but "An Historical Poem," and chooses here to emphasize the value of the georgic over the merely heroic. These choices may suggest that historical poetry has something in common with the georgic and with the particular kind of wonder which it engenders. The explanation that Dryden gives for his generic identification of *Annus Mirabilis* is a formal one: although his subject is not lacking in heroic stature, his narrative or action is "broken," "not properly one," and therefore conforms more to the natural "Laws of History" than to the artificial laws of poetic unity. This claim to historical fidelity prepares the reader for a poem in which the sense of georgic wonder-from-incongruity is conflated with an appreciation of the astonishing incomprehensibility of history itself. Dryden's action is history, the product of time. Our admiration will derive in part from the sheer sublimity of divine creation and in part from the ways in which God both frustrates and fulfills our expectations about what will and should come to pass. Like nature, history is seen as a complex continuum whose anomalies owe their wonderful character fully as much to the incongruity of symmetrically pleasing repetitions and fulfillments as to that of grotesque contrasts and disconfirmations. History is wonderful in the sense that truth is stranger than fiction. *Annus Mirabilis* is historical and not strictly heroic because it relates events so strange and momentous "as nothing can parallel in Story," marvels of unexpectedness which can only be the issue of historical factuality.[3] And Dryden's nominal subject is precisely this, a year filled with wonders.

On the simplest level of significance, however, Dryden's "georgic" wonders are also "historical" only superficially, in that they are uncommon events, remarkable happenings which are forced out of time's "usual" progression into human consciousness. As the subtitle tells us, this "Year of Wonders" contains two principal events, the "Naval War" and the "Fire of London." Dryden uses several different methods to reveal the individual wonder of each of the component parts of these events. One method is the epic simile in which human participants in great actions are compared to animals in characteristic, quasi-naturalistic situations. For the purpose of evoking admiration it is essential that these situations not appear so naturalistic as to obscure the exotic quality of what are also allusions to foreign literature and geography. In *Annus Mirabilis* epic similes often constitute only the barest of similitudes, their primary function being to cast a strange and wonderful glow on the subject with which the exotic has been so tenuously connected. Thus the high-decked Dutch ships and the low English frigates are like elephants and rhinoceroses, and Albemarle is a falcon attacked by the Dutch crows or a lion stalked by *"Lybian Huntsmen"* (59, 86–87, 96–97). Thus Rupert performs the part of a mother eagle in rescuing Albemarle and later is like a panting dog that has an equally exhausted hare at its mercy, yet cannot finish it off (107–8, 131–32). And thus the subtle Dutch lure the English into their shallows just as "the false Spider" might lay a trap for "the strugling Fly" (180–81). Those similes which are not highly exotic achieve the more contemplative wonder of the georgic image which delights in the admirable multiplicity and detail of all natural life, and in its applicability to more strictly human activities. This is the attraction of the figure of the swarming beehive, which Dryden uses to characterize the industrious

3. The idea that history contains wonders not to be paralleled in story was a common one: see, e.g., *Dutch Gazette* (1666?); *HMC Finch*, letter of Oct. 1, 1666, p. 436; Booker, *Telescopium* (1667), sig. B7r.

refitting of the fleet and the later fire fighting (144–50, 228–29).

Other similes, not so formally drawn and developed, are reminiscent more of the "metaphysical" than of the epic aspect of georgic admiration. At first the two fleets are like "floating Nations"; later the disparity in numbers is so great that the English seem "to wander in a moving wood" or fight like a swordfish within the bowels of a whale (57, 78–79). Albemarle is "like some old Oak"; fireships are like "grapling *Aetna's*"; the Great Fire is hydra-headed, like a coven of witches that coalesces out of the darkness, or flaming falcons hooded, eventually, by the divine falconer (61, 84, 248–49, 281). These images all exemplify the way in which Dryden attempts to transform his subjects into prodigies of nature simply by comparing them to prodigies. Other events are sufficiently wonderful in themselves to warrant admiration; Dryden adds only the necessary emphasis and selectivity. This may be said of the attempt at Bergen, a fight in which spices, perfumes, and porcelains are both weapons and the objects for which each side battles (25–30). It also applies to Dryden's brief treatment of the Great Plague and its "poison'd darts."[4] The poem is filled with such prodigies, and frequently Dryden does no more than make their prodigious nature explicit. What interests him about Albemarle, for example, is not his prosperity, but "his eclips'd estate, / Which, like the Sun's, more wonders does afford" (90). Similarly, in his prayer Charles recollects the "wondrous ways" in which God led him from the darkness of exile to the felicity of restoration (262). Dryden's sustained personification of the fire as civil rebellion only confirms what is everywhere apparent, that it is a "prodigious fire."[5] When it reaches the Thames even "wond'ring Fish in shining waters

4. Sts. 267–68. For other contemporary uses of this metaphor see *Runawayes Return* (1665); Trigge, *Calendarium* (1666), sig. C2v; Rolls, *Burning of London* (1667), pt. III, 216. Cf. Dekker, *Wonderfull yeare* (1603?), sig. D2v.

5. St. 215. For similar personifications of plague and the fire see Crouch, *Londinenses* (1666), pp. 4, 9; Ford, *Conflagration* (1667), p. 10; Tomkins, *Inconveniencies* (1667), p. 32. On the rebellious signification of certain natural disasters see Lilly, *Annus Tenebrosus* (1652), p. 5.

gaze" (231). And Britain's triumphant discovery of the "mysterious" secrets of tidal movements, it is prophesied, will be taught to properly "admiring Nations" (161–62).

In a year of such extraordinary developments, it is not surprising that Dryden should keep the factor of celestial influence in the reader's mind. A wonder of precise correspondence at any time, the relations between natural and celestial phenomena were particularly close and observable in periods of great and unusual activities. Thus, two of the comets which preceded the activities that Dryden narrates are twice made the subject of astrological interpretation, and the fixed stars are seen to shine in sympathy with what they witness (18, 278, 291–92). At the lowest points of their fortune, Albemarle and Rupert both berate the stars for denying them a victory in the Four Days Battle (100, 133). And one of the comets, Dryden suggests, may be "that bright companion of the Sun," the star which shone at Charles's birth and then began its new "round of greater years." Its recent return would thus signify the inauguration of a new English age: the felicity which it prefigured in 1630, rendering Charles's nativity an auspicious event, is now fulfilled in the auspicious care of the king and of his own Royal Society.[6] Hence the determinism of amoral astrological influence is not far removed from that of benign providence, an aspect of the poem which was discussed in Chapter 1, and the presence of providence in *Annus Mirabilis* means that the prodigious is often exalted into something resembling the miraculous.

The aura of the Divine Will which invests many of Dryden's wonders is achieved in part by the use of biblical images which have the general effect of identifying the English as God's chosen people, for whom he is usually willing to perform miracles. In the "Verses to her Highness" the natural elements are as subdued, before the Battle of Lowes-

6. See sts. 18, 20, 165, 288. Dryden alludes to Charles's star in *Astraea Redux* (1660), ll. 288–91. For other allusions to its wonderful and auspicious significance, see W. Smith, *To the Kings* (1661), p. 48; *Poem upon his Maiesties* (1661), p. 11; Heath, *Glories* (1662), p. 2. See Hooker's note in Dryden, *Works* (1956), I, 232.

toft, as they were at the parting of the Red Sea, and later York's arm is steadied just as Moses' was when a raised arm miraculously dictated the outcome of the fight. In *Annus Mirabilis* itself, the role of Moses is assumed by Albemarle. His cannon and the smoke they emit are compared with the pillars of cloud and fire by which God both guided the Jews and obscured their way to the Egyptians (92). At this point in the Four Days Battle—the nadir of England's fortune— the sudden sinking of a Dutch ship seems as meaningful as God's smiting of "he that touch'd the Ark," and the remaining Dutch draw back to an "awful distance" (94–95). Rupert's salvation of Albemarle is like the resurrection of Christ.[7] To the fearful Dutch, likened to "fall'n Angels," it is the coming of a "new *Messiah,*" and Albemarle's men now wish for a miracle commensurate with that which God granted to Joshua (114, 118). Finally, throughout *Annus Mirabilis* the Londoners are paralleled with the Jews, whose judgments and trials at the hand of God are chronicled in the Old Testament. At the end of the poem the burning of London is compared to the destruction of Jerusalem, and its restoration is confidently prophesied by the linking of Charles and the people of London with Cyrus and "the *Jews* of old."[8]

What is significant about most of these passages is not simply the parallel with God's chosen people but the emphasis on the performance of miracles, superprodigies whose cause is categorically and exclusively supernatural. Yet because this divine intervention is usually metaphorical or oblique it cannot be said that Dryden clearly portrays England's progress in *Annus Mirabilis* as miraculous. A prodigy such as the blowing up of Admiral Obdam, for example, is rather ambiguous. The extraordinary nature of his fate leads

7. See above, Chapter 1, n8.
8. St. 290. In the lines I have discussed Dryden alludes to the following biblical passages: Exod. 14:21–22, 17:10–13, 13, 14; 1 Chron. 13:9–10; Matt. 27:63, 28:2ff; Josh. 10:12–14; Ezra, 1. The biblical disasters of plague and fire were the occasions of many parallels between England and the Jews: see, e.g., Crane, *Lamentation* (1665), p. 5; Add. MS. 29495, fols. 3–6, "Paralell" (1665?) of W. Lodington; Add. MS. 34363, fol. 57–57v, paper (1666?) of George Cartwright; Crouch, *Londinenses* (1666), p. 2; Wither, *Ecchoes* (1666), pp. 93–94; *Vox & Lacrimae* (1668), pp. 9–10.

the Dutch to think "Heav'n present," but their show of "reverence" is not necessarily evidence of its miraculous quality (22–23). The same must be said of Albemarle's remarkable perseverance in the Four Days Battle, which the Dutch are forced to admit "as when Fiends did Miracles avow" (137). Conventional Homeric devices such as the roll call of heroes, the catalogue of ships, and the direct intervention of "the *British Neptune*" create an atmosphere in which it is difficult to take London's "Guardian Angel" or the "Cherub" recruited by God from the "Heav'nly Quire" as anything more than revitalized literary machinery.[9] On the other hand, when we see God in his "Empyrean Heaven" soften from anger to pity, and devise a wonderfully eccentric means for extinguishing the fire, we must accept the miraculous nature of this "more than natural change."[10] Here Dryden's wonders exceed the realm of nature and demand the status of miracles, events whose causation can be accounted for only in terms of the supernatural.

The wonder of natural prodigies and literary incongruities in *Annus Mirabilis* reinforces the central, historical wonders of the poem which radiate out from the fundamental antithesis of a year that contains both wonderful victories at sea and wonderful devastation at home. It is the inconsistency of the year, the unexpected conjunction of events, which makes 1666 wonderful. This was expressed by the bishop of Exeter in a sermon to the House of Lords one month after the fire: "We have seen *vicissitudes* great and *prodigious*, mixtures and combinations, *marvellous* in our eyes, *horrible destructions* and *wonderful restitutions*, succeeding one another, *raging Plagues* at *home*, and *signal Victories abroad*." And in the bishop's opinion, the heterogeneity of God's dealings

9. Sts. 171–76, 184, 224, 271–72.
10. Sts. 279–83. For versions of the divine extinguishing of the fire similar to Dryden's see Wiseman, *Short Narrative* (1667), p. 11; Guillim, *Akamaton* (1667), p. 12. Cf. R. F., *Letter* (1668), pp. 8–9, who ridicules Dryden's "wonderful Stanza, in his wonderful Poem of the wonderful year 1666. And withall it tells us how the Fire of *London* was put out, which few Countrey people knew before . . ."

with England thus far promised that the low ebb of October 1666 would be balanced by a divine deliverance:

Yet who can tell, but *God* may have *mercy* upon us, but he may *yet* save us from destruction? . . .
. . . God's *signal* Judgments have hitherto been accompanyed with *signs* of mercies, and *this* is *a plain case,* that he is *not fond* of our destructions, and that he had rather that we should *live* . . .
What mean else those *Alternations* and those *mixtures,* and combinations of wonderful *Judgments,* and of wonderful *deliverancies* and *mercies* which our *ears* have heard and our *eyes* have seen?[11]

This way of reading history bears some similarity to the understanding of national judgments as trials. No disaster is so total that it lacks spatial or temporal limitations which are capable of being interpreted as signs of future felicity. But the antithetical quality of history and divine causation is so ambiguous that human interpretation must often appear a vain and subjective exercise. No one was able to give a plausibly disinterested explanation of which specific sins were aimed at in the fire.[12] Royalists most often refuted providential interpretations of pre-Restoration Puritan successes and post-Restoration nonconformist persecution not on the grounds that they were superstitious but because they were erroneous, and defenders of the Restoration settlement felt obliged

to invalidate their pretended Providence, by shewing the falseness of the Application . . . as *Popish* Miracles are no wonders, so *Fanatick* Providence was not prodigious . . .
. . . nothing of strangeness . . . was discoverable in all their undertakings, no not so much as to suspect the least smile of signal Providence, beyond common Dispensations . . .
. . . now the Scene being altered, and the hand of Vengeance beginning to take cognizance of their former sins, our *Fanatick,* like a cunning Ambidexter, inverts the terms, and shifts his place. And what victorious success in 1651. did exhibit, now Persecution

11. Ward, *Sermon* (1666), p. 25.
12. See above, Chapter 4.

(viz. Justice) in 1660. must declare: and now 'tis not Prosperity but Persecution, that is undoubtedly the mark of God's Chosen.[13]

John Spencer, whose distaste for the superstition of all providential interpretations of nature and history was extreme for his age, made a similar point regarding the legalistic citation of prodigies: "Mens minds disturbed with love or hatred (as it falls out in religious differences) each party superstitiously interprets all accidents in favor of it self . . . these Prodigies . . . (like mercenary soldiers) may be easily brought to fight on either side in any case."[14] The invalidation of "pretended Providence," the demonstration that interested readings of providence require the arbitrary inversion of terms, was practiced by all interests even while their own interpretations were tacitly accorded the status of unarguable revelation. In *Annus Mirabilis* Dryden's understanding of the significance of the fire does not preclude his invalidation of the supposed Dutch perspective on their prudent retreat during the St. James' Day Fight, "who call'd that providence which we call'd flight" (192).

If this easy disjunction between objective and partisan understandings of the meaning of events were characteristic of *Annus Mirabilis*, if Dryden merely asserted that any judgment which God cast on England must necessarily have the greater significance of a trial, then it would be foolish to search the poem for a sophisticated attempt to reveal how God works through history, especially the marvelously contradictory history of 1666. But *Annus Mirabilis* is a complex poem, and its structure can be seen to reinforce the complexity of its perspective on the wonderful year. One way of clarifying this structure is by dividing the poem into two parts of equal length which bear a relation to each other similar to that which exists between the Old and New Testaments. This has been done in the following table, where the sequence of stanza numbers has been reversed after the

13. Jenings, *Miraculum basilicon* (1664), introduction, sig. A8r, B2v, B5r–B5v.
14. Spencer, *Discourse* (1665), pp. 15–16.

Stage	Subject	Stanzas numbered in correct order	Stanzas numbered in reverse order	Subject	Stanzas numbered in correct order
	a			b	
1	Restoration of the *London*	151	151	Restoration of the *London*	154
2	Refitting of the fleet	142–50	141–50	Progress of shipping and navigation	155–64
3	Resting in God's will	139–41	139–40	Prophecy of the Royal Society	165–66
4	Fourth day of the battle	120–38	120–38	Preparations for the fight	167–85
5	Third day of the battle	103–19	102–19	St. James' Day Fight	186–203
6	Second day of the battle	72–102	93–101	Vlie and transience of felicity	204–12
			81–92	Birth of the fire	225–37
7	First day of the battle	54–71	68–80	Progress of the fire	225–37
8	Charles delegates his power	47–53	44–67	Charles fights the fire	238–61
9	Charles's diplomacy	39–46	35–43	Charles's prayer: "diplomacy"	262–70
10	Bergen and Münster: inscrutability of fate	24–38	23–34	Fire: prayer answered	271–82
11	Lowestoft: war heroes	19–23	15–22	Fire and war: mutuality	283–90
12	Comets	16–18	13–14	Comets	291–92
13	Prophecy: war and trade	1–15	1–12	Prophecy: end of war and trade	293–304

central passage on the *Loyal London,* indicating a rough correspondence between the first and second halves of the poem. According to this plan, the restoration of the *London* constitutes the central event of the poem and of the history which it relates. It is enclosed on either side by preceding and succeeding events as they are narrated by Dryden, progressions which terminate in the rationale and prophecy of the war on the one hand and in the prophecy of the war's end and England's future on the other. I suggest that *Annus Mirabilis* has the structure of Christian history in that it is organized around a central event of multileveled significance and consists of historical correspondences whose component events derive their own significance from their relations with one another. The wonderful history which the poem narrates, like sacred history, is a dialectic of parallel events the synthesis of whose meaning requires the application of literal, allegorical, and typological techniques of scriptural exegesis.

If the main historical subject of *Annus Mirabilis* is a year or two of English affairs, the poem's historical allusions span the prehistoric invention of ships and the remote future of interplanetary exploration. Dryden's depiction of the present age as one midway between the classical Golden Age and the restored Golden Age of the future grows out of the explicit history and prophecy—the "progress"—of shipping and navigation and the Royal Society at stages 2b and 3b of the table. Within this tripartite division of history the middle, or "present," section is framed by the corresponding prophecies of stage 13: Dryden predicts both a period of war and commerce and the successes necessary for the eventual conclusion of this period. In the first prophecy (stage 13a), mercantile war is proposed as the means by which England may oppose the designs of foreigners and win for herself some of the "Eastern" prizes which Holland's "thriving Arts" have monopolized. In the second prophecy (stage 13b), England's imminent acquisition of "Eastern wealth" and London's knowledge of "the beauteous Arts of Modern pride" subdue and win over foreign competitors, thus making future mercantile wars unnecessary. This knowledge which is London's possession is the same as that which, at stages 2b and 3b, "shall . . . be to admiring Nations taught," the understanding of navigational techniques. England will know the secrets of nature "as Arts Elements" through the auspices of the Royal Society, which, Dryden predicts, will draw from nature the artful rules for her mastery. Thus the progress of the technological "arts" connects the prophecies of stages 2b and 3b with those of stage 13, a connection which suggests that stages 2a and 3a may have some importance in the historical scheme which is developing.

The allegorical significance of the central stages 2 and 3 of *Annus Mirabilis* unfolds from the interpretation of the *Loyal London*'s restoration at stage 1.

> The goodly *London* in her gallant trim,
> (The *Phoenix* daughter of the vanish'd old:)
> Like a rich Bride does to the Ocean swim,
> And on her shadow rides in floating gold.
>
> Her Flag aloft spread ruffling to the wind,
> And sanguine Streamers seem the floud to fire:
> The Weaver charm'd with what his Loom design'd,
> Goes on to Sea, and knows not to retire.
>
> With roomy decks, her Guns of mighty strength,
> (Whose low-laid mouthes each mounting billow laves:)
> Deep in her draught, and warlike in her length,
> She seems a Sea-wasp flying on the waves.
>
> This martial Present, piously design'd,
> The Loyal City give their best-lov'd King:
> And with a bounty ample as the wind,
> Built, fitted and maintain'd to aid him bring.
>
> (151–54)

The ship called the *London*, built in 1656, exploded on March 7, 1665. A subscription by the City of London financed the building of a replacement for her, the *Loyal London*, which was launched on June 10, 1666. The burning of London three months later provided the opportunity, seized by many writers, to regard the phoenixlike renewal of the ship as a presage of the hoped-for, phoenixlike renewal of the city.[15] The symbolic relationship implied by this prophecy backfired in June 1667, when the Dutch burned the *Loyal London* in the Medway. Thus Evelyn built further upon the conceit when he entered, in his diary for June 28, 1667, the comment that "here in the river of Chattam, just before the Towne lay the Carkasse of the *Lond:* (now the 3d time burnt) . . ."[16] *Annus Mirabilis* is dedicated to the City of London, and Dryden's "goodly *London*," "The *Phoenix* daughter of the vanish'd old," clearly stands both for the ship and for the city whose fall and restoration are a major subject of the poem. Thus, insofar as *Annus Mirabilis* is a chronicle of London's fortunes, the four central stanzas of the poem allegorically encapsulate its larger movement.

The allegorical interpretation of stage 1 suggests similar readings of stages 2 and 3. By understanding the "Apostrophe to the Royal Society" in the context of stage 13's prophecies, we saw how the society transmuted the rarefied ideas of God and nature into the gold of technological innovation (stage 3b). This alchemical process is paralleled in stage 3a, where Charles, a pattern of godlike patience, is happy to stand by as "all-maturing time" gradually generates and reveals the consequences of "this early fight," as if he were a miner wise enough to know that time's secret production of gold in the bowels of the earth cannot be hastened by human exertions. In both terms of stage 3, gold is metaphorically generated; but whereas Charles bows to the authority of time and the natural production of gold, the Royal Society uses art to harness nature and speed the technological progress of England and mankind. Since Charles created the Royal Society, it is not entirely distinct from him but rather

15. See the diverse conceits in W. Smith, *Poem On the famous Ship* (1666), pp. 1–2; Crouch, *Poterion* (1666), p. 8, *Londinenses* (1666), p. 9; Hardy, *Lamentation* (1666), p. 22; Guillim, *Akamaton* (1667), p. 14; Settle, *Elegie* (1667), p. 6.
16. *Diary* (1955), III, 486. Cf. *POAS*, Marvell, *Last Instructions* (written 1667, printed 1689), ll. 697–98: "Each doleful day still with fresh loss returns: / The *Loyal London* now a third time burns."

an extension of the royal Charles, a symbol of England's newfound capacities in this new age of instructed navigation whose inauguration is signaled by the central event of London's restoration.

Thus stage 3a, nominally descriptive of the historical period separating the end of the Four Days Battle and the refitting of the fleet, allegorically represents the traditional powers of Charles and his nation before London's restoration, and typologically points forward to a kind of technological fulfillment of those powers (stage 3b) after the restoration of London has made this fulfillment possible. But what has London's restoration to do with technological innovations? On the literal level, stage 2 concerns the rebuilding of ships after the Four Days Battle and the history of shipbuilding and navigation from the dawn of history to the distant future. Yet elsewhere Dryden has used the figure of the ship of state to depict both the unguided wanderings and the constant, dependable progress of which civil government is capable. After wealth and familial security are lost at Bergen, Dryden meditates:

> Such are the proud designs of human kind,
> And so we suffer Shipwrack every where!
> Alas, what Port can such a Pilot find,
> Who in the night of Fate must blindly steer!
>
> (35)

And in the final stanza of *Annus Mirabilis* England sails into a future of peace and wealth like a great ship:

> Thus to the Eastern wealth through storms we go;
> But now, the Cape once doubled, fear no more:
> A constant Trade-wind will securely blow,
> And gently lay us on the Spicy shore.
>
> (304)

Civil states, in other words, are like ships, and government may be represented by navigation. What England learns between stanzas 35 and 304 is allegorically described in the three central stages of the poem. From this perspective, the refitting of the fleet at stage 2a constitutes the repair of England after the battles of the Civil Wars. It is "the Royal work" (144): Charles's "Carpenters" are "the Surgeons" who repair "maim'd ships" (142), laboring, like Charles,

> To bind the bruises of a Civil War,
> And stop the issues of their wasting bloud.
>
> (263)

Charles "restores" "his Navies" with *"English* Oak," the Royal Oak in which the king was miraculously shielded from Cromwell's army at the Battle of Worcester and which became a popular symbol of monarchy preserved by the divine hand in order to be restored to the people of England (143).[17] The restoration of Stuart monarchy permits the return of royalist exiles and the reconciliation of loyalists who had remained in England during the long winter of civil disruption:

> Each day brings fresh supplies of Arms and Men,
> And Ships which all last Winter were abrode:
> And such as fitted since the Fight had been,
> Or new from Stocks were fall'n into the Road.
>
> (150)

The new "Loyal London" is the *"Phoenix* daughter" of the old London; in 1660 she is reborn because she calls for the restoration of the king and thus distinguishes herself, by her "loyalty," from the London which played a major part in rebelling against his father (151, 154).

But the perfection of Charles's government is not achieved by the Restoration of 1660 alone. The central event of *Annus Mirabilis* is not the restoration of Charles and monarchy in

17. See, e.g., the material collected in Broadley, *The Royal Miracle* (1912). This allegorical linking of Charles's restoration of his oaken navy with his miraculous restoration in the Worcester oak receives support from Ogilby, *Entertainment* (1662), p. 37, who describes a depiction—on one of the panels of the first of the triumphal arches erected in London to celebrate Charles's restoration in 1660—of the Royal Oak labeled "ROBUR BRITANNICUM" (British oak) "in allusion to His Majestie's Royal *Navy*, those Floating Garrisons made of Oak."

1660, but the destruction and prophesied renovation of London in 1666. The "Royal work" of the refitting of the fleet is deficient in comparison with the work that will be done by the Royal Society. If stage 2a allegorically depicts the restoration of England after the Civil Wars, stage 2b allegorically depicts man's historical progress in governing the ship of state and his own destiny. The present age, falling in the middle of this progress, Dryden's epic and historical allusions have characterized throughout the poem as the Roman one which followed on Saturn's invention of coin and commerce.[18] It is climaxed by Britain's acquisition of knowledge which constitutes the navigational aid necessary for the "instructed" steering of the ship of state, and therefore the prophetic sense which will obviate the uncertainties of the pilot "who in the night of Fate must blindly steer" and those of the monarch who must wait for the implications of time to manifest themselves (35, 40). As England learns how to navigate and govern securely, she learns how to read the future and even to create the future of unending progress which Dryden prophesies in stage 2b of the poem. The new age forecast by the new "round of greater years" (18) of Charles's birth star and made possible by the scientific study of the Royal Society is one in which prophecy is no longer arbitrary. Dryden affirms this not only in his willingness to prophesy the progress of shipping and navigation and of the Royal Society itself, but also in the central stanzas on the City of London, the prophecy of whose restoration, only implicit in the allegorical reading of the *Loyal London* which I have made here, becomes literal at the end of *Annus Mirabilis*, where the phoenixlike "Maiden Queen" London (288, 295, 297) recalls the "rich Bride" that is the *Loyal London*, "the *Phoenix* daughter of the vanish'd old" of the poem's first stage.

In his treatment of the Royal Society's understanding of "God and Nature" at stage 3b, Dryden conflates the historical and the natural realms and equates, in the society's

18. See st. 158. For Roman allusions see, e.g., the epigraphs, and sts. 5, 15, 21, 50, 63, 67, 88, 173, 175, 191, 194.

alchemical transmutations, the techniques of prophecy and science.

> By viewing Nature, Natures Hand-maid, Art,
> Makes mighty things from small beginnings grow.
>
> (155)

The Royal Society uses art to pierce through natural phenomena to the "Law" which underlies them. To understand nature in this way, to know the "rule of beings in your Makers mind" (166), is to read nature as God's wonderful book, the book of nature corresponding to the sacred history of the Scriptures. When the "mysterious" wonders of nature are traced to God's mind they are understood "as Arts Elements" (162), but they are nonetheless wonderful for that. As the historian of the Royal Society wrote of skeptical philosophers, "If they take from the *Prodigies,* they add to the ordinary *Works* of the same *Author.* And those ordinary *Works* themselves, they do almost rais to the height of *Wonders,* by the exact Discovery, which they make of their excellencies . . ."[19]

The instructed reading of nature, Dryden tells us, is like the instructed reading of history and of *Annus Mirabilis:* to understand the meaning of the phenomena before him the reader must search below the surface and discover the laws that govern them. The discovery of what lies hidden from view is one of the major sources of wonder in *Annus Mirabilis.* The knowledge which the Royal Society gains from its study of God and nature is both theoretical and practical. Knowledge of nature's workings allows one to anticipate and harness them, to predict the consistent success (for example) of navigational techniques. The Royal Society can prophesy what will happen next because it knows the laws which make things happen, unlike Charles after the Four Days Battle, who waits for time to reveal its meaning rather

19. Sprat, *History* (1667), p. 362. See Westfall, *Science and Religion* (1958), chaps. 2, 3. On the literary tradition which treats the evocation of wonder as a means to induce the pursuit of knowledge see Quinn, *ELH,* 36, no. 4 (1969), 626–47.

than divining the meaning of what God has revealed to him in history. By learning to read correctly the revelation that is contained in God's two books, Britain and the Royal Society learn to read the future, to examine the evidence of history and nature empirically for the laws by which they operate. The power of knowledge guarantees that England, once having learned to read the future, will be able to create it. Dryden prophesies that the *translatio studii* of navigational arts will become a *translatio imperii* at the point when England makes the technological breakthrough which inaugurates the coming age (161). Thereafter all informed prophecy will anticipate, and thereby make, the future, since it will be based upon God's intentions. England, like Dryden, will predict unlimited progress to the restored Golden Age and will have the technological capacity to fulfill that prediction. In this way, art "makes mighty things from small beginnings grow."

Thus, what the Royal Society gives to England is a more precise understanding of how God works in nature and history, an understanding which only increases the wonder of those works. If the reader of *Annus Mirabilis* is to understand the meaning of its wonderful history, he must, like the Royal Society, be prepared to search below its surface for the fundamental law which grows from its central event to inform all of preceding and subsequent history. This law contains within itself the antithetical principle which renders prophecy an exercise both in vanity and in wisdom. The examination of this law's operation in *Annus Mirabilis* will benefit from a brief consideration of how some of the poem's stages which have not been discussed so far fit in with the interrelations of the first three and the thirteenth stages of Dryden's historical scheme.

The wonderful history which *Annus Mirabilis* narrates is no more ideally symmetrical than sacred history is: it requires the ingenuity of interpretation and a certain amount of tact as well, lest Dryden's wonders, like God's in the hands of enthusiastic exegetes, seem, despite truth's strangeness, too good to be true. Read literally, the events of the poem appear, like those of the Old and New Testaments, to comprise a fairly linear historical progression. But in both cases, interpretation suggests that the events of the second half of the progression also recapitulate those of the first from a new and more meaningful perspective. A very broad and schematic understanding of how this process of re-capitulation works in *Annus Mirabilis* can be gained from a closer examination of several of its stages; the process is by no means perfectly consistent, and any minute application of such a reading would be useless.

Stage 12 provides a suitable starting point because here the recapitulation occurs even on the literal level, with Dryden self-consciously offering alternative interpretations of the origins—and therefore of the meaning—of the three comets which appeared in the heavens in 1664 and 1665. Stage 12a stands at early 1665, stage 12b at late 1666, in the literal historical progression of the poem. In stanzas 16–18, fanciful or quasi-naturalistic explanations for the first two comets are mixed with the suggestion that one of them is the star that shone at Charles's birth. In stanzas 291–92, the astrological understanding of these two as malevolent warn-ings of plague and fire is balanced by a technical astrological analysis of the third comet's benevolent influence on the renovation of London. Thus stage 12a, while asserting the basic "influence" which celestial bodies have on sublunary occurrences, does not specify the nature of the possible influence, or even the correctness of this interpretation over the alternatives at hand. Stage 12b, however, is consistently astrological in its interpretations and confident in its ability to read the past and future meanings of celestial phenomena. The differences between these two explanations of the sig-nificance of the same events are owing to the influence of the central events in *Annus Mirabilis*. The liberty of prophesy-ing established by the methods of the Royal Society is reflected in Dryden's precise application of the rules of astrological interpretation in stage 12b, a "scientific" method which reveals how seemingly indistinguishable wonders are distinct both in themselves and in what they portend. The antithetical paradigm of London's fall and rebirth reappears in the discordant harmony of the three comets' implications for London, the harsh Law of past judgments and the future Promise of redemption and resurrection.[20]

The informed recapitulation of the past by the future occurs most often, in *Annus Mirabilis,* on a level distinct from that of the literal historical narrative. If stages 2 and 3 present, allegorically, different perspectives on the Restoration settlement, stages 4–11 may be seen as partial recollections of the Civil Wars—but perhaps more comprehensively as archetypal situations in history whose recurrence in the second half of the poem casts them in a new and more satisfactory light without rendering them entirely different. Thus, for example, at stage 11 the precedence of heroes in epic battle is contrasted with the mutuality of prince and people who vanquish the enemy and the warlike fire by working in unison. Stage 10a depicts the ultimate vanity of man's most extraordinary and ambitious enterprises when God's will is not sought and understood; in stage 10b, "th'Eternal heard"—God is seen to be responsive to human will, diverting the fire and then extinguishing it. The international and domestic diplomacy of stage 9a involves Charles in negotiations with other nations and with his own subjects. In stage 9b Charles selflessly negotiates with God through prayer, presenting alternative arguments for England's salvation. Stages 4–8 present England at war, with the Dutch and the fire. At stages 6b and 7b the fire grows into a Cromwellian Protectorate. Charles himself leads the

---

20. Cf. J. B., *Blazing Star* (1665), p. 13: "Thus you see how uncertain the effects of Comets are, sometimes boding the greatest good, sometimes the greatest evil; which alas, cannot be judged signes of any thing, when they are understood by none. What is a sign, signifieth; and what signifieth is known . . . ." Cf. the commentary of Gadbury, *De Cometis* (1665), pp. 51, 65–66: ". . . both these *Comets* are the messengers of *calamities,* and *tristitious events, to befal mankinde* . . . Sure I am, as great a *vein* of *happiness,* is promised unto *mankind* by *this Comet,* . . . as (almost) of *infelicity* denounced, by the *other two;* and the *worser influence* of this. What should the *mixture* of *Jupiter* with *Mars* herein *mean?* unless a *Remonstrance* of *mercy,* from the *God* of mercies, unto *mankinde* in general, after so great *sufferings* and *unhappinesses,* to them *threatened* by the former *Comets?*"

battle against it at stage 8b and manages finally to subdue it with the help of God, to whom he recalls his own labors "to bind the bruises of a Civil War" (263). This personal involvement in war contrasts directly with stage 8a, where Charles delegates his power to his subordinates and runs the risk of losing the battle. In the same way, perhaps, Charles I lost all through his early unwillingness to assert his full power against Cromwell and the parliamentarians. What binds together the two terms of each of the poem's stages is, quite often, not simply the process of recapitulation, but one of fulfillment. The second half of *Annus Mirabilis* is a narrative composed of the archetypal attempts and actions of the first, but executed now with greater efficiency, success, or understanding.

These schematic fulfillments give to *Annus Mirabilis* the kind of structural circularity which the Bible retains despite its doctrinal linearity. The "thriving Arts" of the United Provinces at stage 13a are transmuted by the alchemical art of the Royal Society into the "beauteous Arts" of modernity at stage 13b. The linear progression from an age of mercantile expansion to the restored Golden Age of peace and plenty is clear, but the recurrent themes—arts, ages, war, trade, spices, prophecy—seem to close the gap between the two terms of stage 13 and balance it against the central stages of the poem. In an analogous manner, Genesis builds out of chaos the promise of everlasting life which is lost in man's fall and God's judgment against him; Revelation climaxes man's merciful redemption through Christ's promise by prophesying universal judgment and the return of chaos. "Trade," Dryden says in stanza 2, "like bloud should circularly flow," and the purpose of the war against the Dutch is to restore trade to its rightful revolution.[21] Part of the

21. Contemporary allusions to the wheel of trade and empire, the circulation of commerce, and the centrality of London in this circular motion are plentiful. See, e.g., R. Baker, *Marchants* (1659), pp. 2, 7, 8; *Englands Safety* (1659), p. 19; S. E., *Toutch-Stone* (1659), pp. 3, 11; Dryden, *Astraea Redux* (1660), ll. 298–99; Turnor, *Speech* (Jan. 18, 1667), p. 2; Rolls, *Burning of London* (1667), pt. III, 11, 45; *Answer of the Company* (1667), p. 4; *Et à Dracone* (1668), p. 12; Temple, *Miscellanea* (1680), "Survey . . . in the Year 1671," pp. 26–27, and *Observations* (1673), p. 231.

poem's purpose is to reveal a similar pattern in time, to show how, with the events of 1666, time has "now a round of greater years begun," greater than those which came before, but a necessary recapitulation all the same. The central action of *Annus Mirabilis*, the fall and rise of London, is a circular one which nevertheless holds the promise of a rise exceeding the greatest heights to which the wheel of fortune has raised London thus far. The significance of London's judgment as a divine trial is reflected throughout the history which radiates from her central passion, and it transforms Dryden's prophecies of restoration into an eschatology of unending felicity, a demonstration of how London's fall is fortunate.

In his dedication of *Annus Mirabilis* Dryden tells London: "To you . . . this Year of Wonders is justly dedicated, because you have made it so: You who are to stand a wonder to all Years and Ages . . ." Dryden dedicates to London not only his poem but also the year which is its subject, because the wonders of both the year and the poem are generated by London's sacrifice. She is "a *Phoenix* in her ashes, and, as far as Humanity can approach, a great Emblem of the suffering Deity": in history, a recollection of Christ; in poetry, the central figure whose suffering and triumph, "destruction" and "restoration," give meaning to all that surrounds it. The fundamental pattern of fall and rise in *Annus Mirabilis* can be seen in the antitheses of war versus fire, judgment versus trial. The divine "smile" signified by the war is juxtaposed with the "frown" of the fire: "as by one he did our Nation raise, / So now he with another pulls us down" (211). "Urbs antiqua ruit": but in flames London is a microcosm of the world, "which at the death of time / Must fall, and rise a nobler frame by fire" (212). This pattern pervades the poem in all its parts, drawing the periphery into the center and informing each separate event with the central significance which links them together.

At the beginning of *Annus Mirabilis*, Dryden prophesies that the Golden Age which the Dutch now enjoy must come

Small medal struck in 1666 in remembrance of the wonderful year. The contrast between the two faces reflects the antithetical wonder of the year's events: obverse ("pure goodness") depicts a shrine, fruitful fields, a peaceful shepherd, and St. Paul shaking a viper from his hand (see Acts 28:5); reverse ("so he punishes") shows a city in flames and hailstorm, comets, a leafless tree, and Death and a warrior contending on horseback. Reprinted from Edward Hawkins et al., *Medallic Illustrations of the History of Great Britain and Ireland to the Death of George II* (2 vols., London: Spink & Son, 1969), courtesy of the Trustees of the British Museum, London.

to an end when they, like Carthage, "stoop" to a stronger
Rome-England. This fall will be part of the continuing historical dialectic involving two nations "ingag'd so far, / That
each seav'n years the fit must shake each Land" (7). Thus
the duke of Albemarle, recalling his career as General
Monck, beholds "that *Carthage,* which he ruin'd, rise once
more" (50). When Charles considers the likely consequences of war, he confirms his parentage of the Royal
Society and the antithetical nature of national enrichment
by alchemically estimating cost against benefit and by concluding that "like vapours that from Limbecks rise, / It
would in richer showers descend again" (13). The "stores"
of *Annus Mirabilis* are variously money, ammunition, and
sexuality. On the point of winning the prize of Dutch stores
at Bergen, the English lose it to tempests, but "storms,
repenting, part of it restor'd." The Dutch gain in far-off
Guinea, on the other hand, "was onely kept to lose it neerer
home." Thus Dryden meditates on the vicissitudes of fortune, the inbuilt irony that ambitious and confident designs
end in disaster (31–36).

When Albemarle's potency is drained by the Dutch during the Four Days Battle and his phallic masts have fallen to
the deck, his men "restore" their leader's power by construct-
ing new masts, "whose lofty heads rise higher then before"
(65). Later on in the battle the ghosts of Charles's royal
predecessors find in Albemarle's fallen state the paradoxical
guarantee of his monarch's rise:

> The mighty Ghosts of our great *Harries* rose,
> And armed *Edwards* look'd, with anxious eyes,
> To see this Fleet among unequal foes,
> By which fate promis'd them their *Charls* should rise.
>
> (81)

The wonder that attaches to Albemarle's antithetical state at
this low point in the battle interests Dryden. Having restored Charles from exile to the throne of England, Albemarle is familiar with fortune's reversals. Now he himself
has fallen, but he retains the potential to rise once more:

Let other Muses write his prosp'rous fate,
Of conquer'd Nations tell, and Kings restor'd:
But mine shall sing of his eclips'd estate,
Which, like the Sun's, more wonders does afford.

(90)

Dryden may be confident that Albemarle's rise and his
repetition of earlier naval victories is as certain as the daily
rise of the sun, but Albemarle himself is not. On the eve of
the third day of battle he muses:

That happy Sun, said he, will rise again,
Who twice victorious did our Navy see:
And I alone must view him rise in vain,
Without one ray of all his Star for me.

(100)

But Albemarle's misgivings vanish with the appearance of
the Christ-like Rupert,

Whose waving streamers from afar he knows:
As in his fate something divine there were,
Who dead and buried the third day arose.[22]

(105)

"This new *Messiah*'s coming" marks a rise in English fortunes and correspondingly strikes fear in the hearts of the
Dutch "fall'n Angels" (114).

After the battle Charles "restores" both his fleet and,
allegorically, his nation; London, the ship and, propheti-
cally, the city, rises like a *"Phoenix"* from her ashes; and
Dryden reveals how "mighty things from small beginnings
grow" in his history and prophecy of human progress. England's past aid to the Dutch, like the incidents at Bergen, is
made the occasion for contemplating human blindness to
destiny, yet destiny is seen to be almost dependable in its
wonderful combination of opposites: England checked the
rise of Spain's empire by aiding her Dutch colonies; Spain's
fall was accompanied by the "rising pow'r" of France and

22. See above, Chapter 1, n8.

the Provinces (198–200). The lesson is repeated in the juxtaposition of the burning of the Dutch fleet and the burning of London: the first action "swells" the English, and urges "an unseen Fate to lay us low." God "raises" us to "pull us down"; but in falling we will, like the world "at the death of time," "rise a nobler frame by fire" (210–12). At the end of the poem, Dryden repeats this eschatological phrase which echoes Revelation:[23] London in prophecy "seems to have renew'd her Charters date, / Which Heav'n will to the death of time allow" (294). Contemporary parallels between the Great Fire and the Day of Judgment were plentiful.[24] Dryden draws the parallel more extensively in *Annus Mirabilis* midway between these two anticipations of the apocalypse:

> Night came, but without darkness or repose,
> A dismal picture of the gen'ral doom:
> Where souls distracted when the Trumpet blows,
> And half unready with their bodies come.
>
> (254)

He uses the profound ambiguity of the eschaton—a composite of judgment and mercy—to characterize metaphorically the dual nature of London's experience, the rise which is implicit in her fall. And the eschatological flavor of the fire and its aftermath harmonizes with Dryden's treatment of it as a unique and central event which embraces all of future history just as Christ's passion fulfills the past and preordains the future of humankind.

As Dryden describes it, the rise of the fire entailed the fall of London: he relates in detail the Cromwellian "rise of this

---

23. Rev. 10:6.
24. See, e.g., Henry, *Diaries* (1882), Sept. 2, 1666, p. 193; Evelyn, *Diary* (1955), Sept. 2, 1666, III, 453, 454; Besant, *Survey of London* (1903), letter of Sept. 8, 1666, p. 263; Ward, *Sermon* (1666), p. 2; Stillingfleet, *Sermon* (1666), pp. 13–14; Wiseman, *Short Narrative* (1667), p. 8; Tabor, *Seasonable Thoughts* (1667), p. 36; Doolittle, *Rebukes* (1667), title; Clarendon, *Continuation* (1759), p. 350; Baxter, *Reliq. Baxt.* (1696), III, 17. The plague and the burning of the Dutch fleet at Vlie were similarly compared with doomsday: see Blundell, *Cavalier* (1933), letter of 1665, p. 108; Burney MS. 390, Francis Mundy, "On the Signall Victory," fol. 33v.

prodigious fire," "the flames that to our ruine rose" (215, 217). In the same way, the rise of Cromwell meant the fall of England, but a fall which promised her restoration in that of Charles, whose heroic opposition to the fire Dryden compares to the sun's daily labors:

> Now day appears, and with the day the King.
> . . . .
>
> The days were all in this lost labour spent;
> And when the weary King gave place to night,
> His Beams he to his Royal Brother lent,
> And so shone still in his reflective light.
>
> (238, 253)

Charles is the sun whose fall, like Albemarle's, contains the certainty of future rise, and hence whose "eclips'd estate . . . like the Sun's, more wonders does afford" (90). And like Rupert, he is also the son who dies only to rise again, the Christ with whom London has already been identified.[25]

The heavenly bodies rise "sickly" in sympathy with London's sufferings, and when at last God converts judgment to mercy the stars shine with astrological beneficence, "and high-rais'd *Jove* from his dark prison freed" (278, 292). The "two dire Comets which have scourg'd the Town" die, like abortive phoenixes, "in their own Plague and Fire," while Charles proves loyal to the phoenix London and "will hatch their ashes by his stay" (291, 288). In his allusion to the Jews and their eagerness to rebuild "their Royal City," Jerusalem (290), Dryden brings to a close his continuing parallel between England and the chosen people,[26] whose judgments and trials make up the history of the Old Testament and prepare for the final retribution which comes at the end of the New. The new London will be the New Jerusalem, the eternal city triumphant at the death of time. In a somewhat different manner, the poem's Virgilian epigraph and

25. On the alchemical and astrological significance of this and other imagery in *AM*, and for an argument which substantiates the present one, see Rosenberg, *PMLA*, 79 (1964), 254–58.

26. See above, Chapter 1.

Roman allusions[27] provide a thematic framework for the climactic prophecy that London-Troynovant[28] will be renovated after her necessary destruction. The "Chymick flame" of the fire is the agent that alchemically transmutes London from the base substance of history into the "Gold" of prophecy (293), acting, like the alchemical Royal Society, for England's greater good. In the final allusion to the phoenix legend, London "new deifi'd . . . from her fires does rise": she is the most antithetical and exotic of all georgic wonders, the magical bird whose new life emerges from the old, but whose identity is maintained nevertheless in perpetuity, for "Augusta, *the old name of* London," is now only "more *August*" than before (295). The self-sacrifice and self-renewal of the phoenix was a cyclical phenomenon. Commentators differed on the duration of its life span but agreed that at fixed intervals throughout history the phoenix sank in its spicy nest and rose anew to begin "a round of greater years." Thus too "Augustus" was wonderfully restored from the fires of civil war, inaugurating a new age even while he perpetuated the unbroken line of English kingship.[29]

27. See ibid. And cf. the parallel between the present war and the Trojan War (64).

28. Dryden's comparison of London with Troy does not make use of the popular epithet for England's metropolis, whose appositeness seemed to be confirmed by the fire: see Reeve, *God's Plea* (1657), p. 217; Evelyn, *Diary* (1955), Sept. 2, 1666, III, 454; Tanner MS. 45, fol. 97, T. Flatman to W. Sancroft, Sept. 17, 1666; Hardy, *Lamentation* (1666), pp. 21–22; *London Undone* (1666); Guillim, *Akamaton* (1667), p. 11; Ford, *Conflagration* (1667), p. 18; *Poem On the burning* (1667); Settle, *Elegie* (1667), p. 6; Couch, *New-Englands Lamentation* (1667?); Booker, *Telescopium* (1667), sig. C1r.

29. For examples of the application of the phoenix legend to Restoration history—especially to Charles's restoration and the Great Fire—see Crouch, *Mixt Poem* (1660), p. 1; Saunders, *Apollo Anglicanus* (1661), sig. A7r; Matthew, KAROLOU (1660, 1664), p. 97; *Lamentatio Civitatis* (1665), p. 1; *London Undone* (1666); Crouch, *Londinenses* (1666), p. 9; *Pyrotechnica Loyolana* (1667), sig. A3v; *Poem On the burning* (1667); Briscoe, *Verses* (1667); Gadbury, EPHEMERIS (1667), sig. C8v; Settle, *Elegie* (1667), p. 7; Couch, *New-Englands Lamentation* (1667?), epigraph. On the phoenix legend see Kantorowicz, *King's Two Bodies* (1957), pp. 388–91 and 413, where he describes the medallion struck by royalists in 1649 after Charles I's execution, whose obverse shows the royal martyr in profile and whose reverse bears a phoenix rising from its burning nest and the inscription: "EX CINERIBVS."

At this point in the poem, the reconstruction of the *London* in the *Loyal London*, understood on the level of literal history, has been typologically fulfilled and infused with meaning by the prophesied restoration of her namesake, just as the historical and metaphorical fires of the poem's earlier sections[30] have prefigured the Great Fire of London. At the very center of *Annus Mirabilis*, the *Loyal London's* "sanguine Streamers" seem, by their reflection in the Thames, "the floud to fire" (152), an image which itself reflects its own later actualization (231) and the typological structure that informs much of the poem. The closing prophecy balances that of the beginning, but now the rise which is predicted for England is certain, a wonderful and inescapable concomitant of the fall that she has just undergone. The golden restoration of London and England which is the subject of the final stanzas of *Annus Mirabilis*, already "confirmed" by the historical restoration of Charles and England in 1660 and by the allegorical restoration of the fleet and the *Loyal London* in the central passages of the poem, is ultimately confirmed by Dryden's constant demonstration of how God works in history: after the fall must come a rise.

In a recent article John M. Wallace has discussed the problem of allegory in later seventeenth-century poetry in a way that sheds light on the allegorical reading of *Annus Mirabilis* that I have now completed. Wallace suggests that the overtly historical literary works of this period derive their strong referential quality from their relation to historical writing proper and from the prevailing habit of the times of reading history as exemplary. History teaches by precept and example; readers of history participate directly in their own instruction by applying particular examples they encounter to other cases with which they are familiar. "Historical poetry" works in much the same way, and thus "we need worry less if the discoverable political meanings are 'in'

30. See sts. 67, 82–84, 102, 174, 204.

the work, or if we have put them there. Simply, they are there if we see them, and if we can establish a contemporary background that makes them likely . . ."[31] It should be clear that Wallace does not intend by this argument to license the wholesale "allegorization" of poetry. In fact, his point is that these works are more properly understood as "historical poems" than as "true allegories," that they teach not by metaphorical but by exemplary reference and require a reader who is sensitive to the persuasive historical applications of their substance rather than one who perceives the analogical intention of their author.

These interesting observations invite reflection on *Annus Mirabilis*, which Dryden called a "historical poem" and which I have—with what readers may judge some indiscretion—quite freely allegorized. What Dryden offers us, through the judicious conception and structure of his poem, is an opportunity to apply the particular examples of naval war and domestic disaster to other cases: the history of London during the wonderful year, the history of England from Charles I to Charles II, the history of the world from the immemorial past to the distant future. This process of application is one of gradual generalization, and may be compared to the empirical method associated by Dryden with the Royal Society, which derives the general law from the particular example. On the other hand, the Christian element in *Annus Mirabilis*, once that element has been rightly understood, makes it difficult not to read the poem as a "true allegory." From this perspective, we understand *Annus Mirabilis* according to the deductive method of prophecy, finding that the central and immanent principle of Christ's passion provides a key to the meaning of all particular historical cases with which the poem concerns itself. In making this distinction between the methods of science and prophecy we separate what Dryden's argument, and his historical milieu, would regard as inseparable. We are justified in this anachronism, however, precisely because we are

31. *ELH*, 36, no. 1 (1969), 272.

modern readers who appreciate the value of understanding poetry of the past not only in its own terms but also in others, both contemporary and retrospective.

If *Annus Mirabilis* may be taken as typical, then, the historical poetry of the later seventeenth century can be seen as a transitional form whose mode of teaching characteristically combines the imperatives of allegory with the suggestions of history teaching by example. I do not intend to assert the typicality of Dryden's poem in this respect, but a few observations on some other well-known works of the period may be useful for further thought.[32]

Although Andrew Marvell's "pastorals" of the early 1650s have a variety which makes generalization hazardous, most of them seem to partake of three different kinds of events: a private encounter, an episode drawn from the public history of the times, and the primordial drama in the Garden. Our perception of what each poem is about depends on our willingness to remain with one species of action and on our readiness to move from one species to another. Some poems ("The Mower's Song," "The Mower against Gardens," "The Garden") describe a simultaneously private and primordial fall into artifice and sexual love in terms that extend easily to the public realm of economic experience in mid-century England. Marvell's subtle accentuation of usury, exploitation, enclosure, the ambiguities of "corruption," the rewards and betrayals of industrious labor, gives historical particularity to these pastorals and allows the reader to reflect on the world around him: the agricultural despotism of feudal tenure and Stuart monarchy, the redefinition of property relations in revolutionary England and its promise of individualistic sovereignty and solitude, the obscure but ominous dangers of capitalist improvement. On the other hand, there are poems by Marvell ("Bermudas," "The Nymph Complaining for the Death of her Fawn," "Upon Appleton House") that come closer to being what Wallace calls

32. I am conscious of doing some violence, in the following remarks, to the clarity of Wallace's emphasis on overtly historical literary works, but I hope their interest will justify this obscurity.

"overtly historical" in their more or less explicit allusion to contemporary political events. In these poems, the careful reader's likely movement from Edenic to English history does not exclude the possibility of reversing the initial process of self-instructed reading by applying the particular examples of English history to the general case of Eden.

Milton's "Lycidas" (1645) is a somewhat different instance of the seventeenth-century pastoralist's habit of providing the reader with action on three different levels and allowing him to take either or all as far as he may deem instructive. The private case of the drowned youth, set forth in terms of the classical pastoral, becomes exemplary of the prototypical Christian pastor Christ, and the poet's consolation derives both from the indirect, exemplary bond connecting Christ and Edward King and from the knowledge that Christ's "dear might" is directly responsible for the redemption of Milton's friend, whose fallen classical identity is now also redeemed by his Christian status. Moreover, the speech of the Christian pilot St. Peter enables not only the transition from a private and classical fall to a public and Christian resurrection, but also the introduction of the third level of action, that of seventeenth-century Puritan reformation. For as Milton has promised in his subtitle, "by occasion" of his personal response to his friend's death and with the aid of St. Peter's castigation of bad pastors the poet successfully "foretells the ruin of our corrupted Clergy, then [1637] in their height." This is less an allegory than an assurance that God works both in pastoral poetry and in English history, and one of our responsibilities as readers is to assess the implications of Lycidas's example for the revolution now in progress. *Samson Agonistes* (1671), which Milton probably composed during the 1660s, makes similar demands upon us at a time when the revolution clearly seems, from a mundane perspective, to have failed. Here our historical example is the Old Testament figure Samson, which we may usefully apply in two directions: to the private case of the blinded poet Milton, whose one talent, like Samson's, would appear to be lodged with him useless; and to the public case of the

Puritan cause, now shackled by the chains of monarchy and episocopacy. The two applications serve, of course, to illuminate each other as well, and if it remains the poet's task to determine the applicability of Samson's example to his own fortunes, it is ours to meditate the relevance of Samson's wonderful reversal to the plight of post-Restoration Puritanism.

From Marvell and Milton we may pass to Dryden and Bunyan, in particular to those two works whose formal slipperiness owes to their very different but equally ambiguous claims to the status of "true allegory." In *Absalom and Achitophel* (1681), Dryden's stance as "historian" of the Old Testament denies only that he "invents" his history ("To the Reader"), not that it has modern applications, and other comments in this introductory address do considerably more than Milton's discreet allusions to "saints" and "inward light" to concentrate the reader's attention on one specific application of his Jewish history. That Dryden professes ignorance of how the story will end would seem to confirm that his subject is contemporary. On the other hand, he supplies no ending to the biblical narrative which comprises his poem either, leaving us to recall the fate of Achitophel from our familiarity with Scripture. Whether we then proceed to apply this example to Shaftesbury's case is, Dryden seems to say, left up to us, but the force of historical analogy exists whatever we may do, and the story from Samuel seems not simply to illuminate the Popish Plot but in some manner to predetermine it. Of course, Dryden's ultimate concern is not to propound an abstract theory of history. He hopes to persuade us of two things: first, that the historical analogy before us is a good and proper one; and second, that the analogy is not an allegorical imperative required by the manipulative author but our thoughtful and uncoerced response to the lessons of history. To assure conviction of the second point, Dryden must leave us free to make our own historical applications but be very certain that we accept the principle that history teaches by example and that we are likely to apply the examples we may encounter.

The substantive arguments of the poem, which sharply distinguish legitimate ruler from rebel, provide Dryden with just this assurance that we will perform our proper function as readers. Achitophel bases his argument for Absalom on a repudiation of historical succession as an authenticating principle, elevating the will of the people above "a Successive Title, Long, and Dark, / Drawn from the Mouldy Rolls of *Noah's* Ark." It is Dryden himself who, with greater leisure and eloquence, affirms that historical succession alone can confer moral authenticity on power, an argument which serves simultaneously to legitimate the rule of King David and to justify the reader in making historical analogies—in perceiving Charles II as the moral successor of the Old Testament ruler. Thus we learn the "proper" formal maneuver for reading Dryden's poem by taking to heart its substantive teachings about history; but it is clear that the process may also work in reverse: if we are disposed to read Old Testament history analogically, we have already implicitly acquiesced to the substance of Dryden's defense of Stuart monarchy.

Dryden would like his reader to experience more independence than he really has in applying the historical examples of Scripture. John Bunyan's stance in *The Pilgrim's Progress* (1678, 1684) is quite the opposite, since he openly avows the strict allegorical nature of the personal history which he narrates. His work is, on the face of it, a traditional Christian allegory, whose true substance is the higher level of spiritual meaning, and whose apparent substance—the literal narrative—has the final insubstantiality of a means to an end. The sophistication of this technique is at odds with its pedagogic goal, a paradoxical quality which is strangely reminiscent of the risky but potentially rewarding indirection of Dryden's teaching method in *Absalom and Achitophel*. The concrete materialism of the literal narrative of Christian's history is essential as a means to lure the humble reader's understanding with the attractive bait of the everyday and the commonplace, yet the aim of this process is to persuade the reader to repudiate materialism

for higher things. Thus the idealism of Bunyan's allegorical
intention is, in theory, most effective when the material
"realism" of his historical narrative is most strongly felt.
What is extraordinary about *The Pilgrim's Progress* is that
Bunyan, by fulfilling these formal conditions of Christian
allegory more completely than others had done in the past,
comes dangerously close to subverting his allegorical aim.
The Pilgrim's Progress contains a literal narrative whose
very concreteness, designed to facilitate allegorical "translation" by signifying with clarity the spiritual level of meaning, threatens to preclude the translation process altogether
and to become both signifier and signified. From this perspective we may begin to understand the logic behind modern critics' disconcerting discovery of "realism" and historical concreteness in an author whose unquestionable intent
was to transcend history and to assert the Christian realism
of the spirit.

Bunyan's great work has a general kinship with the poetry
I have been discussing, the "transitional" quality of its
double attraction to the instructive methods of allegory and
history, but it also has a special capacity to reflect on the
future developments of English literature. What is expressed
by the strange formal tendency that we sense in *The Pilgrim's Progress* is not, of course, a subversive doctrinal bias
toward materialism. It is instead the impetus to forgo the
antimaterialism inherent in the allegorical form in order to
exploit more fully the powers of literal narrative to explicitly
instruct its readers in antimaterialism. The novels of Defoe
and Richardson inherit Bunyan's didactic concern with the
relation between flesh and spirit, material and spiritual success, but their didacticism is a direct and substantive expression of literal narrative rather than an implication of allegorical form. All readers of these early novels are familiar
with their insistent and highly conventional claim to the
status of "histories" as opposed to "romances." The seriousness of this claim is evident in the prefaces of a writer like
Defoe, who clearly evinces the belief that the moral justification of his narratives depends on the reader's acceptance

of their historicity, for it is only from history that morally edifying examples may be drawn and applied to one's own experience. This novelistic convention, and its replacement later on in the eighteenth century by a more modern standard of realism, leads us far from the subject of *Annus Mirabilis* and the wonderful year, to which we must now return; but the formal strategies of the early novel shed considerable light on all those transitional works of the later seventeenth century which seem to mediate between the pedagogic methods of allegory and history teaching by example.

Annus Mirabilis reconciles the antithetical wonder of the events of 1666 with God's greater historical plan in a manner that provides ideological support for Charles and his policies, but the reconciliation and its implicit ideology, inseparable in the total experience of the poem, may be distinguished in the process of rhetorical analysis. Many of Dryden's contemporaries were as interested as he in understanding the meaning of 1666. The ideological uses to which they put their understandings varied widely, but in the following chapters I will argue that the common attribute of the prophetic and eschatological frame of mind transcended all secondary differences.

6

DISSENTING PROPHECY

The speculations on the significance of the year 1666 which are my present subject owe their character to different, but reconcilable, traditions and techniques of numerological, astrological, and exegetical interpretation. An eschatological factor is common to all such speculations: not necessarily the belief that 1666 would mark the end of the world, but the belief that in this year would come the end of the old order or series of time and the beginning of the new. I will justify the inclusion of this kind of prophecy within the general category of eschatology by arguing that although the events predicted for 1666 seldom embrace the Day of Judgment or the destruction of all terrestrial life, they always bear a close relation to developments which ancient prophetic works and their exegetes traditionally have associated with the final stages of history—the recollection and conversion of the Jews, the Second Coming of Christ, the thousand-year reign of the saints upon earth, the destruction of Antichrist, and apocalyptic anticipations of Judgment. And when these developments themselves seem not to be forecast for 1666, they are nevertheless so clearly invoked by the language and aura of the prophecies with which we are concerned that what is predicted takes on the significance of eschatology, of the concrete and particular historical events which now fulfill the opaque and ambiguous specifications of ancient eschatological speculation.

In the long history of eschatological literature many dates

have attracted the attention of prophets, and some have
exceeded even 1666 in popularity.[1] The plausible computation of biblical numbers frequently was responsible for the
great popularity of certain dates.[2] In the case of 1666
computation was not even necessary for those exegetes who
had prophetic aspirations, since Revelation 13:18 said quite
clearly: "Let him that hath understanding count the number
of the beast: for it is the number of a man; and his number is
Six hundred threescore and six." That 1666 was equivalent
to 666 was not convincing to all interested observers. As one
cautious writer said, "The number 666, which of late has
made so much noise in the world, and is by many lookt upon
as fatal to this present year, I meet with in that Sacred Book,
but whether it must needs be applied to the course of time, &
if so, whether to our computation of the year, I have neither
the skill nor confidence to assert."[3] The exclusion of temporal schemes from many attempts to clarify the meaning of
the beast of Revelation's number has not lessened the ingenuity or exhaustiveness of exegesis.[4] If seventeenth-century
Puritans derived the number from the names of Anglican
bishops, seventeenth-century royalists were delighted to find
that the members of the rebellious English and Scottish
parliaments, or the words in the Solemn League and Covenant, added up to just 666.[5] And the extraordinary complex-

1. For convenient lists of eschatologically significant dates see Swan,
Speculum Mundi (1635), pp. 18–20, 22–24; Patrick, *Continuation* (1669),
pp. 140, 142; Patrides, *Harvard Theological Review*, 51 (1958), 170, 171;
Cooper, *Baptist Quarterly*, 18 (1960), 351–62, 19 (1961), 29–34.

2. E.g., 1656: see *Clavis Apocalyptica* (1651), pp. 35–36; Vaughan, *Pro-
tectorate* (1838), letter to Thurloe, Mar. 17 or 18, 1655, I, 156–57; Lilly,
Merlini (1656), sig. A4r; Benlowes, *Summary* (1657), sig. A2v; Swan,
Speculum Mundi (1665), p. 484.

3. Tully, *Letter* (1666), pp. 13–14.

4. See, e.g., Bongus, *Petri Bungi* (1591), pp. 623–33; Potter, *Interpretation of the Number 666* (1642), passim (cf. Pepys's reaction to Potter,
Diary, Nov. 4, 10, 1666, VI, 50, 58); Napier, *Plaine Discovery* (1645), pp.
44–45; Sadler, *Times of the Bible* (1667), 2nd pagination, p. 9; Thom,
Number and Names (1848), passim; Begley, *Biblia Cabalistica* (1903),
pp. 119–25.

5. See KLEIS (1660), p. 15; Berkenhead, *Assembly-Man* (1663) (*Harl.
Misc.* [1812], V, 100); Heath, *Brief Chronicle* (1663), p. 832, *Chronicle*
(1676), p. 500; Poor Robin, *Almanack* (1666), sig. C6v, *Almanack* (1667),
sig. A4r. Cf. *List of the Princes* (1652).

ity of medieval numerology and astrological symbolism was often called in to buttress more mundane arguments on the authenticity and morality of contemporary figures.[6] But with the approach of 1666, most commentators who delved into the mysteries of the number of the beast could not avoid the temptation to apply their researches "to the course of time." Other factors—historical, numerological, astrological —gave support to these researches. Was speculation on the wonderful, eschatological significance of 1666 the special province of people who were radically disaffected with the civil and religious settlement of the Restoration, or did it transcend group distinctions and factional affiliations?

After the return of Charles, it was a common royalist-Anglican accusation that those who were dissatisfied with the present state of affairs used the language and even the pretense of religion to conceal their intentions against the civil government. Thus, at the Restoration one writer asserted that "the mask of Religion in the face of Rebellion, will no longer serve to hide some mens detestable deformities in their damnable designes."[7] Another asked: "what hath been the occasion of all our former disturbances for several years together? was it not Rebellion, and Rebellion under a mask of Religion?"[8] In 1662 Clarendon told Lords that "there is a very great Party of those Men in every Faction of Religion, who truly have no Religion but as the Pretence serves to advance that Faction."[9] Roger L'Estrange, the greatest proponent of this argument, gave it a variety of succinct formulations:

A *Tumult* for *Religion*, is within one step of *Rebellion* . . .
   By *PRESBYTERIAN*, I intend a *Faction*, that under colour of setling a Reform'd *DISCIPLINE*, seeks to dissolve the frame of an establish'd *Government* . . .

6. See, e.g., Matthew, KAROLOU (1660, 1664), pp. 64–96. For an extended numerological commentary see Heydon, *Holy Guide* (1662), II passim.
7. Matthew, KAROLOU (1660, 1664), p. 153.
8. Marriot, *Rebellion Unmasked* (1661), p. 3.
9. *LJ*, May 19, 1662, XI, 476.

All Popular Factions take the *Church* in their way to the *State* . . .

. . . what did the late King Grant; or rather, what Deny? . . . what assurance [from the people] Words could give him, he wanted not: Words wrapt up in the most tender and Religious Forms imaginable. But what are Words where a Crown lyes at stake?[10]

Prophesying, either directly or through the publicizing of prodigies whose significations forewarned of God's intentions, constituted for royalists one of the most dangerous of dissent's religious pretenses. As the astrologer John Gadbury observed of contemporary "enthusiasts," "the Visions and Revelations they lay claim unto, and pretend an interest in, proceed rather from Envy then Frenzy; and . . . under pretence of these matters, masking their intentions with the glittering Vizard of Religion, . . . they designe to act over their old Villanies again in these Kingdoms."[11] Any man enamoured of his own "private Party and Opinion," John Spencer wrote, "will need no great Rhetorick to perswade him to receive a Prodigy . . . as a sign from heaven to encourage any seditious endeavours to advance it."[12] This is both the power and the danger of prophecy, as Hobbes testified:

You know there is nothing that renders human counsels difficult, but the uncertainty of future time; nor that so well directs men in their deliberations, as the foresight of the sequels of their actions; prophecy being many times the principal cause of the event foretold. If, upon some prediction, the people should have been made confident that Oliver Cromwell and his army should be, upon a day to come, utterly defeated; would not every one have endeavoured to assist, and to deserve well of the party that should give him that defeat? Upon this account it was that fortune-tellers and astrologers were so often banished out of Rome.[13]

10. *Interest Mistaken* (1661), sig. A7r, pp. 113–14, 170, 171. While L'Estrange and others attribute seditious intent to religious dissenters who use language deceptively, the spiritual discourse of the "enthusiasts" who are satirized in a tract occasioned by Venner's Rising is Swiftian in its unconscious self-reduction to coarse sexuality: see *Holy Sisters Conspiracy* (1661), pp. 3, 4.
11. *Dies Novissimus* (1664), p. 19.
12. *Discourse* (1665), sig. a3v.
13. *Behemoth* (1681, 1889), p. 188.

Sixteenth- and seventeenth-century legislation against prophecy indicates that modern Englishmen, like ancient Ro-
mans, appreciated its self-fulfilling power.[14]

In the restoration year, collections of prodigies—apparitions seen in the air, strange reversals and perversions of
natural laws, the sudden expiration of well-known men—
were already being printed with explanatory commentary
whose interpretation of the prodigies clearly revealed the
collections to be the work of men dissatisfied with the return
of Stuart monarchy and Anglican episcopacy. A notorious[15]
publication of this sort was Henry Jessey's *The Lord's loud
call to England,* which provided a model for the three
Mirabilis Annus tracts of the next two years.[16] The lengthy
history of the seizure and prosecution of these tracts can be
traced in the *Calendar of State Papers, Domestic,*[17] and in
L'Estrange's polemics against published sedition which appeared in the early years of the decade.[18] The first of the
Mirabilis Annus tracts accounted for the large number of
prodigies in the wonderful year of 1660–61 by several different arguments—for example, by suggesting that although
God "hath suffered this year so many *hundreds,* if not

14. See Taylor, *Political Prophecy* (1911), pp. 104–7; Dick, *Tomkis'
Albumazar* (1944), pp. 25–27; Rusche, *Eng. Hist. Rev.,* 84 (1969), 753n2.
15. Cf. Wood, *Life and Times* (1891), I, 322–23, 379; *History and
Antiquities* (1796), II, 703–8; Foulis, *History* (1662), p. 233. See Hart,
Index Expurgatorius (1878), no. 215, p. 179.
16. *ENIAYTOS TERASTIOS. Mirabilis Annus* (1661); *Mirabilis Annus
Secundus; or, The Second Year of Prodigies* (1662); *Mirabilis Annus Secundus: or, The Second Part of the Second Years Prodigies* (1662).
17. Original documents are in PRO SP 29/38(56, 57, 58), 29/39(132),
29/41(40, 41, 42), 29/43(7, 8, 9, 30, 130), 29/45(28, 74, 75), 29/47(55),
29/56(135), 29/75(117), 29/81(73, 731, II, III, IV), *Entry Book,* 5, p. 39.
Earliest documents bear the date June 29, 1661. See also Hart, *Index Expurgatorius* (1878), no. 219, pp. 183–88. These documents refer to the three
Mirabilis Annus tracts by a variety of names, and Kitchin (*L'Estrange*
[1913], p. 113) is incorrect in regarding "*Several Prodigies and Apparitions*"
as distinct from them. Similarly, what Wing (*Short-Title Catalogue* [1951])
calls "Several prodigies & apparitions" (Wing S2798), listing a unique copy
at the Royal College of Physicians, London, is in fact a copy of *ENIAYTOS*
missing the title page (sig. A1r–A1v) and two sheets of illustrations usually
inserted between the "Preface" (sig. A4v) and the beginning of the main
text (sig. B1r). Wing takes the subtitle on sig. B1r as the title, probably
from the card catalogue of the Royal College of Physicians.
18. See *Modest Plea* (1661), pp. 11–15; *King. Intell.,* Oct. 14–21, 1661;
Truth and Loyalty (1662), pp. 57–58; *Considerations* (1663), pp. 5, 16.

Frontispiece to *ENIAYTOS TERASTIOS* (1661), illustrating some of the exotic and ominous prodigies reported or prophesied in the tract. Courtesy of the Harvard College Library.

thousands of our able, godly, *preaching Ministers* to be *removed into corners,* yet the defect of their Ministry hath been *eminently* supplied by the *Lords* immediate preaching to us from *Heaven,* in the great and wonderful works of his Providence . . ."[19] This, and less veiled connections between God's warnings and the sins of the Anglican settlement, neither deceived nor amused unsympathetic readers like the royalist Anthony Wood, the Presbyterian Richard Baxter, and assorted astrologers and court propagandists, who eagerly pointed out the seditious possibilities of this literary form and of the three tracts in particular.[20] In 1665 John Spencer's volume on the timely subject of prodigies countered the tracts' implication of imminent revolutions destructive of the established state by observing—less than candidly, considering the year—that "never did those three National Felicities, *Peace, Health, Plenty,* more bless our habitations in any much longer period of time: so that we have almost seen the *Annus mirabilis* happily refuted by a *Seculum mirabile.*"[21]

Spencer ironically transforms this phrase, whose dissident implications are clear in the isolated context of the *Mirabilis Annus* tracts, into an affirmation of the status quo. Can this somewhat cynical transformation be taken as a model of how Dryden defends court policy in *Annus Mirabilis?* My analysis in Chapter 5 would suggest that it cannot, that when Spencer says the tracts persuade us "that *England* is grown *Africa*"[22] he comes too close to describing the effect of Dryden's poem as well for us to regard it with confidence as the kind of urbane attack on superstition that Spencer's

19. *ENIAYTOS* (1661), sig. A2v.
20. See Wood, *Life and Times* (1891), Jan., Mar. 31, 1661, Feb. 18, Apr. 13, 1662, I, 378, 387–88, 431, 433, 437; Baxter, *Reliq. Baxt.* (1696), II, 432–33; Booker, *Telescopium* (1662), sig. A5r–A6r; Lilly, *Merlini* (1662), sig. A2r–A3r, *Merlini* (1663), sig. A2r–A3r; *Merc. Pub.,* no. 27, July 2–9, 1663. Cf. Petrus Serrarius's favorable notice of the tracts in *Awakening Warning* (1662), pp. 19–20.
21. *Discourse* (1665), p. 102. This passage dates from 1665 and not from the first ed. of 1663. For other allusions to the three tracts see pp. 394ff, 399–400.
22. Ibid., sig. A6r.

work so often is. Our reading of the poem cannot, however, be taken as evidence of its own plausibility. For this we require further study of contemporary prophecy—to begin with, dissident prophecy which is more clearly directed at the wonderful year of 1666.

For many years the prophecy of biblical disasters had been a distinctively Puritan occupation, and its practice did not cease after the Restoration. A multitude of dissenting tracts prophesied the imminent burning of London with startling accuracy but neglected to specify the precise date of the catastrophe.[23] More significantly, there was a long tradition of sectarian prophecy that eschatological revolutions would begin or occur in the year of 1666. These prophecies were most often based upon a computation of biblical numbers much more complex than the addition of a unit to the number of the beast of Revelation. As an interested observer of Fifth Monarchist customs reported, "in their Lectures and chief Conventicles you might have heard such raptures, that you would have thought it were a reading on Astrology, but that the blessed name of our Saviour is so often used by them . . . Months, weeks, daies, and half-times, and such like Chronology alwaies past away their mad hours of meeting . . ."[24]

One of the most influential works that used the mystical numbers of Daniel and Revelation to argue the eschatological significance of 1666 was Henry Archer's *The Personall Reign of Christ upon Earth,* which was printed in 1642 and reprinted for the fourth time in 1661. In a series of computations of the length of the world's great kingdoms Archer revealed the sense of Scripture to be that the deliverance of the Jews would occur in 1650 or 1656, the destruction of Rome—the Antichrist—in 1666, and the Coming of Christ,

23. See, e.g., D. Baker, *Certaine Warning* (1659), pp. 6, 7; J. H., *Englands Alarm* (1659), p. 4; Biddle, *Warning* (1660), p. 1; H. Smith, *Vision* (1660), p. 2; *Strange News* (1661), sig. A3r; *Two most Strange Wonders* (1662), p. 10; Bayly, *Great and Dreadful Day* (1664); Wither, *Memorandum* (1665), p. 12, *Ecchoes* (1666), p. 149; Roe, *God's Judgments* (1666), p. 17. Elias Ashmole was impressed enough by Smith's prophecy to make a copy of it: *Ashmole Collection* (1966), III, 1070n2.
24. Pagitt, *Heresiography* (1662), p. 282.

his raising of the dead, and the inauguration of his thousand-year reign upon earth around 1700.[25] "Thus wee have some comfort, in that there is hope the troubles on us *Gentile Christians* shall cease about 666. But untill those dayes, wee are like to see sad times, even till *Anno Domini* 1666. For it is to be feared, that Poperie shall againe over-run *Europe*, and bring backe under Papall power every Kingdome in *Europe*, and so suppresse all opposers in every Kingdome by Papall power . . ."[26] Archer's prophecy of the Fifth Monarchy of Christ upon earth seems to have been well known in England[27] and generally characteristic of the beliefs of Fifth Monarchy Men and other eschatologically minded radical sectarians. Thus a tract of 1650 that criticized Archer and "the Millenaries" for their belief in Christ's personal reign agreed that Rome would be destroyed around 1666, but placed the conversion of the Jews in the period of 1683–1698 and envisioned in 1700 Christ's salvation of the world through the inspiration of his ministers, "the ministeriall (not personall) Reign and Kingdom of Christ upon Earth," not forever or for a thousand years, "but for a very short time."[28]

During the years of the Civil Wars, proponents of Fifth Monarchist doctrine continued to attribute eschatological significance to 1666. In the idiosyncratic writings of John Rogers, Scripture was explicated with England's eventual escape from the tyranny of the Norman yoke firmly in mind. Rogers disposed of one of the more vexing exegetical problems of Daniel by identifying the little horn of the fourth beast as William the Conqueror; the Norman line and the fourth monarchy thus were extinguished by "the *fatall stroke* given to *Charles Stuart*" in 1649, which prepared the way for the rise of the Fifth Monarchy.[29] As the disappoint-

25. See *Personall Reign* (1642), pp. 46–47, 52, 53–54, 56, 57.
26. Ibid., pp. 54–55.
27. See, e.g., Alsted, *Worlds* (1642), p. 12; Hall, *Revelation Unrevealed* (1650), p. 94; *Brief Description* (1650), sig. A2r–A2v; Pepys, *Diary* (1904), Feb. 18, 1666, V, 226 (pace Braybrooke's note).
28. *Brief Description* (1650), sig. A2v; see also pp. 18–19.
29. Rogers, *Sagrir* (1653), pp. 125, 129. See Dan. 7:8, 8:9.

ments of interregnum government unfolded, Rogers urged England's leaders, with increasing desperation, "to *model* and *conforme* the *Civil affaires* for *Christs coming*," and by 1657 the Protectorate itself had become the last manifestation of the fourth monarchy which the establishment of the fifth would overturn.[30] Cromwell's government, Rogers wrote, revealed "all the Characters of Anti-christ," and he warned London: "thou City! and Seat of the second Beast! next to Rome mayst thou look for the Wrath upon thee!"[31] Thus for Rogers, at any rate, the eschatological inauguration of the Fifth Monarchy had local implications for the commonwealth of England. As far as chronology was concerned, his computations were generally in accord with those of Archer. The time of *"universal restitution"* might be set at around 1690 or 1700, but "within these seaven yeares, by *one Thousand six hundred and sixty*, the worke will get as farre as *Rome*, and by *one thousand six hundred sixty six* this *Monarchy* must be *visible* in all the *earth* . . ."[32] In the analysis of another Fifth Monarchy Man, John Canne, the events of 1666 would have a broader and more absolute significance in the chronology of the last things: "As the *Antichristian State* shall be destroyed before or by the year 1660. and all that fulfilled which is set down, *Rev*. 18. so, not beyond the yeare 1666. shall the *Antichristians* themselves, and *worshippers of the Beast, escape the vengeance of the Lord, and of his Temple* . . . And here the Lord will put an end, and period to all the troubles of the *Gentile* Churches, not to goe beyond, or further then the *yeare* 1666."[33] For the millenarian William Burden, 1666 had an even simpler and more momentous import: "So may it be supposed that Christ will not destroy the power of Sathan the deceiver, until with patience hee hath waited, and born and suffered in himself and members, Sathans evils, 1666. years from his own birth . . . and the living then in the year of Christ,

30. *Sagrir* (1653), p. 136; *Jegar* (1657), pp. 68, 72.
31. *Jegar* (1657), p. 71; Canne, *Time of the End* (1657), preface by Rogers, sig. a6v.
32. *Ohel* (1653), p. 24; *Sagrir* (1653), pp. 124–25, 128–29.
33. *Voice From the Temple* (1653), pp. 24–25.

from the birth of Christ. 1666. shall be partakers of Iesus Christ his glorious reign for that 1000 years of the Devils confinement or imprisonment."[34]

Thus in the years which preceded the Restoration, sectarian yearnings for the restored Golden Age of the Fifth Monarchy frequently were linked to sectarian dissatisfaction with England's government, and frequently anticipated 1666 as an important year of revolutions. As Cromwell's secretary of state was informed in 1655, "Men variously impoverished by the long troubles, full of discontents, and tired by long expectation of amendment, must needs have great propensions to hearken to those that proclaim times of refreshing— a golden age—at hand, &c. Nor is it a wonder that some should willingly listen to those that publish such glad tidings, under the name of the kingdom of Christ and of the saints; . . . Nor need we wonder, if we find some confident that eleven years hence we shall see the fatal change, because of the number 666."[35] In 1656 William Aspinwall looked back to the work of Archer and others and recollected that their prophecies had met with little official alarm, "be[c]ause it was then a little more remote. But now, it is a matter of offence or scorn, to speak of such a Kingdom. And what should be the reason of the difference? The truth is the same then, and now. But the imminent approach of the time, and the publication of it, doth now terrifie carnal Spirits . . ."[36] In the following year Thomas Venner made his first attempt to usher in the Fifth Monarchy. In the paper that was spread about the streets of London to explain the reasons for his more ambitious rising in 1661, Venner wrote of "the great opinions of this year, the wonderfull effects it is like to produce, the sweet harmony and agreement of the Prophecies, . . . the wonderfull undeniable signs of the times . . ."[37] It was the purpose of the first of the *Mirabilis Annus* tracts to publicize these signs of the

34. *Christs Personal Reign On Earth* (1654), pp. 9, 10.
35. Vaughan, *Protectorate* (1838), letter to Thurloe, Mar. 17 or 18, 1655, I, 156–57.
36. *Legislative Power*, p. 50.
37. *Door of Hope* (1661), p. 2.

times, and to "let every one . . . from these things be convinced, that upon us the ends of the world are come, and
that God is now making hast *to consummate* his *whole* work
in the earth, and to prepare the way for his *Son to take unto
himself his great power and reign* . . ."[38] Other anonymous
papers specified the dates on which the great changes in
store would occur. One of these, associated with the abortive
plot to disrupt the coronation ceremonies in 1661, prophesied that "strange things . . . shall come to passe" in the
first decade of the Restoration, and that "in the year one
thousand six hundred and 70 shall be the day of Judgment."[39] Another announced that the "long expected year of
JUBILEE is at hand, wherein our Freedom from the great
Tyrant and *Oppressor* shall be made manifest . . . *The Day
of Vengeance,* and *Year of the Redeemed* are one . . ."
These "dark prophesies," says the writer, will be better
understood by all Englishmen in 1670; by all who suffer
under papal and Turkish tyranny in 1684; and by 1712, "the
very heathen shall appear to be the inheritance of Sions
King . . ."[40] George Fox, the founder of the Quakers, was
unimpressed by the Fifth Monarchy Men he had met, "whoe
lookt for Christ personall comeinge in :66: & some of ym did
prepare ymselves when it thundered & rained & thought
Christ was comeinge to sett uppe his kingedome . . ."[41]
The Dutch chiliast Petrus Serrarius drew a more sympathetic picture of the state of mind of those who perceived
the present conjunction of divine prodigies and biblical
computations:

. . . all the most excellent Chronologers, and Searchers of times,
. . . are become like a woman great with child; which having
passed the time of her reckoning, doth necessarily expect every
hour, the paines and labour of travel. And seeing that the mean
while those signes in Heaven and Earth break forth, and offer
themselves to open view, who cannot conceive that the next

38. *ENIAYTOS* (1661), sig. A4v.
39. Reported in *True Discovery* (1661), p. 3.
40. *News of a New World* (1663), pp. 7, 24.
41. Fox, *Journal* (1911), entry for 1661, II, 12.

change to follow as the expected birth, of which all the Prophets and Apostles have prophesied, is now before the door; and we are now duly warned, that we make our selves ready.[42]

The Fifth Monarchist doctrine, which derived from an allegorical reading of the Book of Daniel, was the basis of most eschatological prophecies regarding 1666, but its influence was not confined to formal adherents to the sect of Fifth Monarchy Men. Prophets who called themselves Independents, Quakers, Levellers, or who refused any denomination whatsoever, knew the language of biblical eschatology and expected great overturnings in 1666.[43]

Once the wonderful year had passed, critics of sectarian prophets were free to attack not only their seditious intent but also—somewhat inconsistently—their fond credulity: "And *you,* who dream't o'th' *Fall* of *Kings,* at last Grow *wise,* now *Sixty-Six* is past."[44] In 1669 Simon Patrick discussed the case of one prophet, who

tells you the 1260. years might begin in 406. or 410. after our Saviours Birth. If you take the former number, then the prophesying in sackcloth ended in 1666. the year when they expected great matters; and of which some confidently cryed to the people out of the Pulpits (before they left them) *Be patient, for 1666. will make an amends for all.* But it failing their expectation and producing nothing according to their mind; that's the reason I conceive why he hath since that, put in the year 410. for the beginning of the years 1260. and so adjourns us for their ending to 1670. which is now approaching.[45]

Those who favored the chronogrammatical technique of prophecy—the extraction of roman numerals from proper

42. *Awakening Warning* (1662), p. 37.
43. For a variety of sectarian prophecies centering on the year 1666 see Llwyd, *Gweithiau* (1899), "1648," p. 22; *Levellers Almanack* (1651), p. 6; Crook, *Glad-Tydings* (1662), p. 5; *Two most Strange Wonders* (1662), pp. 11–12; *Worthington Diary* (1847), I, 254n, Cotton Mather's account of John Sadler's prophecies in 1663; Add. MS. 29495, fol. 2v, W. Lodington, "To my Son E.G. . . ." (1665); *CSPD,* Jan. 5, 1666, p. 191.
44. Ford, *Londini* (1667), p. 9.
45. *Continuation,* pp. 124–25. The prophet is William Bridge: see *Seasonable Truths* (1668), pp. 113–14.

names and popular phrases and the construction of dates
therefrom—had noted frequently[46] the unique perfection of
MDCLXVI, a date which contained sequentially all of the
roman numerals. An antitolerationist recalled in 1668 that
shortly after the Act of Uniformity nonconformists had believed that the depopulation of pulpits would soon result in
their recall.

Then being willing to uphold their Party, (for want of better
things) they catch at the Rush of a fond Prophecy,
MDLLLVVII *BartholoLoMaeVs fLet qIa DesIt Presbyter AngLVs.*
    1662.
MDLCVVVI *ADVentV Laeta est sanCta MarIa tVo.*
    1666.
During the operation of this Prophecy they remained pretty silent;
till the time elapsed, and nothing effected, they saw it necessary
to spread a false report all the Country over, of a *Toleration* prepared for them.[47]

According to this writer, the expectation of change in 1666
was simply one more nonconformist peculiarity, like the
expectation of toleration—foolish but dangerous all the
same.

So far we have reviewed the evidence for regarding eschatological speculation, especially dealing with the year 1666,
as the exclusive practice of people dissatisfied with the
existing civil and religious government. We have recalled
the notoriety of the *Mirabilis Annus* tracts and similar publications of dissident sources and the convergence of Fifth
Monarchist interpretations of Scripture with radical sectarian propaganda and uprisings. Finally, we have seen how
often supporters of the established government attributed
spiritual protestations to civil designs, and how closely they
identified the act of prophecy with the seditious desire for a
change in church and state. But the status of prophecy after
the Civil Wars was unusual. The sectarian revival of He-
braic studies and the slow development of an empirical

46. See, e.g., Sadler, *Olbia* (1660), p. 178.
47. Philotheus, *Anarchie Reviving* (1668), pp. 11–12.

approach to nature and history did much to discredit it among Anglicans and new philosophers, yet Puritanism in its broadest sense altered England fundamentally, and in the seventeenth century the noblest work of empiricists lay in the reconciliation of the new discoveries with the old systems and correspondences. The ambiguous status of prophecy during this period suggests the danger of taking the terms of royalist-Anglican propaganda as an accurate portrayal of the contemporary state of language, not to mention belief. For although we have reviewed the evidence for associating prophecy and eschatology with civil and religious dissent, we have only sampled the store of eschatological thought during this period. In the following two chapters I will present other strains of this thought, some of it problematic in ideology, some of it clearly directed toward the royalist cause, in order to substantiate the argument that prophecy and eschatology were linguistic and epistemological properties of the generality of Dryden's contemporaries.

7

IDEOLOGICALLY
PROBLEMATIC PROPHECY

In 1663 one of the French ambassadors to England wrote home: "Voici le pays de prophètes; nous avons un autre Jérémie que ne parle que de feux et de flammes: on l'a mis en prison."[1] These statements might be taken to confirm the identification of prophecy as a dissenter's occupation, but royal panegyrists, as well as disaffected collectors of prodigies, seem to have been agreed that England was now the "Land of Wonders."[2] Similarly, a royalist collection of prodigies called *The Age of Wonders, or miracles are not ceased* and printed in the restoration year was confident that "not to ravel out the Scriptures which are full of such presidents, we need go no higher then the present times wherein we live, which may not unjustly be called *The Age of Wonders* . . ."[3] For many writers of diverse ideology, "the present

1. Jusserand, *French Ambassador* (1892), Dec. 10, 1663, p. 223. On the popularity of prophesying in England see also D. Lloyd, *Wonders no Miracles* (1666), p. 2; Taylor, *Political Prophecy* (1911), pp. 83, 84; Don Cameron Allen, *The Star-Crossed Renaissance* (Durham, N.C., 1941); Dick, *Tomkis' Albumazar* (1944), pp. 17–47; Rusche, *Eng. Hist. Rev.*, 84 (1969), 753; Royce MacGillivray, "The Use of Predictions in 17th-century Historians," *Cithara*, 8, no. 1 (Nov. 1968), 54–63; Christopher Hill, *Puritanism and Revolution* (London, 1968), pp. 311–23.

2. Cf. *Ourania* (1660) and *Two most Strange Wonders* (1662), p. 3.

3. P. 3. In the English trans. of a French historian, the author calls "this Age, the *Iron Age*, in regard that all the Evills, and Prodigies, have happened in this in grosse, which were in precedent Ages, but in retail": Parival, *Historie of this Iron Age* (1655, trans. 1659), sig. A4r. In explaining the Golden Age allusion in the title of *Astraea Redux*, the editors of Dryden, *Works* (1956), I, 219, use Parival's title as evidence "that the period before the Restoration was thought of as an 'iron age.'" This is

times wherein we live" were an "Age of Wonders."[4] Meric
Casaubon supported his argument to this effect by reference
to the beheading of Charles I, the Royal Oak preservation
and eventual restoration of Charles II, the plague, and the
fire.[5] What were the wonderful events witnessed or expected
in the 1660s which commanded the attention and concern of
people of all persuasions?

By far the most widely publicized wonder of 1666 was
centered not in England but in the Levant. This was the
climax of the career of the famous messianic figure Sabbatai
Sevi, believed by many Jews to be their long-awaited Messiah. According to the numerological calculations of Hebrew
scriptural exegesis, the year 1648 had special status in the
continuing expectation of the coming of the Messiah. At
least one man in the Middle East, Sabbatai, declared himself
to be the Savior in that year, but he achieved little recognition or following. When Sabbatai renewed his claims eighteen years later, the astonishing response to him drew at
least a portion of its force from the coincidence of his
proclamation with diverse Christian expectations for the
wonderful year of 1666, among them the hope that this year
would see the final recollection and conversion of the Jews.
The events surrounding Sabbatai's messianic advent in 1665
occasioned at least ten English tracts devoted entirely to the
subject and scores of shorter notices in a variety of written
forms. Taken together, these sources span a period from the
summer of 1665 to the summer of 1667 and provide the
material for a history of the events in the Levant as they
became known to English observers. This history I have

---

deceptive, since there is no reason to suppose that either Parival or his
translator looked to Charles Stuart's restoration for the return of Astraea.
The history is more precisely understood as evidence that the middle years
of the 17th century were thought of as an Iron Age.

4. See, e.g., O. Lloyd, *Panther-Prophesy* (1662), sig. A2r; Rollins, *Pack
of Autolycus* (1927), "Warning" (1664), p. 135; Charpentier, *Treatise*
(1664), p. 21; Howell, *Poems* (1664), "Upon a Rare . . . TRACY-HIS-
TORY" (1655), p. 35; Glanvill, *Blow* (1668), p. 2.

5. *Of Credulity and Incredulity* (1668), pp. 199–200.

recounted elsewhere,[6] but it will be useful to summarize some of its implications for the understanding of *Annus Mirabilis* and the comprehensiveness of contemporary eschatological thought.

The Sabbatian movement fascinated many English observers because it involved the two vital concerns of eschatology and—since it was widely feared that the wholesale departure of the Jews for the Levant would have commercial repercussions—foreign trade. These concerns are central to *Annus Mirabilis* as well. The history of Sabbatai's great year recalls all of the Old Testamentary elements in Dryden's poem: Albemarle's miraculous means of escaping the Dutch, Rupert's messianic status, the parallel with God's chosen people which extends to the final prophecy of the New Jerusalem in London. And if it is not as difficult to find overtly ironic or suspicious treatments of the eschatological vision in the English reception of Sabbatai's career as it is in *Annus Mirabilis,* the predominant attitude in reports from the Levant and in discussions of their significance is one of sustained and open-minded interest. Of course, official sources like the *Gazette* mixed their accounts with dubious and scornful reflections on the truthfulness of their informants and the rationality of Sabbatai's followers, and the credulity of the English was often directly proportionate to the apparent likelihood that the "Messiah's" ascendancy was an obscure but divine technique for obtaining the conversion of the Jews to Christ. But Scripture testified that the conversion of the Jews was to be one of the last things, and although Sabbatai's history may have appealed most to Fifth Monarchy Men whose beliefs and activities were discredited by the Restoration establishment, contemporary speculation on the Sabbatian movement indicates that in the seventeenth century one need not have been a literal millenarian

6. See my unpublished Columbia University Ph.D. dissertation, "Meanings of Dryden's *Annus Mirabilis*" (1972), pp. 296–300, 378–87. On the general subject of Sabbatai, see Gershom Scholem's monumental work, *Sabbatai Sevi, the Mystical Messiah, 1626–1676,* trans. R. J. Zwi Werblowsky (Princeton, N.J., 1973).

to read the Bible and register interest in the evident signs of the times. People of diverse backgrounds and commitments —royalists, republicans, amateur scientists, professional astrologers, Puritan prophets—were ready to entertain news of him with some enthusiasm, and many made a natural and ingenuous connection in their minds between the news of Sabbatai and the other wonders and judgments which they, among others, anticipated for 1666.[7]

One of these wonders was the case of Valentine Great-rakes, the Irish healer. The brief period of Greatrakes' fame began in the summer of 1665, when the archbishop of Dublin, having heard of his strange but wonderfully success-ful method of curing patients by stroking their diseased parts, sent for him to be examined "by a very eminent divine."[8] A modest and unassuming man, Greatrakes was astounded to have been chosen by God, who had (it would seem) appeared to him one night and announced: *"I have given thee ye gift of healing . . ."*[9] In Dublin he disclaimed the use of charms "or any Contract with the devill," and it was reported that "the Clergy have not yet thought fitt to prohibit him finding him free from endeavoring by his ad-vantage to propagate any ffaction or private opinion and that he Exhorts all he Cures to give the glory to God and oft times casts up a short ejaculation for a blessing on them . . ."[10] Although skeptical himself, the archbishop recommended Greatrakes to the Viscount Conway, whose wife suffered from debilitating headaches. According to the archbishop, the stroker's gift already had gotten the better of

7. See, e.g., *New Letter from Aberdeen* (1665), pp. 2, 6 [mispaginated 3]; *Restauration of the Jewes* (1665), pp. 3–4; *Last Letters* (1665), p. 3; *Jewes Message* (1665), pp. 3–4; Harl. MS. 3785, fol. 66, S. Foster to Dean Sancroft, Dec. 1665; Homes, *Miscellanea* (1666), pp. 3–4; Lilly, *Merlini* (1667), sig. A2r–A4v.

8. Add. MS. 4182, fol. 29v, July 29, 1665 (anon. newsletter journal). Contemporaries spelled the name in a variety of ways, e.g., Greatrakes, Greatrake, Greatricks, Greatrax, Greatrix, Greatres, Greatarick, Greatrixt, Graterix, Gratrix, Grattix, Gertrux, Gretricks, Greotrates.

9. Greatrakes denies having said this in his *Brief Account* (1666), pp. 6–7, but see Bod. B.15.8. Linc., copy of letter from Greatrakes to bishop of Chester, ca. Aug. 1665.

10. Add. MS. 4182, fols. 29v–30, July 29, 1665.

his modesty—"he now dreams of nothing but converting the Jew and Turk"—but unlike some of his followers, Greatrakes lacked any potential for sedition.[11] Conway had heard of him when Greatrakes was curing the earl of Orrery of gout and had sent his friend Dr. George Rust to persuade the healer to journey to England, supplementing this effort with the request made to the archbishop.[12] In September 1665 Henry Oldenburg, the indefatigable joint-secretary of the Royal Society, learned from one of his many correspondents that Greatrakes "has confessd yt formerly he did use charmes, and tis Knowne, yt he did likewise study magick, but as he now sais, he makes use of neither . . . he has attempted the Blind and to raise ye dead, but faild—any woman with child presently miscarries at his first touch, wch he cannot prevent, & therefor gives ym notice."[13] In December Greatrakes prepared for the trip to England and the Conway estate at Ragley.[14]

Anne, Viscountess Conway was a learned woman whose circle of friends included the Cambridge Platonists Henry More, Ralph Cudworth, and Benjamin Whichcote. These distinguished men and others were present at Ragley during the period of the Irish healer's attempt to cure Lady Conway of her headaches, and they observed his method with great interest.[15] But on February 9, 1666, Lord Conway wrote sorrowfully to his friend George Rawdon: "Mr. Greatrax hath been here a fortnight to-morrow, and my wife is not the better for him . . . after all this I am far from thinking . . . that his cures are at all miraculous: but I believe it is by a *sanative virtue* and a *natural efficiency* . . ."[16] Nevertheless, Conway's opinion of Greatrakes' powers remained

11. *CSP Ire.*, Michael Boyle, archbishop of Dublin, to Conway, July 29, 1665, pp. 615–16 (*Conway Letters* [1930], no. 164, pp. 262–63).
12. *Conway Letters* (1930), no. 163, Conway to George Rawdon, July 26, 1665, pp. 260–62 (*Rawdon Papers* [1819], p. 205), no. 168, Conway to Heneage Finch [?], Aug. 1665, p. 266.
13. *Oldenburg Letters* (1965), no. 405, Sept. 4, 1665, II, 496.
14. *Conway Letters* (1930), no. 169, Greatrakes to Rawdon, Dec. 9, 1665, pp. 266–67 (*Rawdon Papers* [1819], pp. 207–9).
15. See ibid., p. 248.
16. Ibid., no. 170, pp. 267–68 (*Rawdon Papers* [1819], pp. 212–14).

high. He was greatly impressed by some of the cures which had been worked during the healer's stay at Ragley, expressed confidence in Greatrakes' ability to cure the aging Jeremy Taylor, and was happy to recommend him to others whose particular complaints might be more susceptible to the stroking which had failed on Lady Conway.[17] Henry More wrote of the benefit that Cudworth's son had derived from Greatrakes' exertions,[18] and later expanded on his virtues: "truly he seems to me such an Exemplar of candid and sincere Christianity, without any pride, deceit, sourness, or superstition; to which let me add his working such wonderful at least, if not properly called Miracles, as the Church of *Rome* in no age could ever produce for their Religion."[19]

In fact the episode at Ragley only improved Greatrakes' reputation, which was beginning now to spread throughout the rest of England. A correspondent of William Sancroft, dean of St. Paul's, enclosed with his own letter one he had received from a fellow Cantabrigian and asked Sancroft for what "you have of More of his Miracles."[20] As this request would suggest, the enclosed letter concerned Greatrakes. It recounted the events at Lord Conway's according to the testimony of three "University" men, who witnessed there the cure, in one day, of "above an 100 of severall diseases." The letter went on to describe Greatrakes as "a civil, Ingenuous, Debonair Gentleman. But very sober & temperate; An honest Protestant, a Conformable man, and in his County High-Sheriff." It concluded with the judgment that the whole matter was "very strange & prodigious" and with the information that the healer planned to return to Ireland after a short stay in Gloucester.[21]

17. Ibid., no. 170, pp. 267–68, no. 176, Conway to E. Dering, June 20, 1666, pp. 274–75, and Conway to Rawdon, Feb. 1666, p. 255; *CSP Ire.*, Rawdon to Conway, Feb. 21, Mar. 3, 1666, pp. 44, 52; *Rawdon Papers* (1819), Greatrakes to Conway, received May 3, 1666, pp. 210–12.

18. *Conway Letters* (1930), no. 174, More to Lady Conway, Apr. 28, 1666, p. 273.

19. More, *Collection* (1712), scholia on *Enthusiasmus Triumphatus*, p. 53.

20. Harl. MS. 3785, fol. 109, S. Foster to Dean Sancroft, Feb. 19, 1666.

21. Harl. MS. 3785, fol. 111–111v, J. Felton to Foster, Feb. 6, 1666.

The true and liuely Pourtraicture of Valentine Greatrakes Esq.r
of Affane in y.e County of Waterford, in y.e Kingdome of Ireland.
famous for curing several Deseases and distempers
by the stroak of his Hand only.

Portrait of Valentine Greatrakes, the Irish stroker. Reprinted from Greatrakes, *Brief Account* (1666), by permission of the Trustees of the British Museum, London.

As Greatrakes' journal for April 6–15, 1666, and its marginal account of wonderful new cures indicates,[22] this plan
was not carried out. The mixed notices of his English strok-
ings which had begun in the fall of 1665 continued through
the following spring,[23] and if some reported that several of
his patients "decry him," others referred to Greatrakes, half
facetiously and half in earnest, as "the man of miracles, the
7th brother, who opens the eyes of those that have been
blind for many years, and cures cancers in the breast, which
he seldom fails in."[24] At the end of February 1666 Greatrakes went to London, and he was soon attracting such
crowds to his lodgings that "scarsly one could enter in."[25]
When Charles heard of the Irish healer's presence he
ordered Arlington to summon Greatrakes to court.[26] According to some sources, Charles hoped to obtain the cure of
Sir John Denham's madness, which had developed suddenly
and was to disappear just as quickly within a year or two.[27]
According to others, Charles thought little of Greatrakes and
his cures.[28] Furthermore, "Sir John Denham is now stark
mad, which is occasioned . . . by the rough striking of
Greatrakes upon his limbs . . ."[29] Whatever the facts surrounding this episode in the famous stroker's career, his
popularity in England continued at least through the end of
the year, when Orrery's son wrote that "Mr. Graterix was

22. See Add. MS. 4293, fols. 50–53.
23. See *Oldenburg Letters* (1965), no. 431, Oct. 10, 1665, II, 561;
Hatton Correspondence (1878), Mar. 1666, I, 49; *HMC* 6th Rept., Apr. 9,
1666, p. 339; *Worthington Diary* (1847), II, 215–17.
24. PRO SP 29/151(23), Muddiman newsletter, Mar. 15, 1666; *HMC*
7th Rept., letter of Feb. 12, 1666, p. 464.
25. Add. MS. 10117, fol. 157v, entry for Apr. 9, 1666; *CSPD*, Muddiman
newsletter, Mar. 1, 1666, p. 281; Greatrakes, *Brief Account* (1666), pp.
39–40.
26. *Rawdon Papers* (1819), p. 210n.
27. *CSP Ire.*, Mar. 3, 1666, p. 52. On Denham's madness see Temple,
Works (1750), letter of Sept. 26, 1667, II, 135; Aubrey, *Brief Lives* (1950),
p. 93; S. Butler, *Poetical Works* (1893), "A Panegyric upon Sir John
Denham's Recovery from his Madness," II, 169–72.
28. *HMC* 6th Rept., letter of Apr. 9, 1666, p. 339.
29. Ibid., letter of Apr. 17, 1666, p. 339.

here for some four or five days and did many *curs* before my father, and I do now believe he can do merickles."[30]

The humorous aspects of Greatrakes' progress in 1666 should not obscure the seriousness with which many observers followed it. Several tracts were printed disputing the miraculous nature of the Irish healer's cures. Henry Stubbe, who later devoted great effort to attacking the Royal Society, published a tract in the form of a letter to Robert Boyle, the intention of which was to provoke fellows of the Society and members of the clergy into public debate.[31] At the end of the tract he wrote: "I might now end this Letter, and leave You, & those other worthy members of the *Royal Society* to determine concerning these Effects, which I apprehend miraculous . . ."[32] Boyle was not amused by Stubbe's baiting, and while he admired Greatrakes, he would never presume to think him a miracle worker.[33] But Stubbe was on firm ground in requiring a justification of their beliefs not only from the Anglican clergy but also from the Royal Society: as Greatrakes said in a letter to Lord Conway of April 1666, "The *Virtuosi* have been daily with me since I writ to your honor last, and have given me large and full testimonials, and God has been pleased to do wonderful things in their sight, so that they are my hearty and good friends . . . I have hardly a testimonial but there is the hands of 2 or 3 doctors of physic to it."[34] Among the well-known figures whose testimonials Greatrakes printed in

30. *HMC* 4th Rept., letter of Dec. 18, 1666, p. 280. Cf. Wood, *Life and Times* (1891), II, 54.

31. See the MS. note on the page preceding the BM copy (551.b.11.[2.]) of Stubbe, *Miraculous Conformist* (1666); Wood, *Athenae* (1692), s.v. "Henry Stubbe."

32. *Miraculous Conformist* (1666), p. 8.

33. Birch, *Life of Boyle* (1741), pp. 157–58. Cf. More's allusion to Stubbe's tract, *Conway Letters* (1930), no. 171, letter to Lady Conway, Mar. 17, 1666, pp. 269–70. Cf. the development in Oldenburg's estimate of Greatrakes in his correspondence with Boyle, *Oldenburg Letters* (1965), nos. 412, 430, 497, Sept. 18, Oct. 10, 1665, Mar. 13, 1666, II, 512–13, 556, III, 59.

34. *Conway Letters* (1930), no. 173, received May 3, 1666, pp. 272–73 (*Rawdon Papers* [1819], pp. 210–11).

his general apology for himself were the Royal Society fellows Rust, Boyle, and John Wilkins, the joint-secretary, whose impromptu experiments on some of the healer's patients are attested to in Greatrakes' tract.[35] The enthusiasm of another fellow, Henry More, has already been noted. In his pamphlet aimed at demonstrating that "such *Miracles* as are only *strange,* and *unaccountable* performances, above the common *methods* of *art* or *nature* are not *ceas'd,*" Joseph Glanvill went so far as to quote Dr. Rust that "the great discourse now at the Coffee-Houses, and every where, is about Mr. G. the famous *Irish Stroker* . . ." and to add that "many of those *matters* of *Fact,* have been since *critically inspected* and *examined* by several *sagacious* and *deep* searches of the ROYAL SOCIETY, whom we may suppose as unlikely to be deceived by a *contrived Imposture,* as any persons extant."[36]

Greatrakes' *Brief Account* of himself was occasioned by a tract which criticized the carelessness with which the word "miraculous" was being applied to the Irish healer's successes: "And to deal plainly with you, Sir, the very time of the pretence is suspicious, it being a time of great Expectations among all men, and of strange Impressions upon very many; the very imagination of strange alterations in the world, makes strange alterations upon mens thoughts and spirits; it's no wonder, when all men look for a year of Miracles, that one man should attempt to begin it." David Lloyd, the author of this tract, was perhaps disturbed at rumors that Greatrakes had attracted a following of undesirables who would be eager to support any scheme, however seditious, which the healer might announce as sanctioned by God: "if the man saith now, *I received a voice from Heaven, bidding me Cure all Diseases;* he *may if this take,* say anon, *I am Commissioned by a Voice from Heaven, to reduce the World to the unity of the* Roman *Church, to teach the infallibility of the Pope, to reveal a Messiah to come, a fifth Monarchy, and what not?*" But so far from

35. See Greatrakes, *Brief Account* (1666), pp. 43–96.
36. *Blow* (1668), pp. 84–85, 89.

doubting that the divine hand ever made itself felt directly in this world, Lloyd considered Greatrakes a dangerous influence for another reason as well—"for men deluded by these jugglers of false Miracles, are shaken in their belief of true ones."[37]

Lloyd is not clear on how the honest man is to distinguish the false from the true miracle, but another tract in this general controversy[38] which may in turn have occasioned Lloyd's was quite content to do without the term "miracle" as long as Greatrakes' wonders received their proper recognition within the context of the wonderful year. The prefatory section of this tract observed that some ascribed his gifts "to the Providence of God, and as Forerunners of those great things which they expect in that great year of Expectation 1666."[39] And one of the following documents made this judgment on the significance of the Greatrakes affair: "Upon the whole, the thing is wonderful, & stupendious, and astonishing, and makes us as men in a dream, when we think or speak of it: And we cannot but conclude, that God is about to do some great work in the World, and that this is but the forerunner of some great things which we may shortly see, unto which we desire to stand prepared. It is clear, that these 1500. years at least, we cannot hear of any instance of the like nature."[40]

In our review of Fifth Monarchist predictions for 1666 we saw that this was the "great year of Expectation" not only because of the appearances of Sabbatai Sevi and Valentine Greatrakes but also because the computation of biblical numbers confirmed its eschatological significance. And it must be noticed here that what Fifth Monarchy Men expected in 1666 was less often the destruction of whichever

37. D. Lloyd, *Wonders no Miracles* (1666), pp. 11–12 (see also p. 21), 4–5, 7.
38. Greatrakes was the subject of a number of more ephemeral polemics: see, e.g., *Rub for Rub: or, An Answer to A Physicians Pamphlet, styled, The Stroker stroked* (1666).
39. Beacher, *Wonders if not Miracles* (1665), p. 3.
40. Ibid., pp. 4–5.

power happened to rule England at the time than the downfall of Rome. The imminent end of the world may have been
implicit in this prophecy,[41] rendering it objectionable not
only to the pope but to whoever else wished to maintain the
present distribution of temporal power, but when Fifth
Monarchy Men connected 1666 with the fall of Rome they
were only continuing an august tradition of Protestant exegesis. This connection itself—without any association between the pope and England's ruler—therefore must be
understood as being ideologically ambiguous.

The identification of the beast of Revelation as Antichrist,
and the further identification of Antichrist as the reigning
pope, was a commonplace even in the Middle Ages.[42] Many
dates were suggested for the future fall of the papal Antichrist,[43] but the number of the beast made 1666 a most
plausible one. The popularity of this prophecy is clear from
the rueful observations of Englishmen that in the year
for which Protestants predicted the destruction of Rome,
Protestant London was reduced to ashes.[44] One writer's
assertion[45] that the prophecy was made only by a few discredited "Enthusiasts" is not supported by the evidence
available, and its divisive implications contradict the same
author's basic argument for unity among Protestants. Indeed, the movement for Protestant unity which was developing in 1666[46] may have lent respectability to some
prophecies of the fall of Rome in that year which otherwise
might have suffered from Fifth Monarchist associations.
Exhortations to observe the Protestant interest in the later
1660s blend very easily with older, eschatological predictions that "Rome can never be destroyed except Protestants

41. See Mommsen, *JHI*, 12 (1951), 348–49, 351.
42. See Cohn, *Pursuit of the Millennium* (1970), p. 80.
43. See, e.g., the 17th-century dates given in Aubrey, *Miscellanies* (1696),
John Pell's "Day-Fatality of Rome," pp. 22–26; and Lee, *Antichristi Excidium* (1664), sig. b7r.
44. See Hardy, *Lamentation* (1666), p. 26; Rolls, *Burning of London*
(1667), pt. III, 156; Wood, *Life and Times* (1891), II, 87.
45. Rolls, *Burning of London* (1667), pt. III, 157–58.
46. On this movement see my unpublished Columbia University Ph.D.
dissertation, "Meanings of Dryden's *Annus Mirabilis*" (1972), pp. 207–26.

lay aside their unnecessary civill contentions, which may
(God so disposing) come to them about *Anno* 1665."[47]

The point is that when we assume a sectarian odor to
pervade prophecies of the fall of the papal Antichrist in
1666, we ignore the effect of contemporary efforts to show
the Protestant orthodoxy of such prophecies, and the effect
of the recrudescence of strong anti-Catholicism during the
years of the Second Anglo-Dutch War. In 1651 *A Voyce Out
of the Wildernes* presented a two-thousand-year-old prophecy and diverse allegorical and numerological readings of
biblical passages in defense of the argument that Rome was
destined to go down in 1666.[48] Luther's *Colloquia* was
translated and glossed to give the impression that the father
of Protestantism had deemed the pope "a right Jew" who
would "be brought to Confusion in the year, 666. according
to the Number of the Beast."[49] The writings of the prophet
Christoph Kotter were resuscitated and shown to foretell the
massacres committed by the Turk and his later conversion;
the downfall of the pope in 1666; and the establishment of
the New Jerusalem in 1680 (the spiritual reign of Christ,
since according to his explicators, Kotter rejected "the error
of the Millenaries").[50] Two of the tracts that describe,
without naming Sabbatai Sevi, the portentous stirrings of
the Jews in 1665 make the following apparent digression
midway through their reports: "As for the great Prophet in
North-Skelton, . . . in the Year 1661. . . . It hapned, that
he being awake in his Bed near Morning he heard a Distinct
Voice telling him, that *Babylon* was to fall in 66. and that at
Midnight, even as it hapnen to *Belthazar;* and that Her Fall

47. *Brief Description* (1650), p. 19. For a great deal more on Rome's
fall in 1666 see pp. 3, 4, 8, 9.

48. T. L., *Voyce* (1651–53), a collection of four separately paginated
tracts: see sig. E6v, E8v, F1r; *To The Church of Rome . . .* , p. 52; *A
Breife Exposition . . .* , pp. 64–65; and *Babylon is Fallen . . .* , p. 25.

49. Luther, *Colloquia* (1652), p. 306; Codrington, *Prophecyes of the
Incomparable* (1664), p. 16, *Several Choice Prophecyes* (1666), p. 16. This
(free) translation, to which Codrington refers, suggests that the pope is the
Antichrist but not a Jew; apparently the equation is Codrington's own.

50. Comenius, *Historia Revelationum* (1659), p. 220; Codrington,
Prophecies of Christopher Kotterus (1664), pp. 12–13, 19.

would cause such a Terror and Consternation to fall upon Men that frdm that time untill 70, there would be a stand in Divine Worship . . ."[51] It would seem natural for the contemporary reader to identify Babylon as Rome and to perceive a connection between this information and news of Jewish commotions in their common status as apocalyptic signs of the times.

A tract printed in 1662 suggested that while the beast whose number is 666 may be Antichrist, the man of Revelation whose number is also 666 must be Christ: thus the reign of the one will be the ruin of the other. Like many other exegetes, the author of this tract argued that "the mystery of that number was only the concealment of the millenary number left out for brevity sake according to the account of all or most Nations," but he buttressed this argument by deriving 1665, the anticipatory year of Christ's coming, from 666 multiplied by the two and a half years of persecution which preceded Christ's death. Having exhausted Revelation 13, the author next applied himself to the mystical numbers of Daniel 12, successfully computing the fall of Antichrist in 1666, the calling of the Jews in 1691, and the beginning of the New Jerusalem in 1711. Although he considered his computations very "seasonable" in view of the recent increase in popish propaganda, the author was forced to admit that "most of my Readers . . . look upon them but as airal [i.e., aerial], and swimmings in the brain of a Phanatick or brain-sick Enthusiast . . .," and he concluded with a frank expectation of the rule of Christ and the saints over the Fifth Monarchy.[52]

The pessimism of this author with regard to the ideological limitations of his appeal cannot be ignored, but neither can the confidence of others whose prophetic message was fundamentally the same. A new edition of a tract predicting the fall of Rome by means of, among other things, a chrono-

---

51. *Last Letters* (1665), p. 3; *Jewes Message* (1665), pp. 3–4. The two tracts are substantially the same.
52. *Christ and Antichrist*, pp. 5, 10, 13–14, 46–47, 53; sig. A2v, pp. 62, 74–75.

grammatical prophecy on Pope Alexander VII,[53] was dedicated to Charles II and dated July 25, 1663, only weeks after Commons had rejected the king's Declaration of Indulgence by asking that he enforce the existing penal laws against Catholics:

ALEXANDER 7. EPISCOPUS ROMAE.				1000.
				500.
ALeXanDer EpIsCopVs RoMae.				100.
				50.
L. X. D.	I.C. V.	M.		10.
				5.
50.10. 500.	1.100.5	1000.		1.

1666. vel sic, MDCLXVI.

When George Wither dated two of his tracts[54] printed in 1666 with the "seasonable CHRONOGRAM LorD haVe MerCIe Vpon Vs," he knew that their contents and other productions of his pen testified that the prophecy related to the destruction of the bestial Roman Church and Empire.[55] And Wither was able to give the Great Fire of London a felicitous significance within the greater eschatological scheme: "This *Author* believes, That the *Saints* last *Purgatory* is now commencing, and that it is made *signal* by the *Fire* which in this year hath eclipsed the glory, and defaced the Beauty of *London* . . ."[56] It is difficult to see why this prophecy of rise after fall should be considered any more essentially or superstitiously eschatological than Dryden's in *Annus Mirabilis*. The increasingly widespread anti-Catholicism of the early 1660s suffused a remarkable prophecy of

53. Windus, *Romae Ruina Finalis, Anno Dom. 1666.* (1663), verso of first sheet. Cf. Windus, *Romae* (1655). Cf. T. Hall, *Chiliasto-mastix redivivus* (1657), p. 93, who alludes to this first ed.

54. See *Ecchoes*, title, and *Sigh*, title.

55. Cf. *Campo-Musae* (1643), Pubs. of the Spenser Society, no. 12, pp. 24–25; *Dark Lantern* (1653), ibid., no. 16, p. 42; *Speculum* (1660), pp. 129–32; *Paralellogrammaton* (1662), Pubs. of the Spenser Society, no. 33, p. 57; *Meditations* (1665), pp. 68–69; *Vaticinia Poetica* (1666), Pubs. of the Spenser Society, no. 18, pp. 8–9; *Ecchoes* (1666), sig. B4r, p. 51 (quoting from *Campo-Musae*). Cf. Charles S. Hensley, *The Later Career of George Wither* (The Hague, 1969).

56. *Ecchoes* (1666), sig. C1v.

220 POLITICS AND POETRY IN RESTORATION ENGLAND

1662, which traced the symbolic subjugation of the estates of England by the Roman Catholic panther and the eventual salvation of the deserving by Christ. A running index to the fortunes of England is the condition of "a city," that is, London, which suffers plague in the middle and fire in the final section of the prophecy, when Christ comes.[57] Prophecies such as this one could not have been very offensive to all those whose concern about the papist threat grew with the disasters of the war years. After the fire, one writer who attributed it to the Catholics looked back sadly to the Protestant chronograms on the fall of Pope Alexander VII, which had provided the Jesuits with a cover for their own designs: the trouble with those chronograms was neither their prophetic form nor their apocalyptic content, but their naive "overconfidence."[58] Thus the consistent antipapism of the eschatological prophecies for 1666 ironically was justified by the great catastrophe of that year, and in a sense the prophecies themselves were thereby fulfilled as well.

Finally, we might consider briefly what the professional astrologers thought of the idea that Rome would be destroyed in 1666. Most of them had some acquaintance with it. John Gadbury, William Andrews, and Thomas Trigge were quite firm in rejecting the possibility.[59] William Lilly doubted the chronological application of the number of the beast but preferred not to speculate on "the fatality of Rome," although in 1667 he noted the nonfulfillment of the prophecy. John Tanner and George Wharton simply observed that "Mutations" in the Church of Rome, or the destruction of "*the* Pope *and* Hierarchy," had been presaged.[60] Joseph Blagrave, on the other hand, provided his

57. O. Lloyd, *Panther-Prophesy*, pp. 3, 6.
58. *Pyrotechnica Loyolana* (1667), p. 125.
59. Gadbury, *EPHEMERIS* (1665), sig. C8r, C8v, *EPHEMERIS* (1666), sig. A4v; Andrews, *Newes* (1665), sig. C8v, *Newes* (1666), sig. C1v, C8v, *Newes* (1667), sig. C2v; Trigge, *Calendarium* (1665), sig. C4r, *Calendarium* (1666), sig. A5r, C2v.
60. Lilly, *Merlini* (1665), sig. A2r, B8v, E3r, *Merlini* (1666), sig. A2r, *Merlini* (1667), sig. A2r; Tanner, *Angelus* (1666), sig. C4r, C4v–C5r, *Angelus* (1667), sig. C3r [misbound after C4]; Wharton, *Calendarium* (1666), sig. A1v.

own numerological calculation of the fall of "the Antichristian power" of the pope in 1666.[61] But no one showed a greater fascination with the problem and a greater conviction of Rome's downfall than John Booker, whose scandalized estimate of the seditious ends of the *Mirabilis Annus* tracts[62] accurately represents his characteristic approach to sectarianism and civil rebellion after 1660. Booker began his prophecies of the destruction of Antichrist in 1666 as early as 1661 and provided his readers with several original verses on the subject and the following chronogrammatical confirmations in 1664 and 1666:

> RoMae DestrVCtIo fInaLIs appropInqVat.
> CaDat Vrbs babyLon MeretrIX.[63]

Far from seeing any sedition in these exercises, Booker evidently engaged in them because he found them enjoyable or because he was convinced of their truth. If his mind should not be taken as representative of the age, neither should the implication of his example, that eschatological prophecy was compatible with more than one ideology, be easily dismissed.

This implication arises not only from comment on the fairly discrete and self-contained phenomena of Sabbatai, Greatrakes, and the prophesied fall of Rome, but also from the great mass of disparate and scattered allusions to the wonders to come in 1666, wonders for London, England, and the world. Nostradamus, Mother Shipton, and numerous more obscure and private sources of speculation were pondered over, updated, and shown to have reference to the war with the Dutch, the Great Fire, the imminent catastrophe in Turkish-Christian relations, and other extraordinary happen-

61. *Ephemeris* (1659), sig. A5r, A5v.
62. See *Telescopium* (1662), sig. A5r–A6r.
63. *Telescopium* (1664), sig. C8r, *Ephemeris* (1666), sig. C1v. See also *Telescopium* (1661), sig. A7v–A8r, *Telescopium* (1663), sig. B6r, *Telescopium* (1664), sig. C2v, *Telescopium* (1665), sig. C7r, *Ephemeris* (1666), sig. C1r. Cf. *Booker Rebuk'd* (1665), p. 6.

ings in the wonderful year. L'Estrange was said[64] to have censored from "most of" the almanacs printed for 1666 all prognostications that London would burn in that year (one of which even "named the month"); what he saw fit to let stand makes interesting eschatological reading all the same. It would be impractical to include all of this diverse prophetical material in the present discussion of ideologically problematic prophecy,[65] which I will conclude here by considering the instructive case of two professional astrologers in particular, Richard Edlyn and William Lilly.

Edlyn was the greatest wonder of all among prognosticators on the year 1666[66] because of what he had achieved in his *Prae-Nuncius Sydereus,* which L'Estrange licensed on March 14, 1663. Not at all fond of "the exasperated spirits of a seditious multitude," Edlyn prefaced the main body of his calculations by saying: "Nor let any mistake me, or think by these eminent transactions I here judge may ensue; that I accord with those erronious Judgements . . . that the consummation of the Universe, or that the calling of the Jewes, or a Fifth Monarchy (as some have vainly conjectured) is thereby signified." Nevertheless he admitted that 1666 was "that year so frequently pointed at by the Learned to be so famous for those eminent Mutations or Transactions . . . to be expected to happen in some parts of the world, but especially in the Church of *Rome.*" From this one might suppose that the "eminent transactions" of which Edlyn warned might touch Rome, but not London; yet this is a sample of what he learned from the stars about England's fate:

me thinks we have too great cause to fear an approaching Plague, and that a very great one, ere the year 1665. be expired . . .

[A certain astrological conjunction] may well signify great Drought, Barrennesse, or Scarcity, Conflagrations, or sudden and

64. See Malcolm, *Lond. Rediv.* (1807), anon. letter of Sept. 1666, IV, 81; J. Ward, *Diary* (1839), information of Sir Edward Walker, p. 94.

65. Interested readers may find it in my unpublished Columbia University Ph.D. dissertation, "Meanings of Dryden's *Annus Mirabilis*" (1972), pp. 317–28.

66. See, e.g., the praise of Booker, *Ephemeris* (1666), sig. C1r, *Telescopium* (1667), sig. C2; Lilly, *Merlini* (1667), sig. A6v.

vehement Desolations by Fire, hot and pestilent Diseases in the bodies of Men, strange Meteors, or fiery Apparitions in the Air; some New Star or Comet appears not long after; some say or conjecture, in the year 1664. I fear a great Plague in sixty five or sixty six.

. . . there will be great Drought and Barrennesse, Conflagrations or great Destruction by Fire, during the effects of that Conjunction, which will continue till the latter end of the year 1666.[67]

Apparently, different people had different ideas of what sort of predictions constituted a danger to the state, and eschatological prophecy was a field broad enough to attract and to satisfy people of very diverse opinions. The same conclusion must be drawn if one considers the long career of the more famous astrologer William Lilly, who prophesied first for the parliamentarian and then for the royalist cause.

During the Civil Wars, Lilly employed his astrological skills in support of the parliamentary cause and in opposition to the calculations of the Cavalier George Wharton (and even, at times, to his fellow parliamentarian John Booker).[68] This support entailed repeated allusions to what the condition of England would be in the 1660s. Thus in 1644 Lilly reproduced a prophecy found in a monastery in 1548, part of which ran as follows:

From *Caesar* did the Tell beginne,
600. yeare ere Will did winne,
66. more makes up the tale.
Remember M. D. C. L. X.
V. and I. then heare a Rex;
Marke the holy written beast,
666. it heast [i.e., hest?][69]

For those who had failed to understand the meaning of this verse Lilly reprinted its most significant lines seven years later, as one of

67. *Prae-Nuncius* (1664), pp. 88, 27, 104, 42, 73, 72; and see pp. 71, 118. As a matter of interest, Edlyn prophesies for London in 1678 "uproars and disturbances about Religion . . . factious spirits do now endeavour to promote their ends and interest . . ." (p. 115).

68. See Harry Rusche, "*Merlini Anglici:* Astrology and Propaganda from 1644 to 1651," *Eng. Hist. Rev.*, 80 (Apr., 1965), 322–33.

69. *Prophecy of the White King* (1644), p. 29.

224 POLITICS AND POETRY IN RESTORATION ENGLAND

severall ancient *English* Prophecies, affirming there shall be no
more *Kings* in *England* . . .
 Remember M.D.C.L.X,
 V and I, then near a REX.
viz. In 1666. there will be no King here, or pretending to the
Crowne of *England*.[70]

Another of Lilly's productions of 1644 asked: "Lord God
how many changes shal this poore Island suffer, & most part
of Europe before 1666 . . . REMEMBER, Religion in its
full purity will hardly flourish untill about 1670.[71] In 1647
he gave a great catalogue of dreadful overturnings, and concluded that "although these things shall be fierce after the
year 1630. yea, more fierce after 1650. yet shall they be most
terrible and rigorous after the year 1660." In the same tract
his combined astrological and biblical calculations brought
him to "1666. near which time the false miracles of the
world shall be discovered, with the change, and destruction
of (almost) all Sects . . ."[72] The following year saw Lilly's
prophecy that in 1656 "or within ten yeers more or lesse of
that time, or within a little time after, [will] appear in this
Kingdom so strange a *Revolution* of fate, so grand a *Catastrophe*, and great mutation unto this *Monarchy* and Government, as never yet appeared . . . it will be ominous to
London, unto her Merchants at Sea, to her Traffique at land,
to her Poor, to her Rich, to all sorts of People inhabiting in
her, or her Liberties, by reason of sundry fires, and a con-
suming *Plague*, &c."[73] Naval wars with the Dutch and the
failure of the Stuarts to regain power figured in Lilly's
predictions of 1652,[74] and as an introduction to a later list of
revolutionary occurrences, he judged "some such *actions,
casualties* or humane *chances* as these . . . will either in

70. *Monarchy or no Monarchy in England* (1651), p. 57. This is repeated in Lilly, *Lord Merlins Prophecy* (1651), p. 4. "Heare" and "near"
probably should be "ne'er," i.e. "never."
 71. *Englands Propheticall Merline*, sig. b4r.
 72. *Worlds Catastrophe, or, Europes many Mutations untill, 1666.*
(1647), pp. 34, 32.
 73. *Astrologicall Prediction* (1648), p. 41.
 74. *Annus Tenebrosus*, pp. 32, 36.

this year 1656, or in 1657, or at or before 1666. come to pass . . ."[75]

At the restoration, Lilly endured a considerable amount of ridicule[76] for—among other things—his prophecy that England would have no more kings, but he dutifully joined the chorus of praise for the miraculous preservation and reinstatement of Charles,[77] meditating on this great revolution in his own and the nation's fortunes as "so conspicuous an example of that great uncertainty whereto all mortall affairs are inevitably Subject, [which] may teach unto mankind a sober Moderatio[n] in their prosperities, and gravely admonish the Transitory *Gods* of Kingdomes, and Nations . . ."[78] Thus when "a Generation of dissatisfied people" predicted great changes in 1663, Lilly denounced their schemes and scorned their faith in numbers. Besides, "the presages of the late Comet, have in a manner, even in full measure performed that great work, for which it was designed, viz. Restauration of his Majesty: therefore from thence no Argument can be drawn to comply with these mens humours."[79] But although he combined attacks on Serrarius and the *Mirabilis Annus* tracts[80] with enthusiastic prophecies and interpretations of prodigies amiable to the new government,[81] Lilly was not entirely successful in shaking his interregnum associations.[82] It would seem, for example, that Arlington's assistant Joseph Williamson, who ran the official *Gazette,* made an erroneous connection between Lilly and Rathbone's Plot of 1665, which must be explained either as a conscious attempt to discredit him or as a reflex assumption that the Astrologer to the Republic must have had some involvement with so seditious an affair.[83]

75. *Merlini* (1656), sig. A5r.
76. See, e.g., *William Lilly Student in Astrologie* (1660); *Lilly Lash't* (1660); Crouch, *Mixt Poem* (1660), p. 2.
77. See, e.g., *Merlini* (1661), sig. A2r, B3v.
78. Ibid., sig. A2v.
79. *Merlini* (1663), sig. A2r, A2v.
80. See *Merlini* (1663), sig. A3r, *Merlini* (1664), sig. B6v.
81. See, e.g., *Merlini* (1666), sig. B2r–B3v, B5r–B5v, B6v.
82. See, e.g., J. B., *Blazing Star* (1665), pp. 2–3.
83. See *Gazette,* no. 48, Apr. 26–30, 1666: ". . . the third of September was pitched on for the attempt, as being found by Lillies Almanack,

This connection was especially unkind since less than three months earlier Lilly had expressly offered his prophetic services to the *Gazette* and to the government which it supported. In a letter of February 12, 1666, to his friend Elias Ashmole, Lilly spoke of a prophecy which he had found among some old papers:

That this prophecy may do his Maty service I conceiue whilst the repoart is fresh, if that it wear putt in the London Gazette, by wch meanes it will pass all over England if not the whole world . . . There may bee also added—Depelletur Rex ffrancia propter Tyrannidem.

I am confident it would putt much corage into his Maty subjects —now in the nick of tyme, when his Maty is preparing his forces if your self and ye freind think fitt, I will English it 2 ways, once Gramatically, the other wth an interpretation—all will go in half one side of the Gazette—I well know, how to humor the people in such like business . . . [I] would bee very willing to serve his Maty wth my penn . . . The English of all nations are most taken with prophecyes . . .[84]

This ancient prediction, which Lilly knew as "St Thomas a Beckets prophecy," was a much-interpreted medieval beast allegory which told of conflict between the Lion (or Lion of the North), the Lily (or Fleur de Lis), and (in some versions) the Eagle, culminating in a messianic intervention by the Son of Man.[85] Its meaning traditionally was explained by assigning to its actors the most plausible or flattering equivalences to European figures who were noteworthy at the time of interpretation, and exegetes as renowned as Merlin, John Baudensis, and Paul Grebner were said to have

and a Scheme erected for that purpose to be a lucky day, a Planet then ruling which Prognosticated the downful of Monarchy . . ." I can find no such indications in Lilly's almanacs for 1665 and 1666. On Rathbone's Plot see above, Chapter 2.

84. Ashm. MS. 423, fols. 256–57. Ashmole's friend was probably Sir Edward Walker of the Herald's Office, who wrote to Lilly on Apr. 12 promising to show the prophecy to Clarendon and to speak to Arlington about it (Ashm. MS. 240, fol. 120–120v). Apparently nothing more came of the project.

85. See a 1559 copy of the prophecy in Harl. MS. 559, fol. 2. For the Son of Man see, e.g., Dan. 7:13, Rev. 14:14, Matt. passim.

attempted its application.[86] A Latin version of the prophecy
and its English translation were printed as a tract in 1666,[87]
accompanied by the testimony of learned men at Oxford
that "Lilium" stood for France, "Leo" for the United Provinces, "Aquila" for the German Empire, "filius hominis" for
England, and "Caput Mundi" for the Turk or the pope.
According to Lilly's manuscript explication of March 1666[88]
the allegory predicts that while England defeats the Dutch
in warfare, French power will decrease, until France is
finally ruled by England. The pope will die in the midst of
these changes, and the prophecy ends with the eschatological apotheosis of England, the Son of Man, accompanied by
signs and foreshadowings of divinity. The three comets, Lilly
says, are intimately related to the working out of the allegory, and "I cannot find by any History that this Prophesy
hath in the least measure had its effects made good even
untill this year 1666. or years 1664 1665. . . ." That it will
be fulfilled in contemporary events is further suggested,
Lilly adds, by similar prophecies by a Dutchman recently
printed in the *Gazette*.[89]

Lilly's own proposals for the *Gazette* never materialized,
but in his almanac for 1667 he wrote an extended piece "*Of
the Numeral Letters 666. and of Christs Temporal Reign
upon Earth one thousand Years . . .*" because there had
been so much speculation on the events of the year 1666:
"Some of these Opinionasters are Fifth-Monarchy-Men;
others have been persons of more refined Judgments, and
Ministers in the Church of *England,* both whose Judgments

86. Taylor, *Political Prophecy* (1911), p. 87, says the prophecy applied
to the period of the French wars of Edward III.
87. *Prophecie of Thomas Becket* (1666). Cf. Tully, *Letter* (1666), who
was cited in the *Prophecie* and here expresses his embarrassment at being
involved in its publicity.
88. See Ashm. MS. 241, fols. 190, 190v, 195, 200.
89. Ibid., fols. 194v, 200. The Dutch prophecies may be those in
Gazette, no. 22, Jan. 25–29, 1666. Similar versions of the Becket prophecy
were printed in Dutch and English in two brs. of ca. 1690: see *Copy Of a
Prophecy* and *Wonderfull Prophesy.* The identifications in both cases are
like those which Lilly made. According to the *Copy,* the prophecy it prints
was sent from France by Algernon Sidney, the exiled republican, to the
Quaker Benjamin Furley in Rotterdam in 1666.

did assure themselves and Proselytes, *Christ his personal coming, and temporally to Reign upon Earth as a Prince in the Year 1666.* This was not all which was expected to happen; but some other extraordinary actions tending to great alteration both in the Church and Kingdom of *England* . . ."[90] Tactfully disregarding both his own prerestoration antimonarchal predictions and his recent interest in the Becket prophecy, Lilly went on to discuss the "great Scholars" and others who had found the number of the beast through chronogrammatical analysis of the names of Martin Luther, William Laud, Oliver Cromwell, Alexander VII, and the Great Turk.[91] Scorning the hopes of Fifth Monarchists, the followers of Sabbatai, and those who had expected Rome's downfall, Lilly added a stern warning to the Provinces: ". . . let them be wary of converting his Majesties Clemency into a just chollerick fury and indignation against them"[92] This patriotic outburst was dated October 10, 1666, but only two weeks later Lilly was called up for examination before the parliamentary committee investigating the causes of the fire,[93] not for any recent offense, but because of the unfortunate woodcuts which had been printed with *Monarchy or no Monarchy in England* in 1651. In his own copy of the tract, Lilly annotated, at an unknown date, the depictions of cities beset by fire and plague to make clear their reference to the events of 1665–66.[94] (At some later date, presumably, Lilly added marginal glosses to his anti-Stuart interpretation of the prophecy of the White King in the

90. *Merlini* (1667), sig. A3r.
91. Ibid., sig. A3v–A4r.
92. Ibid., sig. A2r–A2v.
93. See Lilly, *Life* (written 1667, printed 1774), pp. 141–44; *Ashmole Collection* (1966), I, 158–59. Ashmole's editor suspects that this examination was connected with the suggestion that Lilly's predictions had determined the projected date of Rathbone's Plot (I, 158, and III, 1073n1), but despite the late appearance of the *Gazette* notice, the plot had been set for the 3rd of Sept. 1665, not 1666: see *His Majesties Gracious Speech* (Oct. 10, 1665), Clarendon's speech, p. 18; Abbott, *Amer. Hist. Rev.*, 14 (1909), 699–700.
94. See Ashm. MS. 553 (Lilly's copy, with woodcuts after the text and bearing new pagination), pp. 8–9 [mispaginated 13], p. 15 [mispaginated 11]. Cf. Ashmole's copy of the tract, Ashm. MS. 538. Cf. *Ashmole Collection* (1966), III, 1072n3, 1074n1.

One of the woodcuts William Lilly appended to his *Monarchy or no Monarchy in England* (1651), showing a city on fire and under naval siege. Courtesy of the Harvard College Library.

same tract in order to reconcile it with the Restoration.)[95]

Lilly's efforts to efface the past by alternating between condemnations of what he took to be seditious eschatology, and anticipations of the eschatological triumph of the restored monarchy, only earned him more derision: first, for the inaccuracy of his chauvinistic prophecies in favor of Charles, and second, for the ease with which he seemed to accommodate himself to any government.[96] Dryden wrote in 1667:

> Thus, Gallants, we like *Lilly* can foresee,
> But if you ask us what our doom will be,
> We by to morrow will our Fortune cast,
> As he tells all things when the Year is past.[97]

More than any of his contemporaries, Lilly was in a position to appreciate how serviceable eschatological prophecy might be toward different ideological ends. Our brief review of his checkered career provides a suitable transition from ideologically problematic eschatology to the topic of prophecy whose support of Charles II is quite consistent and unmistakable.

95. See Ashm. MS. 553, pp. 52–53, 64. Cf. Lilly, *Life* (written 1667, printed 1774), pp. 125–27.

96. Cf. *Mr. Lillyes Prognostications* (1667), pp. 11, 14, 17; and *William Lilly Student* (1660), passim.

97. "Epilogue" to *Sr Martin Mar-All,* first acted Aug. 15, 1667.

8

ROYALIST PROPHECY

In 1660 Henry More made the following observation on the nature of millenial expectation: "these good Times, which we expect and hope for, will not be the exaltation of this or that Sect. For the childish conceit of some is, that the future prosperity of the Church will be nothing but the setting up this Forme or that Opinion, and so every Faction will be content to be *Millennists* upon condition that Christ may reign after their way or mode, that is in Calvinisme, in Arminianisme, in Papisme, in Anabaptisme, in Quakerisme, in Presbytery, in Episcopacy, in Independency, and the like."[1] The science of astrology was a prophetic technique which, when properly understood and applied, royalists embraced wholeheartedly. At the Restoration, Clarendon told Parliament:

The *Astrologers* have made us a fair excuse, and truly I hope a true one; all the motions of these last twenty years have been unnatural, and have proceeded from the evil influence of a malignant Star; and let us not too much despise the influence of the Stars: And the same *Astrologers* assure us, that the malignity of that Star is expired; the good *genius* of this Kingdom is become Superior, and hath mastered that malignity, and our own good old Stars govern us again, and their influence is so strong, that with our help, they will repair in a year what hath been decaying in twenty . . .[2]

1. *Explanation*, p. xvi.
2. *His Majesties Most Gracious Speech* (Sept. 13, 1660), pp. 13–14.

The providential relation between celestial and earthly phe-nomena certainly is not invalidated by the fact that some astrologers have been wrong. As John Spencer said, "the greatest and most wonderful change in state that ever hapned, in the restauration of His Sacred Majesty in Peace and honor, was not so much as dreamed of by all the Privy-Councellers to the stars . . ."[3] John Gadbury, a professional astrologer as well as a royalist, came to the defense of his trade by exclaiming, rather enigmatically: "Who could have believed, that so happy and eminent a Turn could have hap-pened among us, without the assistance the Syderial Science affords?"[4] The trouble with many astrologers, according to Gadbury, is that they failed to combine their study of the stars with an enlightened understanding of how God works through Scripture and history. In the words of another royalist, such an understanding would reveal that just as the mark of the beast was the Scottish Covenant, so Charles II was "that *David* the *servant* of the *Lord,* that is to be the great *deliverer* of the *Jews,* out of their long *captivity.*"[5] The deliverer of the Jews chose to present himself to his people in words slightly more muted than these, but equally remi-niscent of *Annus Mirabilis:* "it hath pleased the Divine Providence in so wonderful a manner, and by ways and means no less miraculous, then those by which he did, heretofore, preserve and restore his own chosen people, to restore Us, and Our good Subjects to each other . . ."[6] His panegyrists were not restricted in their language, and one of them evidently felt that the Davidic parallel did not do full justice to his monarch:

Astrologers have made Divinations from the fiery Trigon, and the conjunction of *Saturn* and *Iupiter* as to the condition of Our King and his Kingdoms: bleer eyd men could you not see when Our King was wrapt up in the swadling bands of Majesty, and after *Worcester* Fight laid in a Manger; Could you not see a Star over

3. *Discourse* (1665), p. 320.
4. *EPHEMERIS* (1661), sig. C3r.
5. *KLEIS* (1660), p. 21.
6. *Proclamation against Vicious* (1660).

the place, the Wise men did see it, and did foretel that God had snatcht him as a Fire-brand out of t[h]e Fire, and designed him to be a Crown of Glory in the hand of the Lord, and a Royal Diadem in the hand of his God . . .[7]

If the *Mirabilis Annus* tracts collected prodigies which testified to divine anger at the return of monarchy, royalist collections publicized the deaths of assorted parliamentarians, regicides, and adherers to the Covenant as "the apparent demonstrations of Gods evident and eminent wrath of indignation, expressed against the enemies of the King."[8] Thomas Sprat's later distaste for the vanity of sighting prodigies, "to which the English seem to have bin always subject above others,"[9] was not in evidence in 1659 when he wrote in memory of Cromwell:

> Great Life of wonders, whose each year
> Full of new Miracles did appear![10]

As for "the extraordinary workings of God for *his Majesty,* the many *Miraculous deliverances* wrought for him, Gods *Miraculous Restauration* of him,"[11] these prodigies and their significance held the unflagging attention of numerous royalist writers.[12] Elias Ashmole recorded the following occurrence at the time of Charles's coronation in April 1661: "It is a thing very memorable, that, towards the end of *Diner-*time . . . it began to *Thunder* and *Lighten* very smartly: which, however some sort of People were apt to interpret as *ominous,* and *ill-boding,* yet it will be no difficult matter to evidence from Antiquity, that Accidents of this nature, though happily they might astonish, and amaze the common Drove of men, were by the most Prudent, and Sagacious,

7. Mervyn, *Speech* (1661), p. 7.
8. *Great and Bloody Plot* (1660), p. 5.
9. *History* (1667), p. 362.
10. "To the Happy Memory of the Most Renowned Prince," quoted in Nevo, *Dial of Virtue* (1963), p. 135.
11. Marriot, *Rebellion Unmasked* (1661), p. 18.
12. See, e.g., Matthew, *KAROLOU* (1660, 1664); Jenings, *Miraculum basilicon* (1664); Broadley, *Royal Miracle* (1912).

look'd upon as a *prosperous,* and *happy presage.*"[13] Charles himself was "the Wonder of the *World,*" "the Worlds Wonder, *Englands Charlemain,*" and the narrative of his fortunes a *"Speculum Mirandorum,* the Mirrour of Wonders."[14] The peripeteia of the king's preservation and restoration, like that of Dryden's wonderful year, evoked the admiration owing to that truth which is stranger than fiction. It was

an exhibition of Providence so wonderfully signal, as cannot but at once intrance a Fanatick apprehension, and hush a Loyal intellect into a contented admiration.

. . . wrought by such an admirable chain of events, that if we either regard the *easiness,* or *speed,* or *blessed issue* of the Work; it seems of it self to contain variety and pleasure enough, to make recompence, for the whole Twenty years Melancholy, that had gone before.

. . . never seene in the mention of any history, antient or modern, since the returne of the *Babylonian* Captivity . . .

. . . such miracles that no story can parallel . . .

. . . Grandeurs . . . so far beyond all what Fiction and Invention can offer in *Romantick Hyperboles,* as they come near a Miracle . . .

. . . by such a strange and wonderful providence, as no mortal man could have ever expected; Nor can we consider thereof without much admiration and astonishment, the Work it self being so miraculous, so unexpected, as we are confident no History in the world can ever parallel.[15]

13. *Brief Narrative* (1662), p. 190. On Ashmole's authorship of this piece appended to Ogilby's *Entertainment* see *Ashmole Collection* (1966), I, 139.
14. W. Smith, *To the Kings* (1661), p. 48; Heath, *Glories* (1662), p. 265; Jenings, *Miraculum basilicon* (1664), sig. A6v. On Charles I and II as Charlemagne and the second Charlemagne, see *Manner of Solemnity* (1660); Jevon, *Exultationis Carmen* (1660), p. 2; Brett, *Restauration* (1660), p. 23; Heydon, *Holy Guide* (1662), VI, p. 25; Matthew, *KAROLOU* (1660, 1664), sig. A1r; Howell, *Poems* (1664), p. 6, *PROEDRIA* (1664), frontispiece facing title page; J. H., *Castor and Pollux* (1666); Settle, *Elegie* (1667), p. 5. On prophecies of the messianic reign of a second Charlemagne and expectations of a Golden Age as characteristic of "revolutionary millenarianism," see Cohn, *Pursuit of the Millennium* (1970), pp. 72–73, 106, 126, 198, 203.
15. Jenings, *Miraculum basilicon* (1664), sig. A7v; Sprat, *History* (1667), p. 58; Evelyn, *Diary,* May 29, 1660, III, 246; L'Estrange, *Caveat* (1661), p. 11; Heath, *Glories* (1662), p. 1; W. Andrews, *Newes* (1661), sig. C1v.

In restoring Charles, God overreached the wildest productions of nature and mortal imagination:

> A king! alas I stagger at the name,
> My shallow intellect doth surely frame
> Some strange Chymaera whose most monstrous birth
> Will thunderstrike all nations of the earth.
> The strangest storyes blowne about by fame
> The greatest fictions (former poets theame)
> Will not be wonder'd at, they'l credit gaine
> Now Charles doth ov'r his fathers empires reighne.[16]

". . . For if we search all *Chronologie,* and dig thorow the deep Mine of *Historie,* we shall scarcely find any one thing, so eminently Prodigious and strange, as this——THE HAPPY RESTAURATION OF ENGLAND, SCOTLAND AND IRELAND, TO HER FORMER AND MOST NATURAL GOVERNMENT—MONARCHY! AND THIS PERFORMED . . . WITHOUT THE LEAST BLOUD-SHED!"[17]

In *Annus Mirabilis* the extraordinary nature of the wonderful year seemed to suggest that time itself, like Charles's star, had "now a round of greater years begun." England was moving in a circular motion, continuing forward and returning back, progressing into the restored Golden Age of the future. Dryden was far from being the only panegyrist who understood the Restoration as a restored Golden Age. In the words of one astrologer-poet,

> Thou hast restor'd *Laws, Learning, Arts* and *Trade,*
> And this our Age, a golden Age is made.[18]

The return of Charles not only recalled the bounty of the past but promised the greater wealth and glory of an im-

16. Add. MS. 39866, fol. 5, anon. poem "In Idem subiectum," following "In reditum Caroli secundi &c."

17. Gadbury, *Natura Prodigiorum* (1660), sig. A4r.

18. Saunders, *Apollo* (1661), sig. A6r. See also Jevon, *Exultationis Carmen* (1660), p. 5; Camb. Add. MS. 711, fol. 125v, Anthony Dopping's "upon the same" following "On the happy returne . . . of . . . Charles the second . . . "; *Festa Georgiana* (1661), p. 6; Pordage, *Heroick Stanzas* (1661), pp. 9, 12; *Cities Loyalty* (1661), p. 5; Ogilby, *Entertainment* (1662), pp. 37, 135, 165.

perial future, for to him *"God* has design'd the *Dominion* of the *Ocean,* which renders Your *Majesties Empire Universal* . . . You can bring even the *Antipodes* to meet, and the *Poles* to kiss each other . . ."[19]

> 'Twas by a *Charles, France* once the Empire got:
> 'Twas by a *Charles, Spain* also drew *that* lot:
> Why may not *Britain* challenge the next call,
> And by a *Charles* be made *Imperial?*[20]

Astraea Redux draws toward its conclusion with the following lines:

> And now times whiter Series is begun
> Which in soft Centuries shall smoothly run.

Absalom and Achitophel ends:

> Henceforth a Series of new time began,
> The mighty Years in long Procession ran:
> Once more the Godlike *David* was Restor'd,
> And willing Nations knew their Lawfull Lord.

The idea of restoration combines the apotheosis of absolute eschatology and the revitalization of an end which is only relative, which is simultaneously a renewal, the dawn of a new age which has shed all the bitterness and evil of the old.

For royalist contemporaries, the model of such an eschato-logical event was of course 1660, the restoration of the Golden Age. The conciliatory Presbyterian John Corbet called it "this great turning time": "It is true, that this Nation is not erecting a new Kingdom, nor laying new foundations of Government; yet it is no less true, that this Restauration is as it were life from the dead, and we are in some sort beginning the world anew."[21] In Ashmole's words,

19. Evelyn, trans. of Freart's *Parallel* (1664), sig. a3v.
20. Howell, *Poems* (1664), "Prophetic Poem . . . to his present Majesty then Prince, 1640 . . . ," p. 6.
21. *Interest of England* (1661), p. 22; *Second Part* (1661), pp. 275–76.

"the tyme approacheth, ubi sentire quae velis, et quae sentias dicere licet . . . tis a Tyme for Miracles to worke."[22] In his restoration Charles has "converted *Time*."[23]

> Scarce hath the lazy *Sun* his Circuit gone,
> But! *Revolution! Revolution!*
> Our *King Proclam'd! Restor'd!* and *Crown'd! A Year*
> Like *Plato's*, sets us *Even* as we *Were*.
> Blest be the *Time!* oh may it henceforth be,
> Calendar'd *Englands Year* of *Jubilee!*[24]

The jubilee, recurrent every fifty years, traditionally celebrates the completion of seven Sabbatical cycles in Jewish holiday. On the Day of Atonement a blast of the shofar announces the beginning of the year, as Gabriel's trumpet will signal the final *dies Irae*. Land is restored to its original owners and allowed to lie fallow, and all slaves receive their liberty.[25] Thus the restoration of Charles's birthright, as well as the Act of Indemnity and Oblivion and the nominal remission of lands sold or forfeited during the interregnum, aptly signaled "the year so much desired by all true hearted English men, yea that happy year of *Iub[i]le*, wherein things would again return [into] their right current."[26] The tradition which lies behind the Platonic, or Great, Year is almost as ancient as that of the year of jubilee. Once again, it is a cyclical idea. The eight interior spheres of the heavens, which move in revolutions of unequal duration, achieve simultaneous completions "and the ninth accomplisheth her motion in thirty six thousand, or rather as others say in 49000 years, which is a Jubilee of thousands, commonly called *Plato* his great year, because he affirmed that after this distance of time every thing in this world must

22. *Ashmole Collection* (1966), I, 129.
23. Tatham, *Neptunes Address* (1661), p. 7.
24. Bold, *St. Georges Day* (1661), pp. 1–2.
25. See *Jewish Encyclopedia* (1925), X, 605; *Encyclopedia of Religion and Ethics* (1926), V, 866.
26. Wing, *Olympia* (1661), sig. C5v. On 1662 as a year of jubilee see Tatham, *Londons Triumph* (1662), p. 13; Turnor, *Speech* (May 19, 1662), p. 4.

begin of new again to have being as it was formerly."[27] And like the year of jubilee, Plato's year also had associations with doomsday, for some said that the world "should suffer a total and absolute Destruction and Dissolution at the finishing the great year, or Circle."[28] The idea of the Great Year seemed applicable to many cyclical forms of experience: "For questionlesse it fareth many times with a *Common-wealth*, as with the *Sunne:* which runneth through all the signes of the *Zodiack,* till it return to the place where its motion first began. And the *Platonicke* yeare of reducing all things to the same beginning, continuance, and period; how false soever in the bookes of *Nature*, is in some sort true in the change of Government."[29] Thus Evelyn, in his Restoration panegyric, says "let it be a new year, a new *Aera*, to all the future Generations, as it is the beginning of this, and of that immense, *Platonic* Revolution; for what could arrive more justly, more stupendious, were even the eight[h] sphear it self now hurled about?"[30] 1660 is a revolutionary year, in which time and the heavens have circled back upon themselves, promising the freshness of a second childhood. It is

> The true *Platonick,* when the Sphears are rowl'd
> Back to the *Loyall* points they kept of old.[31]

Restoration has been achieved by a revolution back to the conditions of 1641, the Golden Age before the fall. Charles is accompanied, in his restoration, by the episcopal hierarchy, the continuity of whose succession was just barely maintained by the reinstatement of the superannuated bishops of prewar days.

27. Vaux, *New Almanack* (1665), sig. B6v. Cf. Vaux, *New Almanack* (1661), sig. B3r; Heydon, *El Havarevna* (1665): *Psonthonphanchia*, p. 6 [new pagination].
28. Gadbury, *Dies Novissimus* (1664), p. 30. Cf. Heydon, *Harmony of the World* (1662), p. 244.
29. Heylyn, *Augustus* (1632), pp. 21–22.
30. *Panegyric* (1661), ARS, no. 21 (1951), pp. 4–5.
31. Borfet, *Postliminia Caroli II* (1660), pp. 1–2.

With him returns that beauteous Dame
We *Ecclesia Anglicana* name,
The *Hierarchy* is getting ground
(Its Platonick year's come round).[32]

As in *Annus Mirabilis,* the Restoration idea of circularity is not inconsistent with, and even depends upon, an element of teleology, a sense of reaching the end of a series. Dryden compares the fire with the world's end "at the death of time" (212), and 1666 marks the end of an old and the start of a new age. In the same way, Restoration panegyrists recalled Revelation 10:6 to characterize the unique event which had occurred in 1660:

When he is Crown'd in all your sights,
And takes possession of his rights,
When this is done, and you look on,
Believe a *Resurrection;*
A time when time shall be no more.[33]

When Dryden prophesies that London's charter, now renewed, "Heav'n will to the death of time allow" (294), he only emphasizes the endless continuity which is implicit in the great process of London's renovation. The same effect is achieved by the panegyrists of 1660 when they predict monarchal successions endless to the end of time:

May you abound in hopefull babes, that may
Govern the Nations, and your *Scepters* sway,
Till time shall be no more, and pledges be
Both of our *love,* and our *felicitie.*

The spacious Sea, which does the Earth embrace,
Ne're held so many Princes in one Place;

---

32. Brett, *Restauration* (1660), p. 11. The idea of Plato's Great Year was a popular one. For its use in other contexts see Fuller, *Historie* (1639), p. 278; Brome, *Songs* (1661), "The Royalist," p. 46; Howell, *Poems,* (1664), p. 55; Poor Robin, *Almanack* (1664), sig. B5r, *Almanack* (1666), sig. C6v–C7r; Parker, *Free and Impartial Censure* (1666), p. 87; Milton, *Paradise Lost* (1667), V, ll. 582–83.
33. Brett, *Restauration* (1660), p. 21.

Detail from the first triumphal arch erected in London to celebrate the restoration of Charles II. Below, Charles pursues the many-headed Usurpation into the jaws of Hell, flanked by his divinized predecessors James I and Charles I. Above, he stands against the Royal Oak, which miraculously bears crowns and scepters instead of acorns. The Virgilian tags say, respectively, "successive time [the turning day] does of its own accord" and "leaves unknown / Admiring, and strange apples not her own." Reprinted from Ogilby, *Entertainment* (1662), courtesy of the Harvard College Library.

Princes, whose Father still the Trident bore,
As shall their Sons, till Time shall be no more.[34]

In Dryden's own Restoration offering, the circularity of time
and trade meet in the lines:

Abroad your Empire shall no Limits know,
But like the Sea in boundless Circles flow.[35]

So far we have considered the eschatological elements
that *Annus Mirabilis* has in common with the royalist responses to Charles's restoration, but the prophetic frenzy of
royalists was by no means expended after 1660. Men like
Anthony Wood and John Evelyn wondered at the increasing
prodigies of the next seven years,[36] and James Howell's
poem of 1658, since it was printed in 1664, looked ahead to
both 1660 and 1666 when it observed that "the world is
Hectical, and near/ Its great, and fatal Climacterick year."[37]
The notoriety of the disaffected authorship of the *Mirabilis
Annus* tracts and the knowledge of what actually came to
pass in 1666 have obscured the fact that many men expected
only good from that year:

According to the manifold prophesies, which have been concerning it, —66. should have been a year of *Jubilee*, I had almost said
a time of the Restitution of all things, but, alas! Whilst men lookt
for light, behold darkness . . .
   Many Prodigies there were, as *Josephus* tells us, that went before the destruction of *Jerusalem* by Fire . . . These were dark
Texts for men to expound, yet some did venture to give the sense
and meaning of them, as if each of them had been a token for
good, whereas the event did manifest the quite contrary. So was
the destruction of *London* ushered in with several Prodigies,
Blazing-Stars, and others . . . Neither may we doubt, but there
were some who did put a good construction upon those ill-Signes

34. Brome, *Congratulatory Poem* (1660), p. 18; *To the King, upon his
Majesties* (1660), p. 3.
35. *Astraea Redux* (1660), ll. 298–99.
36. See Wood, *Life and Times* (1891), II, 24, 53–54; Evelyn, *Diary*
(1955), Mar. 10, 1667, III, 477.
37. *Poems,* "*THEROAOGIA* [?]," p. 120.

as if they had been fore-runners of the good things, which they themselves expected in the year —66 . . . Thus far some involved themselves in the same practise with the *Jews* of old, and God hath involved them in the same kind of calamity. It is dangerous doing as *Jews*, lest we suffer as they.[38]

We have seen how many of the prophecies for 1666 looked to that year for the fall of Rome. This in itself might be considered beneficial to England, but the "good things" expected also involved the more positive boon of a Stuart and Anglican ascendancy. In 1653 the Welsh prophet Arise (Rhys) Evans ransacked Revelation to come up with the suggestion that Charles Stuart's approaching reign would constitute the Fifth Monarchy. He found that VVILL LaVD signified 666, and VVILLIaM LaVD signified 1667—"and that is the yeer of rest; for before it be *Anno. Dom.* 1667. most of the world, yea, and Rome it self will acknowledge their error; see the truth, and submit to *William Lauds* rule . . ."[39] Another tract by Evans, printed in 1664, purported to have been written in 1656. In it he recounts an interview which he had with Menasseh ben Israel, the Amsterdam rabbi who was leading the campaign for the official readmission of Jews into England.[40] To Menasseh's suggestion that the Messiah of the Jews could be Cromwell, but never Charles Stuart, Evans recalls having objected strenuously, adding that "he that lives five years to an end, shall see King *Charles Steeward* flourish on his throne to the amazement of all the World, for God will bring him in without blood-shed." Evans goes on to inform his readers that the star which shone at the birth of Christ and Charles is one and the same, and to "predict" a Dutch attempt to foment war, God's punishment of them with plague, the rise of the Jews under Charles and an army of 144,000, their conver-

---

38. Rolls, *Burning of London* (1667), "MEDIATION XXI. *Upon the coming of that most dreadful fire in so Idolized a year, as* 1666," pt. III, 90, 179–80. And pt. III, 92–93, 95. With Rolls's concluding warning against parallels with the Jews of old cf. Wither, *Paralellogrammaton* (1662), title.
   39. *Bloudy Vision* (1653), p. 63.
   40. See Lucien Wolf, ed., *Menasseh Ben Israel's Mission to Oliver Cromwell* (London, 1910).

sion, and the advent and reign of Christ with his viceroy
Charles, king of England.[41] In 1658 Walter Gostelo warned
of God's readiness to burn London and the kingdom for their
obstruction of the "rule of Gods Vice-gerent, *Charles Stuart,
your* only lawful King and Soveraign": "The Unquestionable
Restore of OUR KING *Charles St.* Is Revealed and assured
by God Almighty . . . and look to it that you do Amend, or
assure your selves sudden *Death, Plague, Sword, Fire, Violence,* what not, shall in a very short time burst in upon you,
to *devour,* to *burn* up, to *consume,* and to lay *waste.*"[42]

The traditional language of eschatological prophecy continued to be used in the royalist cause as 1666 approached,
and flowered luxuriously with the militant nationalism of the
Anglo-Dutch War. After the Battle of Lowestoft, one tract
claimed that "such an immediate hand of God hath not in
Battel been so eminent and visible in our daies . . . ,"[43]
reviled "these Pretenders to Celestial Intelligence, that
rather then not to Prophesie at all, will hazard at any thing,"
and concluded with the following verse:

York VICtor Caesars LaVreLL got bII fraCtion ⎫
One VICI hIs ConCIstIng aLL In aCtIon   ⎪
Rests VenI VIDI both for those faInt Foes   ⎬ 1665
KneVV onLII hoVV t'appear, see, flIe, to Lose. ⎭

A poem on the subject of the Four Days Battle observed:

Well did our learned platonists prefix
Wondrous events to the year of sixty six
And now the worlds climaterick fear
But sure I am 'tis no Platonick year
ffor nere was itt, nor nere again must bee
A parellell to this grand Victory
And now th' amazed world at last must find
England to be the Empire of mankind.[44]

41. *Light For the Jews* (1664), pp. 5, 9, 10, 11, 13, 27–28.
42. *Coming of God in Mercy,* sig. D2r, A8r, D8v. Peter Lillicrap was
sent to the Tower in May 1659 for printing this tract: *CSPD,* July 23, 1663,
p. 214.
43. Cliffe, *Abreviate* (1665), "Postscript."
44. Burney MS. 390, fol. 33v, Francis Mundy, "On the Signall Victory."

Praising the English performance in this same battle, another royal poet suggested:

> These are some of those warlike tricks,
> Becket presag'd in sixty six.[45]

Two months later, England "on St. James's day One thousand 666 fought with a Beast with Seven Heads, call'd Provinces."[46] An "English Daniel" gave an interpretation of a dream that had been troubling Johan de Witt, "Hollands Nebuchadnezzar," foretelling the dreamer's ruin at the hands of the *"English Cross,"* the *"Hesperian Lyon,"* and the *"Northern Kings."* The *"Lillies,"* meanwhile, will wither before his eyes and be divided by the *"German Eagle."* The author follows the beast allegory with a prophecy said to have been composed under Queen Elizabeth:

> When *One* and three times *Six* do meet,
> *To* reckon for the Year;
> *The* Bloody *English* Colours shall
> On the *French* Coast appear.
> *June* 10. When *Sol* in *Cancer* enters first,
> On that same very Day,
> The *Ensigns* of these mighty Foes
> Shall in the Field display.
> Twelve Noble Lords that day shall fall,
> With thousands by their *side;*
> And then the *Fates* end and begin
> *The* French *and* English *Pride.*
> *Three* Battels more ere *Christmas Eve,*
> The *Lillies* fight and lose:
> *Then* Peace ensues, and puts an End
> Unto the Subjects Woes.
> Then *High* and *Mighty* look about,
> Your Wooden and Stone-Wall
> Shall not defend you; But shall then
> Begin to *sink and fall.*[47]

45. Firth, *Naval Songs* (1908), "England's Tryumph," p. 66.
46. Berkenhead, *New Ballad* (1666), title. Cf. Berkenhead, *Second Part* (1666), title. Both are reprinted in Firth, *Naval Songs* (1908), pp. 72–79.
47. *Dutch Nebuchadnezzar* (1666), pp. 2–4, 6. The title explains that the "Twelve Noble Lords" are all French. The *"High and Mighty"* (or "Hogen Mogens") are the High and Mighty States-General of the United

A tract of 1666 called *The suspence upon Sixty Six* attacked those astrologers who sat gazing at the evening sky, their minds on the great motions of fate, yet powerless to predict such solid events as the Great Plague or the war with France.

> We'r yet a Nation; O lets joyn in love
> And fight with courage 'gainst our *Belgian* Foes.[48]

A Scottish almanac of 1666 printed "A Strange Prophecie. Uttered by a Marmaid, to a Dutch-Skipper" in 1659, a mild satire which foretells the conversion of all the Provinces to Quakerism and which begins:

> To Thousand add six hundreth sixty six,
> Strange stormes that Year, shall all the World Vex:
> Great share whereof, shall fall upon You, DUTCH.[49]

A broadside "on this Famous Year 1666. Or, The Number of the Beast, so much talked of," presented the following dialogue on the wonderful year:

> Wo to the Year, in which three Sixes meet!
> It doth Portend Disaster to some Fleet;
> Some King to be o'erthrown; some State dispers'd;
> Some Laws Eradicated and Revers'd.
> *Quest.* Then tell me, Fatal Year, What King's foreshown,
> Or here denoted to be overthrown?
> *Answ.* If that you would this Mystery unfold,
> You may in LVDoVICVs him behold.
> *Quest.* Tell me, What State shall be dispers'd? and Who,
> By scattering their Folk, shall it undo?
> *Answ.* The King of *England,* if you will believe
> The Comets, shall the Hogen-Mogens drive.

Provinces, their customary manner of styling themselves. PRO SP 29/143(147) is a MS. "Welsh Prophesy" very similar to this one, but with an additional four lines: "Plauges Pannick feares Prodigious sights/these troubles shall forerunn/And fiue & fifty yeares shall end/Ere this haue well begunn." Anthony Wood's editor prints from a MS. a similar version of the prophecy, with a note attesting to its existence "20 years ago"—i.e., ca. 1645: *Life and Times* (1891), II, 54 and n7.

48. E. G., *Suspence* (1666).
49. Corss, *Almanack* (1666), sig. B4v.

After another exchange, the author proceeds to an explication of the "Mystery" of the king destined to be overthrown:

> The Number is SIX HUNDRED SIXTY SIX:
> Which with the French Kings Name if you compare,
> The Number both with Beast and Man will square.
> LVDoVICVs.
> LeVVIs (the 14.) of FranCe AnD NaVarre.
> DCLVVVI.

After repeating some of this material in Latin on the verso,
the author brings his prognostication to an end with this
postscript:

> *Long Live the Second* CHARLES, *Great Brittains King!*
> *And let Him all His enemies down bring.*   Amen. Amen.
> *And as for those that will not say Amen,*
> *I wish them gone, ne'er to return agen.*   Amen.[50]

The prophetic significance of "Ludovicus" was apparent
to a number of contemporaries, some of whom were slightly
startled to find themselves in the position of inspired seers.
This seems to have been the case, at least, with Capt.
Humphrey Barrowe, who wrote an ingenuous and appealing
account of his experience to Lord Lieutenant Ormonde:

The product of the year 1666 having been the knotty theme of
some laborious, but too many confident pens, which nevertheless
. . . have left us still in the dark, I humbly beg it may not be
accounted a piece of levity in your servant to acquaint your Grace
with a small beam, which lately, yet perhaps seasonably, shined
into his observation. My Lord, I neither pretend to the spirit of
prophecy nor that of interpretation, but on Friday, the first of this
month, about four in the morning, awaking out of a dream (to
which I dare not presume to be the Oedipus) I fell, as above my
station I use to do, into a consideration of the present posture of
affairs betwixt the King and his neighbours, amongst whom the

---

50. R.G., *MDCLXVI* (1666). Part of the Latin version of this prophecy
is given in Eg. MS. 2982, fol. 266, with the addition of the following lines
which somewhat complicate its tone:

> Not[e]: All ye Numerical letters in ye ⎫
> Alphabet and in these Words (Viz:) ⎬ make 1666
> LorDhaVeMerCIe Vpon Vs ⎭

French King was pressed deep into my thoughts, and (as under an impulsive violence) his name (being in the Roman tongue, Ludovicus) made the sole subject of my meditation, which having often revolved in the accusative case, Ludovicum, I fancied the discretion of it, and found it to consist of the numerical letters standing for 1666, viz., M. D. C. L. V. V. V. I. I, with the letter O standing in the body of the name exclamantly calling for the wonder and admiration of the world at what should happen that year . . . After which, retrospecting the nominative Ludovicus, I found its numerical letters, viz., D. C. L. V. V. V. I, being 666, the perfect number of the beast, being the number of a man, Revelations 13th, and last verse. Other observations I made, as that of the evenness of the figurative letters in both cases before and after the letter O, viz., in Ludovicus, before the letter O stands 555, and after it 111, before O in Ludovicum the same 555, and after it 1,111, being just double the number 555, with the addition of a not dividable unit, which last things (by the perusal of some books I then wished for) may, in comparing things with things, be found not without some signification.

After this tour de force Captain Barrowe closed with humility, wishing that

if His Highness . . . shall find anything of God's meaning in these things, he may (pardon, I beseech your Grace, the presumption of a worm to write it) be the better enabled to play his national games with all his neighbour princes and states, to the glory of that God that hath so miraculously restored him . . .[51]

There is an abundance of royalist chronograms on 1666, but some lack any eschatological or even prophetic content, serving simply as a means to proclaim the deviser's patriotism.[52] Yet patriotism constituted an important element in royalist eschatology: if Fifth Monarchy Men envisioned the universal reign of Christ and his saints upon earth, Charles's supporters frequently looked for a magnificent era of imperialism—martial, commercial, and religious—inaugurated by Charles as the instrument or vicegerent of Christ. The

51. *HMC Ormonde*, n.s., letter of Dec. 12, 1665, pp. 199–200.
52. See, e.g., Wood 416, fol. 116[B], a chronogram whose probable author is Robert Whitehall: "In AngLos hoC anno Leo BeLgICVs rVgIebat:/ IsqVe CLVnt saVCIVs stVpens eheV MoX aVfVgIebat./The Belgick *lion* 'gainst England roard this yeare/His *taile* shott off this *lion* return'd a *Bere*."

distinction between these two visions, great in terms of the ideologies that underlie them, in other respects is not so wide as has been assumed. The royalist astrologer Vincent Wing wrote in 1666 that "so *superlative* will the actions of some *Men* be, in this last but worst age of the *World,* that the very Hearts of many will fail for fear . . ." Quoting Scripture to describe the biblical disasters in store for many nations, Wing gave some comfort to his English readers: "see that you be not troubled . . . for all these Things must come to pass, but the End is not yet. There will doubtless, after these grand *Revolutions,* be a *Time* of *tranquility* and *peace,* but it cannot yet be expected; however, great are the Signs portending, that we in England*————*shall not so sensibly feel the Effects of War and Calamity, as some of our Neighbour Nations . . ."[53] He hoped, in fact, that the coming solar eclipse "will much tend to the good and welfare of our Gracious Soveraign and his Dominions, and the final Extirpation of all his Enemies."[54] In a similar manner, a 1659 collection of the most diverse sort of eschatological prophecies concluded with the words: "all these prophesies . . . cry out a Conquerour and Reformer of the universal Church of Christ, from the *Brittains* or Island of Great *Brittain* . . . According to the real in[t]ention and hearts integrity of these Prophesies, I make bold to minde you, day and night to square your lives as becometh chosen Instruments for bringing to pass the glorious works here destinated for you . . ."[55] Charles Stuart may have been very far from the savior who this author imagined might lead the chosen people of England, but this vision is quite compatible with that of Charles's ardent supporters—for example, a poet of the Anglo-Dutch War:

> Ere many years, all *Christendome* shall see
> *Great Britaines* King Gods Instrument to be;
> Christs Sacred Gospel Truth he will advance,

53. *Bloody Almanack* (1666), pp. 3–4. Cf. Wing, *Olympia* (1666), sig. C4v.
54. *Bloody Almanack* (1666), p. 2.
55. *Forraign and Domestick Prophesies,* pp. 180–81.

Throughout all *Holland,* and wide-skirted *France.*
And with his own right hand will tumble down
Base *Antichrist,* and take from him his Crown.
False Sects and Schismes, with all vain opinions,
Shall not take root or bide in his Dominions.[56]

This kind of prophetic ending, a device favored by many royalist poets and by Dryden as much as any, denies the possibility of an end to the wonders of England's monarch— not, at least, until the death of time. It suggests that the triumphs of Charles related in the poem which is now ending will be recapitulated endlessly in future time. The greatest wonder of Charles's fate, like that of London and England in *Annus Mirabilis,* is that it is revolutionary: eschatological yet circular.

One of the most extravagant royal panegyrics of the period, one that combines iconography, numerology, and occult symbolism in praise of the restored monarch, uses sibylline prophecy and the beast allegories of Daniel to predict that Charles, glorious as he now may be, is destined to rule the fifth and final empire which will rise on the ruins of the Assyrian, the Persian, the Greek, and the Roman. Writing in 1660, the author prophesied that

the time draweth near, and is even at hand, when as a miraculous Change in Kingdoms and Nations shall manifest it self, in *Europe,* . . . as ever did in any part of the world, since the universal Deluge in Noah's time, and these so great and formidable actions, are to be performed by the Power and Atchievments of one eminently excellent Person, whom God hath ordained for that purpose, to do wonders, wheresoever he shall come, both in Church and State . . .

The day of his Majesties glorious renown now begins to dawn, And before the number of years which equalls the number of Stars in the . . . Celestiall sign *Pleiades,* appearing at his Majesties Nativity, be expired, shall shine most brightly throughout *Europe,* and other parts more remote . . .[57]

56. Eliot, *English-Duel* (1666).
57. Matthew, *KAROLOU* (1660, 1664), pp. 34–35, 61.

It would be difficult to justify any great linguistic or epistemological distinctions between a vision such as this and the
expectation of Christ's millenial reign on earth.

I have been concerned to show the similarities between
royalist and antiroyalist uses of eschatological prophecy in
order to argue that the eschatological elements of *Annus
Mirabilis* should be taken on their own terms rather than as
a quasi-ironic reaction to an alien ideology. The common
"political" interpretation of the poem depends ultimately on
the significance that has been attributed to the *Mirabilis
Annus* tracts. If Dryden took his very title from a well-
known set of Fifth Monarchist prophecies, then the idea that
his prophetic stance in *Annus Mirabilis* was intended on
some important level as an ironic reflection on deluded and
deluding sectarians gains a good deal in plausibility. There
is no reason to suppose, however, that Dryden owed any real
debt to these tracts. We have seen that their prophetic conventions were universally acceptable and universally employed, and I hope to show that even their titles were
available from other writings of varied ideologies.

Perhaps the most wonderful year previous to 1666 had
been 1588, the year of two eights, the Spanish Armada, and
terrible signs in heaven and earth. John Harvey called it the
"Greatwoonderful, and Fatall yeere of our Age" and devoted
himself to abating, or at least to prophesying, the wonders
"*Anni famosi magis, quàm mirabilis, 1588.*"[58] A poem written on this wonderful year contained the lines:

> Quis verum neget augurium mirabilis anni?
> Aurea iam redijt post ferrea secula proles.[59]

Part of the fame that this year had acquired was owing to a
prediction by a certain Regiomantus which had circulated
widely, and whose third line referred to "Octogesimus

58. *Discoursive Probleme* (1588), title, p. 132.
59. J. Case, *Sphaera civitatis* (1588), sig. gg5v, quoted in Yates, *Jour.
Warb. and Court.*, 10 (1947), 61.

octauus mirabilis annus."[60] When Thomas Dekker chose to assert the precedence of the plague year of 1603 as the most wonderful year of all, he found it necessary to argue specifically against *"Octogesimus, Octauus Annus"*: ". . . That same terrible 88. . . . which had more prophecies waiting at his heeles, tha[n] euer *Merlin* the Magitian had in his head, was a yeare of *Iubile* to this. *Platoes Mirabilis Annus,* (whether it be past alreadie, or to come within these foure yeares) may throwe *Platoes* cap at *Mirabilis,* for that title of wonderfull is bestowed vpon 1603."[61] Thus many years earlier the idea of the *annus mirabilis* was being associated with Plato's revolutionary Great Year, the restored Golden Age, and, if only negatively so far, the year of jubilee.

The prophecy of Regiomantus continued to be remembered and quoted during the next half century. In his manuscript collection of occult materials, William Sancroft, dean of St. Paul's and later bishop of London, copied out the prophecy, noting that 1588 "had many hundred years before been much spoken of by Astrologers."[62] But as the extraordinary events of the seventeenth century unfolded, people began to claim "the title of wonderfull" for more recent years. This was part of the message in Stephen Marshall's sermon of 1641:

. . . This one yeer, this wonderfull yeer, wherein God hath done more for us in some kinds, then in fourescore yeers before, breaking so many yokes, giving such hopes and beginnings of a very Jubilee and Resurrection both of Church and State: *This yeer* wherein we looked to have been a *wonder* to all the world in our *desolations,* and God hath made us a *wonder* to the world in our *preservation* . . .

. . . this yeer have we seen broken *the yokes* which lay upon our estates, Liberties, Religion, and Conscience . . .

Quadragesimus primus mirabilis annus. Oh wonderfull yeer!

60. See, e.g., Geveren, *Of the ende* (1577), p. 19; R. Harvey, *Astrological Discourse* (1583), p. 45; Bacon, *Essays* (1597), XXXV, "Of Prophecies."

61. *Wonderfull yeare* (1603?), sig. B4v–C1r.

62. Sancroft MS. 51, p. 39. For Regiomantus's prophecy see also Swan, *Speculum Mundi* (1635), p. 19; Booker, *Ephemeris* (1666), sig. C1r.

and so much the *more wonderfull* that all these things are done for us, *when* our *neighbour Nations* round about us see no such dayes . . . And which is *most wonderfull,* all this done for the most unworthy and unthankfull Nation in all the world . . .[63]

The wonder of Marshall's great year, like Dryden's, resides not simply in the felicity of some of its events but in its antithetical quality, the fact that preservation has come when people expected and deserved only desolations. Another Puritan divine, Nathanael Homes, who twenty-five years later was to help in the publicizing of Sabbatai Sevi's messianic movement, chose the same revolutionary year 1641 to expand upon the great historical principle of perpetual renovation which binds the present age to sacred history. Homes reviews the earlier stages of renovation; "finally, when the Church had that great blow in *Babylon,* whereof shee lay sicke seventy yeares, then was Christ promised, the *magnus instaurator.* The stay of all stayes forever. So that when Christ came, and began the new Testament, was *Mirabilis annus,* the admired period of the Church . . . But this great restitution of the Church of the New Testament hath severall particular periods before it come to that *instaurationem maximam;* O that greatest and inaugmentable restitution at the end of the world."[64] Thus the term whose connotations we are investigating was deemed applicable even to the central event of Christian history, the first coming of Jesus Christ. In 1651 William Lilly hinted darkly at the coming of "the wonderfull yeare of the World." A calendar of marvelous events—sea victory, plague, great wars, drought, famine, the advent of Christ— was prefaced by the remark that "the certaine yeare of these monthly Predictions is not to be revealed, but such there will be in that great yeare before the wonderfull *Catastrophe* of this world shall happen . . ."[65] In two tracts printed within a year of Lilly's, Nicholas Culpeper an-

63. *Peace-Offering* (1641), pp. 40, 45, 46.
64. Homes, *New World* (1641), p. 11.
65. *Monarchy or no Monarchy* (1651), pp. 70–73. Cf. Lilly, *Lord Merlins Prophecy* (1651), pp. 10–11.

nounced 1652 to be "a Year of Wonders," "The Year of Wonders: Or, The glorious Rising of the fifth Monarch."[66] Culpeper's efforts coincided with those of *The Levellers Almanack: for, The Year of Wonders, 1652. . . . prognosticating, The ruine of Monarchy throughout all Christendom* (1651).

These scattered citations indicate that before 1660 there was ample precedent for the use of the terms "*annus mirabilis*" and "wonderful year" to describe events that were neither uniformly dreary nor necessarily sectarian in their appeal. What is most clear from the diversity of usage we have noticed, however, is that the terms seem to have been acceptable for the characterization of any marvelous concatenation of occurrences, whatever their ideological or ethical tendency. This conclusion seems even more likely when we juxtapose the usage of the *Mirabilis Annus* tracts with reference to 1661 and 1662, and that of royal panegyrists with reference to the restoration and coronation years of 1660 and 1661. In his relation of the entertainments which accompanied Charles's coronation ceremony in April 1661 John Ogilby printed the speech which was addressed to the king by one of the blue-coat boys of Christ's Hospital, who expressed great joy at "Your safe arrival to us, and Your presence among us. This Year may well be called *The Year of Wonders;* and this Day of Your Solemnity may be termed *The Birth-day of England's Happiness* . . . We have seen all those *Magnalia Dei* plainly discovered, and have observed the Wheels of Divine Providence in a seeming contrariety; yet the motion at last to be true and regular."[67] The date of April 22 on which this address is said to have been made precedes the earliest mention of the first *Mirabilis Annus* tract, on June 29, by over two months. In his entry for December 31, 1659, Evelyn writes: "Settling my domestic affaires in order, blessed God for his infinite mercies and

---

66. *Ephemeris* (1651), title, *Year of Wonders* (1652), title.
67. Ogilby, *Relation* (1661), pp. 31–32. The speech was printed separately as well: *Speech spoken By a Blew-Coat Boy* (1661).

preservations the past Yeare: ANNUS MIRABILIS."[68]
Since this heading cannot date from before the restoration
day of May 29, 1660, it seems most likely that Evelyn went
back and added it, in one of his customary reviews of the
past year, on December 31, 1660, in the entry for which he
wrote: "I gave God thankes for his many signal mercies to
my selfe, Church & Nation this wonderfull Yeare."[69] In one
of the earlier pages of his *History of the Royal Society* (a
large portion of which was composed before the fire and
hence before the appearance of *Annus Mirabilis*), Thomas
Sprat recalled the restoration year and its many felicities:
". . . Philosophy had its share, in the benefits of that glorious Action: For the *Royal Society* had its beginning in the
wonderful pacifick year, 1660."[70]

Knowing that royal panegyrists were referring to the
restoration year as an *annus mirabilis* at about the same time
that Fifth Monarchy Men were prophesying their own
annus mirabilis, it is extremely hard to tell from which
source Gadbury, in 1665, derived the phrase for his own
highly antithetical treatment of the three comets—if indeed
the phrase did not come from Regiomantus or some other
prophet likely to be familiar to a practising astrologer: "It is
a thing so *rare* and *unusual*, for to have *three Comets* in a
year; nay, sometimes in an *Age:* that we may properly term
this, wherein we live, not only, ANNUS (*sed* AETAS)
MIRABILIS! not only a WONDERFUL YEAR, but AGE."[71]
The term seems to have been conventional enough to allow

68. *Diary* (1955), III, 239.
69. Ibid., III, 265. Cf. III, 246, entry for May 29, 1660: ". . . it was
the Lords doing, *et mirabile in oculis nostris* . . ." Evelyn's editor believes
that the heading in question probably was added when Evelyn transcribed
this portion of the *Diary* from his original notes into the MS. "K"—i.e.,
after Dec. 8, 1680 (see I, 73)—perhaps deriving it from the titles of the
Mirabilis Annus tracts or Dryden's poem (III, 239n1). But Evelyn is
known to have made changes continuously in his original notes for the
Diary (see I, 74–79), and it is more plausible that he added the heading
on May 29 or Dec. 31, 1660, when the significance of the year was fresh
in his mind, than twenty or more years later.
70. *History* (1667), p. 58. On the hiatus in Sprat's composition of the
History see p. 120.
71. *De Cometis* (1665), p. 62. For Gadbury's treatment of the comets
see above, Chapter 5, n20.

a punning (and favorable) reference to it in the diary of an Anglican rector who wrote at the end of the plague year of 1665: "This year was memorabilis annus in Horsted Caines, for there were only two persons buryed in the parish . . ."[72] And one of the tracts entirely devoted to reporting the messianic movement of Sabbatai Sevi contained a letter which bore the following heading: *"Lift up your Heads, this is the Wonderful Year, Feb. 26, 1666."*[73]

The almanacs for 1666, which were printed in the fall of 1665 over a year before the appearance of *Annus Mirabilis*,[74] provide the most positive evidence that Dryden's title should not be seen a priori as a reaction to Fifth Monarchist doctrine. The royalist astrologers William Andrews and Richard Saunders announced that "the Prodigious Year of 1666. is now at hand . . ."; "So that this is like to be a *Year* of *Wonders*, though I mention not the *Popes* 1666."[75] Booker's subject was "the wonderful year, 1666": he referred to Regiomantus's prophecy for 1588 and chose as a suitable title-page chronogram for 1666—the chronogrammatic device itself being not unusual in his almanacs—"MIrabILIs est DeVs In SanCtIs sVIs . . ."[76] Gadbury promised "a general judgement upon this (supposed wonderful) year," indicating his uncertainty about the ideological implications of this supposition, and later exclaimed: "We're come to th' Year of Wonders! Sixty six!"[77] The lesser-known astrologer Thomas Nunnes wrote consistently modest and inoffensive almanacs. In 1666 he discussed the Sabbatian movement and then brought his predictions for the year to a close with this paragraph: "There are many other places in the world, I have not room here to mention, that will be Actors in this Comi-Tragedy, as *Tartaria, Muscovia, Westphalia,* &c. And

72. Moore, "Extracts" (1848), entry for Dec. 30, 1665, I, 97.
73. *New Letter Concerning the Jewes* (1666), p. 5.
74. Almanacs regularly appeared in the fall of the year preceding the one for which they were written: see Thomason's dating of almanacs in the Thomason Tracts collection at the BM, 1640–1661. Cf. Malcolm, *Lond. Rediv.* (1807), anon. letter of Sept. 1666, IV, 81.
75. Andrews, *Newes* (1666), sig. C1r; Saunders, *Apollo* (1666), sig. C3v.
76. *Ephemeris* (1666), sig. C6r, C1r, title.
77. *EPHEMERIS* (1666), title, sig. A3v.

many others, This being *Mirabilis Annus*, but I will conclude with These words, being a Prophesie of the year 1666:
Totum operit mundum terror & Ira Dei."[78] "Comi-Tragedy"
aptly describes Dryden's, and many other contemporaries',
conception of the antithetical wonder of the wonderful year.

Finally, we have the almanac of Vincent Wing, the professional among professionals whose mathematical calculations
provided the basis for many of his fellow astrologers' yearly
tables, a loyal supporter of monarchy whose almanacs always included the lines:

> God save King Charles, His foes destroy;
> And such as do his Realms Annoy.[79]

Early in his offering for 1666, Wing wrote: "Erithic [?]
Annus verè mirabilis. This is like to be a strange year, in
regard of the manifold Actions and Mutations depending
thereon . . ."[80] And at the top of each of the fourteen pages
of the appendix to his almanac, Wing placed, as a general
heading to his comments: "*Annus Mirabilis, 1666.*"[81]

There is no more reason to suppose that Dryden took the
title for his poem from the *Mirabilis Annus* tracts than there
is to think that he borrowed the image of the phoenix from
the seditious tract of that name, which reminded Englishmen that their newly restored king had once pledged to
abide by the phoenixlike Solemn League and Covenant and
which received virtually as much adverse publicity as the
Fifth Monarchist collections.[82] *Annus Mirabilis, The Year
of Wonders, 1666* is a poem whose title is as conventional as
the eschatological prophecies which it contains. Its "political" dimension cannot be found in any implicit opposition to

78. *Almanack* (1666), sig. C8v.
79. E.g., *Olympia* (1666), sig. A2v.
80. Ibid., sig. A5r.
81. And cf. the title of *Bloody Almanack* (1666), probably by Wing.
Cf. Pepys, *Diary* (1904), Dec. 31, 1666, VI, 119: "Thus ends this year of
publick wonder and mischief . . ."
82. See *Phenix, or, The Solemn League and Covenant* (1660?). Charles
himself may allude to this tract in *His Majestie's Declaration* (Oct. 25,
1660), p. 6.

sectarian epistemology and language. Rather, the critic must seek, like Dryden's contemporaries, a rhetorical understanding of the poem, a response which combines conventional and ideological perspectives, collective and individual levels of understanding.

9

HISTORY AND PROPHECY

In my Introduction I suggested that modern historians of religion have perpetuated the general distinction between the pragmatic rationalism of dominant social groups and the fantastic millenarianism of those who have sought to shift the social balance of power. H. R. Trevor-Roper has developed this distinction in a recent discussion of the intellectual foundations of the English Civil Wars. According to Trevor-Roper, the Thirty Years War was the end of an era, and the intellectual survivals of this apocalypse therefore must be seen as "anachronisms," "out of date," the productions of "crackpots." The prophetic utopianism of Hartlib, Dury, and Comenius is owing (in this analysis) entirely to the milieu of the early part of the seventeenth century; the fellows of the Royal Society extended their social and scientific philosophy, but "never having experienced the disasters of the 1620s, they were exempt from its peculiar metaphysics." Cromwell's concern for the Protestant cause, moreover, was an anachronism derived from the antiquated counsel of his contemporaneous advisers, and entailed policies which turned "aghast" all those sober realists who "understood present politics or national interest." Trevor-Roper concludes that "the life work of . . . all those enthusiastic prophets of the Protestant Millennium, would seem, after 1660, irrecoverably dated."[1] One of the aims of the present

1. Trevor-Roper, *Religion* (1967), pp. 282–83, 293.

study has been to cast doubt on the easy disjunctions between religious enthusiasm and ideas of political interest which confirm modern historians in their preconceptions. Eschatological prophecy in the 1660s was no more an anachronism, or a mark of ideological dissent, than a concern for the Protestant cause was.[2] The confident revelation of anachronisms, foreshadowing, fulfillments, and inheritances in history presupposes, no less than Fifth Monarchist doctrine, a preconceived plan of how history works. Whether the result is called fantasy, truth, or something less absolute depends on the perspective from which the estimate is made.

All people who attain a fundamental level of historical consciousness seek patterns in history, births, deaths, and continuities which may constitute fantasy or villainy for those who are not convinced that such patterns accurately describe reality. The epistemological similarities between the ideas of millenarianism, utopianism, and continuous progress are fully as striking as the diversity of ideological ends on which they have been focused.[3] The Protestant Reformation, and all of its denominational offspring, was built upon an eschatological rupture, the end of a corrupt age and the beginning of a new one which would witness the renovation of the primitive Church.[4] Thus Milton's eschatological understanding of the Reformation, if not the parallel which he used it to draw in 1644, was orthodox English

2. For an extended discussion of Restoration advocacy of the Protestant cause and interest as an intellectual posture which reconciled motives of religious belief and political expediency, see my unpublished Columbia University Ph.D. dissertation, "Meanings of Dryden's *Annus Mirabilis*" (1972), pp. 207–26. In his recent book *Religion and the Decline of Magic: Studies in Popular Beliefs in Sixteenth- and Seventeenth-Century England* (London, 1971), Keith Thomas discusses with great learning those questions concerning the relation between enthusiastic belief, rationalism, and the new science which are my subject in Part II of the present study. In my revision of this study for publication I have chosen simply to recommend Thomas's important work to interested readers rather than to enter into extended dialogue with it.

3. See Tuveson, *Millennium* (1949), chap. 3; Ladner, *Idea of Reform* (1967), pp. 30, 31.

4. See Tuveson, *Millennium* (1949), pp. 25–26; Burrell, *Scott. Hist. Rev.*, 43 (1964), 4–5.

Protestantism: "Now once again by all concurrence of signs, and by the generall instinct of holy and devout men, as they daily and solemnly expresse their thoughts, God is decreeing to begin some new and great period in his Church, ev'n to the reforming of Reformation it self . . ."[5]

Contemporaries' testimony regarding the ideological comprehensiveness or limitations of seventeenth-century eschatological prophecy is problematic. For the most part, the Anglican clergy were not seriously troubled by the inconsistency with which they attacked credulity and superstition on principle and marveled over the wonders of prodigies and prophecies which had the correct ideological tendencies. As for the Royal Society, eschatological speculation was not at all a discredited, "unscientific" occupation. Throughout the Restoration, the commonplace distinctions that have since developed between scientific empiricism and inspired or witty interpretation were only potential. According to the professional astrologer John Gadbury, the "honor & excellency" of his trade consists in "that it argueth from the *cause* to the *effect;* and that alone proveth it a *Physical and demonstrative Science.*"[6] Like natural prodigies, the discoveries of the Royal Society seemed to many of its members to be products of divine revelation: God sometimes chooses to reveal himself through a scientist-prophet whose function it is to interpret the book of nature just as exegetes interpret the book of Scripture.[7] Astrology and the astronomical calculations which it employed brought to eschatological speculation by biblical exegesis a tone of scientific objectivity, and many fellows of the society had an avid interest in astrology (and alchemy) which apparently did not conflict with their other concerns.[8] There is no reason to suppose that Dryden himself, a fellow of the Royal Society,[9] was not

5. *Works* (1940), *Areopagitica* (1644), IV, 340.
6. *EPHEMERIS* (1666), sig. A3v.
7. Cf. Rusche, *Eng. Hist. Rev.*, 84 (1969), 756–57.
8. See Tuveson, *Millennium* (1949), p. 55; *Ashmole Collection* (1966), V, index, s.v. "Lilly," "Booker," "Gadbury," "Wharton," etc. (see also I, 135–36).
9. See *List of the Royal Society* (1666), list of fellows as of Apr. 11, 1666.

"sincere" in his many expressions of interest and belief in astrology.[10] Belief is a complex phenomenon which will foil all attempts to reduce its seeming contradictions to unitary or static consistency. In the 1660s eschatological prophecy had the ambiguous status of a slightly suspect indulgence which was simultaneously a natural and indispensable area of human inquiry. Its ethical and intellectual value depended entirely on the context in which it was used or encountered, that is, on the ideology toward which it was directed. When Swift satirized religious enthusiasm in the eighteenth century, he also parodied the enthusiastic experiments of the Royal Society; both seemed misguided, overly zealous methods to attain a truth which was merely secular and dependably accessible to systematic diligence. The technological control of nature eventually obviated the necessity of learning God's truth by reading his works, as long as the works continued to be understood and exploited on their own terms. Collective material progress became possible whether or not individual spiritual progress accompanied it, and as human wonder at nature lessened and the spiritual significance of natural events waned, the principle of material progress itself came to be imbued with the spiritual dynamism which organized religion no longer was capable of mediating.

A comprehensive understanding of the eschatological prophecy of the later seventeenth century requires an appreciation not only of the common element of belief which transcends ideological distinctions but also of the common element of ideological purpose which underlies belief. Common to all eschatological expectations with which we have been concerned was the belief that the great event would be, in some manner, a circular one. The specification of what was

10. Cf. Ashmole's casting of the nativities of Dryden and his son, Ashm. MS. 243, fol. 209. See the story of Dryden's predictions on the basis of his son's nativity: Dryden, *Critical Works* (1800), I, i, 405–19. And see Dryden, *Letters* (1942), no. 47, to his sons, Sept. 3, 1697, pp. 93–94. See generally Gardner, *SP*, 47 (1950), 506–21.

to be renewed constituted the criterion of ideological differentiation. Speculators on 1666 had the added knowledge that 6 was a great number of change; a "perfect" number, the sum of its divisors exclusive of itself; most of all, a "circular" number, which perpetually reproduced its last digit when raised to its powers.[11] For Dryden's contemporaries, the word "revolution" had the same connotation in civil as in astronomical contexts: a restoration or renovation, a return to a former state,[12] and it was this kind of revolution that they looked for in 1660, 1666, and 1688. The change which was expected in the year of change was a conservative one, a revolution in time back to first principles of pristine purity. In this sense, the "conservative myth"[13] was a more or less universal aspect of belief during the Restoration—but ideology differed even as myth and language remained the same. The Fifth Monarchy Man John Rogers combined the commonplace of the serial *translatio* with the cyclical overturning of Ezekiel 21:27 when he exhorted the saints to "rend up by the very roots the *foundations* of these persecuting *Nimrods, . . .* til there be such a *trembling,* shaking, and *consternation,* yea a . . . translation, overturning and total *amotion* of them, that the *Beasts Government* may never have a *being* more in *England . . .*"[14] The astrologer William Andrews celebrated the revolution of 1660 with these words: ". . . And thus did the great God, Overturn, overturn, overturn, the Government of *England, Scotland* and *Ireland,* until he came whose right it was, and he hath given it him."[15] The Hesiodic and Danielic prophecies of the great monarchies fed very different ideologies with identical

11. Cf. Swan, *Speculum Mundi* (1635), p. 21; Sadler, *Olbia* (1660), p. 181, and *Times of the Bible* (1667), p. 6 [2nd pagination]; C. Butler, *Number Symbolism* (1970), p. 8.

12. See Snow, *Hist. Jour.,* 5, no. 2 (1962), 168, 172, 174. Pace Zagorin, *Court and Country* (1969), p. 16, and Lasky, *Encounter,* 34, no. 3 (1970), 37–38, this means not that the word "revolution" had no political use or meaning but that its political meaning was not controversial, since all agreed that revolutions must be conservative and that revolutions such as this are desirable.

13. See above, Introduction.

14. *Jegar* (1657), p. 141.

15. *Newes* (1661), sig. A3v.

visions, so that the conventional presentation of the Western *translatio imperii* by a republican eschatologist might pale beside the inspired messianism of a royal panegyrist.[16] Another Restoration panegyric said, with little irony,

> If a *Fifth Monarch* there must be,
> Let *Englands* Emperour be He,[17]

and Henry More wrote with no irony at all,

whatever grand matters the fervid Parturiency and amuzed Expectation of the very Fanatick part of this Nation was big withall, may come to a more safe and mature birth by the restoring this long-afflicted Prince to his ancient Right, then by any other way conceivable. For those words of so great sound, and of no less import, namely the *Millenium*, the *Reign of the Saints*, the *New Jerusalem*, and the like, to them that are not very wild or ignorant can signifie nothing else but the recovery of the Church to her ancient Apostolick purity . . .[18]

The restoration of Charles and the Anglican Church was, to royalists, a circular renewal of the past, a death and a rebirth. George Rust, one of the fellows of the Royal Society who was so impressed by Greatrakes' stroking, recalled 1660 in the following terms: "By this time the Wheel of Providence brought about the King's happy Restauration, and there began a new World, . . . and all the Three Nations were inspir'd with a new Life . . ."[19] Looking back on the Civil Wars, Hobbes was tempted to discover a circular symmetry in those events which proved fortune's wheel to be providential: "I have seen in this revolution a circular motion of the sovereign power through two usurpers. father and son, from the late King to this his son. For (leaving out the power of the Council of Officers, which was but tempo-

16. Cf. *Brief Description* (1650), p. 36; and Matthew, *KAROLOU* (1660, 1664), pp. 34–35, 61. Kantorowicz, *King's Two Bodies* (1957), p. 83, observes that transferences like that of Charlemagne to Charles II, or of Jerusalem to London, had a significance in men's minds which exceeded that of mere metaphor.
17. Brett, *Restauration* (1660), p. 25.
18. *Explanation* (1660), pp. xii–xiii.
19. *Funeral Sermon* (1668), pp. 15–16.

rary, and no otherwise owned by them but in trust) it moved from King Charles I. to the Long Parliament; from thence to the Rump; thence to the Long Parliament; and thence to King Charles II., where long it may remain."[20] English sovereignty revolved through the traditional typology of governmental forms only to return finally to the first and best form, monarchy. And if royalists saw the Restoration as a return of the Golden Age before the wars, or as a renewal of "Apostolick purity," Fifth Monarchy Men looked to their own eschatons not for the destruction of the world or the Day of Judgment but as "a time of *restoring all things* . . . , a making all things new," a "reforming" and "restitution,"[21] "a good *Reformation*," "the *restoration* of our *Primitive Liberties*."[22] The millennial reign of Christ upon earth, a renewal of all that was lost at the Fall, at the bureaucratization of primitive Christianity, and at the Norman usurpation, would be a "golden age, and the highest top of holy felicity, and happiness, which mortal men may expect."[23] The terms in which revolutionary hopes were expressed were, like the eschatological circularity of those hopes, universal; only the nature of what was to be restored varied from man to man. There were few revolutionaries whose desire for a new start did not envision, as a foundation for the future, a return to the past.

Dryden was fascinated by this idea of the revolution in time which gives birth to a new age simultaneously old, and he used every means he could think of to express it adequately. At the end of his life he published a panegyric to Mary Somerset, duchess of Ormonde, which compared her to the woman whom he imagined Chaucer to have used as a model of beauty:

> Thus, after length of Ages, she returns,
> Restor'd in you, and the same Place adorns;

20. *Behemoth* (1681, 1889), p. 204.
21. Archer, *Personall Reign* (1642), p. 10.
22. Rogers, *Sagrir* (1653), pp. 3, 13.
23. Thomas Brightman, quoted in Cooper, *Baptist Quarterly*, 18 (1960), 354–55. Cf. Alsted, *Worlds* (1642), pp. 7ff.

Royalist vision of the circularity of the Civil Wars. On the right, law and church sink beneath the soldier's ire; on the left, the gentry rise with the aid of judge and bishop. Two-faced Janus, his temple shut, benignly halts the revolution of time's globe at this present point of felicity. The Virgilian legend says, "the turning day." Reprinted from James Heath, *Brief Chronicle* (1663), courtesy of the Harvard College Library.

Or you perform her Office in the Sphere,
Born of her Blood, and make a new Platonick Year.
. . . . .
   As when the Dove returning, bore the Mark
Of Earth restor'd to the long-lab'ring Ark,
. . . . .
So, when You came, with loud repeated Cries,
The Nation took an Omen from your Eyes,
And God advanc'd his Rainbow in the Skies,
To sign inviolable Peace restor'd;
The Saints with solemn Shouts proclaim'd the new accord.
   When at Your second Coming You appear,
(For I foretell that Millenary Year)
The sharpen'd Share shall vex the Soil no more,
But Earth unbidden shall produce her Store:
The Land shall laugh, the circling Ocean smile,
And Heav'ns Indulgence bless the Holy Isle.

. . . . .
All other Parts of Pious Duty done,
You owe Your *Ormond* nothing but a Son:
To fill in future Times his Father's Place,
And wear the Garter of his Mother's Race.[24]

Like his London, Dryden's duchess is wonderfully antithetical in the way she completes the circle of fall and rise, past
and future. Human history, like nature and Scripture, is a
complex continuity of anticipations which are also fulfillments, deaths which are also births, ends which are also
beginnings.

24. "To Her Grace the Dutchess of Ormond" (1700), ll. 26–29, 70–71,
75–85, 165–68.

CONCLUSION:
RHETORICAL ANALYSIS AND
DIALECTICAL CRITICISM

At the beginning of this study I formulated a plan for a rhetorical analysis of *Annus Mirabilis* through a deliberate reaction to what I suggested were two common but distinct ways of approaching the poem. It is now time to ask what this analysis has achieved and what are the main questions that it has raised.

Modern critics frequently praise the epic generality of *Annus Mirabilis*. Whether or not they are specifically interested in the historical context from which the poem emerged, critics who value its generality tend to ascribe their own evaluation of *Annus Mirabilis* to the audience which first read it as well. The poem is taken to create the conditions for its appreciation "as poetry": Dryden's contemporaries and his critics apprehend his rhetorical appeals to national interest and unity as uncontroversial "poetic" commonplaces, and the poem rises from political particularity to poetic generality. I have suggested, however, that rhetorical appeals may be apprehended not only as poetic but also as political strategies. *Annus Mirabilis* can be read with a consciousness of the ideological ends toward which rhetorical commonplaces argue, and Dryden's contemporaries were well equipped to understand the language of interest and unity simultaneously as commonplace and ideology. Hence there is no reason to suppose that the audience of *Annus Mirabilis* was easily disposed to undergo the proc-

ess of persuasion to which modern critics often are susceptible.

When critics choose to emphasize the poem's political
particularity, on the other hand, they take the language of
and belief in eschatological prophecy as one controversial
target against which Dryden launches his political attack. In
this view, Dryden's ideological end is not only to undermine
antiroyalist sedition but to do so in part by tacitly discrediting the enthusiastic state of mind which is characteristic of
the seditious. Yet this understanding of eschatological
prophecy, I have tried to show, does not necessarily reflect
its status either in *Annus Mirabilis* or in seventeenth-century
thought. It is more convincing to understand the poem as an
ideological attack on sedition whose rhetorical strategy requires a complete and unquestioning acceptance of eschatological prophecy as a valid frame of reference. Moreover, an
examination of other Restoration sources fully substantiates
this view of eschatological prophecy as a commonplace of
the age, a rhetorical fundamental which in itself commanded
most people's assent even if its simultaneous ideological use
did not.

Some aspects of my rhetorical analysis of *Annus Mirabilis*
are specific to this particular poem and to its historical
context, while some appear to be capable of extension to
other instances of poetic production. First, I do not intend to
suggest that the perspectives with which I have associated
the poet and his audience respectively have the character of
absolute aesthetic categories. Thus, it need not be a matter
of the "poetic definitions" of the poet versus the "political
definitions" of his audience. In my first reading of *Annus
Mirabilis* I identified the general, transcendent understanding of the poem as Dryden's own definition of it, to be
countered by the ideological understanding discoverable by
adopting the perspective of his historical audience. Another
poem, however, might seem to be defined by the poet in a
totally different manner. In *The Last Instructions*, for example, Marvell frequently is intent on revealing the political
specificity of much that Dryden hopes to generalize in

Annus Mirabilis. The poet, in other words, is not bound by his status "as poet" to define his work as generalized "poetry" rather than as particular "politics." If, as the preceding study seems to suggest, Marvell's ideological stance is fundamentally closer than Dryden's is to the mood that was prevailing in 1667, a rhetorical analysis of his poem might require a finer dissection of the growing opposition to Stuart rule. By distinguishing degrees of disaffection, the critic might determine the nature and substance of the historical audience which Marvell sought to turn from tentative dissatisfaction to his relatively radical position.

Furthermore, it must be emphasized that my own analysis has concentrated on two spheres of public discourse—those of group consciousness and eschatological prophecy—which seem to be important in *Annus Mirabilis* and in the two common readings which were my starting point. It may be that a fuller analysis would study other spheres of discourse as well. I have limited my task to the prior necessity of demonstrating that any given sphere of discourse must be understood both on its primary (or commonplace) and on its secondary (or ideological) levels. Criticism that emphasizes one *level* of discourse in distinction from the other is partial in a way that the limitation of analysis to one or more of several operative *spheres* of discourse is not. This is because it is most basically the dialectic of levels, rather than the interrelation of discourses, that constitutes the poem as a historical event—levels on which Dryden sought to be understood and those on which his contemporaries took the language of *Annus Mirabilis,* both acceding to and resisting its author's persuasions. And it is from our understanding of this historical dialectic, through the reconstruction of contemporary dispute within any given sphere of discourse, that our understanding of the meaning of poetry will derive. The goal of comprehensiveness which is served by rhetorical analysis is thus a qualitative, not a quantitative, value. It should be confused neither with the exhaustive search for all modes of thought and expression that exist in a poet's milieu and that are discernible in his poetry, nor with the eclectic acceptance of all, "equally valid" meanings that can be found in a poem.

Do these observations have relevance only for Dryden's (and Marvell's) discourse, or might they apply to other kinds of poetry as well? It may be tempting to limit rhetorical analysis to the "public," "occasional" poetry of the Restoration, or at least to those ages whose poetic practice was as closely linked with classical rhetorical theory, but I am not sure that this limitation would be warranted. All poems, whatever the aesthetic theories held by the poet, are "public" acts in the sense that they are outward expressions of inner states, written in language that has public significance, and partially dependent, for their meaning, on what their audiences make of them.

Yet what is most essential to my purpose in this study is certainly not the critical terminology which was formulated in the Introduction, and the idea of "rhetorical analysis" itself is simply a convenient means of getting at problems of literary criticism which bear on, but which extend beyond, the "political poetry" of the Restoration. These problems are expressed by the familiar dichotomies which engage all critics who try to come to a full understanding of the literature they study: form vs. content, generality vs. particularity, eternal vs. temporal, transcendent vs. concrete, original creativity vs. historical representativeness. It is commonly held by literary critics that the most successful works of literature reveal not a disjunction but a close interaction of form and content. My aim here is to suggest that high achievement in literature depends, as well, on an especially fruitful dialectic of the transcendent and the concrete. The opposition between the general and the particular which is implied by the generality theory of value takes poetic success to be a transcendence of all questions of political success. A consistently dialectical mode of criticism, however, must recognize that the two kinds of achievement are interdependent, and that poetic transcendence is therefore in some manner the fulfillment, rather than the obliteration, of the concrete historical existence of the poem.

One of the most pressing questions raised by this suggestion is that of critical relativism. How can aesthetic value
have any autonomous meaning if it is dialectically related to
political value? How can the critic perform the task of
aesthetic evaluation if his judgments are limited by his
political orientation? These questions must be answered first
in the clear and inescapable terms dictated by the critical
premises that have led us this far. Aesthetic value cannot
have any such autonomous meaning. There is a difference
between judging a poem "good" and demonstrating its aesthetic value according to autonomous aesthetic criteria.
Most critics are content to do the first while assuming,
without justification, that they must be doing the second,
and thereby performing a primary function of literary
criticism.

Even so, a conviction that the autonomy of the aesthetic
domain is a fiction of idealist critical theory need not render
the idea of aesthetic value a meaningless one or the act of
evaluation an exercise in private subjectivity. Nor must the
recognition that the critic's political partiality affects his
artistic understanding be perceived as a limitation. The
critic's passage from an unaccustomed consciousness of the
ideological persuasiveness of a poet to an awareness of his
own customary submission to this persuasive power takes
him a step closer to assessing the comprehensive value of
poetry than the proponent of the generality theory of value,
for customary submission implies the existence of an alternative perspective that can acquire plausibility only when the
reflex of critical submission is resisted. In my Introduction I
suggested that it is only the adoption of the audience's
perspective which gives meaning to the idea that the poem
is written from the poet's perspective. The critical act of
juxtaposing reductive with dogmatic readings of poetry does
not make either interpretation or evaluation any more
autonomous, but it does make them more objective in two
simple respects.

First and most important, by this act the critic succeeds in
identifying, and in systematically balancing, his own par-

tiality as it tends to be manifested in his understanding of poetry. Thus, the acknowledgment of partiality leads not to its effacement or negation, but to its conscious incorporation within a dialectical mode of understanding which is characterized by what I have called a qualitative comprehensiveness. Criticism that regards the poet's meaning as a sufficient basis for objective understanding of poetry is, in these terms, unobjective not only because it is inadvertently partial as a critical method, but also because it obscures an essential quality of the object it studies, the constitution of its meaning by the dialectic of authorial and audience perspectives. This is one kind of objectivity, then, that is not dependent on a belief in aesthetic autonomy. Second, the antithetical perspectives that provide the focus for this dialectical understanding need not be abstract or subjective categories of the critic's own construction. His inquiry may entail (as mine has done) a concrete historical investigation whose end is knowledge about the meaning of language for a particular poet and for those whom he addresses. It is of no consequence that an understanding of "history as it really was" is unobtainable; knowledge of this sort is determinate, to a large degree discoverable, accessible to many, and in this sense objective. And here too, critical objectivity does not depend on aesthetic autonomy, but on the contrary becomes possible only when the idea of autonomous interpretation and evaluation has been discarded. In fact, far from dissolving in the face of critical relativism, objectivity of the sort I have described derives its strength from the perception that poetic meanings and values are always located in a relation. For if relativism frees the critic from the illusory search for meanings and values that transcend history, it does not abandon him to the realm of personal history where criticism is relative solely to the quality of his own private and subjective response. The task of the critic who is conscious of the relativity of his statements regarding poetry is, instead, to define with precision the objectivity of that necessary relation—that is, to insure that his statements are relative to the particular historical dialectic of poetic production and consumption with which they are concerned. And in establishing his objective relation to this historical dialectic, the critic establishes the conditions for confronting the problem of objectivity not only for the poem but also for criticism itself. The dialectic embodies in its very structure both the ontology (or "meaning") of the poem, and the comprehensive epistemology required to overcome customary partiality and to "comprehend" this meaning.

Throughout the body of this study I have been interested in examining the historical dialectic of *Annus Mirabilis* in order to discover its meaning, and the related question of its aesthetic value has been deferred during the course of this examination. One might expect, however, that the standards according to which dialectical criticism attributes value to the poetry it studies would resemble closely the standards by which I have suggested it can be appreciated as a valuable approach to poetry. For dialectical criticism, aesthetic value is not simply the label that critics attach to works by which they have been persuaded politically, but a function of the degree to which the poet has grounded the specific necessities of his persuasive task in a larger conception of the ideological possibilities that inhere in his general historical context. A dialectical criticism is, in the qualitative sense of the term that I have discussed, a comprehensive perspective on literary production, one for which aesthetic value is, similarly, a matter of comprehensiveness: the power of great literature to go beyond itself, to express the largest capabilities of its age even as it argues for a dogmatic and ideologically limited version of historical possibilities.

Clearly, the ideological bias which is inescapable in poetic production is insufficient alone to guarantee this power of historical representativeness. But just as dialectical criticism demands in the critic a sense of the relative character of aesthetic interpretation and evaluation, so a sharply realized ideological bias is a necessary precondition, in poetry, for its own transce.idence. The nature of this transcendence differs radically from the achievement of aesthetic excellence which is envisioned by the generality theory of value, a critical premise which is applied by the dogmatic elevation of commonplace at the expense of ideology. All poetry amounts to a dialectic of commonplace and ideology. What is required for high poetic achievement in any period is so intense an engagement in the concrete demands and conflicts of the poet's particular age that the limited expression of group interest which must result from this engagement is capable of becoming—however undeliberately—the basis for the broadest and most inclusive conceptualization of contemporary historical conflicts and of their potential resolution. Poetic success is a complex function of political success because it consists in the expansion of ideological argument to the most general and all-embracing levels of discourse possible within any given historical context.

For dialectical criticism, then, aesthetic value is inseparable from the historical context of literature and amounts to the transcendence of closely circumscribed ideology and the attainment of a broad and inclusive historical representativeness. The preceding argument has sufficient generality, I think, to be applied usefully to a variety of literary forms and historical periods; but such an application would go far beyond the scope of this study, which I will conclude instead with a brief attempt to assess the aesthetic value of *Annus Mirabilis* from the perspective of dialectical criticism.

We have seen that Dryden's court ideology in *Annus Mirabilis* involves a partisan characterization of social and political conflict in Restoration England. His constant concern is to dissolve class, party, and sectarian distinctions by defining "things as they are" to be in the national interest or according to the benign will of God—the outcome, that is, of political or providential necessity. This strategy of "decategorization," whereby all minor interests are subsumed under that of Charles and all particular oppressions pale beside those of his impersonally suffering London, seems to reach its climax in Dryden's utopian vision of the internationalist Golden Age of the future, the universal collective made

possible by the discovery of "a more exact measure of
Longitude":

> Instructed ships shall sail to quick Commerce;
> By which remotest Regions are alli'd:
> Which makes one City of the Universe,
> Where some may gain, and all may be suppli'd.

(163)

It is interesting to inquire just what Dryden intends by these
undeniably visionary lines. Is his utopia no more than a
Restoration commonplace (like the ideas of national interest
and circular revolution), directed here to a specific ideological end?

First of all, it is important to recognize what Dryden does
not intend by them. The universal city "where some may
gain, and all may be suppli'd" is very far from the socialist
state which triumphantly will inscribe on its banners (in the
words of Karl Marx): "From each according to his ability, to
each according to his needs!" What Dryden envisions is a
society whose sophisticated technology and communications
owe to the discovery of divine and natural laws and permit a
liberty of opportunity and achievement which, it is implicit
in these prophetic lines, are denied to his own age. In this
future society, the possibility of outstanding individual gain
will be compatible with the capacity for adequate collective
supply. Scientific progress will obviate the restrictions that
are necessary, at present, to protect the national interest
against individual acquisitiveness, and the international balance against the dominance of single nations. The supply of
all thenceforth will proceed easily with the healthy gain of
some. The outlines of this vision are hazy enough, and, as we
might expect of a vision, the details of its realization are
lacking altogether. I think it would not be misleading to look
to another source for a clarification of what is only obscurely
set forth in Dryden's poem.

One hundred years after the publication of *Annus Mirabilis* Adam Smith brought out his great work which refuted

English economic policies under Charles II and other Stuart monarchs by uncovering what he held to be the true and natural laws of economic intercourse. It is worth quoting passages from this refutation at some length. One of its principal tenets was that it is not the satisfaction of the public interest which guarantees the well-being of all private interests but precisely the reverse:

> Every individual is continually exerting himself to find out the most advantageous employment for whatever capital he can command. It is his own advantage, indeed, and not that of the society, which he has in view. But the study of his own advantage naturally, or rather necessarily leads him to prefer that employment which is most advantageous to the society.
>   . . . He generally, indeed, neither intends to promote the public interest, nor knows how much he is promoting it . . . he intends only his own gain, and he is in this, as in many other cases, led by an invisible hand to promote an end which was no part of his intention. Nor is it always the worse for the society that it was no part of it. By pursuing his own interest he frequently promotes that of the society more effectually than when he really intends to promote it.

Inseparable from Smith's pragmatic defense of individual selfishness is his opposition to all forms of governmental protectionism, which mistakenly are designed to further the national interest. In fact, "the natural effort of every individual to better his own condition, when suffered to exert itself with freedom and security, is so powerful, that it is alone, and without any assistance, not only capable of carrying on the society to wealth and prosperity, but of surmounting a hundred impertinent obstructions with which the folly of human laws too often incumbers its operations . . ." For Dryden, the creation of "one City of the Universe" will depend upon continuing scientific exploration and technological development. A century later, what stands in the way of Smith's somewhat similar ideal is little more than the inveterate blindness of legislators: "Were all nations to follow the liberal system of free exportation and free importation, the different states into which a great continent was divided would so far resemble the different provinces of a great empire."[1]

Dryden's argument throughout *Annus Mirabilis,* of course, is no more sustaining of economic individualism and a laissez faire economy than it is of parliamentary democracy. Perhaps what is most crucial to the way in which his ideology seems to go beyond itself even as it solidly buttresses the economic and political policies of Charles II is Dryden's attitude toward revolution and the new science.

Dryden's conservative idea of political revolution seems harmonious enough with his enthusiasm for the nascent scientific revolution of his age, but there is a suggestive uneasiness in the relationship nonetheless. The Royal Society represents the progressive spirit of the new science—the quest for practical knowledge and the inexorable mastering of nature—for which Bacon and others had prepared at the beginning of the century, and in *Annus Mirabilis* the Royal Society undoubtedly serves the interests of the royal Charles. But as Dryden indicates,[2] even England's monarch has something to learn from the revolutionary methods of the new science, whose talents are described thus in the "*Apostrophe to the Royal Society*":

> O truly Royal! who behold the Law,
> And rule of beings in your Makers mind,
> And thence, like Limbecks, rich Idea's draw,
> To fit the levell'd use of humane kind.

(166)

We are given to understand that as a wise ruler Charles will encourage the Royal Society's explorations into uncharted areas of intellectual and material promise. Yet the consequences of these explorations were as unforeseeable and revolutionary in social and political spheres as they were in the scientific. As men like Dryden were just beginning to understand, the Golden Age of the future, the establishment of "one City of the Universe, / Where some may gain, and

1. Smith, *Wealth of Nations* (1776, 1937), IV, ii, 421, 423; v, 508, 506.
2. See above, Chapter 5.

all may be suppli'd," would have no precedent in the history
of humankind—however apposite the literary commonplaces might continue to appear. The wonder of this distinctively urban Eden is that universal peace and plenty will be
re-created, in a world grown unimaginably complex, not by
teaching humans to temper their sinful and selfish desires
but by regulating nature to accommodate those desires to
the fullest extent.

In this utopia of unfettered private interests, the role to be
played by the national monarch could only be uncertain.
One consequence of the scientific inquiry which Dryden
praises in *Annus Mirabilis* was the discovery of "natural
laws" that had profound political implications—such as
Adam Smith's warning that "to hinder . . . the farmer from
sending his goods at all times to the best market, is evidently
to sacrifice the ordinary laws of justice to an idea of public
utility, to a sort of reasons of state; an act of legislative
authority which ought to be exercised only, which can be
pardoned only in cases of the most urgent necessity."[3] When
national policies are identified with "reasons of state," they
have a sanctity which overrides mere private interests in a
way similar to the transcendence, in the medieval theory of
kingship, of the king's body politic over his body natural.
And Dryden's conservative idea of political revolution—
Charles II restoring England to the prelapsarian days of his
father—had a considerable appeal which drew strength
from this notion of the uninterrupted translation of monarchal authority. Yet the principle that the king cannot err still
was being given lip service in 1667 less because it retained
much of its traditional serviceability than because of the
harshness of Charles's laws on sedition and printing. During
the Civil Wars the monarchist doctrine of the king's two
bodies was used by republicans to justify rebellion against
Charles I "in his private capacity," and after the Restoration
the doctrine was generally and tacitly discredited as a dis-

3. *Wealth of Nations* (1776, 1937), IV, v, 507.

tinction whose idealism allowed a more comprehensive license with reality than royalists had intended.

The beheading of Charles I's body natural inspired the gradual realization that the unique sanctity of the public interest lay not in its spurious identification with governmental policy but in the fact that public interest was a practical function of how all private interests—including that of the king—interacted in their pursuit of different rewards.[4] The year 1649 is a revolutionary date in the special sense that it marked, with extraordinary force and finality, a milestone in the development of the idea of political revolution away from its strict association with conservative circularity and toward its modern connotation. In much the same way, the seventeenth-century discovery of scientific revolution—at once obscure, tantalizing, and portentous for contemporaries—severed unalterably the Golden Age of the past from whatever technological utopias the world might anticipate in times to come. Once again, Adam Smith describes not only the economic, but also the political, fruits which were to germinate from the seeds of Dryden's panegyric to the new science:

All systems either of preference or of restraint, therefore, being thus completely taken away, the obvious and simple system of natural liberty establishes itself of its own accord. Every man, as long as he does not violate the laws of justice, is left perfectly free to pursue his own interest his own way, and to bring both his industry and capital into competition with those of any other man, or order of men. The sovereign is completely discharged from a duty, in the attempting to perform which he must always be exposed to innumerable delusions, and for the proper performance of which no human wisdom or knowledge could ever be sufficient; the duty of superintending the industry of private people, and of directing it towards the employments most suitable to the interest of the society.[5]

4. For an extended analysis of the seventeenth-century transformation of the idea of public interest, see J. A. W. Gunn, *Politics and Public Interest in the Seventeenth Century* (London, 1969).

5. *Wealth of Nations* (1776, 1937), IV, ix, 651.

We need not share Smith's conviction that "natural liberty" is a concomitant of free-enterprise capitalism to appreciate the perspective which his critique provides on *Annus Mirabilis*. But although *The Wealth of Nations* is a convenient and lucid account of capitalist principles, it is possible, as the foregoing speculations on seventeenth-century science and revolution will have suggested, to perceive Dryden's oblique relation to them without having recourse to later formulations. In *Annus Mirabilis*, Dryden exalts the national interest, identifying it with governmental interest and distinguishing this collective ideal from all varieties of individualistic, merely private self-interest. Monarchal absolutism protects the national interest by limiting the "liberties" claimed by divisive interest groups—antimonopolists, tolerationists, the poor—and by restraining the selfish motives of individual acquisitiveness and aggrandizement which feed such claims. In order to lend special credence to this quite traditional conception of the national interest, Dryden erects, as the cornerstone of his argument and of his poem, the anticipated achievements of the new science, the marvels of material progress which will proceed under the absolute and beneficent patronage of Charles II. Yet the empiricist premises of the new science are totally subversive of authoritarianism in the realm of natural knowledge and, by necessary implication, in the realm of received political and socioeconomic wisdom as well. Scientific method is rigorously individualistic in its commitment to the discovery of "natural laws" ("a more exact measure of Longitude," a more exact system of economic intercourse and political management) which call into question traditional ideas about what constitutes the natural. "The law of nature," R. H. Tawney once observed, "had been invoked by medieval writers as a moral restraint upon economic self-interest. By the seventeenth century, a significant revolution had taken place. 'Nature' had come to connote, not divine ordinance, but human appetites, and natural rights were invoked by the individualism of the age as a reason why self-interest should be given free play."[6] Because it is so closely identified with scientific method in *Annus Mirabilis,* Dryden's bold liberty of prophesying is far bolder than he intends. It prepares not for the renovation of prelapsarian absolutism and "reasons of state," but for the ascendancy of individualism and the commonplace invocation of "individual rights" in all spheres of public life.

It is with the aid of this broad perspective that *Annus Mirabilis* can be seen to have a historical representativeness which is larger than its poetic commonplaces and its political ideology. The technique of decategorization, the sheer expansiveness which underlies Dryden's advocacy of mercantilist nationalism and the passive reliance on monarchal authority, gives an ideological breadth to his account of England's condition and prospects in the wonderful year which is no part of his present purpose. In his attempt to resolve the difficult problems besetting the reign of the restored monarch, Dryden employs strategies that aim directly at the preservation of Charles II's interests as the poet best understands them. And these strategies play a clear and useful role in Dryden's ideological defense of things as they are, even as they transcend this defense by pointing forward to things—radically different—as they must necessarily be in the not-so-distant future.

6. *Religion and the Rise of Capitalism* (1937, 1958), pp. 152–53.

BIBLIOGRAPHY   INDEX

BIBLIOGRAPHY

The Bibliography constitutes a comprehensive list of the "primary" sources used in this study and of the "secondary" sources used in any detail. It is divided into three sections: (1) Manuscripts, (2) Works Printed through 1700, and (3) Works Printed after 1700. Although none of the post-seventeenth-century printing dates of certain government publications (*Commons Journal, Lords Journal, Calendars of State Papers, Statutes of the Realm, Reports of the Historical Manuscripts Commission*) have been given in the footnotes, bibliographical references to these works will be found in section 3.

I have aimed at precision in transcribing names of authors of seventeenth-century tracts as they appear (or do not appear) on title pages. Hence I have used the dash (————.) only in those cases where a name appears exactly as it is given in the preceding entry. Thus, when the name of the author in the preceding entry is in brackets, a dash signifies that the following tract also was printed anonymously.

Despite the fact that almanacs customarily were printed at the end of the year preceding the one for which they were written, the dates of almanacs are given here as they appear on their title pages.

In section 2 London should be understood to be the place of publication unless another place name is given. If place of publication is unknown, this fact is signified by "n.p." All known places of publication, including London, are given in section 3.

No publication information other than place and date is given for works printed through 1800. Name of publisher is given for works printed after 1800.

Hebrew words and letters have been omitted from titles, and Greek titles have been transliterated and silently amended. No attempt has been made to reproduce unusual type fonts, italicization, and so forth. With these exceptions language and format have not been modernized or "corrected."

In section 2 the British Museum should be understood to be the location of all tracts whose location is not given in parentheses. For these latter tracts I have given the names, or abbreviations of the names, of the libraries in which each one was used.

The letters "brs." after a work in section 2 indicate that it is a broadside—printed on a single sheet.

1. *Manuscripts*

Bodleian Library, Oxford

Ashmole MSS.

240: Letter of Sir Edward Walker to Lilly concerning Becket prophecy.
241: Lilly's "Paraphrase" on Becket prophecy.
243: Dryden's and son's nativities.
423: Letter of Lilly to Ashmole concerning Becket prophecy.
538: Ashmole's copy of Lilly's *Monarchy or no Monarchy in England* (1651).
553: Lilly's copy of *Monarchy or no Monarchy in England* (1651).

B.15.8. Linc.: Greatrakes' letter to Dr. Hall, bishop of Chester.

Clarendon MS. 83: Miscellaneous letters and papers of state, 1665.

Sancroft MS. 51: Sancroft's book of prophecies, dreams, divinations, etc.

Tanner MS. 45: Miscellaneous letters and papers, 1665–1667.

Wood 416: Robert Whitehall's [?] poem and chronogram on 1666.

British Museum, London

Additional MSS.

4182: Unsigned newsletter journal, Jan. 1664–Nov. 1665.
4293: Documents relating to Greatrakes.
5810: Letters of Simon Patrick to Mrs. Gauden, 1665–66.
6331: Seal of Company of Royal Adventurers trading into Africa.
10116: Thomas Rugge's "Diurnal," May 1659–Dec. 1661.
10117: Thomas Rugge's "Diurnal," Dec. 1661–Mar. 1672.
29495: Poems of William Lodington, Quaker, 1653–1698.
32094: State papers, 1660–1676, including William Coventry's secret paper on a Dutch war.
33770: Documents on the Yorkshire Plot, 1663.
34362: Copy of poem "Couer la feu ye Hugonotts," circulated after the Great Fire.
34363: George Cartwright's "Upon the deplorable fire at London . . . 1666."
39866: Two anon. poems on the restoration of Charles II.
40712: Letters, 1666, to Sir George Oxinden in Surat.
40713: Letters, 1666–67, to Sir George Oxinden in Surat.

Burney MS. 390: Miscellaneous poems, 1660s.

Egerton MSS.

627: "Relation D'Angleterre" (1666).
2982: Miscellaneous letters and papers, 1660s.

Harleian MSS.
559: Copy of Lily prophecy, 1559.
3785: Letters to Sancroft, 1660s.
7010: Letters to and from Sir Richard Fanshawe, English ambassador to Spain, 1665–66.
Stowe MS. 744: Miscellaneous letters and papers, 1660s.

Cambridge University Library, Cambridge
Additional MS. 711: Two poems by Anthony Dopping.

Chetham's Library, Manchester
Mun. A.3.123: Abstract, notes, and collections from diary of Henry Newcome, covering 1646–1695.
Mun. A.4.14: Copy of poem "Couer la feu ye Hugonotts," circulated after the Great Fire.

Longleat, Wiltshire
Coventry MS. 102: William Coventry's notes on the causes of the Second Anglo-Dutch War and how to win a future one.

Public Record Office, London
Privy Council Registers (PC 2/): Papers concerning trade and the Company of Royal Adventurers trading into Africa.
State Papers, Domestic (SP 29/): Miscellaneous letters and state papers.
State Papers, Foreign, Flanders (SP 77/): Letters to and from William Temple in Flanders, 1665–66.

2. *Works Printed through 1700*

Adams, Edward. *A Brief Relation of the Surprizing several English Merchants Goods, by Dutch Men of Warre* . . . 1664.
The Advantages of the Kingdom of England, both abroad and at home . . . 1662 [?].
An Advertisement As touching the Fanaticks Late Conspiracy and Outrage attempted and Acted partly in the City . . . T.T. Jan. 28, 1661.
The Age of Wonders, or miracles are not ceased . . . 1660.
[Alsted, Johannes Heinrich.] *The Worlds Proceeding Woes and Succeeding Joyes* . . . Ed. by William Burton. 1642.
Andrews, William. *Newes From the Stars* . . . 1661. (Bod.)
———. *Newes from the Starrs* . . . 1665. (Bod.)

———. *Newes from the Starres* . . . 1666.

———. *Newes from the Starrs* . . . 1667.

Answer of the Company of Royal Adventurers of England trading into Africa . . . 1667. (National Library of Scotland)

Archer, Henry. *The Personall Reign of Christ upon Earth. In a treatise wherein is fully and largely laid open and proved, that Jesus Christ, together with the saints, shall visibly possesse a monarchicall state and kingdome in this world* . . . 1642. (Bod.: 5th ed., 1661)

Articles of Peace & Alliance Between the most Serene and Mighty Prince, Charles II . . . *And the High and Mighty Lords, The States General Of the United Netherlands, Concluded the 4th day of September, 1662.* 1662.

[Ashmole, Elias.] *A Brief Narrative of his Majestie's Solemn Coronation* . . . 1662. [Printed with continuous pagination after Ogilby, *Entertainment* (1662), q.v.]

A[spinwall], W[illiam]. *The Legislative Power is Christ's Peculiar Prerogative.* 1656.

Aubrey, J[ohn]. *Miscellanies* . . . 1696.

B., J. *The Blazing Star: or, A Discourse of Comets, Their Natures and Effects: in a letter from J. B. to T. C. concerning the late comet seen on Sunday December the 11. 1664* . . . 1665.

B., J. *The Shepherds Lasher Lash'd, Or a Confutation of the Fugitives Vindication.* 1665. brs.

Baker, Daniel. *A Certaine Warning from a naked Heart* . . . 1659.

[Baker, Richard.] *The Marchants Humble Petition And Remonstrance, To his late Highnesse. With an Accompt of the Losses of their Shipping, and Estates, since the War with Spain* . . . *A General Remedy proposed for the restauration of the Trade* . . . 1659.

Baxter, Richard. *A Key for Catholicks, To open the Jugling of the Jesuits* . . . 1659.

———, *Reliq. Baxt.: Reliquiae Baxterianae: or, Mr. Richard Baxter's Narrative of The most Memorable Passages of his Life and Times* . . . Ed. by Matthew Sylvester. 1696.

B[ayly], W[illiam]. *The Great and Dreadful Day of the Lord God Almighty* . . . *once more proclaimed, That All People may again be warned to Repent with speed, and so be left without excuse.* 1664. brs.

[Beacher, Lyonell.] *Wonders if not Miracles or, A Relation of the Wonderful Performances of Valentine Gertrux of Affance neer Yonghall In Ireland. Who Cureth all manner of Diseases with a stroak of his hand and Prayer, as is testified by many eare and eye Witnesses.* 1665.

Bedloe, William. *A Narrative and Impartial Discovery of the Horrid Popish Plot* . . . 1679.

Benlowes, Edward. *The Summary of Wisedome.* 1657.

[Berkenhead, John.] *The Assembly-Man. Written in the Year 1647.* 1663. [Reprinted in *Harl. Misc.*, V (1810), 98–104, q.v.]

———. *A New Ballad Of a famous German Prince and a renowned English Duke, who on St. James's day One thousand 666 fought with a Beast with Seven Heads, call'd Provinces* . . . 1666. brs. (Bod.)

———. *The Second Part Of the New Ballad Of the Late and Terrible Fight on St. James's day One Thousand 666* . . . 1666. brs. (Bod.)

[Bethel, Slingsby.] *Observations On the Letter Written to Sir Thomas Osborn; Upon the Reading of a Book called the Present Interest of England Stated* . . . 1673.

Biddle, Ester. *A Warning from the Lord God of Life and Power, unto thee O City of London, and to The Suburbs round about thee* . . . 1660.

Blagrave, Joseph. *Blagrave's Ephemeris For the Year 1659* . . . 1659. (Bod.)

Bold, Henry. *St. Georges Day Sacred to the Coronation of his Most Excellent Majesty Charles the II* . . . 1661.

Bongus, Petrus. *Petri Bungi Bergomatis Nvmerorvm Mysteria* . . . 2nd ed. Bergamo, 1591.

Booker, John. *An Ephemeris* . . . *for the year of Christ's Incarnation M.DC.LXVI.* . . . . *MIrabILIs est DeVs In SanCtIs sVIs, Psal. 68.36.* 1666.

———. *Telescopium Uranicum: Or* . . . *An Almanack and Prognostication for* . . . *M.DC.LXI.* . . . . 1661.

———. *Telescopium Uranicum* . . . 1662.

———. *Telescopium Uranicum* . . . 1663.

———. *Telescopium Uranicum* . . . 1664. (Bod.)

———. *Telescopium Uranicum* . . . 1665. (Bod.)

———. *Telescopium Uranicum* . . . 1667.

Booker Rebuk'd for his Telescopium Uranicum . . . 1665. (Bod.)

Borfet, Abdiel. *Postliminia Caroli II. The Palingenesy, or, Second-Birth, of Charles the Second to his Kingly Life* . . . 1660.

[Boyle, Robert.] *Occasional Reflections upon Several Svbiects. Whereto is premis'd A Discourse About such kinds of Thoughts.* 1665.

Brett, Arthur. *The Restauration. Or, A Poem on the Return of the Most Mighty and ever Glorious Prince, Charles the II. to his Kingdoms.* 1660.

Bridge, William. *Seasonable Truths in Evil-Times: in Several Sermons, lately preached, in and about London* . . . 1668.

A *brief Description Of the future History of Europe, from Anno 1650 to An. 1710. Treating principally of those grand and famous Mutations yet expected in the World, as, The ruine of the Popish Hierarchy, the final annihilation of the Turkish Empire, the Conversion of the Eastern and Western Jews, and their Restauration to their ancient Inheritances in the holy Land, and the Fifth Monarchie of the universall Reign of the Gospel of Christ upon Earth. With principal Passages upon every of these, out of that famous Manuscript of Paul Grebner extant in Trinity-Colledge Library in Cambridge* . . . 1650.

A *Brief Narrative Of that Stupendious Tragedie Late intended to be Acted by the Satanical Saints of these Reforming Times* . . . 1662, 1663. (Bod.)

Briscoe, William. *Verses, Presented to his Masters in the Ward of St. Giles's Cripplegate, within the Freedom.* 1667. brs.

Brome, Alex[ander]. *A Congratulatory Poem, on The Miraculous, and Glorious Return of that unparallel'd King Charls the II. May 29. 1660.* 1660.

———. *Songs and other Poems.* 1661.

Burden, William. *Christs Personal Reign On Earth, One Thousand Yeers with his Saints* . . . 1654. (Houghton Library, Harvard University)

By the King. A Proclamation commanding All Jesuits and Popish Priests To depart this Kingdom. Apr. 9, 1663.

By the King. A Proclamation Concerning the Acts of Navigation, and Encouragement of Trade. Aug. 26, 1663.

By the King. A Proclamation For Banishing all Popish Priests and Jesuites, and putting the Laws in speedy and due Execution against Popish Recusants. Nov. 10, 1666.

By the King. A Proclamation Forbidding Foreign Trade and Commerce. Mar. 1, 1665.

By the King. A Proclamation, Prohibiting all unlawful and Seditious Meetings and Conventicles under pretence of Religious Worship. Jan. 10, 1661.

By the King. A Proclamation Prohibiting the Importation of all sorts of Manufactures and Commodities whatsoever, of the Growth, Production, or Manufacture of France, and of all places in the Possession of the French King. Nov. 10, 1666.

By the King. A Proclamation Requiring some of His Majesties Subjects in the parts beyond the Seas, to return into England . . . Apr. 21, 1666.

By the Mayor. Dated the 27 of October, 1665. And in the 17 year of His Majesties Reign. 1665. brs.

Canne, John. *The Time of the End* . . . 1657. [With "Epistolary Perambulations" by John Rogers.]

————. *A Voice From the Temple to the Higher Powers. Wherein is shewed, that it is the work and duty of the Saints, to search the Prophesies and Visions of holy Scripture, which concern the Later Times . . . Also Severall Prophesies are here opened, concerning the Time of the End . . .* 1653.

Casaubon, Meric. *Of Credulity and Incredulity, In things Natural, Civil, and Divine . . .* 1668.

A Catalogue of the Damages for which the English Demand Reparation from the United-Netherlands. As also A List of the Damages . . . for which Those of the United-Netherlands demand Reparation and Satisfaction from the English . . . 1664.

The Cavaleers Letany. 1661. brs. (Chet. Lib.)

The Cavaliers Complaint . . . [and] *An Echo to the Cavaliers Complaint.* brs. 1660.

[Charpentier, François.] *A Treatise Touching the East-Indian Trade: or, A Discourse* (*Turned out of French into English*) *Concerning the Establishment of a French Company For the Commerce of the East-Indies . . .* 1664.

Christ and Antichrist: or, 666. Multiplied by 2½. Whereby the true Number of Antichrists Reign Is discovered. 1662.

The Cities Loyalty Display'd: or the Four Famous and Renowned Fabricks in the City of London . . . 1661.

The Citizens Joy For the Rebuilding of London. 1667. brs.

[Clarendon, Edward Hyde, Earl of.] *Second Thoughts; or the Case of a Limited Toleration, Stated according to the present Exigence of Affairs in Church and State.* 1663.

Clarke, John. *The Plotters unmasked, Murderers no Saints, or, a Word in season to all those that were concerned in the late Rebellion against the peace of their King and Country, on the sixth of January last at night, and the ninth of January.* T.T. Jan. 12, 1661.

Clavis Apocalyptica: A Prophetical Key: by which The great Mysteries in the Revelation of St. John, and the Prophet Daniel are opened; It beeing made apparent That the Prophetical Numbers com to an end with the year of our Lord, 1655. Written by a Germane D[octor]. and now translated out of High-Dutch [by Samuel Hartlib] *. . .* 1651.

Cliffe, E. *An Abreviate of Hollands Deliverance By, and Ingratitude To the Crown of England and House of Nassau . . .* 1665.

[Codrington, Robert.] *His Majesties Propriety, and Dominion on the Brittish Seas Asserted . . .* 1665.

C[odrington], R[obert]. *Prophecies of Christopher Kotterus, Christiana Poniatovia, Nicholas Drabicius. Three Famous German Prophets . . . Predictions concerning the Pope, Emperor, and King of France, with the sudden destruction of the Popish Religion in the year 1666* . . . 2nd ed. 1664. (Bod.)

————. *The Prophecyes Of the Incomparable and Famous Dr Martin Luther* . . . *As also, The Remarkable Prophecy of the Learned and Reverend Musculus* . . . 1664.

————. *Several Choice Prophecyes Of the Incomparable and Famous Dr Martin Luther, as also, The Remarkable Prophecy of the Learned and Reverend Dr Musculus.* 1666. (Bod.)

C[omenius], J[an] A[mos]. *Historia Revelationum Christophori Kotteri, Christinae Poniatoviae, Nicolai Drabicij. & qvae circa illas varie acciderunt, usqve ad easundem Anno 1657 publicationem, & post publicationem* . . . N.p., 1659. [First printed in 1657 as *Lux in Tenebris* . . .]

Copy of a Prophecy sent to B: F: in the Year 1666 from Montpelliers by the late honourable Algernon Sidney Esqr. & by him Accidentally found among old Papers this 18/28 February 1689. Rotterdam[?], 1690[?]. brs.

Corbet, John. *The Interest of England In the Matter of Religion, The First and Second Parts. Unfolded in the Solution of Three Questions.* 2nd impression. 1661.

Corbet, J[ohn]. *The Second Part of the Interest of England, In the Matter of Religion, Unfolded in a Deliberative Discourse, Proving, That it is not agreeable to sound Reason to prefer the Contracted and Dividing Interest of one Party, before the general Interest of Protestantism, and of the whole Kingdom of England, in which the Episcopal and Presbyterian Parties may be happily United.* 1661. [2nd part of above entry, with continuous pagination.]

Cornelius, Peter [Cornelius Plockhoy]. *A Way propounded to make the Poor in these and other Nations happy* . . . 1659.

[Corss, James.] *An Almanack Or, New Prognostication, For the Year of our Lord and Saviour, 1666* . . . Aberdeen, 1666.

Couch, Robert. *New-Englands Lamentation For the Late Firing of the City of London.* 1667[?]. brs.

Cradocke, Francis. *An Expedient For Taking away all Impositions, and For Raising a Revenue without Taxes* . . . 1660.

C[rane], R[ichard]. *A Lamentation Over thee O London with thy rulers and people, who hast slighted the day of thy Visitation, and resisted the Spirit of the Lord* . . . *and now must receive thy reward at the hand of the Lord.* 1665.

[Crook, John.] *Glad-Tydings Proclaimed to the Upright in Heart* . . . *and Judgment pronounc'd against Babylon, and her Merchants* . . . 1662.

Crouch, John. *Londinenses Lacrymae. Londons Second Tears*

mingled with her Ashes. Chronogram. Vrbs LonDon CoMbVsta fVIt. M.DC.LXVI. 1666.

C[rouch], J[ohn]. *A Mixt Poem, Partly Historicall, partly Panegyricall, upon the Happy Return of His Sacred Majesty Charls the Second* . . . 1660.

Crouch, John. *Poterion glukhupikhzon. Londons Bitter-Sweet-Cup of Tears For Her late Visitation: and Joy for The Kings Return* . . . 1666.

Culpeper, Nich[olas]. *An Ephemeris for the Year 1652. Being Leap-year, and a Year of Wonders* . . . 1651.

[Culpeper, Nicholas?] *The Year of Wonders: Or, the glorious Rising of the fifth Monarch: Shewing the greatness of that freeborn Prince, who shall Reign and govern; and what shall happen upon his Coronation* . . . 1652.

D[arell], J[ohn]. *A True and Compendious Narration; or (Second Part of Amboyna) of Sundry Notorious or Remarkable Injuries, Insolencies, and Acts of Hostility which the Hollanders Have Exercised from time to time against the English Nation* . . . 1665.

Davenant, William. *Poem, to the King's most Sacred Majesty.* 1663.

[Dekker, Thomas.] *The Wonderfull yeare. 1603* . . . 1603[?]

Dolus an Virtus? Or, An Answer to A Seditious Discourse concerning The Religion of England: and The Settlement of Reformed Christianity in its due Latitude . . . 1668.

D[oolittle], T[homas]. *Rebukes for Sin By God's Burning Anger: by the Burning of London: by the Burning of the World: by the Burning of the Wicked in Hell-Fire* . . . 1667.

A Door of Hope: or, A Call and Declaration for the gathering together of the first ripe Fruits unto the Standard of our Lord, King Jesus. 1661. [Thomason writes on the 2nd blank sheet following this tract: "This libell [w]as Scattered about the Streett that night those bloody Villaines intended their Massacre in London which was upon Sunday night ye 6th of January 1660 [1661] . . ."]

[Dury, John.] *The Plain Way of Peace and Unity in Matters of Religion. Shewed* . . . *for the preserving and promoting of the Protestant Religion* . . . 1660.

The Dutch Armado A meer Bravado. A poem upon the late engagement at sea . . . 1665. brs.

The Dutch Drawn to the Life . . . 1664.

The Dutch Gazette: or, The Sheet of Wild-Fire, that Fired the Dutch Fleet. 1666[?]. brs.

The Dutch Nebuchadnezzar; Or, A Strange Dream of the States-

General: With the Interpretation thereof. And a famous Prophecy of Mr. Powel, Writ in the first Year of the Reign of Queen
Elizabeth of ever blessed Memory; Fore telling the great Warrs
betwixt England, France, and Holland, this present Year, 1666
. . . 1666. (Bod.)

E., S. The Toutch-Stone of Mony and Commerce: Or an Expedient For increase of Trade, Mony, and Shiping in England
. . . 1659.

Edlyn, Richard. Prae-Nuncius Sydereus: an Astrological Treatise
of the effects of the great conjunction of the two superiour
Planets, Saturn & Jupiter, October the Xth. 1663 . . . 1664.

Eliot, George. An English-Duel: or Three to Three . . . 1666.
brs. (PRO SP 29/)

Englands Safety in the Laws Supremacy. 1659.

ENIAYTOS TERASTIOS. Mirabilis Annus, or The year of Prodigies and Wonders, being a faithful and impartial Collection of
several Signs that have been seen in the Heavens, in the Earth,
and in the Waters; together with many remarkable Accidents
and Judgments befalling divers Persons, according as they have
been testified by very Credible Hands; all which have hap-
pened within the space of One Year last past, and are now
made publick for a seasonable Warning to the people of these
Three Kingdoms speedily to repent and turn to the Lord, whose
Hand is lifted up amongst us. 1661.

Et à Dracone: Or, some Reflections Upon a Discourse Called
Omnia à Belo comesta. Containing Some Animadversions from
the North, upon the Letter out of the West . . . 1668.

Evans, Arise. The Bloudy Vision of John Farley, Interpreted by
Arise Evans. With another vision signifying peace and happiness. Both which shew remarkable alterations speedily, to come
to pass here in England. Also a refutation of a pamphlet, lately
published by one Aspinwall: called a brief discription of the
fifth Monarchy. Showing: . . . that the fifth Monarchy will
shortly be established in the person of Charls Stewart. 1653.

[Evans, Arise.] Light For the Jews: Or, the Means to convert
them, in Answer to a Book of Theirs, called The Hope of Israel,
written and printed by Manasseth Ben-Israel, Chief Agent for
the Jews here. 1650. Shewing the Time of King Charles coming
in; his War with Holland, and the issue of it: also the Emperour[s] wars with the Turk, and the Event of it; given as a
Sign to the Jews, to know when to stand up in their own Land,
and how to prevail . . . This book was written eight years ago
. . . and never published till now. 1664. 1664.

[Evelyn, John.] An apology for the Royal Party: Written in a
Letter To a Person of the Late Councel of State . . . 1659.

Evelyn, John. *A Panegyric to Charles the Second.* 1661. [Reprinted in *The Augustan Reprint Society,* no. 28, with an introduction by Geoffrey Keynes. Los Angeles: William Andrews Clark Memorial Library, 1951.]

―――, trans. *A Parallel of the Antient Architecture with the Modern* . . . [by Roland Freart]. 1664.

An Exact Narrative of the Tryal and Condemnation of John Twyn, for Printing and Dispersing of a Treasonable Book . . . 1664. (Bod.)

[F., R.] *A Letter from a Gentleman To the Honourable Ed. Howard Esq; Occasioned By a Civiliz'd Epistle of Mr. Dryden's, Before his Second Edition of his Indian Emperour.* 1668. (Victoria and Albert Museum, London)

Fair-Warning: or, XXV. Reasons Against Toleration and Indulgence of Popery . . . *With an Answer to the Roman-Catholicks Reasons for Indulgence. Also the Excellent Reasons of the honourable House of Commons against Indulgence; with Historical Observations thereupon.* 1663.

Fair Warning: The Second Part. Or XX. Prophesies Concerning the Return of Popery . . . *With the several Plots laid* . . . *for Restoring Popery, now Discovered. To justifie the King's most Excellent Majesty, and the Right Honourable the Parliament of Englands Just Resolution to maintain the Act of Uniformity, that Onely Great Remedy against the Growth of Popery.* 1663.

Festa Georgiana, or the Gentries & Countries Joy for the Coronation of the King, on St. Georges Day. 1661.

A few Sober Queries Upon the late Proclamation, For enforcing the Laws against Conventicles, &c. and the late Vote of the House of Commons, for Renewing the said Act for three years more . . . 1668. (Bod.)

[Ford, Simon.] *The Conflagration of London: Poetically Delineated* . . . 1667.

―――. *Londini quod Reliquum. Or, Londons Remains: in Latin and English.* 1667.

Forraign and Domestick Prophesies: Both Antient and Modern. Fore-telling The several Revolutions which shall yet befall the Scepter of England . . . 1659.

Fortrey, Sam[uel]. *Englands Interest and Improvement. Consisting in the increase of the store, and trade of this Kingdom* . . . Cambridge, 1663.

Foulis, Henry. *The History Of the Wicked Plots and Conspiracies of Our Pretended Saints* . . . 1662. (Bod.)

[Fox, George, et al.] *A Declaration from the Harmles & Innocent People of God called Quakers. Against all Plotters and Fighters in the World* . . . *in Answer to that Clause of the Kings late*

Proclamation, which mentions the Quakers . . . Feb. 21, 1661.

A Free Conference Touching the present State of Enland Both at home and abroad: In order to the Designs of France. 1668.

Fuller, Thomas. *The Historie of the Holy Warre.* Cambridge, 1639.

G., E. *The suspence upon Sixty Six: or the Astrologers Prerogative.* 1666. brs.

G., R. *MDCLXVI. A Prognostick on this Famous Year 1666. Or, The Number of the Beast, so much talked of, Dialogue-wise, Chronogrammatically Explained.* 1666. brs. (National Library of Scotland)

G., Z. *Excise Anotomiz'd, and Trade Epitomiz'd: Declaring, that unequall Imposition of Excise, to be the only cause of the ruine of Trade, and universall impoverishment of this whole Nation.* 1659.

Gadbury, John. *De Cometis: or, A Discourse of the Natures and Effects of Comets, As they are Philosophically Historically & Astrologically Considered. With a brief (yet full) account of the III late comets, or blazing stars, visible to all Europe. And what (in a natural way of Judicature) they portend* . . . 1665.

————. *Dies Novissimus: or, Dooms-Day Not so Near as Dreaded. Together with something touching the present invasion of the Turk into the German Empire; and the probable success thereof.* 1664.

————. *EPHEMERIS: or A Diary Astronomical And Astrological For the Year of Grace 1661* . . . 1661.

————. *EPHEMERIS* . . . 1665.

————. *EPHEMERIS* . . . *Containing* . . . *a general judgement upon this (supposed wonderful) year* . . . 1666.

————. *EPHEMERIS* . . . 1667.

————. *Natura Prodigiorum: or, A Discourse Touching the Nature of Prodigies. Together with the kinds, causes and effects, of Comets, Eclipses, and Earthquakes* . . . 1660.

Gazette: The Oxford Gazette. Published by Authority. [Commenced printing Nov. 16, 1665. Entitled *The London Gazette* after no. 24, Feb. 1, 1666.]

[Geveren, Shetoo à.] *Of the ende of this world, and second comming of Christ* . . . Trans. by Thomas Rogers. 1577.

[Glanvill, Joseph.] *A Blow at Modern Sadducism In some Philosophical Considerations about Witchcraft* . . . *By a Member of the Royal Society.* 1668. (Bod.)

Goodman, Godfrey. *The Fall of Man, or the Corruption of Nature, proved by the light of our naturall Reason* . . . 1616.

Gostelo, Walter. *The Coming of God in Mercy, in Vengeance;*

beginning with Fire, to convert, or consume, at this so sinful City London: Oh! London, London. 1658.

Graunt, John [and William Petty]. *Natural and Political Observations Mentioned in a following Index, and made upon the Bills of Mortality . . .* 1662.

A great and Bloody Plot discovered against His Royal Majesty, Charles, by the Grace of God King of Great Brittain, France, and Ireland . . . 1660.

Greatrakes, Valentine. *A Brief Account of Mr Valentine Greatraks, and divers of the Strange Cures By him lately Performed. Written by himself in a Letter Addressed to the Honourable Robert Boyle Esq. Whereunto are annexed . . . Testimonials . . .* 1666.

G[uillim], J[oseph]. *Akamaton Pur. Or, the Dreadful Burning of London: Described in a Poem.* 1667.

H., J. *Castor and Pollux: or, An Heroique Poeme Upon his Majesties Victorious, and Princely Generals, The Dukes of Cumberland [Prince Rupert], and Albemarle. [With] The Famous Prophecy of Grebnerus (Reflecting upon the Norwest Isles) paraphrasd in Verse, and Englishd.* 1666. brs. (Bod.)

H., J. *Englands Alarm, the State-Maladies, and Cure: a Memento to the Soldiers, and a parallel of Egypts Plagues with Englands Sinnes . . .* 1659.

[Hall, Joseph.] *The Revelation Unrevealed. Concerning The Thousand-Yeares Reigne of the Saints with Christ upon Earth. Laying forth the weak Grounds, and strange Consequences of that plausible, and too-much received Opinion.* 1650.

Hall, Tho[mas]. *Chiliasto-mastix redivivus, Sive Homesus enervatus. A confutation of the millenarian opinion, plainly demonstrating that Christ will not reign visibly and personally on earth with the Saints for a thousand yeers either before the day of Judgement, in the day of Judgement, or after it . . . With a word to our Fifth Monarch-men, whose dangerous practices of late, clearly shew that this opinion leads to schisme, and sedition in Church and State.* 1657.

Hammond, Charles. *Truth's Discovery; or the Cavaliers Case clearly stated by Conscience and Plain-dealing . . .* 1664. [Reprinted in *Somers Tracts*, VII (1812), 557–67, q.v.]

Hardy, Nath[aniel]. *Lamentation, Mourning and Woe. Sighed forth in a Sermon Preached . . . On the 9th day of September. Being the next Lords-Day after the Dismal Fire in the City of London.* 1666.

[Harvey, John.] *A Discovrsive Probleme concerning Prophesies . . . Deuised especially in abatement of the terrible threaten-*

ings, and menaces, peremptorily denounced against the kingdoms, and states of the world, this present famous yeere, 1588.
supposed the Greatwoonderful, and Fatall yeere of our Age.
1588.

Harvey, Richard. An Astrological Discourse . . . 1583.

H[eath], I[ames]. A Brief Chronicle Of the Late Intestine Warr
in the Three Kingdoms of England, Scotland & Ireland . . .
2nd impression. 1663.

Heath, James. A Chronicle of the Late Intestine War in the Three
Kingdoms of England, Scotland and Ireland . . . To which is
added A Continuation to this present year 1675 . . . By J.
P[hilips]. 2nd ed. 1676.

————. The Glories and Magnificent Triumphs of The Blessed
Restitution of His Sacred Majesty K. Charles II. From His
Arrival in Holland 16 59/60 Till this Present . . . 1662.

Heydon, John. The Harmony of the World . . . 1662.

————. El Havarevna or the English Physitians Tvtor In the
Astrobolismes of Mettals Rosie Cruican . . . Whereunto is
added, Psonthonphanchia [separate pagination] . . . 1665.

————. The Holy Guide: Leading the Way to the Wonder of the
World . . . 1662.

[Heylyn, Peter.] Avgvstvs. Or, An Essay of those Meanes and
Counsels, whereby the Common-wealth of Rome was altered,
and reduced unto a Monarchy. 1632.

His Majesties Declaration to All His loving Subjects, December
26. 1662. 1663.

His Majestie's Declaration To all His Loving Subjects of His Kingdom of England and Dominion of Wales concerning Ecclesiastical Affairs. Oct. 25, 1660.

His Majesties Gracious Message to the House of Commons.
Wednesday, June 20, 1660 . . . 1660.

His Majesties Gracious Speech To both Houses of Parliament, On
Wednesday, February the 18th 1662 [1663] . . . 1663.

His Majesties Gracious Speech to Both Hovses of Parliament, Together with the Lord Chancellor's Delivered In Christ Church
Hall in Oxford, The 10th of October, 1665. Oxford, 1665.

His Majesties Gracious Speech to the Honorable House of Commons, In the Banquetting-house at White-Hall, March 1. 1661
[1662]. 1662.

His Majesties Gracious Speech to the Lords & Commons, Together with the Lord Chancellor's, At the opening of the Parliament, On the 8th day of May, 1661. 1661.

His Majesties Most Gracious Speech, To both Houses of Parliament, at their Prorogation, On Monday the Seven and twentieth of July, 1663. 1663.

His Majesties Most Gracious Speech to Both Houses of Parliament; On Monday the One and twentieth of March, 1663/4. 1664.

His Majesties Most Gracious Speech, Together with the Lord Chancellors, to the two houses of Parliament; On Thursday the 13 of September, 1660. 1660.

[Hodges, John.] *The true and onely Causes of the great Want of Moneys in these Kingdoms; and the Remedies mentioned, in these General Assertions, in order to more particular Demonstrations, how these Kingdoms may grow Rich, and Powerful.* 1666. brs. (University Library, University of London)

The Hollanders Unmasked. 1665. brs. [Printed as 2nd item on sheet headed by *The Dutch Boare Dissected . . .*]

The holy Sisters Conspiracy against their Husbands, and the City of London, designed at their last Farewell of their Meetinghouses in Coleman-street; Together with their Psalm of Mercy. T.T. Jan. 26, 1661.

Homes, Nathanael. *Miscellanea: Consisting of Three Treatises . . .* 1666. [Part III has new pagination.]

Homes, Nath[anael]. *The New World, or The New Reformed Church. Discovered out of the second Epistle of Peter the third chap. verse 13 . . .* 1641. (Houghton Library, Harvard University)

[Howell, James.] *Mr. Howel's Poems Upon divers Emergent Occasions.* Ed. by P. Fisher. 1664.

———. *PROEDRIA-BASILIKE: A Discourse Concerning the Precedency of Kings . . .* 1664.

The Humble Apology Of some commonly called Anabaptists . . . with their Protestation against the late wicked and most horrid treasonable Insurrection and Rebellion acted in the City of London . . . T.T. Jan. 28, 1661.

The Humble Representation and Petition Of the Lords and Commons Assembled in Parliament, Concerning Romish Priests and Jesuits; Presented to His Majesty by both Houses . . . 1663.

An humble Representation of the sad Condition of many of the King's Party, who since his Majesty's happy Restoration have no Relief, and but languishing Hopes; together with Proposals how some of them may be speedily relieved, and others assured thereof, within a reasonable time. 1661. [Reprinted in *Somers Tracts,* VII (1812), 516–20, q.v.]

[Humfrey, John.] *A Defence of the Proposition . . .* 1668.

[Humfrey, John?] *A Proposition for The Safety & Happiness of the King and Kingdom both in Church and State, and prevention of the Common Enemy; By way of Accommodation and Indulgence in matters of Religion . . .* 1667.

The Intelligencer, published for Satisfaction and Information of the People. With Privilege. Aug. 1663–Jan. 1666.

The Interest of England in the Protestant Cause. 1669. (Bod.)

J[enings], A[braham]. *Miraculum basilicon: or the Royal Miracle, Truly Exhibiting The wonderful Preservation of His Sacred Majesty in, with his miraculous Escape after, the Battel of Worcester . . . Whereunto is added Some Essayes, by way of Introduction . . .* 1664.

J[essey], H[enry]. *The Lords Loud Call to England: being a true relation of some late, various, and wonderful Judgments, or Handy-works of God, by Earthquake, Lightening, Whirlewind, great multitudes of Toads and Flyes; and also the striking with Sudden Deaths, of divers persons in several places; for what causes let the Man of Wisdome judge, upon his serious perusal of the book it self. Also of the strange Changes, and later Alterations made in these Three Nations . . .* 1660.

Jevon, Rachel. *Exultationis Carmen to the Kings Most Excellent Majesty upon his most Desired Return.* 1660.

The Jewes Message to Their Brethren in Holland . . . 1665. (Houghton Library, Harvard University)

A Judgment and Condemnation of the Fifth-Monarchy-Men, their Late Insurrection. Also, how far the Guilt of that fact may justly be imputed to those that are commonly distinguished by the Names of Independents, Presbyterians, Anabaptists and Quakers . . . T.T. Jan. 17, 1661.

[Keymor, John.] *John Keymors Observation made upon the Dutch Fishing About the year 1601 . . . Printed from the Original Manuscript, for Sir Edward Ford in the year, 1664.* 1664.

The Kingdome's Intelligencer of the Affairs now in agitation in England, Scotland, and Ireland: together with Foraign Intelligence: to prevent False Newes. Published by Authority. Apr. 1660–Aug. 1663. [*Parliamentary Intelligencer* before Jan. 1661.]

KLEIS PROPHETEIAS or, The Key of Prophecie: whereby The Mysteries of all the Prophecies from the Birth of Christ until this present, and so forward, are unlocked and opened . . . And the speedy Resurrection of King Charls the II. out of Banishment into Advancement, is certainly foreshewn. T.T. Jan. 28, 1660.

L., T. *A Voyce Out of the Wilderness crying, With many Tears and strong perswasions to the World for Repentance . . .* 1651–1653. [Consists of four tracts bearing separate pagination and original dates of publication, and two postscripts signed J. E. and J. W.]

Lamentatio Civitatis. or, Londons Complaint Against her Children in the Countrey . . . 1665.

The last farewel to the Rebellious Sect Called the Fifth Monarchy-Men on Wednesday January the Ninth . . . *With the total dispersing, defeating, and utter ruining of that Damnable and Seditious Sect in general.* T.T. Jan. 16, 1661.

The Last Letters, To the London-Merchants and Faithful Ministers concerning The further Proceedings of the Conversion and Restauration of the Jews . . . 1665. (Houghton Library, Harvard University)

[Lee, Samuel.] *Antichristi Excidium.* 1664.

[L'Estrange, Roger.] *A Caveat to the Cavaliers: or an Antidote against Mistaken Cordials* . . . 1661.

L'Estrange, Roger. *Considerations and Proposals In Order to the Regulation of the Press* . . . 1663.

————. *Interest Mistaken, or the Holy Cheat; Proving From the undeniable Practises and Positions of the Presbyterians, that the Design of that Party is to enslave both King and People under the Masque of Religion* . . . 1661.

————. *A Modest Plea Both for the Caveat, and The Author of It. With some notes upon Mr. James Howell, and his Sober Inspections.* 1661.

————. *Truth and Loyalty Vindicated, From the Reproches and Clamours of Mr. Edward Bagshaw* . . . 1662.

The Levellers Almanack: for, The Year of Wonders, 1652 . . . *prognosticating, The ruine of Monarchy throughout all Christendom* . . . 1651.

Lilly, William. *Annus Tenebrosus, Or the Dark Year* . . . 1652.

————. *An Astrologicall Prediction of the Occurrences in England, Part of the Yeers 1648, 1649, 1650* . . . 1648.

————. *Englands Propheticall Merline, Foretelling to all Nations of Europe untill 1663* . . . 1644.

[Lilly, William.] *The Lord Merlins Prophecy Concerning the King of Scots* . . . *With The Lady Sybilla's Prophecy* . . . *Likewise, The Prophecy of Paul Grebner* . . . 1651. (Bod.)

Lilly, William. *Merlini Anglici Ephemeris. Astrologicall Predictions for the Year 1656.* 1656.

————. *Merlini Anglici Ephemeris* . . . 1661.

————. *Merlini Anglici Ephemeris* . . . 1662.

————. *Merlini Anglici Ephemeris* . . . 1663.

————. *Merlini Anglici Ephemeris* . . . 1664. (Bod.)

————. *Merlini Anglici Ephemeris* . . . 1665.

————. *Merlini Anglici Ephemeris* . . . 1666.

————. *Merlini Anglici Ephemeris* . . . 1667.

————. *Monarchy or no Monarchy in England. Grebner his Prophecy concerning Charles Son of Charles, his Greatnesse, Victories, Conquests. The Northern Lyon of the North, and*

Chicken of the Eagle discovered who they are, of what Nation. English, Latin, Saxon, Scotish and Welch Prophecies concerning England in particular, and all Europe in generall . . . 1651. (Bod.: Lilly's copy)

———. *A Prophecy of the White King: and Dreadfull Dead-man Explaned* . . . 1644.

———. *The Worlds Catastrophe, or, Europes many Mutations untill, 1666. The fate of Englands Monarchy untill its Subversion. Government of the World under God by the Seven Planetary Angels; their Names, Times of Government* . . . 1647.

Lilly Lash't with his own Rod. Or, an Epigram On the Quaint Skill of that Arch Temporizing Astrologer Mr. William Lilly . . . 1660. brs.

A List of the Princes, Maior Generalls, &c. and Colonells, of the Scots Kings party slaine and taken Prisoners . . . 1652. brs.

A List of the Royal Society. His Sacred Majesty King Charles II. Founder and Patron. 1666. (Bod.)

A Lively Pourtraict of our New-Cavaliers, Commonly Called Presbyterians, clearly shewing, That His Maiesty came not in upon their Account . . . 1661. (Bod.)

[Lloyd, David.] *Wonders no Miracles; or, Mr. Valentine Greatrates Gift of Healing Examined, upon occasion of a sad effect of his stroaking, March the 7. 1665. at one Mr. Cressets house* . . . 1666.

[Lloyd, Owen.] *The Panther-Prophesy, or, A Premonition to all People, of Sad Calamities and Miseries like to befal these Islands* . . . 1662.

Lluelyn, Martin. *To the Kings most excellent Majesty.* 1660.

Londini Lachrymae; or, London's Complaint against her Fugitives. 1665. brs.

Londons Flames Discovered by Informations Taken before the Committee, Appointed to Enquire after the Burning of the City of London. And after the insolency of the Papists, &c. 1667. [Reprinted in *State Tracts* (1693), pt. II, 27–48, q.v.]

Londons Glory, or, The Riot and Ruine Of the Fifth Monarchy Men, and all their Adherents. Being a true and perfect Relation of their desperate and bloody Attempts and Practises in the City of London on Monday, Tuesday, and Wednesday last, Jan. the ninth, 1660 [1661] . . . T. T. Jan. 25, 1661.

London Undone; or, A Reflection upon the Late Disasterous Fire. 1666. brs.

A Looking-Glass for England. Being An Abstract of the Bloody Massacre in Ireland . . . *in the Year 1642* . . . 1667. (Bod.)

The Loyall Subjects Lamentation for Londons Perversenesse, in the Malignant Choice of some Rotten Members, on Tuesday the 19. of March 1661. 1661. brs.

[Luther, Martin.] *Dris Martini Lutheri Colloquia Mensalia: or, Dr Martin Luther's Divine Discourses At his Table, &c* . . . Trans. by Capt. Henry Bell. 1652.

M., H. *A Letter to a Person of Honour in London, From an Old Cavalier in Yorkshire, concerning the Papists.* 1663.

Manley, Thomas. *Usury At Six per Cent. examined, and Found unjustly charged by Sir Tho. Culpepper and J[osiah] C[hild] with many Crimes and Oppressions, whereof 'tis altogether innocent* . . . 1669.

The manner of the Solemnity of the Coronation of His most Sacred Majesty King Charles . . . 1660. brs.

Marriot, Thomas. *Rebellion Unmasked Or a Sermon preached at Poplar in the parish of Stepney . . . upon occasion of the late Rebellious Insurrection in London. Wherein is opened the Resemblances between Rebellion and the Sins of Witchcraft and Idolatry, as also the Pretences for Rebellion answered.* T.T. Jan. 26, 1661.

Marshall, Stephen. *A Peace-Offering to God. A Sermon Preached to the Honourable House of Commons assembled in Parliament . . . For the Peace concluded between England and Scotland.* 1641.

Matthew, Edward. *KAROLOU trismegistou epiphania. The Most Gloriovs Star, or Celestial Constellation of the Pleides, or Charles Waine* . . . 1664.

Mede, Joseph. *The Key of the Revelation . . . Translated into English by Richard More . . . With a Praeface written by Dr [William] Twisse* . . . 1643.

Mercurius Publicus, comprising the Sum of all Affairs now in Agitation in England, Scotland, and Ireland, together with Foraign Intelligence; for Information of the People, and to prevent False News. Published by Authority. Apr. 1660–Aug. 1663.

Mervyn, Audley. *A Speech Made by Sir Audley Mervyn his Majesties Prime Serjeant at Law in Ireland, the 11th day of May in the House of Lords* . . . 1661. (Bod.)

Mirabilis Annus Secundus: or, The Second Part of the Second Years Prodigies . . . Together with many remarkable Accidents, and signal Judgments which have befel divers Persons who have apostatized from the Truth, and have been Persecutors of the Lord's Faithful Servants . . . 1662.

Mirabilis Annus Secundus; or, The Second Year of Prodigies . . . now published as a Warning to all Men speedily to Re-

pent, and to prepare to meet the Lord, who gives these Signes of His Coming. 1662.

[Monck, George.] *A Collection of Several Letters and Declarations, sent by General Monck* . . . 1660. [Pagination highly irregular; cited according to actual order of pages.]

More, Henry. *An Explanation of The grand Mystery of Godliness* . . . 1660.

Moulin, Peter Du. *A Vindication of the Sincerity of the Protestant Religion In the Point of Obedience to Sovereignes* . . . 1664.

Mun, Thomas. *England's Treasure by Forraign Trade. Or, The Ballance of our Forraign Trade is The Rule of our Treasure.* 1664. [1st ed.; written in 1620s.]

Mr. Lillyes Prognostications Of 1667 . . . 1667.

Napier, John, Lord of Marchiston. *A Plaine Discovery of the whole Revelation of St. John* . . . 5th ed. Edinburgh, 1645. ["Epistle dedicatory" dated Jan. 29, 1593.]

The Newes, published for Satisfaction and Information of the People. With Privilege. Aug. 1663–Jan. 1666.

A New Letter Concerning the Jewes, written by the French Ambassador, at Constantinople, To his Brother the French Resident at Venice. Being a true Relation of the Proceedings of the Israelites, the wonderful Miracles wrought by their Prophet, with the terrible Judgments that have fallen upon The Turks. 1666.

A new Letter from Aberdeen in Scotland, Sent to a Person of Quality. Wherein is a more full Account of the Proceedings of the Jewes, Than hath been hitherto Published. 1665. (Mocatta Library, University College, University of London)

News of a New World: or, The Mystical Prison-Door Opened, Whereby The Outwardly Bound are Inwardly Free, While The Seemingly Free are still Really Bound . . . 1663.

Nunnes, Thomas. *An Almanack or Ephemerides For the Year of our Lord, 1666* . . . 1666.

Ogilby, John. *The Entertainment of His Most Excellent Majestie Charles II, in His Passage through the City of London to his Coronation* . . . 1662.

————. *The Relation of His Majestie's Passing through the City of London, To His Coronation: with a Description of the Triumphal Arches, and Solemnity.* 1661.

Omnia Comesta a Bello. Or, An Answer Out of the West to A Question Out of the North . . . 1667.

Ourania: The High and Mighty Lady the Princess Royal of Aurange Congratulated On Her Most Happy Arrival September the 25th. M.D.C.LX. 1660. brs.

Owen, John, Bishop of St. Asaph. *Herod and Pilate reconciled: or the Concord of Papists, Anabaptists, and Sectaries, against Scripture, Fathers, Councils, and other Orthodoxal Writers, for the Coercion, Deposition, and Killing of Kings* . . . 1663. (Bod.)

Pagitt, Epraim. *Heresiography, Or a Description and History of the Hereticks and Sectaries Sprang up in these latter times . . . The sixth edition, Whereunto is added the last year 1661* . . . 1662.

Parival, J[ean Nicholas de]. *The Historie of this Iron Age* . . . Trans. by B. Harris. 2nd English ed. 1659.

Parker, Sam[uel]. *A Free and Impartial Censvre Of The Platonick Philosophie* . . . Oxford, 1666.

[Patrick, Simon.] *A Continuation of the Friendly Debate.* 1669.

Peace Concluded and Trade Revived in An Honourable Peace betwixt the English and Dutch, &c. Vnited now in one, all discords cease, The Gentrys quiet, Farmers joy, and Trades encrease. 1667. brs.

The Petition of the Lord Mayor, Aldermen, and Common-Council-men of the City of London . . . to the Parliament, For the Reducing of all Forein Trade under Government; as also the Petition, together with the Proposals of several Merchants of London, on the behalf of themselves and the Merchants of England. Humbly tendred to the Grand Committee of Parliament for Trade; containing the desired manner and method for such regulation. 1662.

The Phanatiques Creed, or a Door of Safety; in answer to a bloody pamphlet intituled A Door of Hope . . . T.T. Jan. 18, 1661.

A Phenix, or, The Solemn League and Covenant. Whereunto is annexed, I. The Form and manner of His Majesties Coronation in Scotland . . . II. A declaration of the Kings Majesty to all his loving subjects of the Kingdoms of Scotland, &c. in the yeare 1650. III. The great danger of covenant-breaking, &c. Being the substance of a sermon preached by Edm. Calamy the 14. of Jan. 1645 . . . Edinburgh, 1660[?].

Philoprotest. *The Protestant Almanack for the Year From The Incarnation of Jesus Christ, 1668* . . . 1668. (Bod.)

Philotheus, Abraham. *Anarchie Reviving, or, the Good old Cause on the Anvile. Being a Discovery of the present Design to retrive the late Confusions both of Church and State, in several Essays for Liberty of Conscience.* 1668.

The Plea, Case, and Humble Proposals Of the Truly-Loyal and Suffering Officers. 1663. (Bod.)

A Poem On the burning of London. York, 1667. brs.

A Poem upon his Maiesties Coronation the 23. of April 1661. Being St. Georges day. 1661.

Poor Robin. *1664. An Almanack After a New Fashion* . . . 1664.

———. *1666. An Almanack* . . . 1666. (Bod.)

———. *1667. An Almanack* . . . 1667.

Pordage, Sam[uel]. *Heroick Stanzas On his Maiesties Coronation.* 1661.

Potter, Francis. *An Interpretation of the Number 666. Wherein, not onely the manner, how this number ought to be interpreted, is clearely proved and demonstrated; but it is also shewed, yt this number is an exquisite and perfect character, truly, exactly, and essentially describing that state of government, to wch all other notes of Antichrist doe agree* . . . Oxford, 1642.

Proclamation Against all Meetings of Quakers, Anabaptists, &c. Edinburgh, Jan. 22, 1661.

A Proclamation against Vicious, Debauch'd, and Prophane Persons . . . May 30, 1660. brs.

The Prophecie of Thomas Becket . . . *Concerning the Wars betwixt England France and Holland; Lately found in an ancient Manuscript at Abington, by Dr. Ailsworth; and by him sent as a Rarity to the University of Oxford* . . . 1666. (Bod.)

A Prophecy, Lately found amongst the Collections of famous Mr. John Selden. Faithfully rendred in the originall Latine, and translated for the English Reader. 1659.

A Pulpit to be let . . . *With a just applause of those worthy Divines that stay with us* . . . 1665.

Pyrotechnica Loyolana, Ignatian Fire-works. Or, the Fiery Jesuits Temper and Behaviour. Being an Historical Compendium of the Rise, Increase, Doctrines, and Deeds of the Jesuits. Exposed to Publick view for the sake of London. 1667.

The Reasons Humbly offered to Consideration, Why the Incorporating the whole Trade of the Woollen Manufactures of this Kingdom to the Company called The Merchant-Adventurers of England, is and will prove more and more detrimental . . . *to the Country in general* . . . *And also how a Frank and Free Trade to all English Merchants, will be far more advantagious to the whole Land.* 1662[?].

Reasons offered by the Merchants Adventurers of England and Eastland Merchants residing at Hull for the preservation of their Societies and Regulations, as being reasonable, just, and necessary to the liberal and profitable Vent of our Native Manufactures in the Forreign Parts limited to them by their Charters. 1662.

Reeve, Thomas. *God's Plea for Nineveh: or, London's Precedent for Mercy* . . . 1657.

Rege Sincera. *Observations both Historical and Moral upon the Burning of London September 1666* . . . 1667.

A Remonstrance, Proving that the Confinement of Trade, to particular Companies, is of general Losse to His Majesty, and His People. 1661. brs.

A Renuntiation and Declaration of the Ministers of the Congregational Churches and Publick Preachers of the same Judgment, Living in, and about the City of London: Against the late Horrid Insurrection and Rebellion Acted in the said City. T.T. Jan. 25, 1661.

The Restauration of the Jewes: Or, A true Relation of their Progress and Proceedings in order to the regaining of their Ancient Kingdom. Being the Substance of several Letters viz. From Antwerp, Legorn, Florence, &c. 1665. (Mocatta Library, University College, University of London)

R[oe], D[aniel]. *God's Judgments still Threatned Against Thee, O England, For the great Abominations that have been, and are committed in Thee; and Thy Sad Estate Lamented* . . . 1666.

[Rogers, John]. *Jegar-Sahadvtha: An Oyled Pillar. Set up for Posterity, Against the present Wickednesses, Hypocrisies, Blasphemies, Persecutions and Cruelties of this Serpent power (now up) in England* . . . 1657.

Rogers, John. *Ohel or Beth-shemesh. A Tabernacle for the Sun: or Irenicum evangelicum. An idea of church-discipline. in the theorick and practick parts* . . . 1653.

————. *Sagrir. Or Doomes-day drawing nigh, With Thunder and Lightening To Lawyers. In an Alarum For New Laws, and the Peoples Liberties from the Norman and Babylonian Yokes. Making Discoverie Of the present ungodly Laws and Lawyers of the Fourth Monarchy, and of the approach of the Fifth; with those godly Laws, Officers and Ordinances that belong to the Legislative Power of the Lord Jesus* . . . 1653.

Rohan, [Henri,] Duc de. *A Treatise of the Interest of the Princes and States of Christendome.* Trans. by Henry Hunt. 1663.

Rolle [Rolls], Samuel. *The Burning of London in the year 1666. Commemorated and improved in a CX. Discourses, Meditations, and Contemplations* . . . 1667. [Parts I–II, III, and IV have separate pagination.]

Rolls, Samuel. *Londons Resurrection or the Rebuilding of London Encouraged, Directed, and Improved, In Fifty Discourses* . . . 1668.

The Royal Victory, Obtained (with the Providence of Almighty

God) against the Dutch-Fleet, June the 2d. and 3d. 1665 . . . 1665.

The Run-awayes Return: or, The Poor Penniless Pilgrim. 1665. brs.

The Run-awayes Routed. or, A Whip for Momus. Being an Answer, and a Confutation, Against the Run-awayes, and their Vindication. 1665. brs.

The Run-awayes safe Refuge: or the Poor Penniless Pilgrims Answer to Their Miserable Comforters their Fellow Citizens in London. 1665. brs.

Rust, George. *A Funeral Sermon, Preached at the Obsequies Of the Right Reverend Father in God Jeremy [Taylor] Lord Bishop of Down* . . . 1668.

[Sadler, John]. *Olbia. The New Iland Lately Discovered* . . . *The First Part* . . . 1660. [No 2nd part printed.]

————. *Times of the Bible. Veyled in Cubits, Shekels, Talents, Furlongs, Chapters, Verses, Letters, of the Scripture: with the Days, Hours, Watches, Weeks, and Months of the Jewish Year.* 1667.

Saunders, Richard. *1661. Apollo Anglicanus: The English Apollo* . . . 1661.

————. *1666. Apollo Anglicanus* . . . 1666.

Serrarius, Petrus. *An Awakening Warning to the Wofull World, By a Voyce in three Nations; Uttered in a brief Dissertation Concerning that Fatal, and to be admired Conjunction of all the Planets, in one, and the same sign* . . . *Sagitarius, the last of the Fiery Triplicity, to come to pass the 1/11 day of December, Anno 1662. In which It is clearly evinced, as well by S. Scriptures, as by the Nature of the Conjunction it self, and other Antecedents, Concomitants and Circumstances, that the Glorious Coming of Jesus Christ is at hand. Whereby 1. He will recollect the Dispersed Nation of the Jews. 2. Abolish the man of Sin* . . . *And, 3. At length erect his Glorious Kingdom on Earth.* Amsterdam, 1662.

Settle, E[lkanah]. *An Elegie On the late Fire And Ruines of London.* 1667. (Library of the Guildhall, London)

The several Declarations of the Company of Royal Adventurers of England trading into Africa, Inviting all His Majesties Native Subjects in general to Subscribe, and become Sharers in their Joynt-stock. Together With His Royal Highness James Duke of Yorke['s] . . . *Letter to the Right Honourable Francis Lord Willoughby of Parham, &c. Intimating the said Companies Resolutions to furnish his Majesties American Plantations with Negroes at certain and moderate Rates. As also a List of the Royal Adventurers* . . . 1667.

Sir Robert Holmes his Bonefire: or, the Dutch Doomsday. 1666. brs.

Smith, Humphrey. *The Vision of Humphrey Smith, Which he saw concerning London, In the Fifth Month, in the year 1660. being not long after her King came into her.* 1660.

Smith, John. *The Trade & Fishing of Great-Britain Displayed* . . . 1661.

Smith, William. *A Poem On the famous Ship called The Loyal London. Begun at the charge of the* . . . *City of London, in the year 1665. and Lanched June 10. 1666. which they presented to His Majesty as a testimony of their Loyalty and dutiful affection* . . . 1666.

[Smith, William.] *To the Kings most Excellent Majesty, and to the Right Honourable, the Lords And others of Your Majesties most Honourable Privy Councel. An Essay for Recovery of Trade* . . . 1661.

The Speeches, Discourses, and Prayers, of Col. John Barkstead, Col. John Okey, and Mr. Miles Corbet; Upon the 19th of April, being the Day of their Suffering at Tyburn . . . 1662.

A Speech spoken By a Blew-Coat Boy of Christs Hospital to His Most Sacred Majestie Charles the Second In His Passage from the Tovver to White-hall. April 22, 1661. Being the Day before His Coronation. 1661.

Spencer, John. *A Discourse concerning Prodigies: wherein The Vanity of Presages by them is reprehended, and their true and proper Ends asserted and vindicated* . . . *To which is added a short Treatise concerning Vulgar Prophecies* [with separate pagination]. 2nd ed. Cambridge, 1665.

Sprat, Thomas. *History of the Royal Society.* 1667. Ed. by Jackson I. Cope and Harold W. Jones. St. Louis: Washington University Studies, 1958.

———. *Observations on Monsieur de Sorbier's Voyage into England* . . . 1665.

State-Tracts . . . *From the Year 1660. to 1689. Now Published in a Body, to shew the Necessity, and clear the Legality of the late Revolution* . . . 1693.

Stillingfleet, Edward. *A Sermon Preached before the Honourable House of Commons, At St. Margarets Westminster Octob. 10. being the Fast-day appointed for the late dreadfull Fire in the City of London.* 1666.

[Stirling, James, and James Stewart.] *Naphtali, or The Wrestlings of the Church of Scotland for the Kingdom of Christ* . . . N.p., 1667.

Strange News from the West, being a true and perfect Account of several miraculous Sights . . . 1661.

Stubbe, Henry. *The Miraculous Conformist: or An account of severall Marvailous Cures performed by the stroaking of the Hands of Mr Valentine Greatarick* . . . Oxford, 1666.

Swan, John. *Speculum Mundi or A Glasse representing the Face of the World* . . . Cambridge, 1635.

——. *Speculum Mundi* . . . 3rd ed. 1665.

Tabor, Joh[n]. *Seasonable Thoughts in Sad Times, Being some Reflections on the Warre, the Pestilence, and the Burning of London. Considered in the Calamity, Cause, Cure.* 1667.

Tanner, John. *Angelus Britannicus An Ephemeris for the Year of our Redemption 1662* . . . 1662.

——. *Angelus Britannicus* . . . 1666.

——. *Angelus Britannicus* . . . 1667.

[Tatham, John.] *Londons Triumph* . . . *Celebrated in Honour of* . . . *Sr. John Robinson, Knight and Baronet, Lord Mayor of the City of London* . . . 1662.

——. *Neptunes Address to His Most Sacred Majesty Charls the Second* . . . *Congratulating His happy Coronation Celebrated The 22th. Day of Aprill, 1661. In several Designements and Shews npon the Water, Before White-hall, At His Majesties Return from the Land-Triumphs.* 1661.

Temple, William. *Letters Written by Sir W. Temple, Bart. and other Ministers of State* . . . 2 vols. Ed. by Jonathan Swift. 1700.

[Temple, William.] *Lettre d'un Marchand de Londres A son amy à Amsterdam depuis la derniere Bataille de Mer. Sur l'occasion & le remede de la Guerre presente.* Amsterdam[?], 1666.

——. *Miscellanea* . . . 1680.

Temple, William. *Observations upon the United Provinces of the Netherlands.* 1673.

[Tomkins, Thomas.] *The Inconveniencies of Toleration, or an Answer To a late Book, Intituled, A Proposition Made to the King and Parliament for the Safety and Happiness of the King and Kingdom* [by John Humfrey ?, q.v.]. 1667.

To the King of these Nations, the Humble Representation of Several Societies, commonly called by the Name of Anabaptists, where in short they Declare their Innocency, Sufferings, Desires & Resolutions. T.T. Jan. 30, 1661.

To the King, upon his Majesties Happy Return. 1660.

Trigge, Thomas. *Calendarium Astrologicum: or an Almanack for the Year of our Lord, 1665* . . . 1665. (Bod.)

——. *Calendarium Astrologicum* . . . 1666. (Bod.)

——. *Calendarium Astrologicum* . . . 1667. (Bod.)

A True and Exact Relation of The Araignment, Tryal, and Con-

demnation of Tho. Tongue, George Philips, James Hind, Francis Stubbs, John Sallows, Nathaniel Gibbs . . . Being a full discovery of the whole plot. 1662. (PRO SP 29/: incomplete copy)

A true and faithful Account of the several Informations exhibited to the Honourable Committee appointed by the Parliament to inquire into the late dreadful Burning of the City of London. Together with other Informations touching the Insolency of Popish Priests and Jesuites, and the Increase of Popery, brought to the Honourable Committee appointed by the Parliament for that purpose. 1667. [Reprinted in *Somers Tracts* (1812), VII, 615–33, q.v.]

A true Discovery of a Bloody Plot Contrived by the Phanaticks against the Proceedings of the City of London, in order to the Coronation of the High and Mighty King, Charles the Second . . . 1661.

[Tully, Thomas.] *A Letter Written to a Friend in Wilts, Upon occasion of a late Ridiculous Pamphlet, Wherein was inserted a pretended Prophecie of Thomas Becket's, &c.* 1666. (Bod.)

[Turnor, Edward.] *The Speech of Sr Edw. Turnor, Kt. Speaker of the Honorable House of Commons, to the Kings Most Excellent Majesty, Delivered on Monday the Nineteenth day of May, 1662* . . . 1662.

———. *The Speech of Sr. Edw. Turnor . . . on Friday the Eighteenth day of January 1666* [1667]. 1667.

Two most Strange Wonders; the one is a true Relation of an Angel appearing to Mr. James Wise . . . and the many strange and wonderful Visions which he at that time beheld; as also his Prophecies . . . The other being a most fearful Judgment which befell Dorothy Mattey . . . 1662.

Vaux, John. *1661 . . . A New Almanack for the Year of the Worlds Redemption, 1661* . . . 1661. (Bod.)

———. *Vaux . . . A New Almanack* . . . 1665. (Bod.)

V[incent], T[homas]. *Gods Terrible Voice in The City: wherein you have I. The sound of the Voice, in the narration of the two late dreadful judgments of plague and fire . . . II. The interpretation of the Voice* . . . 1667.

The Votes and Orders Of the honourable House of Commons, Passed February 25, and 26, 1662 [1663]. *Upon reading His Majesties Gracious Declaration and Speech* . . . 1663.

Vox & Lacrimae Anglorum: or, The True English-mens Complaints, To their Representatives in Parliament. Humbly tendred to their serious Consideration at their next sitting, February the 6th. 1667/8. 1668.

W., J. *A Friendly Letter to the Flying Clergy, Wherein Is Humbly*

Requested and modestly Challenged the Cause of their Flight.
1665. (Bod.)

[W., W.] *The English and Dutch Affairs Displayed to the Life:
Both in matters of Warr, State, and Merchandize . . . 1664.*
[Apparently the same tract, except for the title page, as W. W.,
*An History of the Transactions Betwixt the Crown of England
And the States of the Netherlands . . . 1664.*]

[Ward,] Seth, Bishop of Exeter. *A Sermon Preached before the
Peers, in the Abby-Church at Westminster: October 10th.
M.DC.LXVI. 1666.*

[Waterhouse, Edward.] *A Short Narrative Of the late Dreadful
Fire in London: together With certain Considerations Remarkable therein, and deducible therefrom; Not unseasonable for
the Perusal of this Age. 1667.*

Wharton, George. *Calendarium Carolinum: or, A New Almanack.
After the Old Fashion, For the Year of Christ 1666 . . . 1666.*

*William Lilly Student in Astrologie, His past and present Opinion
touching Monarchy In these Nations: And his Decision of the
Controversie between the Normans and The Long-Parliament.*
1660.

W[indus], J[acobus]. *Romae Ruina Finalis, Anno Dom. 1666.
Mundiq; finis sub Quadragesimum quintum post Annum. Sive,
Literae ad Anglos Romae versantes datae, quibus (vel ex Ponti-
ficiorum Scriptis evicto, Babylonis in Apocalypsi nomine,
Romam Pontificiam designari, Papamque Romanum ipsissimum
esse Anti-Christum, Scripturis praedictum) & Bestiam derelin-
quere, & Babylone, urbe nempe Romanâ anno jam dicto, Mil-
lesimo sc. Sexcentisimo, Sexagesimo Sexto, excidio, & incendio
delendâ, atq; funditus evertendâ confestim exire admonentur.*
1655. (Bod.: issue of 1663)

[Wing, Vincent?] *The Bloody Almanack For the Year, 1666. And
The Fiery Trigon; Wherein is set forth, the great Changes and
Revolutions, extraordinary Events and Alterations, that may
come to pass, and be acted upon the Stage of the World, in
this [supposed Wonderful] Year . . . Also . . . The great and
Warlike Actions amongst Foreign Princes; The approaching
Ruine of the Hollanders; And a Famous Monarch to arise from
the Islands of Great Brittain, who shall both begin and go forward in that Mighty Work of Conquest and Reformation,
throughout France, Spain, the Netherlands, and other Habit-
able Places of the World. 1666.*

Wing, Vincent. *Olympia Damaza. Or, an Almanack and Prognostication for the year of our Lord, 1661 . . . 1661.*

———. *Olympia Damaza . . . 1666.*

[Wiseman, Samuel.] *A Short and Serious Narrative of Londons Fatal Fire, with its Diurnal and Nocturnal Progression, From Sunday Morning (being) the Second of September, Anno Mirabili 1666. Until Wednesday Night following. A Poem* . . . 1667.

Wither, George. *Campo-Musae, or The Field Musings of Captain George Wither* . . . 1643. [Reprinted in Publications of the Spenser Society, no. 12 (1872).]

––––––. *The dark Lantern, containing a dim Discoverie* . . . 1653. [Reprinted in Publications of the Spenser Society, no. 16 (1874).]

[Wither, George.] *Ecchoes from the Sixth Trumpet. Reverberated by a Review of Neglected Remembrances: abreviating Precautions and Predictions heretofore published at several times* . . . *Imprinted in the Year chronogrammatically expressed in this Seasonable Prayer LorD haVe MerCIe Vpon Vs.* 1666.

––––––. *Meditations upon The Lords Prayer* . . . 1665. (Houghton Library, Harvard University)

Wither, George. *A Memorandum to London, Occasioned by the Pestilence there begun this Present Year MDCLXV, and humbly offered to the Lord Maior, Aldermen and Commonalty of the said City* . . . 1665.

––––––. *Paralellogrammaton. An Epistle to the three Nations of England, Scotland, and Ireland; whereby their Sins being Parallel'd with those of Judah and Israel, they are forewarned, and exhorted to a timely Repentance, lest they incur the like Condemnation* . . . 1662. [Reprinted in Publications of the Spenser Society, no. 33 (1882).]

––––––. *Sigh for the Pitchers: Breathed out in a Personaf Contribution to the National Humiliation the last of May, 1666. In the Cities of London and Westminster, upon The near approaching Engagement Then expected, Between the English and Dutch Navies* . . . *Imprinted in the sad year expressed in this seasonable CHRONOGRAM LorD haVe MerCIe Vpon Vs. MDCLXVI.* 1666.

––––––. *Speculum Speculativum: or, a Considering-Glass; being an Inspection into the present and late sad Condition of these Nations* . . . 1660.

––––––. *Vaticinia Poetica* . . . 1666. [Reprinted in Publications of the Spenser Society, no. 18 (1875).]

[Wither, George.] *Vox Vulgi. A Well-come home from the Counties Citties an[d] Burroughs to their prevaricating Trustes; with a premised Savinge of the honor of everie faithfull and discreet Member of Parliament* [written 1661]. In *Anecdota Bodleiana: Gleanings from Bodleian MSS.*, pt. II, Ed. by W. D. Macray. Oxford: James Parker and Co., 1880.

A wonderfull Prophesy taken out of an old Church Book in Rome . . . Rotterdam, 1690. brs.

[Wood, Anthony.] *Athenae Oxonienses . . . Dom. 1500, to . . . 1690 . . . To which are added, The Fasti or Annals, of the said University, For the same time.* 2 vols. 1691, 1692.

3. *Works Printed after 1700*

Abbott, W. C. "English Conspiracy and Dissent, 1660–1674." *American Historical Review*, 14 (1908–9), 503–28, 696–722.

Abernathy, George R., Jr. "The English Presbyterians and the Stuart Restoration, 1648–1663." *Transactions of the American Philosophical Society*, n.s., pt. 2 (1965).

Ailesbury, Thomas, Earl of. *Memoirs of Thomas, Earl of Ailesbury, Written by Himself.* Ed. by W. E. Buckley. 2 vols. London: The Roxburghe Club, 1890.

Andrews, Charles M. *British Committees, Commissions, and Councils of Trade and Plantations, 1622–1675.* Johns Hopkins University Studies in Historical and Political Science, ser. 24, nos. 1–3. Baltimore: Johns Hopkins University Press, 1908.

Arlington's Letters: The Right Honourable the Earl of Arlington's Letters . . . Ed. by Thomas Bebington. 2 vols. London, 1701.

Ashley, Maurice. *John Wildman, Plotter and Postmaster: A Study Study of the English Republican Movement in the Seventeenth Century.* London: Jonathan Cape, 1947.

Ashmole Collection: Elias Ashmole (1617–1692): His Autobiographical and Historical Notes, His Correspondence, and Other Contemporary Sources Relating to His Life and Work. Ed. with a biographical introduction by C. H. Josten. 5 vols. Oxford: Clarendon Press, 1966.

Aubrey, John. *Aubrey's Brief Lives.* Ed. with an introduction by Oliver L. Dick. 2nd ed. London: Secker and Warburg, 1950.

Barbour, Violet. *Henry Bennet, Earl of Arlington, Secretary of State to Charles II.* Washington, D.C.: American Historical Association, 1914.

Barlow's Journal of His Life at Sea in King's Ships, East and West Indiamen and Other Merchantmen from 1659 to 1703. Transcribed by Basil Lubbock, 2 vols. London: Hurst & Blackett, 1934.

Bate, Frank. *The Declaration of Indulgence, 1672: A Study in the Rise of Organized Dissent.* London: A. Constable, 1908.

Begley, Walter. *Biblia Cabalistica; or, The Cabalistic Bible.* London: David Nutt, 1903.

Bell, Walter G. *The Great Fire of London in 1666.* London: John Lane, 1920.

————. *The Great Plague in London in 1665.* London: John Lane, 1924.

Besant, Walter. *The Survey of London.* Vol. 5, *London in the Time of the Stuarts.* London: Adam & Charles Black, 1903.

Birch, Thomas. *The Life of the Honourable Robert Boyle.* London, 1741.

Blundell, Margaret, ed. *Cavalier: Letters of William Blundell to His Friends, 1620–1698.* London: Longmans, Green, 1933.

Bosher, Robert S. *The Making of the Restoration Settlement: The Influence of the Laudians, 1649–1662.* London. Dacre Press, 1951.

Boyle, Robert. *The Works of the Honourable Robert Boyle.* 6 vols. London, 1772.

Boyle, Roger, First Earl of Orrery. *A Collection of the State Letters of the Right Honourable Roger Boyle, the First Earl of Orrery, Lord President of Munster in Ireland . . .* London, 1742.

Broadley, A. M., ed. *The Royal Miracle: A Collection of Rare Tracts, Broadsides, Letters, Prints, and Ballads Concerning the Wanderings of Charles II after the Battle of Worcester (September 3–October 15, 1651).* London: Stanley Paul, 1912.

Bryant, Arthur, ed. *The Letters, Speeches and Declarations of King Charles II.* London: Cassell, 1935.

Buck, Philip W. *The Politics of Mercantilism.* New York: Henry Holt and Co., 1942.

Budick, Sanford. *Dryden and the Abyss of Light: A Study of Religio Laici and The Hind and the Panther.* New Haven: Yale University Press, 1970.

Burnet, Gilbert. *Burnet's History of My Own Time.* Ed. by Osmund Airy. Pt. I, *The Reign of Charles the Second.* 2 vols. Oxford: Clarendon Press, 1897.

Burrell, S. A. "The Apocalyptic Vision of the Early Covenanters." *Scottish Historical Review,* 43 (Apr. 1964), 1–24.

Butler, Christopher. *Number Symbolism.* London: Routledge & Kegan Paul, 1970.

Butler, Samuel. *The Poetical Works of Samuel Butler.* Ed. by Reginald B. Johnson. 2 vols. Aldine Editions of the British Poets. London: George Bell & Sons, 1893.

Butt, John. *The Augustan Age.* London: Hutchinson's University Library (no. 43), 1950.

Calendar of State Papers, Colonial Series, America and West

Indies, 1661–1668. Ed. by W. N. Sainsbury. London: Her
    Majesty's Stationery Office, 1880.
*Calendar of State Papers, Domestic Series, of the Protectorate
    and the Reign of Charles II. 1655–1667; 1670; and Addenda,
    1660–1670.* 15 vols. Ed. by M. A. E. Green. London: Her
    Majesty's Stationery Office, 1860–66, 1882–86, 1895.
*Calendar of State Papers, Domestic Series, of the Reign of
    Charles II. Addenda, 1660–1685.* Ed. by F. H. Blackburne
    Daniell and Francis Bickley. London: His Majesty's Stationery
    Office, 1939.
*Calendar of State Papers, Ireland: Calendar of State Papers Re-
    lating to Ireland Preserved in the Public Record Office. 1663–
    1665, 1666–1669.* Ed. by R. P. Mahaffy. London: His Majesty's
    Stationers Office, 1907, 1908.
*Calendar of State Papers, Venetian: Calendar of State Papers
    and Manuscripts, Relating to English Affairs, Existing in the
    Archives and Collections of Venice, and in Other Libraries of
    Northern Italy.* Vols. 33–35, *1661–1668,* ed. by A. B. Hinds.
    London: His Majesty's Stationery Office, 1932–35.
*Calendar of the Clarendon State Papers Preserved in the Bodleian
    Library.* Vol. 5, *1660–1726,* ed. by F. J. Routledge. Oxford:
    Clarendon Press, 1970.
Carlyle, E. I. "Clarendon and the Privy Council, 1660–1667."
    English Historical Review, 27 (1912), 251–73.
Chalker, John. *The English Georgic: A Study in the Develop-
    ment of a Form.* London: Routledge & Kegan Paul, 1969.
Chaudhuri, K. N. "Treasure and Trade Balances: The East India
    Company's Export Trade, 1660–1720." *Economic History Re-
    view,* 2nd ser., 21 (1968), 480–502.
Chernaik, Warren L. *The Poetry of Limitation: A Study of
    Edmund Waller.* New Haven: Yale University Press, 1968.
Christie, W. D. *A Life of Anthony Ashley Cooper, First Earl of
    Shaftesbury, 1621–1683.* 2 vols. London: Macmillan and Co.,
    1871.
Clarendon, *Continuation: The Life of Edward Earl of Clarendon.
    Lord High Chancellor of England . . . Containing, I. An Ac-
    count of the Chancellor's Life from his Birth to the Restoration
    in 1660. II. A Continuation of the Same, and of His History of
    the Grand Rebellion, from the Restoration to His Banishment
    in 1667.* [Part II has separate pagination.] Oxford, 1759.
Clarendon, Edward Hyde, Earl of. *The Miscellaneous Works of
    the Right Honourable Edward, Earl of Clarendon* . . . 2nd ed.
    London, 1751.
Clark, G. N. *The Seventeenth Century.* 2nd ed. Oxford: Claren-
    don Press, 1947.

Clarke, J. S. *The Life of James the Second, King of England, &c.* 2 vols. London: Longman, Hurst, Rees, Orme, and Brown, 1816.

Cohn, Norman. *The Pursuit of the Millennium: Revolutionary Millenarians and Mystical Anarchists of the Middle Ages.* 3rd ed. London: Paladin, 1970.

Colenbrander, H. T. *Bescheiden uit vreemde archieven omtrent de groote nederlandsche zeeoorlogen, 1652–1676.* 2 vols. Rijks geschiedkundige publicatiën, kleine serie, nos. 18, 19. The Hague: Martinus Nijhoff, 1919.

Commons Journal: Journals of the House of Commons. Vols. 8–9. Apr. 25, 1660–Apr. 28, 1687.

Conway Letters: The Correspondence of Anne, Viscountess Conway, Henry More, and Their Friends, 1642–1684. Ed. by Marjorie H. Nicolson. London: Oxford University Press, 1930.

Cooper, Brian G. "The Academic Re-Discovery of Apocalyptic Ideas in the Seventeenth Century," *Baptist Quarterly,* 18, 19 (1960, 1961), 351–62, 29–34.

Cosin Correspondence: The Correspondence of John Cosin, D.D., Lord Bishop of Durham: Together with Other Papers Illustrative of His Life and Times. 2 vols. Publications of the Surtees Society, vols. 52, 55. Durham: Andrews & Co., 1869, 1872.

Davies, Godfrey. *The Restoration of Charles II, 1658–1660.* San Marino, Calif.: Huntington Library, 1955.

Davies, K. G. *The Royal African Company.* London: Longmans, Green and Co., 1957.

Davison, Dennis. *Dryden.* London: Evans Brothers, 1968.

Dick, Hugh G., ed. *Thomas Tomkis' Albumazar: A Comedy (1615).* University of California Publications in English, vol. 13. Berkeley: University of California Press, 1944.

Dictionary of National Biography. Ed. by Leslie Stephen and Sidney Lee. 63 vols. London: Smith, Elder & Co., 1885–1900.

Dryden, *Critical Works: The Critical and Miscellaneous Prose Works of John Dryden . . .* Ed. by Edmond Malone. Vol. I, pt. I. London: T. Cadell and W. Davies, 1800.

——, *Essays: John Dryden, Of Dramatic Poesy and Other Critical Essays.* Ed. with an introduction by George Watson. 2 vols. London: Everyman's Library, 1964.

——. *The Letters of John Dryden with Letters Addressed to Him.* Ed. by Charles E. Ward. Durham, N.C.: Duke University Press, 1942.

——. *Poems of John Dryden.* Ed. by James Kinsley. 4 vols. Oxford: Clarendon Press, 1958.

——. *The Works of John Dryden.* Vol. I, *Poems 1649–1680,* ed. by Edward N. Hooker and H. T. Swedenberg, Jr. Vol. III,

Poems 1685–1692, ed. by Earl Miner. Berkeley: University of California Press, 1956, 1969.

Dryden Collection: Dryden: A Collection of Critical Essays. Ed. by Bernard N. Schilling. Englewood Cliffs, N.J.: Prentice-Hall, 1963.

Dryden's Mind and Art. Ed. by Bruce King. Edinburgh: Oliver and Boyd, 1969.

Echard, Laurence. *The History of England* . . . 3 vols. London, 1718.

Edie, Carolyn A. "The Irish Cattle Bills: A Study in Restoration Politics." *Transactions of the American Philosophical Society*, n.s., 60, pt. 2 (1970).

Ellis, Henry, ed. *Original Letters Illustrative of English History* . . . 2nd ser., vol. IV. London: Harding and Lepard, 1827.

Elloway, D. R., ed. *Dryden's Satire*. London: Macmillan, 1966.

Encyclopaedia of Religion and Ethics. Ed. by James Hastings et al. 13 vols. Edinburgh: T. & T. Clark, 1909–26.

Essential Articles for the Study of John Dryden. Ed. by H. T. Swedenberg, Jr. N.p.: Shoe String Press, 1966.

Evelyn, John. *The Diary of John Evelyn*. Ed. by E. S. de Beer. 6 vols. Oxford: Clarendon Press, 1955.

Feiling, Keith. *British Foreign Policy, 1660–1672*. London: Macmillan and Co., 1930.

————. *A History of the Tory Party, 1640–1714*. 1924. Reprint. Oxford: Clarendon Press, 1965.

Firth, C. H., ed. *Naval Songs and Ballads*. Publications of the Navy Records Society, vol. 33. London, 1908.

Fox, George. *The Journal of George Fox*. 2 vols. Cambridge: At the University Press, 1911.

Foxcroft, H. C. *The Life and Letters of Sir George Savile, Bart., First Marquis of Halifax &c*. 2 vols. London: Longmans, Green, 1898.

Gardner, William B. "John Dryden's Interest in Judicial Astrology." *Studies in Philology*, 47 (1950), 506–21.

Gee, Henry. "The Derwentdale Plot, 1663." *Transactions of the Royal Historical Society*, 11 (1917), 125–42.

Geyl, Pieter. *The Netherlands in the Seventeenth Century*. 2 pts. London: Ernest Benn, 1964.

Grassby, Richard. "English Merchant Capitalism in the Late Seventeenth Century: The Composition of Business Fortunes." *Past & Present*, no. 46 (Feb. 1970), 87–107.

Grey, Anchitell. *Debates of the House of Commons, from the Year 1667 to the Year 1694*. 10 vols. London, 1769.

Haley, K. H. D. *The First Earl of Shaftesbury*. Oxford: Clarendon Press, 1968.

Hardison, O. B. *The Enduring Monument: A Study of the Idea of Praise in Renaissance Literary Theory and Practice.* Chapel Hill: University of North Carolina Press, 1962.

Harleian Miscellany: A Collection of Scarce, Curious, and Entertaining Pamphlets and Tracts, as Well in Manuscript as in Print. Selected from the Library of Edward Harley, Second Earl of Oxford . . . Ed. by William Oldys and Thomas Park. 10 vols. London: John White, John Murray and John Harding, 1808–13.

Hart, W. H. *Index Expurgatorius Anglicanus.* 5 pts. London: John Russell Smith, 1872–78.

Harth, Phillip. *Contexts of Dryden's Thought.* Chicago: University of Chicago Press, 1968.

Hartmann, Cyril H. *Clifford of the Cabal: A Life of Thomas, First Lord Clifford of Chudleigh, Lord High Treasurer of England (1630–1673).* London: William Heinemann, 1937.

Hatton Correspondence: Correspondence of the Family of Hatton, A.D. 1601–1704. Ed. by Edward M. Thompson. 2 vols. Camden Society, n.s., 22–23. London, 1878.

Hawkins, Edward, Augustus W. Franks, and Herbert A. Grueber, eds. *Medallic Illustrations of the History of Great Britain and Ireland to the Death of George II.* 2 vols. London: Spink & Son, 1969.

Heckscher, Eli F. *Mercantilism.* Trans. by Mendel Shapiro. 2 vols. London: George Allen & Unwin, 1935.

Henry, Philip. *Diaries and Letters of Philip Henry, M.A., of Broad Oak, Flintshire, A.D. 1631–1696.* Ed. by Matthew H. Lee. London: Kegan, Paul, Trench & Co., 1882.

Historical Manuscripts Commission Reports:
  4th Rept.: App., MSS. of the earl de La Warr.
  5th Rept.: App., MSS. of the duke of Sutherland.
  6th Rept.: App., MSS. of Sir R. Graham, Bart., and Sir Henry Ingilby, Bart.
  7th Rept.: App., MSS. of Lord Sackville and Sir H. Verney.
  Beaufort: 12th Rept., App., pt. IX, MSS. of the duke of Beaufort.
  Finch: Rept. on the MSS. of A. G. Finch, Vol. I.
  Gawdy: 10th Rept., pt. II, MSS. of the family of Gawdy.
  Hastings: Rept. on the MSS. of R. R. Hastings, vols. II, IV.
  Le Fleming: 12th Rept., app., pt. VII, MSS. of S. H. Le Fleming.
  Lonsdale: 13th Rept., app., pt. VII, MSS. of the earl of Lonsdale.
  Ormonde: 14th Rept., app., pt. VII, MSS. of the marquis of Ormonde, vol. II.
  Ormonde, n.s.: Calendar of the MSS. of the marquess of Ormonde, n.s., vol. III.

Portland: 14th Rept., app., pt. II, MSS. of the duke of Portland, vol. III.

Hobbes, Thomas. *Behemoth; or, The Long Parliament.* 1681. Ed. by Ferdinand Tönnies. London: Simpkin, Marshall, and Co., 1889.

Holdsworth, William S. *The History of English Law.* 14 vols. London: Methuen & Co., 1903.

Jack, Ian. *Augustan Satire: Intention and Idiom in English Poetry, 1660–1750.* Oxford: Clarendon Press, 1965.

The Jewish Encyclopedia. 12 vols. New York: Funk and Wagnalls, 1925.

Josselin, Ralph. *The Diary of the Rev. Ralph Josselin, 1616–1683.* Ed. by E. Hockliffe. Camden Society, 3rd ser., vol. 15. London, 1908.

Jusserand, J. J. *A French Ambassador at the Court of Charles the Second: Le Comte de Cominges from His Unpublished Correspondence.* London: T. Fisher Unwin, 1892.

Kantorowicz, Ernst H. *The King's Two Bodies: A Study in Mediaeval Political Theory.* Princeton, N.J.: Princeton University Press, 1957.

Kennet, White. *A Complete History of England* . . . 3 vols. London, 1706.

[Kennet, White.] *A Register and Chronicle Ecclesiastical and Civil* . . . Vol. I. London, 1728. [No more volumes published. The original materials, bringing the register to 1679, are in BM Lansdowne MSS. 1002–1010. Published volume ends at Dec. 1662.]

Kenyon, J. P., ed. *The Stuart Constitution, 1603–1688, Documents and Commentary.* Cambridge: At the University Press, 1966.

Kinsley, James. "Dryden and the Art of Praise." *English Studies* (Apr. 1953), 57–64.

———. "The 'Three Glorious Victories' in *Annus Mirabilis.*" *Review of English Studies,* n.s., 7 (Jan. 1956), 30–37.

Kitchin, George. *Sir Roger L'Estrange: A Contribution to the History of the Press in the Seventeenth Century.* London: Kegan Paul, Trench, Trübner & Co., 1913.

Lacey, Douglas R. *Dissent and Parliamentary Politics in England, 1661–1689.* New Brunswick, N.J.: Rutgers University Press, 1969.

Ladner, Gerhart B. *The Idea of Reform, Its Impact on Christian Thought and Action in the Age of the Fathers.* New York: Harper Torchbooks, 1967.

Lasky, Melvin J. "The Birth of a Metaphor: On the Origins of Utopia and Revolution (II)." *Encounter,* 34 no. 3 (Mar. 1970), 30–42.

The Lauderdale Papers. Ed. by Osmund Airy. 3 vols. Camden Society, n.s., 34, 36, 38. London: Nichols and Sons, 1884–85.

Lilly, *Life: The Lives of Those Eminent Antiquaries Elias Ashmole, Esquire, and Mr. William Lilly, Written by Themselves* . . . London, 1774.

Lipson, E. *The Economic History of England.* Vols. II and III, *The Age of Mercantilism.* 5th ed. London: Adam and Charles Black, 1948.

Lister, T. H. *Life and Administration of Edward, First Earl of Clarendon; with Original Correspondence* . . . 3 vols. London: Longman, Orme, Brown, Green and Longmans, 1837–38.

Llwyd, Morgan. *Gweithiau.* Ed. by Thomas E. Ellis. University of Wales Guild of Graduates, Reprints of Welsh Prose Works, no. 1. London: J. M. Dent & Co., 1899.

Lords Journal: Journals of the House of Lords. Vols. 11–12. Apr. 25, 1660–June 9, 1675.

Lovejoy, A. O., and George Boas. *Primitivism and Related Ideas in Antiquity.* Baltimore: Johns Hopkins University Press, 1935.

Ludlow, Edmund. *The Memoirs of Edmund Ludlow* . . . *1625–1672.* Ed. by C. H. Firth. 2 vols. Oxford: Clarendon Press, 1894.

MacPherson, James, ed. *Original Papers; Containing the Secret History of Great Britain, from the Restoration, to the Accession of the House of Hanover. To which Are Prefixed Extracts from the Life of James II. as Written by Himself.* 2 vols. London, 1775.

Macray, W. D., ed. *Notes Which Passed at Meetings of the Privy Council between Charles II. and the Earl of Clarendon, 1660–1667, Together with a Few Letters.* London: Nichols and Sons, 1896.

Malcolm, James P. *Londinium Redivivum; or, an Ancient History and Modern Description of London. Compiled from Parochial Records, Archives of Various Foundations, the Harleian MSS. and Other Authentic Sources.* 4 vols. London: John Nichols & Son, 1802–7.

Marvell, Andrew. *The Poems and Letters of Andrew Marvell.* Ed. by H. M. Margoliouth. 2 vols. 2nd ed. Oxford: Clarendon Press, 1952.

Milton, John. *The Works of John Milton.* Ed. by Frank A. Patterson. 18 vols. New York: Columbia University Press, 1931–40.

Milward, John. *The Diary of John Milward, Esq., Member of Parliament for Derbyshire, September, 1666, to May, 1668.* Ed. by Caroline Robbins. Cambridge: At the University Press, 1938.

Miner, Earl. "Dryden and the Issue of Human Progress." *Philological Quarterly*, 40 (Jan. 1961), 120–29.

———. *Dryden's Poetry*. Bloomington: Indiana University Press, 1967.

Miscellanea Aulica; or, A Collection of State-Treatises, Never before publish'd . . . Ed. by Thomas Brown. London, 1702.

Mommsen, Theodor E. "St. Augustine and the Christian Idea of Progress: The Background of the City of God." *Journal of the History of Ideas*, 12 (1951), 346–74.

Moore, Giles. "Extracts from the Journal and Account Book of the Rev. Giles Moore, Rector of Horstead Keynes, Sussex, from the Year 1655 to 1679." In *Sussex Archaeological Collections*, ed. by Robert W. Blencowe, I, 65–127. London: John Russell Smith, 1848.

More, Henry. *A Collection of Several Philosophical Writings* . . . 4th ed. London, 1712.

Muddiman, J. G. *The King's Journalist, 1659–1689: Studies in the Reign of Charles II*. London: John Lane, 1923.

Nevo, Ruth. *The Dial of Virtue: A Study of Poems on Affairs of State in the Seventeenth Century*. Princeton, N. J.: Princeton University Press, 1963.

Nichol Smith, David. *John Dryden*. Clark Lectures on English Literature, 1948–49. Cambridge: At the University Press, 1950.

Nuttall, Geoffrey F., and Owen Chadwick, eds. *From Uniformity to Unity, 1662–1962*. London: Society for Promoting Christian Knowledge, 1962.

Ogg, David. *England in the Reign of Charles II*. 2nd ed. London: Oxford University Press, 1963.

Oldenburg Letters: The Correspondence of Henry Oldenburg. Vols. 1–4, 1641–68. Madison: University of Wisconsin Press, 1965–67.

[Oldmixon, John.] *The History of England, during the Reigns of the Royal House of Stuart* . . . London, 1730.

Oxford History of English Literature: Sutherland, James. *English Literature of the Late Seventeenth Century*. Oxford History of English Literature, vol. 6. Oxford: Clarendon Press, 1969.

The Oxinden and Peyton Letters, 1642–1670: Being the Correspondence of Henry Oxinden of Barham, Sir Thomas Peyton of Knowlton and Their Circle. Ed. by Dorothy Gardiner. London: Sheldon Press, 1937.

Patrides, C. A. "Renaissance and Modern Thought on the Last Things: A Study in Changing Conceptions." *Harvard Theological Review*, 51 (July 1958), 169–85.

Pepys, Samuel. *The Diary of Samuel Pepys* . . . *with Lord Braybrooke's Notes, Edited with Additions by Henry B. Wheatley*. 9 vols. [With a supplementary volume of Pepysiana.] London: George Bell & Sons, 1904, 1903.

————. *Further Correspondence of Samuel Pepys, 1662–1679.* Ed. by J. R. Tanner. London G. Bell & Sons, 1929.

Poems on Affairs of State. Vol. I, *1660–1678.* Ed. by George deF. Lord. New Haven: Yale University Press, 1963.

Priestley, Margaret. "Anglo-French Trade and the 'Unfavourable Balance' Controversy, 1660–1685." *Economic History Review,* 2nd ser., 4, no. 1 (1951), 37–52.

Quinn, Dennis. "Donne and the Wane of Wonder." *ELH,* 36, no. 4 (Dec. 1969), 626–47.

[Ralph, James.] *The History of England: During the Reigns of K. William, Q. Anne, and K. George I. With an Introductory Review of the Reigns of the Royal Brothers, Charles and James; in Which Are to Be Found the Seeds of the Revolution.* 2 vols. London, 1744–46.

The Rawdon Papers, Consisting of Letters on Various Subjects, Literary, Political, and Ecclesiastical, to and from Dr. John Bramhall, Primate of Ireland . . . Ed. by Edward Berwick. London: John Nichol and Son, 1819.

Recueil des instructions données aux ambassadeurs et ministres de France depuis les traités de Westphalie jusqu'a la révolution française. Ed. by J. J. Jusserand. Publié sous les auspices de la Commission des Archives Diplomatiques au Ministère des Affaires Etrangères. Vols. 24–25, *Angleterre.* Paris: E. de Boccard, 1929.

The Restoration of the Stuarts, Blessing or Disaster? A Report of a Folger Library Conference Held on March 12 and 13, 1960. Washington, D.C.: Folger Shakespeare Library, 1960.

Roberts, Clayton. *The Growth of Responsible Government in Stuart England.* Cambridge: At the University Press, 1966.

————. "The Impeachment of the Earl of Clarendon." *Cambridge Historical Journal,* 13, no. 1 (1957), 1–18.

Rollins, Hyder E., ed. *The Pack of Autolycus . . . Broadside Ballads of the Years 1624–1693.* Cambridge: Harvard University Press, 1927.

Roper, Alan. *Dryden's Poetic Kingdoms.* London: Routledge and Kegan Paul, 1965.

Rosenberg, Bruce A. "*Annus Mirabilis* Distilled." *PMLA,* 79 (June 1964), 254–58.

Rusche, Harry. "Prophecies and Propaganda, 1641 to 1651." *English Historical Review,* 84 (Oct. 1969), 752–70.

Sainsbury, Ethel B., ed. *A Calendar of the Court Minutes Etc. of the East India Company, 1664–1667.* Introduction by Sir William Foster. Oxford: Clarendon Press, 1925.

Schilling, Bernard N. *Dryden and the Conservative Myth.* New Haven: Yale University Press, 1961.

Scott, William R. *The Constitution and Finance of English, Scottish and Irish Joint-Stock Companies to 1720*. 3 vols. Cambridge: At the University Press, 1912, 1911.

Select Charters of Trading Companies, A.D. 1530–1707. Ed. by Cecil T. Carr. Selden Society Publications, vol. 28. London: Bernard Quaritch, 1913.

Sharpe, Reginald R. *London and the Kingdom*. 3 vols. London: Longmans, Green & Co., 1894–95.

Skeel, Caroline A. J. "The Canary Company." *English Historical Review*, 31 (1916), 529–44.

Smith, Adam. *The Wealth of Nations*. 1776. Ed. by Edwin Cannan. New York: Modern Library, 1937.

Snow, Vernon F. "The Concept of Revolution in Seventeenth-Century England." *The Historical Journal*, 5, no. 2 (1962), 167–74.

Somers Tracts: A Collection of Scarce and Valuable Tracts . . . Selected from an Infinite Number in Print and Manuscript, in the Royal, Cotton, Sion, and Other Public, as Well as Private, Libraries; Particularly That of the Late Lord Somers. Ed. by Walter Scott. 2nd ed. 13 vols. London: T. Cadell and W. Davies, 1809–15.

The Statutes of the Realm . . . from Original Records and Authentic Manuscripts. Vol. 5, *1625–1680*. N.p., 1819.

Steele, Robert, ed. *A Bibliography of Royal Proclamations of the Tudor and Stuart Sovereigns and of Others Published under Authority, 1485–1714*. Vol. I, *England and Wales*. Bibliotheca Lindesiana, vol. 5. Oxford: Clarendon Press, 1910.

Swedenberg, H. T., Jr. "Dryden's Obsessive Concern with the Heroic." In *Essays in English Literature of the Classical Period Presented to Dougald MacMillan*. Ed. by D. W. Patterson and A. B. Strauss. *Studies in Philology*, extra ser., no. 4 (Jan. 1967), 12–26.

Tawney, R. H. *Religion and the Rise of Capitalism: A Historical Study*. 2nd ed., 1937. Reprint. New York: New American Library, 1958.

Taylor, Rupert. *The Political Prophecy in England*. New York: Columbia University Press, 1911.

Temple, William. *The Works of Sir William Temple, Bart*. 2 vols. London, 1750.

Thom, David. *The Number and Names of the Apocalyptic Beasts . . .* London: H. K. Lewis, 1848.

Thomason Tracts: Catalogue of the Pamphlets, Books, Newspapers, and Manuscripts Relating to the Civil War, the Commonwealth, and Restoration, Collected by George Thomason, 1640–

1661 [at the British Museum, London]. Ed. by G. K. Fortescue. London: By Order of the Trustees of the British Museum, 1908.

Trevor-Roper, H. R. *Religion, the Reformation and Social Change, and Other Essays*. London: Macmillan, 1967.

Trickett, Rachel. *The Honest Muse: A Study in Augustan Verse*. Oxford: Clarendon Press, 1967.

Turner, Edward R. *The Privy Council of England in the Seventeenth and Eighteenth Centuries, 1603–1784*. 2 vols. Baltimore: Johns Hopkins University Press, 1927, 1928.

Tuveson, Ernest L. *Millennium and Utopia: A Study in the Background of the Idea of Progress*. Berkeley: University of California Press, 1949.

Vale, V. "Clarendon, Coventry, and the Sale of Naval Offices, 1660–8." *Cambridge Historical Journal*, 12, no. 2 (1956), 107–25.

Van der Welle, Jojakim A. *Dryden and Holland*. Groningen: J. B. Wolters, 1962.

Vaughan, Robert, ed. *The Protectorate of Oliver Cromwell and the State of Europe during the Early Part of the Reign of Louis XIV. Illustrated in a Series of Letters* . . . 2 vols. London: Henry Colburn, 1838.

Viner, Jacob. *Studies in the Theory of International Trade*. London: George Allen & Unwin, 1937.

Walker, James. "The Yorkshire Plot, 1663." *Yorkshire Archaeological Journal*, 31 (1934), 348–59.

Wallace, John M. *Destiny His Choice: The Loyalism of Andrew Marvell*. Cambridge: At the University Press, 1968.

————. "Dryden and History: A Problem in Allegorical Reading." *ELH*, 36, no. 1 (Mar. 1969), 265–90.

Ward, Charles E. *The Life of John Dryden*. Chapel Hill: University of North Carolina Press, 1961.

Ward, John. *Diary of the Rev. John Ward, A.M., Vicar of Stratford-upon-Avon, Extending from 1648 to 1679* . . . Ed. by Charles Severn. London: Henry Colburn, 1839.

Wasserman, George R. *John Dryden*. New York: Twayne Publishers, 1964.

Wedgwood, Cecily V. *Poetry and Politics under the Stuarts*. Ann Arbor, Mich.: Ann Arbor paperbacks, 1964.

Welch, Charles. *History of the Monument: With a Brief Account of the Great Fire of London, Which It Commemorates*. London: Printed under the direction of the City Lands Committee of the Corporation of the City of London, 1893.

Westfall, Richard S. *Science and Religion in Seventeenth-Century England*. New Haven: Yale University Press, 1958.

Whiting, Charles E. *Studies in English Puritanism from the Res-*

toration to the Revolution, 1660–1688. Published for the Church Historical Society, n.s., no. 5. London: Society for Promoting Christian Knowledge, 1931.

Wilson, Charles. *Profit and Power: A Study of England and the Dutch Wars.* London: Longmans, Green and Co., 1957.

Wing, Donald. *Short-Title Catalogue of Books Printed in England, Scotland, Ireland, Wales, and British America and of English Books Printed in Other Countries. 1641–1700.* 3 vols. New York: For the Index Society by Columbia University Press, 1945–51.

Witcombe, D. T. *Charles II and the Cavalier House of Commons, 1663–1674.* Manchester: At the University Press, 1966.

Wood, Anthony. *The History and Antiquities of the University of Oxford.* 2 vols. Oxford, 1792–96.

————. *The Life and Times of Anthony Wood, 1632–1695.* Ed. by Andrew Clark. 5 vols. Oxford: Clarendon Press, 1891–1900.

Worthington Diary: The Diary and Correspondence of Dr. John Worthington . . . Ed. by James Crossley. 3 vols. Publications of the Chetham Society, vols. 13, 36, 114. Manchester, 1847–86.

Yates, Frances A. "Queen Elizabeth as Astraea." *Journal of the Warburg and Courtauld Institutes,* 10 (1947), 27–82.

Youngren, William H. "Generality, Science and Poetic Language in the Restoration." *ELH,* 35, no. 2 (June 1968), 158–87.

Zagorin, Perez. *The Court and the Country: The Beginning of the English Revolution.* London: Routledge & Kegan Paul, 1969.

Zook, George F. *The Company of Royal Adventurers Trading into Africa.* [Reprinted from the *Journal of Negro History,* 4, no. 2 (Apr. 1919).] Lancaster, Pa.: New Era Printing Co., 1919.

INDEX

Achitophel, 186

Adams, Edward, 118–19

Admiration, literary, 154–55, 156, 157

Ailesbury, earl of (Robert Bruce), 82

Albemarle, duke of (George Monck), 49, 51, 64, 86, 105, 177; at Four Days Battle, 53, 66, 156, 157, 158, 159, 160, 178, 180, 207; and Rupert, 57, 60, 76, 178; as leader, 61, 62, 63; on factionalism, 79–80; plots against, 91, 93, 96; as assistant in Royal Company, 112n39, 113

Alexander VII (pope), 219, 220, 228

Allegory, 182–88, 202, 217; in *AM,* 164, 165–66, 167–68, 169–70, 183–84; in *Absalom and Achitophel,* 186–87; beast allegory, 226–27, 244, 249

Amboyna, massacre at (1623), 99

Amsterdam, 127, 128n98, 242

Anabaptists, 231; and other sects, 84, 86, 87, 88, 89, 91, 92, 93; in United Provinces, 127; and Roman Catholics, 133

Andrews, William, 220, 255, 262

Anglesey, earl of (Arthur Annesley), 112n39

Anglican Church, 83n21, 95, 132, 134, 136, 192–93, 231, 255; restoration of, 81, 132, 133, 137, 142, 194, 196, 238–39, 263; attitude of, toward Protestant dissent, 84, 134 (*see also* Protestant dissent); and eschatologi-

cal prophecy, 152, 191, 204, 227, 228, 242, 260; and Greatrakes, 213. *See also* Uniformity, Act of (1662)

Anglo-Spanish War (1655–1659), 100

Animal imagery, 57–58, 156–57, 226–27, 244, 249. *See also* Beehive emblem; Phoenix emblem; Revelation, Beast of

Antichrist, 190, 216, 218, 249; as Rome, 197, 221; as Cromwell's government, 199; as the pope, 216, 217, 221. *See also* Revelation, Beast of

Archer, Henry, 197–98, 199, 200

Argyle, marquis of (Archibald Campbell), 90

Arlington, earl of (Sir Henry Bennet), 112n39, 123, 125, 137, 225; on civil unrest, 91, 92; and Clifford, 118; and Greatrakes, 212; and Lilly, 226n84

Arminianism, 231

Ashley, Baron (Anthony Ashley Cooper; later earl of Shaftesbury), 136, 146, 186

Ashmole, Elias, 197n23, 226, 233, 236

Aspinwall, William, 200

Audience, literary: and parochial response to poetry, 5; poetic persuasion of, 7, 14, 18; "ideal," 12–13; poet's consciousness of, 24; historical, 38, 39, 40–41, 267; and resistance to poet's persuasion, 77–78; and historical poetry, 182–83, 185, 187; and